D0893365

Comparative
Economic Systems

Comparative Economic Systems

Ninth Edition

WILLIAM N. LOUCKS
Emeritus Professor of Economics
Wharton School, University of Pennsylvania

WILLIAM G. WHITNEY
Assistant Professor of Economics
Wharton School, University of Pennsylvania

Harper & Row, Publishers
New York, Evanston, San Francisco, London

Sponsoring Editor: John Greenman
Project Editor: Betsy Dilernia
Designer: Michel Craig
Production Supervisor: Valerie Klima

COMPARATIVE ECONOMIC SYSTEMS, Ninth Edition

Library of Congress Cataloging in Publication Data

Loucks, William Negele, 1899–
    Comparative economic systems.

    1. Comparative economics. I. Whitney,
William G., joint author. II. Title.
HB90.168 1973   330.1   73-2706
ISBN 0-06-044045-7

With the hope that their generation
may retain and enlarge the spirit of free
inquiry in controversial areas of thought,
this volume is dedicated to

> *William Loucks Harvey*
> *Scott Charles Harvey*
> *Susan Mary Harvey*
> *Jennifer Louise Whitney*
> *Andrea Marie Whitney*
> *Katherine Frances Whitney*

Contents

Foreword to the First Edition

It is, perhaps, because "life is a swallow, and theory a snail," as Richard H. Tawney once wrote, that a text has not heretofore appeared for college and university courses in the field of comparative economics. The maze of economic experimentation and the rapidity of economic change have made it difficult to develop a mature point of view in this field. Recently, however, many courses have been established which deal with subjects covered in this volume. It is needless to say that we frankly regard the present book as a first effort in a difficult and controversial field, and that we shall welcome suggestions from teachers and students.

It is our hope that the pages which follow may show something of the fruits of free inquiry amid considerable difficulties in the gathering

*of facts swirled by the rip-tides of controversy. It should be clear that
we advocate the priciples of a liberal education. The purpose of such
education is to free the mind from arbitrary restraints and to assist it in
the arduous process of thinking. Training in how to think, rather than
indoctrination in what to think, is more likely to develop a capable
individual and one useful to society. The "ostrich principle" must be
ruled out of education, so that facts may be faced without regard to
their palatability. To do this is to face the future where the problems
to be solved lie, and to avoid facing the past. In this connection it is
well to recall Tawney's description of the ruling classes at the time of
the French Revolution: "They walked reluctantly backward into the
future, lest a worse thing should befall them." If one all-important
conclusion is to be drawn from this volume it can be this: That if the
pace of social and economic change of the past twenty years projects
itself into the future, the central problem will be to make the economic
adaptations which the course of events may require—without the loss
of cherished freedoms.*

WILLIAM N. LOUCKS
J. WELDON HOOT
Philadelphia—August, 1938

Foreword to the Ninth Edition

*"How can history be interpreted
without recognizing the differences
between different economic systems?"*
Joan Robinson

The thirty-plus years that have passed since the publication of the first edition places this book among the senior citizens of the textbook population. The new and modified forms of economic organization and processes that have sprung up since that time make the earliest editions curiosities of a bygone era. That will also soon be the fate of this ninth edition, for the one persistent factor in economic affairs has been change.

One objective of this book is to slow down the blurring motion of a modern economic system momentarily in order to appreciate and ponder about the intricate institutional platform on which it is built. A bold and much-needed renaissance of institutional economics is beginning to emerge from the realization that much of currently accepted economic theory has very little to say about how economic decisions are made and how economic power is exercised in the real world. Wherever possible, an institutional perspective continues to be incorporated in the economic analysis of this edition. Like the dowager who saved her Tiffany lamps, we take some pride in seeing our insistence on a central role for economic institutions come back into fashion again.

Periodic revisions of a book of this nature are imperative to take account of developments in the structure of economic systems. Revision also provides an opportunity to assess future directions economic systems may take. This edition reflects the authors' concern for and commitment to change in basically capitalist economic institutions as the best means, at least in the United States, of meeting new demands on economic arrangements to promote human well-being. Admittedly this commitment becomes more difficult amid what appears to us to be a growing reluctance and inability of participants in economic and political institutions to see that long-term welfare may sometimes consist of some degree of moderation in advancing narrow, short-run interests. It will be cruel irony if the United States—a nation that has traditionally demonstrated more idealism and receptivity to change than the world's norm—should become so cynical, so apprehensive, and so incapable of admitting error that we fail to respond to the human needs and aspirations that new technology, new political realities, and new standards of integrity and decency create. The record of American involvement in the problems of Indochina does not provide very much basis for hope.

Our view remains, nevertheless, that people are capable of learning from their past experiences, even if the lessons may be painfully and slowly absorbed. This involves a responsibility for everyone to make value judgments weighing the costs and benefits—the "bads" and "goods"— found in economic systems as they exist and are in the process of becoming. For us that responsibility consists of dropping the fiction that economics is, or can be, a value-free, completely objective science in favor of stating our own personal views and evaluations, at various points, of the issues under discussion. These personal views connote neither implied omniscience nor dogmatic rejection of differing positions. They are injected to give students something concrete from which they may depart in shaping their own ideas and programs for changing economic and political institutions. If major changes are to be made in American capitalism, as we believe they must be, it is our hope that this book can make some contribution toward an open and informed discussion, in the broadest possible context, of the issues involved.

The people who assisted in the preparation of this edition deserve public recognition of our gratitude. Phillis Kaniss and Charles Movit served as research assistants, with the latter's knowledge of the Soviet economic system amounting to shared authorship of that section. Our colleagues, Herb Levine and Don Green, were helpful in offering both their professional expertise and their vision of how a discussion on comparative economic systems should be organized. Linda Thornburg transformed the language of felt-tipped pens into the language of typed manuscript—languages that differ in spelling, grammar, and legibility.

The name of Andrea Marie Whitney remains on the dedication page even though a tragic and senseless pedestrian accident confined her spirit of free and joyous inquiry to a span of five years. Her loss is one more reminder of how great the gap sometimes is between how things are and how we would like them to be.

WILLIAM N. LOUCKS
WILLIAM G. WHITNEY

Comparative
Economic Systems

PART I: INTRODUCTION

1. The comparative study of economic systems

A casual glance around the world reveals that man uses various forms of economic organization to gain a livelihood. The underlying purpose of every form is the same: to ensure that the goods and services required for physical existence and social cohesiveness are provided on a regular basis. The way man attempts to achieve this basic purpose differs from age to age and from place to place. We are interested here in the different forms of economic organization—that is, the different *economic systems*—through which man seeks to fulfill his material needs.

THE VARIETY OF ECONOMIC SYSTEMS

Man does not live by (or for) bread alone, and every economic system is deeply embedded in a complex web of social patterns. One extreme of the spectrum is the type of system that emphasizes freedom and incentive for the individual to follow his own interests as worker, investor, consumer, or business entrepreneur. At the other extreme is a system in which group values play the leading role in organizing, planning, and carrying on economic activity.

Most actual economic systems operate at a considerable distance from either extreme. Family structure, for instance, imposes limitations on individuals when a customary internal division of labor exists. The family group may also be the relevant unit of decision making in supplying labor services or acquiring goods for consumption outside the family circle. In some societies the range of family obligation extends to distant cousins and in-laws for whom sustenance or employment must be furnished upon request.

Employment relations are another area in which social norms influence individual behavior. College students beginning summer jobs are often advised by fellow workers to "make the work last" if they go about their tasks too energetically. American workers readily move from one employer to another, while Japanese workers usually enter into a lifetime employment relationship with a single firm that guarantees not only employment but also housing, recreational facilities, and sometimes a focus for family and religious life.[1]

Loyalty is an elusive commodity which, according to economist Kenneth Arrow, "if you have to pay a price for, you probably haven't bought." Yet loyalty—to family, village, ethnic group, or nation—is a powerful cohesive force in allowing economic systems to operate smoothly. As economic systems become more complex and impersonal, they must rely more heavily on a legal structure to regulate economic arrangements between individuals that were previously a matter of social rights and obligations.

By means of the following three examples, we will attempt to illustrate the diversity of conceivable economic systems and to jar the reader loose from the unconscious ethnocentricity that tends to equate one's own economic system with the way things necessarily ought to be done. These examples, one each from utopian fiction, from economic anthropology, and from the contemporary world, serve our purposes better than would any listing of economic categories and definitions.

Edward Bellamy's Utopian Economic System

The novel *Looking Backward* caused tremendous popular excitement in the years immediately following its publication in 1888. The plot is simple enough. Julian West, a young Bostonian, falls into a deep sleep in an underground chamber in 1887. He is discovered by Doctor Leete and his beauti-

---

[1]James Abegglen, *The Japanese Factory,* Glencoe, Ill.: Free Press, 1958.

ful daughter Edith in the year 2000. The remainder of the book, with the
exception of some romantic thoughts and heavy breathing by the young
couple, consists of an attempt to explain to Julian the economic and political system that had peacefully evolved during the intervening century.

Looking Backward stands out among the visionary novels of its period
in its attention to the traditional areas of economics—consumption, production, market exchange, and income distribution—and as an attempt
to integrate the economic and political institutions of contemporary society. Dr. Leete explains that each citizen is given a bank balance equal
to his per capita share of national product and a credit card to use for all
purchases. This sum proves more than adequate to meet typical consumption needs. Military, police, advertising, merchandising, and financial expenses are eliminated. The consumer chooses products from sample stores
resembling modern discount warehouses, and the goods are dispatched via
pneumatic tubes (the technology of the future in 1888) to his home. Meanwhile, information of the sale is relayed back to the factory (the equivalent
of a computer inventory system) to alert production managers of changes
in customer tastes.

Bellamy projected the movement toward formation of large-scale
industrial trusts occurring in the late nineteenth century to what he regarded as its logical conclusion—the One Great Trust in which the government acquired ownership and control of all the nation's industrial capacity. This action, he claimed, came about peacefully sometime in the
twentieth century. Citizens recognized that economies of scale were inherent in ever-larger units of production.

Problems of labor supply were also solved in a creative way: the
principle of universal military training, or the draft, was "expanded" to
cover the 20–45 age bracket for all men and women. People were free at
age 24 to choose an occupation. Since all citizens received an identical
income credit, supply and demand forces in each area of employment
were aligned by making hours shorter in types of work attracting too few
volunteers—a two-hour shift for garbage collectors, for example. The first
three years of national service were reserved for tasks that older workers
still could not be persuaded to take up; interestingly, Bellamy thought that
necessary personal service jobs such as that of waiter in a community din-
ing hall would be considered demeaning. These jobs would be assigned
to new entrants to the labor force. Any citizen could spend a trial year in
a professional school such as a lay or medical school until age 30. An artist,
author, composer, or inventor could devote full time to his or her craft
as long as there existed sufficient popular demand for that unique creative
talent.

Finally, the functions of government were performed by those who
retired at age 45. Representation was based on occupation, with each occupational guild administered by workers who had performed best while

they were economically active. The national government was conducted by those who excelled at guild administration.

Bellamy displays admirable awareness of the complex interrelationships between the component parts of an economic system. Consumer preferences are matched with the assortment of goods produced, and occupational preferences are matched with employment opportunities. All economic activity occurs within a framework of minimal governmental coercion and without differences in personal income serving as a motivating factor. The problems associated with the transitional period from the old to the new system are slighted, however, as are the problems of dealing with "deviant" behavior in the form of resistance to the labor draft. Bellamy relies heavily on the fashionable idea of evolutionary change to bring forth a new era of enlightenment and cooperation in economic relationships. All in all, the creation of a relatively complete and innovative economic system in the mind of a single individual is a remarkable accomplishment. *Looking Backward* deserves a place with Skinner's *Walden Two* and Vonnegut's *Player Piano* as entertaining presentations of economic systems in fictional form.

The Tribal Economic System of the Trobriand Islanders

Bellamy's *Looking Backward* was chosen as an example partly because his economic system dealt separately and explicitly with each of the categories of traditional economic analysis. Such clear-cut distinctions are not available for the anthropologist who studies subsistence and peasant economies. There the economic system functions as a by-product of noneconomic institutions rather than as a separate set of practices and relationships. Such economic systems are sometimes called primitive because of the relatively simple level of technology and because resource limitations or social behavior discourage capital formation. As we shall see, however, the absence of machine technology does not preclude highly functional and complex ways of organizing production and exchange in subsistence economies.

The economic system of the Trobriand Islands, lying off the eastern end of New Guinea in the South Pacific, was the subject of a famous anthropological study conducted half a century ago by Bronislaw Malinowski.[2] Their society illuminates the extent to which economic systems can function with tradition, rather than markets, providing the signals that organize effort and determine relative shares in the resulting output. It is also an example of a system that antedates the impact of transistor radios and other instruments of Western culture.

[2]Bronislaw Malinowski, *Argonauts of the Western Pacific*, London: Routledge & Kegan Paul, 1922.

A Trobriand Islander learns and follows the rules of *economy* in his society almost like an American learns and follows the rules of *language* in his. An American is born into an English-speaking culture. In no sense does he "choose" to speak English because no real alternative is presented to him. So too, the Trobriander is born into a yam-growing economy. He does not "choose" to plant yams rather than broccoli. The question does not arise in this form, but rather in the form of how much of each of very few conventional crops to plant or how to apportion a given work day to several tasks.

In the Trobriand subsistence economy, labor, land and other resources are not purchased, and produce is not destined for sale to others, so it is personal taste within the *ecological* constraints set by resource endowment, the *technological* constraints set by known techniques of production, and the *social* constraints set by the obligation to provide sister's husband with yams that dictate how much of each crop is to be planted.[3]

Several aspects of this economic system deserve special mention. First, even though it is called a subsistence economy, the sweet potatoes that form the main crop are regarded not merely as food but for their prestige value as well (one is reminded of hunting and fishing trophies). Before the yams are collected in private storehouses that display the quantity and quality of the owner's possessions, a magical spell is invoked to make the appetites of the inhabitants poor; if the magic works well it is hoped that half the yams will rot before they are replaced by the new crop.

Second, the wealth in yams that an individual possesses is not what he has produced through his own labor but what he has received from relatives-in-law as part of a life-long obligation of each man to work for the families of his sisters and other female relatives. These obligations, including the ability to be summoned to do communal work, are reciprocated with countergifts that fall far short of the value of the work performed. Chiefs, through a series of marriages, have the right to receive payments of yams from the male relatives of their many wives and to assemble them for communal tasks requiring large numbers of workers.

The giving and receiving of gifts permeates Trobriand society; every performance of a service or favor must be repaid with a ceremonial gift. The effect of this web of exchange is to bind the society more closely together in traditional patterns of behavior, including the patterns of work organization and distribution of goods and services that constitute the economic system.

The social nature of the Trobriand Islanders' economic activity is most apparent in their *kula* trading system. A circular network of islands extending over thousands of miles participates in the ceremonial exchange

[3]George Dalton, "Theoretical Issues in Economic Anthropology," in George Dalton, ed., *Economic Development and Social Change: The Modernization of Village Communities*, Garden City, N.Y.: Natural History Press, 1971, pp. 188–189.

of shell necklaces, which travel clockwise, and armshells, which travel counterclockwise, around the circle. These items, which have no practical use, are exchanged according to very strict rules. "A firm and lifelong relationship is always established between any participant in the *kula*, and a number of other men, some of whom belong to his own community, and others to overseas communities. Such men call one another *Karayta'a* ("partner," as we shall designate them), and they are under mutual obligations to trade with each other, to offer protection, hospitality, and assistance whenever needed.[4] Each member of a sailing expedition moving from one island to the next one in the circuit will present his trading partner with, say, a pair of armshells in anticipation of a return visit. The next year the partner will return the visit, bearing either a necklace of equivalent value or a temporary gift of a smaller necklace to serve until he comes into possession of one of adequate size and quality. All of this is accompanied by considerable ceremony and narrative concerning the history of the particular object. The whole system of equivalent exchange is enforced only by tradition and the sense of trust and honor between partners.

Our mental excursion to the Trobriand Islands has demonstrated the strength of reciprocal obligations, reinforced by ceremonial practices and a sense of longstanding tradition, in supplanting private gain as the focus of economic activity. We may speak of "owing" someone a dinner invitation or a thank-you note, but it is difficult to imagine devoting the bulk of one's productive effort to meeting such responsibilities. That is because a market economy is impersonal in a way that would equally confound the Trobriand Islanders.

The Idealistic Economic System of the Israeli Kibbutz

From the Trobriand Islanders' economic system, which took centuries to reach the state that Malinowski observed, we turn for our final example to a system that was created more or less instantaneously. The *kibbutz* may serve as an instructive example of the creation of economic institutions within a context of religious idealism and political necessity. The survival of the kibbutz as part of the modernizing economy of Israel shows the adaptability of economic systems. It thus serves as a bridge to the subsequent discussion of how economic systems change.

The Israeli kibbutz is a collective settlement in which members jointly own the means of production, provide their own labor for all work, and share in the allocation of goods and services according to need. In 1971 there were 229 kibbutzim located throughout the rural areas of Israel,

[4]Bronislaw Malinowski, "Kula: The Circulating Exchange of Valuables . . .," in George Dalton, ed., *Tribal and Peasant Economies*, Garden City, N.Y.: Natural History Press, 1967, p. 173.

with some 85,000 inhabitants (2.8 percent of the Israeli population). The average population of a kibbutz is 350.

The first kibbutz, *Kvutsa Degania*, was founded in 1910 on the banks of the Sea of Galilee. Degania and the small communal settlements that developed later differed from the fleeting utopian experiments that had been attempted elsewhere in that they were part of a larger struggle to establish a homeland for the Jewish people. Zionists returning to Palestine at the end of the nineteenth century were faced with a desolate land and an impoverished Jewish population of little more than 25,000. All attempts at Jewish colonization through the method of private ownership and wage labor had failed, forcing the first pioneers to employ cheap Arab labor or to accept support from philanthropists abroad. The communal life eventually was seen as the most viable way of colonizing the wastelands, developing Jewish agriculture, and maintaining physical security. The kibbutzim, as they came to be called, were the vanguard of a movement that culminated in the creation of the independent state of Israel in 1949.

Though formed out of practical necessity, the kibbutzim were designed to fulfill the Zionist-Socialist vision of a new society. The new pioneers sought a return to the soil and productive labor for the Jewish people, who had for so long been divorced from agricultural occupations. They were also eager to leave behind the ghetto exploitation of their Eastern European background and establish a more egalitarian society along Marxist lines. The kibbutz fulfilled these goals and over the years succeeded in absorbing hordes of immigrants into the new society and facilitating the transition of the Jewish people to an agricultural life.

The kibbutz is organized around the Marxian principle "from each according to his ability to each according to his needs" within the possibilities of the commune. A newly formed kibbutz leases nationally owned land and is provided with public funds for capital which it eventually repays. All means of production are owned by the group. Wages, private property, or private economic activity are not allowed. There are no class divisions between employer and employee. The administrators of the farm are democratically elected but enjoy no special privileges; all decisions on the economic and social life of the commune are made by the members themselves.

Each kibbutz is run as a single competitive farm; given the prices of inputs and outputs it faces, the kibbutz acts as a profit-oriented unit, with the major exception that, in principle, it will not hire workers. Thus labor inputs are limited to those that can be provided by the members of each kibbutz.

Profits, however, are not the only goal of the kibbutz. Most of the economic activity of the kibbutz has as its aim development of the community and the country as a whole providing a decent standard of living for its members. Noneconomic considerations often govern the economic sphere. This can be seen in the following considerations:

1. Settlements are often located in new and undeveloped areas
   rather than in populated areas where economic prospects would
   be better. The locations of these new kibbutzim are often decided on the basis of strategic needs rather than economic viability.
2. The kibbutz does not calculate whether borrowed capital will
   in every case leave a profit after interest has been paid. It is often
   considered sufficient if a loan develops a farm or industry,
   allows for the employment of older people, etc.
3. While many kibbutzim would be large enough to produce one or
   two commercial crops efficiently, the ideology of the kibbutz
   has fostered a commitment to intensive mixed farming. Pioneers
   were anxious to avoid specialization in export crops that
   would have identified them as a colonial economy. They also
   believed that mixed farming would allow for the distribution of
   risk, for rotation of crops, as well as for more equal distribution of labor during the year and a larger range of job opportunities for members.

In recent years many kibbutzim have been turning away from an exclusive concern with agriculture to development of a broader economy
based on industry. Because of increased efficiency in agricultural production, much of the kibbutz labor has become available for nonagricultural
activities. The profitability and growth potential of industry is seen as a
means of providing the kibbutz with a better chance than with agriculture
to be economically self-sufficient. Industry also provides a range of skilled
occupations as well as less rigorous jobs for older people no longer able
to work in the fields. Nearly two-thirds of the kibbutzim have started at
least one factory. Most of these factories are small scale, with an average
of about 50 workers per plant. In 1968, 171 factories (producing metals,
wood, plastics, agricultural machinery, irrigation pipes, and the like) accounted for 30 percent of kibbutz income compared to only 10 percent
in 1960.

Factories are run democratically, incorporating group rather than
individual decision making wherever possible. Top management officers
are elected; although management training is offered, skills are usually
learned on the job. Studies have shown that these cooperatively administered industrial enterprises can be as efficient or more efficient than man-
agerially controlled units. A 1965 survey found that kibbutz labor was 26
percent more productive than private wage earners and that capital was
invested more productively by kibbutz factories.

Future growth of kibbutz industry is threatened, however, by a severe
labor shortage. At present, an estimated 50 percent of kibbutz factory
workers are hired labor, an ideological anathema to kibbutz members.
Some regard mergers and joint ventures with neighboring kibbutzim as a
means of overcoming this problem; other solutions involve growth of the

kibbutz from an average population of 350 to one of a few thousand, forming large agricultural-industrial complexes.

Almost half of the kibbutz members work in the service sector—the kitchens, laundries, schools, and so forth. The work of the kibbutz is outlined by work committees, which submit to the kibbutz an overall plan for the year; this is broken down into smaller units. Jobs are assigned by a work organizer, and in order to avoid establishing power elites the top jobs are rotated. Efforts are also made to rotate undesirable jobs. There are no wages and no material bonuses for work well done—the only incentive is the respect of the community, the only punitive measure public opinion.

The collective consumption of the kibbutz operates under two main principles: provision of all the needs of the population, as determined collectively, and equal distribution regardless of what type of work the member is doing. Collective consumption encompasses all the major and minor needs of the individual and family—food, housing, clothing, medical care, culture, entertainment, vacations, full social security in illness and old age. The method of distribution varies according to the commodity involved. While items such as work clothes, toilet requirements, and cigarettes are given freely on the basis of need, housing is allocated on a more complicated basis—a point system based on seniority, age, health, and family status. Many kibbutzim try to allow for a degree of personal choice in items such as clothing and furnishings by specifying only a given price range for certain items. Gifts from outside the kibbutz are usually allowed.

Though the kibbutz autonomously decides its living standards according to its financial situation at the time, pressures to keep up with outside trends make it difficult to lower those standards. Thus, planning of consumption becomes a more difficult problem than planning of production, since in consumption there is more emphasis on satisfying needs and tastes than on running a sound economic operation.

Though austerity characterized the kibbutz from its beginnings until Israeli statehood, the picture has changed considerably. Living standards rose in the 1950s, paralleling the general trend throughout the country. Today many kibbutzim are quite affluent operations. The kibbutz has succeeded in keeping pace with and exceeding the very high growth rate of Israeli agriculture. Output per worker on the kibbutz has risen roughly fourfold in the past 20 years. In the early 1950s the kibbutz enjoyed a seller's market, straining to feed the quickly growing population of Israel. By the end of the decade, agricultural surpluses began to grow, leading to more careful planning in the 1960s to meet home needs. Industrial crops, products for canning, and especially exports received greater stress. Though Israel is a capitalist country, its public sector—the part owned by the government, the Zionist institutions, and the *Histadrut* (General Federation of Labor)—account for nearly half of its gross national product

(GNP). Ninety percent of the land in Israel is nationalized, belonging to the nation through a joint body of the government and the Jewish National Fund. It is leased to settlers for long terms at relatively low rents. Because of the national ownership of land and public financing, there is a high degree of agricultural planning. Each branch of agriculture works according to production quotas for the whole country. The government also fixes prices and is a decisive factor in determining the relationship of prices to production costs through its credit policy, interest rates, subsidies, import and export duties, and the like.

Government policy over the years has been directed specifically toward developing agriculture, even at the expense of economic efficiency. Tariffs, subsidies, and quantitative import restrictions have been used to increase the viability of the agricultural sector. Loans have been made at low interest rates, frequently so low that the real rate of interest was negative; a major part of the fixed and working capital needs of kibbutzim have been provided by the public sector. Also, public development projects such as irrigation and afforestation have been provided to the kibbutzim.

The kibbutz is run through a weekly general meeting in which members who are over high school age are entitled to vote. The general meeting elects a secretariat, including a secretary and coordinators in such areas as finance, economics, labor, education, culture, and so forth. These coordinators run the day-to-day operations of the kibbutz, consulting regularly with committees of elected kibbutz members.

The kibbutz system of child rearing and education, one of its most controversial aspects, aims to introduce children to the values and habits of collective life. From birth onward, children live in dormitories organized by age group. However, attachment to parents is reinforced from the beginning. For the first six weeks of a baby's life, the mother does not work but feeds and cares for her child. In addition, a trained nurse, who will stay with the same child through adolescence, looks after the baby. Though children generally live apart from their parents, they return to their parents' home after the workday ends and stay with them until bedtime.

As children grow, they are organized into groups of five or six supervised by their nurse. Within these groups, children are taught proper eating habits, cleanliness, and discipline. They are exposed systematically to a wide variety of sports, crafts, nature tours, educational games, and the like, so that all children, irrespective of parental leanings, have equal access to all forms of expression. All kibbutz children receive a full high school education. Some very large kibbutzim have schools of their own, but two or more settlements usually operate a regional boarding school from which children come home for weekends and once or twice a week.

In kibbutz society, the relationship of the family to society is completely changed. It has no economic functions, since collective production and consumption have replaced the family as the basic economic unit.

Though the family raises children, its function is no longer dominant among the factors shaping collective education. The family remains at the center of communal life, however, and is still the basic unit.

The kibbutz style of life has freed women from many of the duties and chores traditionally assigned to them. The woman is no longer economically dependent on her husband and is no longer tied down to full-time care of her children. She is guaranteed equal rights in the community. Despite these freedoms, the reality of the kibbutz shows that women have to a great extent remained in subordinate roles. Though some women occupy top kibbutz jobs, the majority continue to work in traditionally female-oriented jobs such as child care, education, and services (sewing, laundry, kitchen work).

Inhabitants of kibbutzim often cite the impressive fact that 80 percent of their youth choose to remain in the kibbutz after growing up, thus demonstrating the continued viability of the collective way of life. Yet doubts have begun to creep in as to whether increasing affluence and the disappearance of the pioneer spirit will lead to a reemergence of property instincts.

The threat exists that without a real material struggle to engage youth, communalism will give way to careerism and individualism. There also remains the question of whether the egalitarian system developed in the commune can survive too much industrial growth, with its parallel risks of managerial cliques and depersonalization.

Given the adverse political and economic circumstances in which the kibbutz movement was begun, however, it must be regarded as an unusually successful experiment in creating a new type of economic system. It has allowed settlers to pursue their religious and philosophical ideals. American visitors to a kibbutz often report that they find the prevailing sense of cooperation, community, and egalitarianism a pleasant experience.

The kibbutz economy seems to have surmounted many of the problems that plagued nineteenth-century American economic experiments: Continuity from generation to generation seems assured; internal production and consumption patterns are meshed with the outside economic world; prosperity has not destroyed the idealism and social position that developed under conditions of economic hardship. "As Israel's economy has surged, the kibbutzim are becoming burgeoning industrial complexes and tourist attractions."[5]

THE EVOLUTION OF ECONOMIC SYSTEMS

It is now time to begin a more orderly approach to the investigation of economic systems. We must erect boundary markers around the economic aspects of human existence that our three examples showed to be so firmly

[5]*Time*, July 3, 1972, p. 40.

interwoven with the organization of noneconomic activities. This is what the economic theorist accomplishes by invoking the *ceteris paribus* assumption, holding all things constant except for the specific factors allowed to change. In practice this has meant ignoring the social setting in which economic activity occurs to a degree incompatible with an in-depth comparison of economic systems. We turn to the concept of economic institutions for the building blocks from which economic systems are formed and linked with other institutions.

Economic Institutions

Institutions are ways in which the actions of social units occur through interaction with other units under repetitive, typical conditions. The units may be individuals, families, business firms, political parties, or other groups. The interaction must be repetitive so that we know what to expect of others. The "rules of the game" define the rights and obligations of participants as they play their roles in that situation. Dating is an institution facilitating mate selection in our society; the funeral institutionalizes expressions of grief; the family provides, among other things, for rearing children.

Economic institutions are devoted primarily to gaining a livelihood, although they may also serve other functions in the society, such as political action. Thus labor unions allow members to exert collective pressure in negotiating terms of employment. Business firms assemble factors of production and create the channels of communication needed for internal decision making. Trade associations and lobby groups promote the economic interests of their members in dealing with governmental agencies and with the public.

The most important economic institution in Western economies is the self-regulating market, in which price signals attract or repel customers and producers. The market as a way of organizing production and distributing the rewards of the production process has shown tremendous adaptability and resiliency in the face of the geographical and technological changes that have occurred since Adam Smith observed that "it is not from benevolence of the butcher, the brewer, or the baker that we expect our dinner, but from their regard of their own interest."

Market institutions so permeate the economic systems of the nations of North America and Western Europe that the participants are largely unaware of the uniqueness of their particular way of conducting economic activity. Capitalism, the economic system to be described in the following chapters, has evolved since the eighteenth century with the self-regulating market at the center of its set of economic institutions. Karl Polanyi, a famous economic historian and economic anthropologist, demonstrated in his book *The Great Transformation* the limited historical and geographical context in which unregulated markets for products, labor, and land have actually prevailed. Polanyi was interested in the trading activities of ancient societies, in the reciprocal gift exchanges of primitive people such as the Trobriand Islanders, and in peasant economic systems whose products (such as cocoa or rubber) were often destined for worldwide markets but who relied on nonmarket methods of bringing land and labor together. Thus he saw market economies as historical anomalies that tend to revert to various forms of nonmarket regulation, especially by the government, when the socially disruptive effects of the impersonal market system become as great as they did during the Great Depression of the 1930s.

One essential of an economic system is that its institutions "fit together," both with one another and with noneconomic institutions, in a way that avoids operating at cross-purposes. This means that a change in some aspect of society seemingly remote from the economic system may set up shock waves that require an accommodation in economic institutions (as in Max Weber's account of the influence of religious beliefs on the economic motivations of Calvinists) or that changes in a part of the economic system may similarly cause upheavals in social institutions (as demonstrated by the impact of mechanized cotton harvesting in the American South).

The Dynamics of Institutional Change

Change is a complex and imperfectly understood phenomenon. We can confidently expect (and hope) that a significant portion of human behavior will remain outside the ability of social scientists to comprehend fully or to predict. The diversity of economic systems occurring within areas of roughly similar environmental conditions gives rise to the conclusion that we are dealing with a nondeterministic subject.[6] We can only hope to sketch an outline of possible ways in which the process of change may occur.

Imagine first an economic system that is in equilibrium, meaning that whatever inconsistencies exist between economic institutions can be explained away by appeals to tradition or to prevailing moral values without significant changes in the regular pattern of economic activity. Next, imagine a change either outside or inside the economic system—a series of bad harvests, for instance, or a decline in infant mortality—that creates basic inconsistencies between economic institutions.[7]

Reactions to strain may take the form of unrest resulting from an unacceptable ratio of unemployment, or it may be felt in the rise of a new

[6]George Dalton, ed., *Tribal and Peasant Economies*, p. 65.
[7]This approach follows the general pattern presented in Neil J. Smelser, *The Sociology of Economic Life*, Englewood Cliffs, N.J.: Prentice-Hall, 1963, which builds, in turn, on the more detailed (and less comprehensible) theory of social systems in Talcott Parsons and Neil J. Smelser, *Economy and Society*, New York: Free Press, 1956.

group of potential entrepreneurs. New political movements may spring up, or social deviance such as crime, alcoholism, or juvenile protest may increase. Whatever the form in which the strain manifests itself, the economic system must adjust to the situation before a new equilibrium can result.

Authorities within prevailing economic institutions can react to strain in either of two basic ways. First, they can attempt to *repress* it in various ways. Institutions for social control such as the court system or the police can be used; public opinion can be rallied in opposition; protest leaders may be discredited or coopted while their cause is given lip service. Second, they can *accommodate* existing institutions to ease the strain. Economic rewards may be shared with those who were formerly excluded, or new institutions may be created that allow the system to function smoothly once again.

Either solution creates indirect effects that cannot be fully anticipated. Favorable positions in the economic hierarchy are usually not relinquished voluntarily or without an attempt at least to mold new institutions to the advantage of those already holding economic power. The history of "reform" movements in the United States and other countries records the divergence between original ideals and actual results in such diverse areas as antitrust regulation, medical care, and civil rights.

As Karl Marx observed, change occurs through a dialectical process that incorporates neither the total result desired by the reformers nor the situation clung to by defenders of the status quo. Even "good" innovations such as the polio vaccine and the no-press shirt must have caused ambivalent feelings on the part of artificial-lung manufacturers and hand laundry operators.

Once we recognize that situations of economic change both create new profit opportunities and threaten the economic and social positions of those holding economic power, the question of whether economic systems are "man-made" can be considered. Economic systems are man-made in the sense that change comes about through human actions; we can even agree that the greater the potential reward for "inventing" a new institutional form for achieving economic goals, the more likely that someone will discover a means of doing it.[8] But we must also remember that binding constraints on human inventiveness are operative in the inertia of tradition, in the obstructionism of vested interests, and in the feedback impacts on other institutions which economic change sets off. The amazing thing is not the unchanging aspects of economic systems; it is rather the ability of economic systems to adapt in the face of profoundly altered circumstances.

These circumstances, the facts of life to which economic systems

---

[8]This view has been persuasively argued in Lance E. Davis and Douglass C. North, *Institutional Change and American Growth*, London: Cambridge University Press, 1971.

must conform, include the principles of economics that should be included in a basic course in economics. These principles are derived from the essential fact that resources are *scarce* relative to the potential range of social and individual wants. Thus the concept of *opportunity cost* states that the true cost of devoting resources to one use lies in the output sacrificed from alternative uses; the concept of a *production function* relates output with required inputs, given the technology and organizational institutions that exist at a particular historical moment; and the principle of *diminishing marginal utility* states that additional satisfaction gained from consuming more of a given commodity occurs in smaller and smaller increments.

THE STUDY OF COMPARATIVE ECONOMIC SYSTEMS

The heart of the study of comparative economic systems is the analysis of the institutional structure of each type of economy and of the ways in which basic economic principles working through such a structure produce economic results. We seek to understand the reasons for the similarities and differences of institutional structures in general types of economic systems, the problems that arise out of each, and the attempts to create new institutions to solve these problems.

A word of warning should be inserted here. The current level of interest in the study of economic systems originated partially in certain cataclysmic events of the twentieth century, including the Russian Revolution of 1917–1918, the rise of Nazi Germany in the 1930s, and the Cold War politics of the postwar era. Some people regard the study of economic systems as an opportunity for nationalistic propaganda and for instilling "right" viewpoints in the minds of supposedly impressionable students. This book seeks to avoid the excesses of sloganizing and moralizing while pursuing a more objective view of economic systems and their functioning. Value judgments implicit in words like good or bad, successful or unsuccessful should be reached *after* an attempt has been made to understand how a particular economic system actually operates. From time to time we will attempt to offer our own value judgments concerning aspects of modern economies, but the reader should remember that his or her own value judgments are equally justified and equally valid. Differing economic priorities and goals cause genuine differences concerning suggested public policy, for instance, although they may be based on evaluations of an agreed-upon set of facts.

Finally, we believe the comparative study of economic systems is both potentially fun and vitally important for a present and future understanding of the real world. Enjoyable learning is not a contradiction of terms: In fact, we really learn only what we are curious enough and challenged enough to want to know. In one sense, economic systems are intellectual puzzles in which the pieces "fit" together in a variety (but not an infinite variety) of interesting ways. The questions for class discussion at the end of each chapter are designed to stretch imaginations and expose value judgments of students who are willing to play intellectual games for the fun of it.

At the same time, most of us place a fairly high value on wanting to live in a world that is somewhat more humane and less hassled than the one in which we find ourselves. Many of the proposals that compel our attention deal with the creation or alteration of economic systems, Can communal organizations replace "selfishness" with concern for group welfare as a primary source of economic motivation? Should the government operate rail passenger service in the United States? Is health care just another economic commodity, or is it too vital to trust entirely to the market mechanisms? Can Russian economic "reforms" increase the quality and quantity of consumer goods? We view human comfort, security, peace, and happiness as worthwhile goals which, in some modest way, an understanding of economic systems can help achieve.

QUESTIONS FOR CLASS DISCUSSION

1. What forces create economic systems? Which of these are within and which outside of man's control?

2. In what ways can a student of economic systems attempt to disassociate himself mentally from the economic system in which he lives? Is this desirable?

3. What is a "good" economic system? How does one weigh the various aspects of economic systems to form a judgment about the entire system?

4. The citizens in *Looking Backward* do not spend all of their available funds because they supposedly have all they want. Is this believable economic behavior? Could consumers be conditioned to want less than they could afford? If so, how?

5. Name some occupations in which nonmaterial rewards partially offset relatively low salary levels. Name some occupations in which high salary levels partially offset unfavorable working conditions. Could Bellamy's system of equal incomes work in America?

6. Why do Trobriand Islanders work so hard to grow yams if they have to give them away to in-laws? Why do receivers of yams allow them to rot? Are there any parallels of reciprocal gift obligations in the American economic system?

7. In what sense is the long-distance *kula* trade of the Trobriand Islanders beneficial to the participants? Do Americans derive nonmaterial advantages from participation in economic activities?

8. What are the economic advantages of the kibbutz form of organization? Could these advantages exist if an unequal distribution of income existed among kibbutz members?

9. How would you expect the increasing industrial activities of kibbutzim to affect the style of life for their members? Are prosperity and

economic success detrimental to communal forms of economic
organization?

10. Is the evolutionary path of economic systems inevitable? If
so, what determines the path? If not, how can deviations occur?

11. What functions do the following social institutions serve:
graduation exercises, family reunions, presidential news conferences? What
functions do the following institutions serve: strikes, auctions, apprentice-
ship requirements?

12. What are the advantages and disadvantages of an impersonal
market system in which producers and ultimate consumers often have no
face-to-face interaction?

13. Why have self-regulating markets arisen in Western Europe
in the past two or three centuries? Are land and labor less easily
exchanged through market institutions than other commodities?

14. Is our outline of how economic change occurs persuasive?
Does change ever occur without opposition? Can pressure for change be
completely repressed so that no change at all results? What is meant by
the term "dialetical process?

15. Can economic systems be studied objectively? enjoyably?
purposively?

SUGGESTIONS FOR FURTHER READING FOR PART I

Bellamy, Edward, *Looking Backward*, New York: Modern Library, 1951.
Dalton, George, ed., *Economic Development and Social Change: The
    Modernization of Village Communities*, Garden City, N.Y.: Natural
    History Press, 1971.
Dalton, George, ed., *Primitive, Archaic, and Modern Economies: Essays
    of Karl Polanyi*, Garden City, N.Y.: Doubleday, 1968.
Dalton, George, ed., *Tribal and Peasant Economies*, Garden City, N.Y.:
    Natural History Press, 1967.
Herskovits, Melville J., *Economic Anthropology*, New York:
    Norton, 1965.
Ilekman, Warren F., and Norman Thomas Uphoff, *The Political
    Economy of Change*, Berkeley: University of California Press, 1971.
Leon, Dan, *The Kibbutz, A New Way of Life,* London: Oxford
    University Press, 1969.
Malinowski, Bronislaw, *Argonauts of the Western Pacific*, London:
    Routledge & Kegan Paul, 1922.
Parsons, Talcott, and Neil J. Smelser, *Economy and Society*, New
    York: Free Press, 1956.
Polanyi, Karl, *The Great Transformation*, Boston: Beacon, 1957.
Skinner, B. F., *Walden Two*, New York: Macmillan, 1948.
Smelser, Neil J., *The Sociology of Economic Life*, Englewood Cliffs,
    N.J.: Prentice-Hall, 1963.
Vonncgut, Kurt, Jr., *Player Piano*, New York: Avon, 1967.

PART II: CAPITALISM

2. Capitalism as a theoretical concept

This chapter will describe the theory of capitalism as it was developed by Adam Smith and other classical economists. This description may seem remote from today's world, but its major purpose is to present the concept in its purest theoretical form so that we can assess its relevance to modern capitalist societies. That was the goal of the classical economists: Their theoretical model, though based on the historical situation they perceived in the aftermath of the British Industrial Revolution, is an abstract ideal rather than a portrayal of some economic golden age that disappeared with the passage of time.

The pure theory of capitalism has two parts—an institutional stage and a repertoire of economic scenarios that are acted out upon that stage.

Economic theorists have at times been so fascinated by the dramatic action of capitalism that they have taken for granted the elaborate institutional arrangements that make the action possible. Economic institutions, as the previous chapter argued, are the building blocks from which economic systems are constructed; we must therefore take a thorough look at the economic institutions of capitalism in this chapter. Paradoxically, they are so familiar that we are largely ignorant of their operational significance.

First, however, we need a few definitions. It is especially important to distinguish between capital and capitalism. *Capital* means tangible things that are not used directly for consumption but, instead, assist in the production of other goods. The distinguishing feature of capital is the use to which it is put—a bicycle used for pleasure is a consumption good, but used by a delivery service it is a capital good. Machines, tools, factory buildings, and farm equipment are all examples of capital. In recent years economists have begun to talk about *human capital formation*—that is, the investment of resources in training and education of people who utilize their human capital in the production of other goods and services.

The essential point about capital is its usefulness in "roundabout" methods of production. Economics textbooks will probably always use the example of Robinson Crusoe sacrificing a day's fishing to acquire capital in the form of a fish trap yielding more fish than the old method; modern factories, in effect, divert labor from current production to build machines, which likewise increase the yield of whatever the factory turns out. Since all modern production requires at least some use of capital, "roundaboutness" is a relative concept. More capital-intensive methods are usually assumed to be more productive as well, but those who have tried to straighten out an error by a computerized billing service or to place a call when automated equipment is malfunctioning will question the universal validity of that assumption.[1]

The economic system of *capitalism* is not distinguished by the mere physical presence of capital or the use of relatively capital-intensive methods of production. The Soviet Union would qualify under those criteria. Capitalism can be defined and distinguished from other economic systems only with reference to its institutions. Capitalism is a system of economic organization in which individual persons, singly or in groups, privately own the factors of production and possess the right to use those economic resources generally in whatever manner they choose.

It should be noticed that in defining capitalism we required all *factors of production* to be privately owned and controlled instead of just capital. Thus an economic system in which the government owns all land and

---

[1] Rube Goldberg machines dreamed up by the cartoonist to perform simple tasks with farfetched sequences of operations are examples of the potential wastefulness of roundabout methods of production pushed beyond the limits of economic rationality.

rents it to the highest bidder is theoretically plausible, but this institutional arrangement would not fit within our definition of capitalism. Implicit in the definition of capitalism is the right of the individual to employ his talents and energies in the manner he deems best to promote his personal interests. Slavery is inconsistent with capitalism because the slave does not control the use of the labor resources he possesses. The organization and management of economic activity is such an essential part of capitalism that entrepreneurship is sometimes considered a factor of production distinct from other forms of human labor.

Our concept of capitalism emphasizes economic aspects. This does not imply that noneconomic institutions have no significant bearing on capitalism or its development. The process of economic change described in the introductory chapter applies to capitalism as well as to other economic systems. Likewise, one should not identify capitalism exclusively with such noneconomic institutions as freedom of speech or religion, a free press, or democratic government; these noneconomic institutions can be associated with other types of economic systems. We shall focus our attention on the economic institutions of capitalism considered separately, remembering that the relationships between economic and noneconomic institutions are both complex and important.

ECONOMIC INSTITUTIONS OF CAPITALISM

Private Property

Private property is an institutional arrangement fundamental to capitalism. It involves the right of an individual to acquire, use, or dispose of something of economic value in any legitimate way the owner wishes and the right to enjoy the economic rewards that result. Under capitalism, ownership of property is a matter of right. It is the responsibility of government to define the scope and nature of this right and, in the event of its violation, to enforce and protect the owner's claim. A major part of the legal system is composed of institutions for adjudicating disputes arising over the exercise of property rights.

Private property does not refer solely to tangible things; intangible forms of property such as contracts or patent rights are included. Contracts are legally enforceable agreements for the performance of economic activity. Since contracting for the use of land, capital, and labor services (largely, but not exclusively, in return for money income) is the means used for organizing production under capitalism, the rules of contract are an intrinsic part of the institution of private property. Of course, the right to use private property as one pleases is not unrestricted. The government reserves the right of eminent domain to secure ownership of property for which there is a compelling public need, even if the original owner would prefer not to sell. The law also limits the unfavorable effects a property owner may impose on his property. A Philadelphia home owner, for instance, is still forbidden to construct a "soap, candle, glue, starch, lampblack, bone boiling or skin dressing establishment, blacksmith shop, slaughter house, cattle pens, piggery, or other buildings for offensive purpose or occupation" on his property. Each technological era creates its own legal definition of public nuisances; present efforts to abate air, water, and noise pollution must deal with the present-day counterparts of piggeries and lampblack establishments.

One function of private property is to encourage the accumulation and conservation of wealth in the form of capital goods. The one means of capital accumulation that is wholly consistent with capitalism is the private saving of personal and corporate income. Saving presumedly will not occur extensively unless individuals and corporations have incentives to save. Failure to accumulate capital via the process of saving would probably impose a technological barrier on the growth potential of a capitalist economy.

Given the crucial connection between private property and capital accumulation the question of intergenerational transfers of wealth through inheritance becomes important. Inheritance can be treated as an institution of capitalism separate from private property or, as we choose to treat it, as one of the rights attached to private property. If the owner has a right to designate to whom property shall pass at the time of his death and if the designated individual has a legally enforceable claim to that property, then inheritance becomes a powerful mechanism for accumulating wealth.

It also becomes a potential source of conflict with other values in a capitalist society. If the society claims to reward individual "merit," what is the merit of being lucky enough to have had wealthy ancestors? If the society as a whole seeks to redistribute income in the direction of greater equality through taxation, can income arising from inherited wealth be taxed without destroying the original motivation to accumulate? Even if inheritance taxes are levied, the opportunity to make substantial gifts while still living and the provision of training and education can make "equality of opportunity" a very hazy concept in a private-property economic system.

Thus it is imperative to note that even in a purely theoretical approach to capitalism the right to private property cannot be regarded as completely unrestricted. Controls on the use of private property and conflicts with other institutions of a capitalist system are as old as the institution of private property itself, and with the development of capitalism they have multiplied enormously. Nevertheless, they do not negate the basic right of the owner of productive resources to employ them as he sees fit. The other institutions of capitalism derive from and depend on the cornerstone of private property to a large degree.

Freedom of Enterprise

Freedom of enterprise is, in fact, an extension of the concept of private property. It gives the individual owner, or group of owners, the right to select the *type* of economic activity in which their resources will be employed. In the broadest sense, freedom of enterprise is not confined strictly to economic entrepreneurship—it also includes every individual participating in the operations of a capitalist system, whether as wage worker, owner of natural resources or capital, or holder of liquid financial resources.

It is a basic tenet of capitalism that the indvidual, acting alone or collectively, is the best judge of his own interests. Self-interest is a broad concept, but in the theory of capitalism it means primarily *economic* self-interest. This is commonly referred to as the "economic man" concept. In consumption activities the individual is assumed to maximize the satisfaction he derives from the choices he makes; in production activities the entrepreneur is assumed to maximize his profits by striving to increase revenues and decrease costs. If productive resources are directed toward their most remunerative use, there are, as we shall see, important consequences for the overall economic efficiency of the capitalist economic system.

The entrepreneur is assigned the key role in the capitalist economic system; he is assumed to be one who sees the opportunities, takes the risks, gathers the needed factors of production, and gains the profit or suffers the losses that result from the venture. Yet there is no intrinsic reason why a group of workers, capital owners, or landlords should not hire a manager to supervise a project and thus reserve for themselves the profits. Farmers in many Midwestern towns, for example, market their grain cooperatively and then divide the surplus remaining after expenses, including the salary of a professional manager, have been paid.

Some entrepreneurial activity is undoubtedly of the kind that the late Joseph Schumpeter placed at the center of the process of economic development—the *first* breakthrough in the introduction of a new product, a new technology, a new marketing scheme, a new structure of business organization, and so forth.[2] When we look at an advanced capitalist economic system, however, we see that most economic activity is conducted by managers of business firms instead of by individual entrepreneurs. Most business firms, moreover, are engaged in fairly routine production and distribution processes rather than in spectacular Schumpeterian innovations.

The modern corporation is the institutional form in which freedom of enterprise most often manifests itself in the real world. And yet the pure theory of capitalism has no specific role for the corporation to perform; it is regarded simply as a collective form of "economic man" intent on

---

[2]Joseph A. Schumpeter, *The Theory of Economic Development*, New York: Oxford University Press, 1961. See especially chaps. II and IV.

profit maximization like the solitary, decision-making entrepreneur. The reason for this seeming oversight is contained in the next essential institution of theoretical capitalism, the competitive market. We will have more to say about the economic role of the modern corporation.

Competitive Markets

Capitalism, as a concept, assumes the existence of competition in markets where factors of production are bought or leased, as well as in consumer-goods markets. Competition refers to the existence of independent buyers and sellers for a given product or service; no one is coerced either to buy or to sell at the prevailing market price. This price, which is assumed to fluctuate up or down in response to changes in underlying supply and demand conditions, serves two crucial functions.

The *rationing* function tends to allocate goods and services to those who are willing to pay the prevailing price. Willingness depends on the intensity of desire and the purchasing power of the prospective customer. Many college professors would be "in the market" for a Rolls Royce if the price were one-tenth of the current level; the rationing function of price signals tends to cause professors to seek out other modes of transportation. Factors of production are similarly rationed among those producers who are able to make more efficient use of productive resources. Those who "can't afford" to hire more workers or rent more land at the going factor prices are excluded from the utilization of scarce resources.

The *motivating* function of prices also operates in both product and factor markets. The rising price of a commodity for which demand has increased alerts prospective new producers of possible profit opportunities in that area. Existing multiproduct firms can shift resources into activities with favorable price signals. Declining prices may squeeze profit levels for some firms to a point at which they will shift to other products or even go out of business completely. The punishment meted out by competitive capitalist markets to producers who misjudge demand for a new product, are slow in adopting a new production technique, or suffer adverse effects of an unforeseeable change in consumer preferences is often understated. There must be losers as well as winners in order for participants in competitive markets to adapt to changing conditions. When markets fail to function effectively in capitalist economies, it is often because producers have found some way of insulating themselves from the harsh consequences of an unfavorable market situation.

Factor prices also serve—more effectively than most people realize—to affect career choices and the uses to which land and capital are put. Falling birth rates signal prospective obstetricians toward psychiatry or other medical specialties for which continued demand seems assured; farmland is turned into shopping centers; more new investment goes into the trucking industry than into railroads. Specialized occupational skills already acquired are often less easily shifted into other areas of employment (as barbers and aerospace engineers have discovered in recent years); an adjustment lag may exist in factor markets during which resources are temporarily unemployed while market forces work themselves out.

One more aspect of competitive markets warrants discussion. Adam Smith's famous pin factory served to illustrate the specialization of production activities that large-scale markets allow. This division of labor permits those who control factors of production to channel them into most productive uses. Human labor, especially, can stick to one line of work where skills and practice can be brought to bear—imagine the wastefulness of training someone to perform a single brain operation, for example. Benefits from the division of labor arise only because the operation of a market economy provides a regular supply of goods and services. We would each become a combination farmer, weaver, lawyer, and so forth, with resulting losses in specialized talents and skills, if we did not trust the market system to provide those needs. The chaos arising from a disruption of electric service or from a transportation strike shows the web of human independency spun by a market economy.

Government

Despite the presumption of a general absence of governmental interference in a smoothly functioning theoretical capitalist economy, it should be stressed that the system cannot operate without the aid of a government possessing sovereign powers. In this sense government per se is an institution of capitalism, and its role as such should be understood.

Milton Friedman, a forceful and intellectually consistent adherent of a minimal role for government in economic affairs, nevertheless advances this extensive roster of activities:

> A government which maintained law and order, defined property rights, served as a means whereby we could modify property rights and other rules of the economic game, adjudicated disputes about the interpretation of the rules, enforced contracts, promoted competition, provided a monetary framework, engaged in activities to counter technical monopolies and to overcome neighborhood effects widely regarded as sufficiently important to justify government intervention, and which supplemented private charity and the private family in protecting the irresponsible, whether madman or child—such a government would clearly have important functions to perform.[3]

This list shows that government involvement is essential to preserve social values. Without regulatory measures, there is danger that a capitalist

[3]Milton Friedman, *Capitalism and Freedom*, Chicago: University of Chicago Press, 1962, p. 34.

system based on individual self-interest could run amok, degenerating into a disorderly scramble in which neither the values of the society nor the rights of the individual would be safeguarded. Restrictions on the institutions of capitalism, even in its purest theoretical form, are essential to keep those institutions from destroying themselves.

Government intervention in a capitalist economy is never "neutral" because it always has different impacts on various individuals. Antipollution laws that provide recreational benefits or decrease medical costs for consumers, for example, impose economic hardships on producers. The point to remember is that once government performs its necessary functions such as defining property rights, it is possible for competitive markets to operate in such a way as to achieve efficient results. Firms liable for damages caused by pollution may choose to install control devices, to compensate those affected, or to change locations; potential victims can choose to limit their exposure, to collect deliberately for injuries incurred, or to move elsewhere.[4] The economic role of government under theoretical capitalism resembles decisions concerning traffic rules—it matters less whether traffic drives on the right or left than that a single rule is selected and consistently enforced

THE RESULTS OF PERFECTLY COMPETITIVE CAPITALISM

We are now ready to wind up the institutions of theoretical capitalism and watch their simultaneous performance under ideal conditions. The ideal conditions are fairly restrictive, but they are necessary to demonstrate the economic efficiency achieved by theoretical capitalism. In later chapters we will investigate the claim that theoretical socialism can achieve an equivalent degree of efficiency if similar ideal conditions are postulated.

The conditions can be stated in five brief categories. More rigorous and elegant statements could be used, especially in mathematical form, but we are using economic theory to highlight economic systems, not the other way around. The five conditions are:

1. Consumers maximize their total utility or satisfaction instantaneously and without cost; firms likewise maximize their total profits and factor owners their incomes.
2. Consumers, firms, and factors of production can enter or exit from any market without cost or penalty.
3. There are sufficient numbers of firms, customers, and owners of factors of production in each market so the activities of any

[4]See R. H. Couse, "The Problem of Social Cost," *Journal of Law and Economics,* October 1960. This important article is the basis of current thinking about the economic effects of property rights and their violation. The adjustment process is complicated if transactions are costly, a point to be discussed later.

individual buyer or seller are too inconsequential to affect the prevailing market price. Individuals are price takers, not price makers, in the market.

4. Consumers experience declining marginal utility, meaning that as they consume more and more of any given product they get smaller and smaller doses of additional satisfaction. Firms experience increasing marginal costs, meaning that as they produce more and more of any given product they incur larger increments of additional cost.

5. There are no technological or organizational economies of scale within the firms, no barriers to price flexibility in either direction, no governmental interference, and no other conditions that would impede the operation of perfectly competitive markets.

Product Markets

The market mechanism allows each consumer, operating in his own self-interest, to determine the unique combination of goods and services that provides the greatest achievable satisfaction within his spendable income. Like the system used by Boy Scouts at a jamboree, this process could occur through bartering or swapping in the absence of price signals. After a mutually advantageous swap, the law of diminishing marginal utility decrees that each partner attaches lower utility to the last unit of the item he acquires and higher utility to the last remaining unit of the item he gives up. Eventually his remaining supply of the bartered commodity becomes too "valuable" to part with relative to what he can get for it, and further trade ceases.

Prices perform exactly the same function as repetitive bartering, without the monumental confusion that would exist if a complex capitalist economy had to rely extensively on face-to-face exchange through barter. Consumers divert their dollars away from goods giving little additional satisfaction and toward goods yielding more additional satisfaction at prevailing market prices. Diminishing marginal utility again sets a stopping place—an individual equilibrium in which the marginal utility per dollar expended is the same for each commodity. Each consumer, in effect, barters away potential purchases of less preferred goods.

Perfectly competitive firms also operate within a framework of prevailing product prices. Firms maximize their profits by producing a level of output in each product line so that the additional cost of the last unit of each product is precisely equal to the price received from its sale. If price is above marginal cost for some products and below in others, the firm will shift the resources at its command into producing more of the profitable goods and less of the unprofitable ones. The law of increasing marginal costs ensures that the individual firm will use this process of internal barter to stop at a profit-maximizing equilibrium in its production mix.

Since it is assumed that consumers and producers are unable to affect prices by solitary actions, it is evident that prices will change only through the cumulative effects of a change in underlying demand conditions (reflecting consumer tastes) or supply conditions (reflecting production costs). Once any price in the product universe changes, all consumers and producers face the task of adjusting their activities to achieve equilibrium once again. Included in this adjustment process is the entry or exit of some firms and some consumer markets for particular products.

Factor Markets

Factor markets under theoretical capitalism parallel product markets in responding to supply and demand conditions, but for some reason students have more trouble understanding how factor markets work. First, even in the absence of a price system in factor markets, firms could swap factors just as consumers could swap products if it were mutually advantageous to do so. Firms using identical factors of production would test to see whether they could gain more additional production (called marginal physical product) by acquiring more of one factor than they would lose by giving up the required amount of another factor. Barter would occur when a firm with relatively more productive potential uses for one of two factors found a firm in the opposite situation. Moreover, if marginal physical product declines as more and more of a factor is added, the bartering will halt when the ratio of marginal products is the same in each firm.

Factor prices, like product prices, circumvent the inconvenience of bartering. Each firm, facing an array of factor prices that it cannot influence, chooses to acquire additional units of factors whose additional contribution to output per dollar expended is high and to divest itself of factors whose marginal product per dollar of factor cost is relatively low. A little thought will show that a firm minimizes its total costs, under conditions of declining marginal physical product, when it chooses an equilibrium in which the marginal product per dollar spent on each factor is equal. A firm following this rule of maximum output per dollar of costs is also minimizing additional costs per unit of output, thus ensuring that the pattern of marginal costs for each product is as low as possible. A profit-maximizing firm must logically also be a cost minimizer.

Demand for factors of production is thus related to their relative effectiveness in producing final products. What determines the supply of factors of production? If factors are conceived of in the broadest categories of land, labor, and capital, then the supply is pretty much fixed at any moment and changes only in response to slow changes in population behavior or land-settlement patterns. If, however, factors of production can choose among alternative occupations, then a higher factor price will bring forth a greater quantity of that factor. For example, workers confronted with prevailing wage rates in various occupations choose according to their earning skills and the attractiveness or unattractiveness of working conditions in each.

Since no single buyer or seller can influence factor prices under conditions of perfect competition, a prevailing set of equilibrium factor prices will change only if the basic supply or demand conditions change. And again, as in the case of product prices, a change in one or more factor prices means that all participants must at least check to make sure that they are demanding or supplying the individually optimal pattern of resources.

Income Distribution

Economists studying capitalist economic systems are often accused of neglecting the topic of income distribution. Their defense is that under *theoretical* capitalism there is little to discuss—perfectly competitive markets determine factor prices and hence factor earnings. Often a value judgment is slipped in at this point, stating that incomes determined by competitive markets are "fair" and that therefore individuals at the lower end of the income scale have no legitimate complaint about their economic status.

This argument is inadequate in at least two respects. First, it says nothing about how the *ownership* of productive resources is distributed. If land, physical capital, and human capital are concentrated in a small sector of the total population, it follows that income from those factors will be similarly concentrated so that effective demand for commodities will be tilted toward recipients of nonwage income. An economic theory that has so little to say about how the distribution of factor ownership came about in the first place is vulnerable to criticism.

Second, political power often parallels concentrations of economic power. Theoretical capitalism assumes that government does not interfere in competitive markets. This noninterference is, at the very least, likely to preserve existing concentrations of economic and political power or even to facilitate a trend toward greater concentration. These are issues to consider even in the most abstract discussions of theoretical capitalism. When we relax our assumptions to allow imperfections and interferences in factor markets, they will assume major importance.

We should also keep in mind that the abstract factor of production called labor is made up of flesh-and-blood human beings whose rational powers of observation make them aware of their economic situation. While it might be economically rational to withhold one's labor at a low prevailing market wage, it might not be realistic in terms of survival.

Economic Balance and Pareto Optimality

We have demonstrated the solution provided by perfectly competitive capitalism for each of the major questions that every economic system must answer: what to produce, what factor combinations or techniques of production to use in producing it, and how to divide up access to what is produced. It remains to show how the final proportions of goods produced are selected and how the perfectly competitive economy is economically efficient.

Imagine an extreme case in which all factors of production are fully employed in producing a single product—ashtrays. Under these circumstances it is more than likely that the marginal utility derived by the typical consumer from his last ashtray is very low. Likewise, the marginal cost of producing the last ashtray is very high because some factors of production are very ill-suited for ashtray production. To shift some of these factors to another product, say doughnuts, would sacrifice few ashtrays and would involve a gain in consumer satisfaction due to the high marginal utility of the new product for doughnut-starved consumers. In the process the income of factors specially suited to doughnut production rises and that of factors stuck in ashtray production falls.

As doughnuts and other new products are introduced, the marginal utility gained from additional units will decline and the marginal costs connected with their production will rise. An equilibrium will be established where the ratio of marginal utility to marginal cost for the last unit of each product, including ashtrays, is equal. One of the strongest claims for competitive markets is their ability to relate the mental preferences of individual consumers and the facts of relative factor scarcity (as reflected in the cost curves of individual firms) in one global, simultaneous, frictionless system.

The system is also economically efficient in the sense that no individual can be made better off without reducing the total satisfaction of some other individual. The sources of potential slack—a reallocation of goods among consumers, a reallocation of factors among firms, a change in the consumer's own product mix or the firm's own factor mix—are all ruled out when the competitive system achieves equilibrium prices and quantities in every market. This situation, called Pareto Optimality, is a standard of comparison for judging other theoretical systems. It is also a basis for discussion of the effects of market failure in causing the capitalist system to fall short of the potential output achievable under efficient conditions.

QUESTIONS FOR CLASS DISCUSSION

1. Discuss reasons why the British Industrial Revolution and Adam Smith's description of the model of capitalism occurred at about the same time.

2. What are the relations between capitalist institutions and the operation of a capitalist economic system?

3. In what ways is human capital similar to, and in what ways different from, physical capital? College expenses are treated as a consumption item like housing or recreation in national income accounts. In what ways is your college education a consumer good? In what ways is it an investment?

4. Give examples of multistage roundabout methods of production

in which, for example, machines are used to make other machines.

5. What are the essential elements in a definition of capitalism? Can true capitalism exist if most people work for others? if everybody works for a single employer? if a tax rate of 80 percent is imposed on all incomes? a tax rate of 10 percent?

6. How is the dividing line between allowable and unallowable uses of private property determined by society? Should airplanes be allowed to fly over my property at an altitude of 30,000 feet if I don't want them to? at an altitude of 300 feet? if they discourage my hens from laying eggs? if they wake me on Sunday morning after a long Saturday night? if they might crash? if they won't crash, but I worry that they might?

7. In what ways is entrepreneurial freedom different from the freedom of any other owner of factors of production to act in his own self-interest?

8. Can stiff inheritance taxes be compatible with the basic institutions of theoretical capitalism? Does having to pay estate taxes significantly alter or reduce economic motivation? Does receiving an inheritance significantly alter or reduce economic motivation?

9. Imagine an economic system in which self-interest expressed itself primarily in noneconomic goals. Is such a system viable?

10. How does society benefit from acts of Schumpeterian entrepreneurship when so many people are inconvenienced or even ruined when old ways of doing things are replaced?

11. Distinguish between the rationing and motivating functions of the price system in both product and factor markets. Is it fair that people suffer from adverse market conditions that are in no way their fault?

12. Give examples of how career choices are affected by conditions prevailing in factor markets.

13. If government cannot be "neutral" in applying economic policy, on what basis should policy choices be made?

14. How are factor markets and product markets linked in a perfectly competitive capitalist economy?

15. Do your parents know that they are spending good money to allow you to discuss questions like these?

3. Capitalism as an existing system

This chapter will consider developments in American capitalism that, to a greater or lesser degree, take account of departures from the theoretical concept of capitalism embodied in the preceding chapter. Most abberations of theoretical capitalism are best observed by studying the causes of imperfections in otherwise perfectly competitive markets. These have two primary origins: They may be either generated in the private sector or attributable to government. Since flaws in the institutions of private property and free enterprise have their effects through the market system, we will concentrate on instances of market failure in a realistic assessment of capitalism. After that we will be ready to take a comprehensive look at the strengths and weaknesses of American capitalism.

PRIVATE SOURCES OF MARKET FAILURE

Transaction Costs

Our discussion of theoretical capitalism explicity assumed that market transactions occurred instantaneously and without cost to either buyer or seller. But such is not the case in the real world. There are search costs in finding the least costly factors of production or final products, negotiation costs of settling contract terms, costs of litigation, and costs of maintaining distribution networks through which goods move from producer to consumer. Some of these costs are unavoidable and some are incurred on purpose to avoid the even higher costs of striving for perfectly competitive markets. Either way, some resources that could have been used to produce goods and services for final consumers will be absorbed in the unavoidable friction created in a market system.

Advertising expenditures represent one controversial form of transaction cost in the American economy. Advertising can increase consumer satisfaction by reducing the search costs of finding preferred goods; in many cases, however, competing advertising claims simply cancel each other out. It was widely reported that American cigarette companies secretly welcomed the 1971 ban on television advertising of their product; they were said to feel that potential new brands would be the only ones hurt significantly by the regulation.

The presence of transaction costs also interferes with market responsiveness in adjusting to the economic effects of one individual's actions on others. These *externalities* are dealt with when property rights are assigned and damages assessed. Transaction costs, however, may prevent the victims of pollution or other unwanted side effects from organizing effectively to remedy the situation to the mutual advantage of everyone.

The point about transaction costs, to repeat, is that they serve as barriers to achieving efficient production methods or patterns of consumer satisfaction. One potential case for government intervention in a capitalist economic system exists when transaction costs are too large for the self-correcting feature of markets to operate.

Economies of Scale

The second source of market failure is the existence of economies of scale, which are assumed absent in the model of theoretical capitalism. These exist when an increase in the output of a firm does not require a proportionate increase in productive resources. If the costs required for each unit of output continue to fall as output increases, monopoly conditions may result and a single firm or small number of firms may dominate an entire industry. The theoretical model of capitalism requires that no firm can influence market price by its own actions alone; a monopoly firm can increase its profits by limiting output and raising prices to a more profitable level.

Some economies of scale arise from technological causes; the efficient scale of a modern steel mill or oil refinery is very large indeed. Equally important, perhaps, are economies of scale from other sources—information flows, research and development activities, and managerial expertise. If information is assembled on consumer receptivity to a new product or the probability of finding oil in a new area, for instance, that information is probably applicable to large-scale projects at no greater cost than for limited utilization. The same is often true of the scientific effort needed to develop new production techniques or new products—once developed, they can be duplicated with little additional effort. Finally, the special skills that go into executive decision making probably do not vary proportionately with the magnitude of the decision being made.

Corporate Business Organization

We are now ready to discuss why the organization of business firms is such a neglected topic in the pure theory of capitalism. It is because the firm can reduce transaction costs and take advantage of economies of scale by forming an "island of planning" insulated from the market system. "Outside the firm price movements direct production, which is co-ordinated through a series of exchange transactions on the market. Within a firm, these market transactions are eliminated and in place of the complicated market structure with exchange transactions is substituted the entrepreneur-coordinator, who directs production."[1] When transaction costs and economies of scale are nonexistent, as assumed in the pure theory of capitalism, market prices alone determine all decisions for the profit-maximizing firm; there is no latitude remaining for entrepreneurial planning.

A distinguishing feature of the American economy has been the rise of the corporate form of business organization. Corporations enjoy status as legal entities and provide limited liability so that no individual stockholder is financially responsible for losses beyond his initial investment. They are particularly suited for large-scale ventures because of the ability to consolidate amounts of private funds in excess of those available to individual entrepreneurs and because professional managers can develop techniques that effectively organize productive activities.

One such technique is the multidivisional structure in which semi-autonomous divisions are responsible for day-to-day operations, leaving the central office free to concentrate on long-term entrepreneurial policy choices.[2] This provides the essential separation of routine administration

---

[1] R. H. Coase, "The Nature of the Firm," *Economica*, November 1937. Reprinted in Wayne A. Leeman, ed., *Capitalism, Market Socialism, and Central Planning*, Boston: Houghton Mifflin, 1963, p. 322.

[2] Alfred D. Chandler Jr., *Strategy and Structure*, Cambridge, Mass.: MIT Press, 1962. This book presents the historical circumstances under which four giant American corporations adopted the multidivisional corporate structure.

from overall policy determination that is needed to operate a diversified corporation. One might even argue that the recent trend toward creation of conglomerate corporations through the acquisition and merger of firms involved in widely disparate types of economic activity would be impossible without some reliance on a multidivisional structure.

The motivation to merge may be to ensure an increased availability of finance beyond the separate availabilities of the merging firms; one or more component parts of a given merger may be unable to obtain further credit from its bankers. Again, a merger may be for the purpose of realizing economies of large-scale production or distribution. Varieties of tax avoidance or tax benefits provide motives for some kinds of mergers. Frequently, a desire to reduce or eliminate competition of one kind or another is the preponderant motivation.

The concentration of economic power in giant corporations, whether arising from mergers or from internal growth, is a fact of American economic life. More than half of manufacturing activity is accounted for by the nation's 500 largest manufacturing corporations. In addition, these firms have become a major political force in the United States, both because of their ability to lobby effectively for their economic interests and because of the potential impact on employees, suppliers, and investors of a serious economic setback or failure. The question arises as to whether the obvious reduction in transaction costs and internalization of economies of scale realized by the modern corporation are gained at the expense of distortions in competitive markets of so great a magnitude that the survival of the capitalist economic system is endangered. If one makes the value judgment that the balance of power should be shifted toward competitive markets, very difficult questions immediately appear concerning how such changes should, and even could, be carried out.

Labor Unions

A labor union is a merger of a sort in that individual workers join together to achieve a better bargaining position. This may mean that labor can charge for its services a price higher than would otherwise be a competitive wage. It is public policy in the United States, however, that labor unions not be prosecuted as violators of the antitrust statutes that nominally apply to business firms.

The Taft-Hartley Act of 1947 made illegal some labor practices such as secondary boycotts and jurisdictional strikes. Nevertheless, within these limitations unions have considerable power to influence wages by means—including political means—inconsistent with the nature of a truly free market. From a public-policy standpoint, collective bargaining by unions is regarded as approximately equalizing the respective bargaining positions of employers and employees. One may make the value judgment that this is desirable public policy, but it does constitute another inroad to the existence of theoretically perfect free markets in the American capitalist economy.

GOVERNMENT SOURCES OF MARKET FAILURE

We now turn our attention to those sources of market imperfections that either arise from or are correctable only through government intervention. It is paradoxical that government, which attempts to promote competition through antitrust action and other devices, should deliberately distort other prices from their perfectly competitive norms. In some cases the paradox is explained by reference to the underlying goal of protecting the general interests of society; in others it boils down to the ability of special groups to exercise political power to advance their economic interests at the expense of other groups.

Public Goods

Heading the list of candidates for governmental intervention are a special type of commodity called public goods. Pure public goods have the quality that, unlike bread or other nonpublic goods, use by one person does not detract or disallow use by other people; national defense and malaria-spraying programs are often cited as examples in which the protection afforded one person is equally available to everybody in the relevant area. If these services are provided at all, there is no way in which coverage can be withheld from nonsubscribers. If a voluntary collection were taken, each person would tend to understate the value of being protected in the hope that others would care enough to provide the service. Since each individual is tempted to be a "free rider," public goods are *underproduced* by a market system, if they are produced at all, relative to the amount consumers really desire. Only the government, using the legal coercion implicit in sovereign power, can tax customers for the full cost of public goods. An ideal tax system would charge each person according to the hidden satisfaction derived from the public good.

There are public-goods features in many other activities. Although individual beneficiaries of police, fire, and public health activities could theoretically be charged on a fee basis, the utility gained from living in a protected environment is a public good that all can enjoy. Even education, which is definitely an individually consumed product, creates a public good in the form of a more culturally and politically sophisticated populace. In each of these cases the public-goods aspect will cause some degree of market failure unless governmental action is forthcoming.

The free-rider problem is potentially present in any form of collective activity.[3] One example is the American Association of University Pro-

[3]Mancur Olson Jr., *The Logic of Collective Action*, New York: Schocken Books, 1968.

fessors (AAUP), which exists to advance the interests and protect the academic freedom of college teachers. Dues are approximately $25 a year, which is undoubtedly a bargain relative to the value of the benefits arising from AAUP activities. Yet most professors do not belong to the organization—those benefits are enjoyed whether or not an individual chooses to pay his or her dues. Many appeals from private groups for governmental intervention arise from the free-rider problem. The government may be called upon to enforce participation (compulsory union membership, for instance) or to provide services (such as agricultural research or vocational training) that sometimes cannot easily be organized on a private basis.

Public Utilities

Many services can be produced and distributed efficiently only by monopolies because of the cost of establishing the distribution network or of the inconvenience for customers excluded from access to the entire system. Gas, electricity, and telephone service are examples of natural monopolies that are often regulated as public utilities with government control of rates and quality of service. Thus, customer prices and investor return presumably are kept in line with what would prevail if competitive markets could exist in these industries.

The regulatory activities of the United States government—the Interstate Commerce Commission, the Federal Communications Commission, the Federal Aviation Agency, and so forth—can be regarded as quasipublic utilities in which there would have to be costly duplication of services in order for competitive conditions to prevail. Accordingly, it is judged to be in the public interest to protect consumers from the consequences of market failure in these industries.

Public-utility regulation vividly demonstrates how difficult it is to restore economic efficiency by governmental edict when the market system breaks down. By imposing rate-of-return-on-investment criteria in setting prices for public utilities, there is a bias toward capital-intensive techniques of production and less incentive for labor-intensive maintenance and customer-service activities. By setting rates on one activity, the regulating agency may upset the competitive balance with a competing industry—cargos carried by rail, inland waterways, and motor trucks, for example, are all subject to regulatory control in the United States. Finally, there is a persistent tendency for regulatory activities to be turned into a means of protecting the economic interests of those supposedly being monitored. Appointments to regulatory agencies become politically sensitive; employees of regulatory agencies often find lucrative jobs in the industry they formerly supervised; lobbying activities and political contributions are major activities of trade associations. The public interest can easily get lost in so much maneuvering for private advantage.

Indirect Controls and Subsidies

American capitalism departs from freely competitive market conditions in the multitude of governmental activities that have indirect ramifications on economic decisions made by firms or individuals. Monetary and fiscal policy, for instance, plays a major role in determining what happens in the economy, as does a wide range of safety and consumer-protection legislation that did not originate primarily for economic reasons.

Monetary policy, administered by the semigovernmental Federal Reserve System, manipulates one of the most important prices in our economy—the interest rate on borrowed money. In regulating the flow of money throughout the economy, different industries are affected disproportionately. Residential construction, for instance, is so sensitive to increases in interest rates that tight monetary policy aimed at slowing down an overheated economy may send the housing industry into a disastrous slump.

Fiscal policy, likewise, cannot be neutral in its effects. Additional spending to achieve full employment has its initial impact on industries closely linked with the types of goods and services the government decides to purchase—military expenditures help aircraft manufacturers, educational expenditures help textbook publishers, and so forth. When it comes to the revenue side of fiscal policy, the differential impact of taxation is abundantly clear. The type of tax selected, the progressiveness of rates, and the creation of tax loopholes for selected groups all influence the distribution of the actual tax burden. One example will serve to show the tendency of the tax base to erode with the passage of time and lobbying tactics: The depletion allowance originally granted to oil producers with the questionable rationale of compensating for using up the asset has now been extended to cover other minerals, timber, beef cattle, and even professional football players. Some of the best minds in America are devoted to exploiting "tax angles"; a simplified and more equitable tax system would free this human capital for more productive purposes.

Government subsidies often take indirect forms. Grants for airport construction may appear nondiscriminatory until it is remembered that a high portion of air travel is done by business executives who benefit to the extent that costs are shifted from their firms to the general taxpayer. Government medical treatment of miners who contract black-lung disease relieves coal companies of an occupationally related expense; preventive measures might be adopted more readily if liability were assigned to employers. Unemployment-compensation payments to striking workers represent an indirect subsidy to union strike funds.

These examples illustrate the substantial advantages to be gained from having the government bear some of the social costs created by private enterprise. The government has another set of favors to grant to private enterprise: It can enforce the ability of one group to impose transaction costs on another in excess of what they would be if market forces were allowed to operate more freely. Building codes require work to be done by registered plumbers and electricians. Barbers and beauticians (and schools training them) benefit from occupational licensure laws. Lawyer-dominated legislatures have been slow to institute no-fault automobile insurance or to reform probate and divorce laws; all of these areas involve considerable transaction costs in the form of legal fees. Milton Friedman goes so far as to recommend that licensing of doctors should be ended in order to allow market forces greater influence in providing health care.[4]

CAPITALISM'S STRENGTHS

The list of sources of market failure—private and public—should be sufficient to indicate that there is a large discrepancy between the world of pure capitalism, which logically implies maximum welfare and economic efficiency, and the more realistic world in which markets are flawed by internal imperfections and outside interference. An assessment of the real capitalist economy, then, requires us to go beyond pure theory to weigh the strengths and weaknesses of the system as it actually operates. Since every type of economy must be judged in terms of net human benefits, the final reckoning becomes a personal matter highly charged with subjective values. We begin with a discussion of the strengths of capitalism as it has developed in the United States.

Flexibility

The capitalist system of the United States has demonstrated a flexibility and adaptability permitting it to conform institutions and processes to innumerable environmental changes. In substantial measure, it has adapted itself to war and then to peace, to new technology, to basic shifts in consumer preferences and needs, and to increasing urbanization and industrialization. These adaptations have occurred through the decisions of business entrepreneurs, workers, consumers, unions, owners of investment securities, and so on. The point for emphasis is that a capitalist institutional framework has permitted the free play of forces producing those decisions.

The rise of the corporate form of business is but one of the many possible illustrations of this process of adaptation. Business corporations have been woven so completely into the fabric of our capitalist system that we forget that the system once existed without them. Similarly, the institution of private property has evolved from a context once consisting almost exclusively of land, buildings, livestock, machinery, and durable consumption goods to a maze of intangible possessions, contractual rights, and pa-

---

[4]Milton Friedman, *Capitalism and Freedom*, Chicago: University of Chicago Press, 1962, chap. IX.

per claims essential to the integrated functioning of highly specialized industrial and business firms.

Such institutional changes in capitalism come to be embodied in legislation and court decisions, but they originate with entrepreneurs, owners, workers, investors, or consumers who sense their own needs for institutional change and instigate modifying legislation and court cases. Not the least important aspect of this flexibility has been capitalism's adaptation to increasingly numerous and complex governmental controls. Today our capitalist system retains its basic reliance on private economic enterprise as the mainspring of productive energy and action—despite the enormous absolute growth of socially imposed restraints.

Rising Standards of Living

There is no doubt that the people of the United States have experienced a remarkable rise in their material living standards. The rise in per-capita standards, along with an increasing population, implies that our productive system has been operating at a high level of efficiency. Moreover, in spite of the existing inequality of income and wealth among families, there are few sections of our society that have not shared the rise in living standards. However, we must not identify material or economic prosperity with human happiness. Economic betterment is one important factor in human happiness, but whether rising living standards have made our population happier, on balance, involves factors outside the scope of our inquiry. Also, it is necessary to recognize that capitalist institutions per se must not be given sole credit for raising our standards of living. Scientific research outside the business system, for example, has played an important supplemental role in the development of technology and scientific knowledge.

Individual Opportunity

It is one of the most noteworthy strengths of the U.S. economy that its capitalistic framework has generated massive forces of ability and desire to activate, organize, and direct the factors of production, thus adding to the stock of wealth and the flow of goods and services. In combining the available productive resources into organized units, entrepreneurship occupies a strategic role. The continuous adaptations of economic activity to changing conditions depends on the quality of available entrepreneurship.

Capitalism's strength arises partially from its close identity with individualism. The profit motive and the individual's relative freedom to pursue his own interests have channeled these efforts into the productive employment of natural resources, labor, and capital funds. Under the spur of individual reward for success (and penalty for failure), business and industrial enterprises have sought new forms of economic organization, new processes, and new products to the end that our economy has yielded a remarkable increase in standards of living. The individualistic institutions of private property and inheritance have encouraged risk taking, thereby stimulating the creation and preservation of productive wealth for future use. Individualism is a basic characteristic of capitalism, and much of capitalism's strength is attributable to it.

American capitalism has provided upward social and economic mobility for literally millions of immigrants and their children. Access to public education and the opportunities that rapid economic growth creates for new managers and members of professions have combined to provide favorable chances of intergenerational movement to better positions in the economic hierarchy.

Technological Progress

The rapidity and nature of advances in machine technology in the United States is one of our most impressive accomplishments. This technology has progressed from the introduction of simple mechanical devices or machines, through the substitution of power-producing machinery for human and animal muscle power, to a point at which automated equipment can perform a whole series of complex operations. Technological advances have occurred and continue to be developed over the entire range of economic activity.

Again, the mere form of our economic organization per se is not creating this technological progress. Physicists, chemists, engineers, mathematicians, and production technologists are responsible for expansion of the scientific base underlying our industrial expansion. The important point is that the capitalist setting in which technological progress has taken place provides motivation for cost-reducing technological developments. It also provides an institutional setting in which basic and applied research can be conducted on a scale beyond the means of the typical researcher.

CAPITALISM'S WEAKNESSES

An examination of our contemporary capitalist economy reveals two types of weaknesses. The first comprises failures of the various sectors of the economy to function as efficiently as they should; these are excluded from consideration here. The second type consists of significant shortcomings of the *basic institutions* of our capitalist economy in promoting human welfare. If these failures become sufficiently acute, correction can occur only by means of drastic modification or replacement of the fundamental institutions of capitalism, thus altering the character of the capitalistic free-enterprise system.

Pecuniary Versus Human Values

Business success in the capitalist system is judged by measures such as profit and loss, price and cost—concepts that are pecuniary and in many instances may have little or no necessary relationship to human welfare. Economic activity has as its main purpose the creation of human well-being, but the entrepreneurial decisions that guide the operations of our economy are based on calculations and considerations framed in dollar terms. The absence of any consistent inherent relationship between the dollar and human welfare may cause economic decisions to depart widely from those indicated by the sole criterion of human welfare. What will benefit or injure the consumer is frequently a minor consideration, relative to potential monetary profit, in entrepreneurial decisions. In short, elements of immediate or long-range importance to the well-being of people as human beings are neglected or obliterated by entrepreneurial decisions as to *what* will be produced and *how* it will be produced.

This point is vividly illustrated by comparison with the flexibility demonstrated by primitive economic systems in meeting nonmaterial needs:

> It is because of the absence of Western market and technological constraints that work *can be* arranged to express social relationships. The tribal producer does not have a payroll to meet. It is *not* that he is indifferent to material abundance or efficiency; rather, unlike the West, there is no larger economy to compel producers to seek cost minimization, or provide them with economic directives (factor and output prices) to make economizing decisions in work arrangement.[5]

The other side of the coin of technological progress is the monotonous, alienating tasks that mechanization often imposes on production workers. Economists are just beginning to explore the relationship between material abundance and individuals' perceptions of their own happiness, but it seems likely that they will find considerable willingness to sacrifice income for jobs that are interesting, socially relevant, and varied. It is also a good bet that they will discover that feelings of benevolence or malevolence toward others play a larger role in motivating human behavior than the individualistic calculus of neoclassical economic theory would indicate.[6]

A recent book argues that the richer an economy becomes, the more frantic the pace of life will seem and the less really idle time will be avail-

[5]George Dalton, ed., *Tribal and Peasant Economies*, Garden City, N.Y.: Natural History Press, 1967, pp. 69 70.

[6]Charlie Chaplin's motion picture *Modern Times*, which was made in the 1930s, is a funny but chilling portrayal of the dehumanization resulting from pushing pecuniary values to extreme limits. Richard Easterlin discusses results of survey research on perceived happiness in an unpublished paper written in 1971 and entitled "Does Economic Growth Improve the Human Lot?" Economists are even becoming aware of that greatest among nonmaterial sources of utility, love! See Charlotte D. Phelps, "Is the Household Obsolete?" *American Economic Review*, May 1972.

able for people to enjoy. If productivity is rising, then an hour "wasted" away from working sacrifices a greater amount of production; if the act of consuming takes time, as it undoubtedly does, then a rising level of affluence absorbs more time. Either way, time becomes more valuable and it becomes increasingly extravagant to use it in noneconomic pursuits such as musing, praying, or sheer idleness. Only poor societies can afford the luxury of not being enslaved by the clock.[7]

Unemployed Resources

It was generally believed by the classical economists that the capitalist society generates forces that keep the economy in a state of balance. An oversupply of a particular type of good could not exist for long because the suppliers of this good would soon note a drop in sales and profits, causing them to move to more profitable areas of production. This shift would also cause a reallocation of productive resources from less profitable to more profitable, and therefore more needed, employment. An important conclusion of this line of reasoning is that the free play of capitalist institutions could not permit involuntary unemployment of any productive factor throughout the economy for an extended period. If productive agents were mobile and if all prices reacted quickly and surely to changes in demands and costs, the economy would so adjust itself as to operate at a level of full utilization of productive resources and perfect balance.

However, as the Great Depression of the 1930s showed, this is not the case. Labor acquires specialized skills and becomes attached to specific geographic locations; highly durable equipment is designed for very specialized purposes; wage rates become crystallized by custom and union-company agreements; interest rates and land rents are frozen in long-term contracts. Varying degrees of immobility impede productive agents, and the price flexibility requisite to full coordination of economic activity is absent. Changes occur in one part of the economy, and the other parts are not attuned to adjust to those changes, which brings about less than full utilization of resources in one or more sectors of the economy.

The market imperfections discussed earlier in this chapter insulate firms and factor suppliers from the need to react quickly to changing economic circumstances. This "slack" probably exists in any economic system to some extent, but in a capitalist system monopoly elements find it possible to pass along the consequences of their inefficiency to consumers in the form of higher prices, lower quality, and reduced auxiliary services.[8]

---

[7]Staffan B. Linder, *The Harried Leisure Class*, New York: Columbia University Press, 1970.

[8]Albert Hirshman, *Exit, Voice, and Loyalty*, Cambridge, Mass.: Harvard University Press, 1970. Hirshman shows that consumer protest (which he calls "voice") is sometimes more feasible than not buying the product (exit) when monopoly forces are operating.

Attempts to pull unemployed resources back into productive use through government fiscal policy involves American capitalism in two further dilemmas. The first is that inflationary pressures seem to be generated by labor unions and giant firms whenever full employment is being approached, thus presenting the choice between continuous erosion of real income for groups lacking economic and political power or else the establishment of wage and price controls with attendant enforcement problems. The second dilemma revolves around military spending as a means of achieving full-employment levels of resource utilization. One Marxist analysis of twentieth-century American economic history sees a norm of chronic depression and unemployment offset only by the economic build-ups connected with military preparedness and the pent-up consumer demand following wars.[9] Most economists believe, however, that the American economy could successfully achieve a considerable shift away from defense spending *if* other politically acceptable sources of aggregate demand were found and *if* the political opposition generated by industries and geographical regions hardest hit by the reallocation could be overcome. Those are big "ifs"!

Inequality

Amid the bounty that accompanies America's status as the richest nation in the world, it is an anomaly that approximately one out of every five citizens is too poor to be considered realistically as sharing in those riches. Chronic poverty extends beyond the pocketbook to the spirit, creating a life-style of despair that offers little hope of escape for those caught up in the system or for their children. Rather than quibble in search of some rigid income level defining poverty, it is more important to ask whether the existence of substantial poverty is an inherent weakness in the capitalist economic system or whether it is a defect that could be remedied.

The largest identifiable groups among the poor—older people, women heading families, school dropouts, the technologically unemployed—could be helped by specific types of expenditure programs. It is also evident that the required pensions, child-care facilities, remedial training programs, and so forth might be regarded as social costs of production that firms could be made to absorb. The culmulative effects of low skill levels, racial and other forms of discrimination on noneconomic grounds, and the trend toward increasing mechanization create a situation in which market forces operating unhindered probably create a core of marginal participants in the economic system. Their relative powerlessness, economic and political, under modern capitalism stands in stark contrast to the ability of those at the top end of the *earned*-income scale to supplant the advantages of

[9]Paul A. Baran and Paul M. Sweezy, *Monopoly Capital: An Essay on the American Economic and Social Order*, New York: Monthly Review Press, 1966.

superior natural ability and training with tax advantages and other political favors. Corporate managers' pay levels and fringe benefits are determined by their fellow managers operating largely outside market controls; professions are often self-regulating in a way that limits participation and allows monopoly influence over fees and other sources of income.

There is even greater inequality of *unearned* income. Most of the nonresidential wealth in the United States is concentrated in the richest 5 percent of the population. This represents a disproportionate power to direct society's resources and to enjoy the income these resources yield. Extreme disparities in living standards may create class antagonisms and strife, which, in turn, endanger the close cooperation essential to the functioning of a complex economy. The institution of inheritance perpetuates and sharpens these tendencies, as do the tax advantages on capital gains and municipal bonds enjoyed by upper income groups.

THE FUTURE OF AMERICAN CAPITALISM

From the preceding assessment of its strength and weaknesses emerges the question, What is capitalism's future in the United States? When the question is posed in the abstract, the people of the United States overwhelmingly desire to preserve capitalism as our form of economic organization. Its emphasis on the rights and freedoms of individuals, alone or combined into groups, to pursue their individual goals seems to accord with our basic values and philosophic predilections. It appears to many of us to be the form of economic organization that is most fundamentally consistent with the preservation of democratic political institutions. Pragmatically, it has served us well in material terms by creating living standards as high as, or higher than, any others in the world.

However, the *desire* and the *ability* to preserve capitalism indefinitely are two different matters. The ability does not derive automatically from the desire. Even today we have imposed politically enforced controls, restraints, compulsions, and guidance upon both pure capitalist institutions and single-purpose pursuit of profits. Misguided or not, these represent democratic political decisions that in very many respects capitalistic institutions and processes per se fail to yield generally accepted patterns of economic achievement. Will these modifications of pure capitalism in the United States continue to multiply in number and variety? If so, is it imperative now to visualize a future predominance of political control over private profit-seeking enterprise and to prepare a smooth evolutionary transition to a socialist economy?

For present-day students of economic systems, this is a major issue that can by no means be evaded or easily answered. Direct consideration requires satisfactory answers to two questions: (1) What should be the long-range achievement goals of economic activity in the United States? (2) What means of politically assisting our economy to these achievements will be effective and consistent with preservation of the basic institutions of capitalism? These questions are much too complex to yield simple answers. The dilemma is the ancient one of bringing about orderly change under conditions in which rapid change would be disorderly, and yet maintaining perfect order serves as a rationale for those who benefit from the status quo.

Long-Range Achievement Goals

There appears to be little basic difference of opinion in the United States today on what, practically speaking, we demand of our capitalist system in the future. We seek from it a substantial—say, 4 percent—annual rate of growth in real national income, with the benefits of such economic growth diffused widely over all sectors of the population. These goals are to be achieved through a combination of advancing production technology and full employment of all potentially productive resources. The full-employment aspect of this goal has special application to wage labor in our economy, since it is abhorrent to us to have physically and mentally able people seeking to earn their own living and unable to do so. In addition, the goal of relative price stability enters in because of the erosion of assets that occurs under conditions of constant inflation. These are the absolute minimum goals and are generally accepted as practicable "musts."

Political Methods of Achieving Goals

On the second question, there is general consensus in the United States today that capitalism in its pure theoretical form cannot be relied upon to generate these long-run goals for our economy. The huge size of the production unit in many industries, the size and influence of the principal banking and financial institutions, the reality of oligopolistic or administered pricing in many industries, the size and bargaining power of certain unions, and the influence of trade associations and other forms of cooperation for the promotion of limited group aims characterize the context within which present-day capitalism functions in the United Staes. Their presence has effectively replaced the classical theory of competition, forcing our society to take refuge in the modification of capitalist institutions and their regulation by government or its affiliated agencies. Thus, the various types of regulatory measures described earlier, plus the active operation of fiscal and monetary policies, are the avenues through which capitalism may be so guided as to achieve our economic goals.

Herein lies the deepest and most difficult dilemma of the capitalist system in the United States. Increasing modification and regulation of capitalist institutions may seriously impair the basic fabric of capitalism, yet without these modifications and regulations capitalism may not be effective enough to meet our goals. If there is a solution for it, it must be one that will (1) substantially alleviate or eradicate from our functioning economy the adverse propensities described above, and (2) retain the essential character of capitalism by preserving each private interest's right to manage its own affairs as it sees fit. Both of these qualifications are necessary within a new context of national fiscal and monetary policies that are capable of realizing basic economic goals.

This whole matter may be phrased differently. In our single-purpose attempts to maximize private-interest gains from each set of circumstances, have we not simply assumed that the institutions of capitalism will continue to exist and function regardless of the context our actions create for their functioning? If so, that assumption is now fallacious. At one time private interests could make such an assumption—during the period when small business and industrial units predominated, when it was easy for a new unit to be created or an old one liquidated because the capital needed for entry into and continued operation in an industry was small. That was the era of "automistic" competition. Today, the predominance of the large firm in many industries, the large capital investment necessary for entry by a new firm into an industry, and the size and power of the economic units among which "competition" occurs have worked major changes in the setting within which a private interest presses its own immediate advantage. The economic impact of an inflationary wage settlement or price increase in a major industry has too many repercussions to ignore the public's stake in such decisions. The threatened bankruptcy of a giant firm such as a railroad or a defense contractor is now a matter for immediate governmental action to protect employees and stockholders.

Like most solutions, the answer appears to lie in compromise. We cannot trade our political freedom and individual liberty for the promise and glitter of economic prosperity, nor are we willing to surrender our economic goals to unlimited freedom and unrestricted liberty. What the exact nature of the compromise will be is yet to be seen. It appears, however, that we will have to rely on monetary and fiscal controls utilizing the very best of recent developments in econometrics and related fields and develop the political sophistication necessary to enable us to use these tools in a politically democratic setting. We will have to develop, furthermore, some self-discipline in large corporate business units, labor unions, and other power centers, to the end that economic power will be tempered by greater concern for the common good. Combined with such developments, modern capitalism can serve us long and well in the United States.

QUESTIONS FOR CLASS DISCUSSION

1. What distortions occur in markets subject to especially high transaction costs? Can we be sure that consumer welfare will be maximized in an economy with transaction costs?

2. Imagine the structure of the American economy if no economies of scale existed.

3. Discuss the economic advantages of the multidivisional form of corporate organization.

4. Should conglomerate mergers be outlawed in the United States?

5. In what ways do labor unions resemble and differ from large corporations? If the goal of corporations is profits, what is the goal of union activity?

6. Are all goods and services provided by the government *public goods* according to our definition? Are all public goods provided by the government instead of by private suppliers?

7. Why are public goods underproduced by a market system without government intervention? Can you imagine a society in which everyone revealed his true preference and there were no free-rider problem?

8. Milton Friedman argues against regulation of public utilities by the government because the economic distortion created by intervention may exceed that created by unregulated monopoly behavior. Do you agree?

9. Organized crime often exists by bribing public officials, in effect, to grant exclusive franchises for drug pushers, prostitutes and boot-leggers. Discuss the market-failure aspects of the following situations: (1) entry is restricted; (2) new entrants can enter if they pay the bribe; (3) the activities are suddenly legalized.

10. Is there any question that the American standard of living has risen substantially in this century? How about the American standard of happiness? Has the capitalistic form of our economy been responsible for these developments?

11. How did market capitalism facilitate or hinder the tremendous shift from a primarily agricultural economy to a primarily industrial and service economy that has occurred in the United States?

12. How would you judge whether individual opportunities for upward economic and social mobility are increasing or decreasing at this time in the United States?

13. Don't nonpecuniary values get registered in the American economy through the exercise of consumer and occupational choice?

14. For those who have seen it, what is the source of humor in Charlie Chaplin's *Modern Times?*

15. What is a "fair" and "necessary" degree of economic inequality in the United States today? Are these two criteria compatible?

SUGGESTED SUBJECTS FOR STUDENT REPORTS FOR PARTS I AND II

1. The mingling of economic and noneconomic institutions in a selected primitive economy.

2. The problems of modernizing peasant agriculture.

3. The relatons between economic and noneconomic institutions under capitalism.

4. The effects of inheritance taxes on estate-planning behavior.

5. The degree of competition prevailing in a selected industry and the forms that competition takes.

6. A history of the corporate form of business organization.

7. The effects of the separation of ownership from managerial control in the modern corporation.

8. The social consequences of inequality.

9. The taxation of unearned income in the United States.

10. Empirical attempts to measure economies of scale.

11. The history of a selected antitrust case.

12. A study of the merger activity of a selected conglomerate corporation.

13. An estimate of the bargaining power of a selected union.

14. The relationship between taxes paid and benefits received by various economic groups.

15. The role of public opinion and social pressure in dealing with the free-rider problem.

16. A debate on the overall performance of the American economy, pro and con.

17. The economic implications of Arthur Miller's *All My Sons* and *Death of a Salesman*.

18. A comparison of the evolution of American capitalism as presented in the *National Review* and the *Monthly Review*.

19. A study of job alienation among different occupational groups.

20. A report on the economic status of women under American capitalism.

21. A report on the problems of defining poverty.

22. The role of pressure groups in American capitalism.

SUGGESTIONS FOR FURTHER READING FOR PART II

Baran, Paul A. and Paul M. Sweezy, *Monopoly Capital: An Essay on the American Economic and Social Order*, New York: Monthly Review Press, 1966.

Dobb, M. H., *Studies in the Development of Capitalism*, London: Routledge & Kegan Paul, 1963.

Friedman, Milton, *Capitalism and Freedom*, Chicago: University of Chicago Press, 1962.

Galbraith, John Kenneth, *The Affluent Society*, Boston: Houghton Mifflin, 1958.

Galbraith, John Kenneth, *The New Industrial State*, Boston: Houghton Mifflin, 1967.

Ginsberg, E., *The Pluralistic Economy*, New York: McGraw-Hill, 1965.

Hacker, Louis M., *The Triumph of American Capitalism*, New York: McGraw-Hill, 1965.

Harrington, Alan, *Life in the Crystal Palace*, New York: Avon, 1967.

Heilbroner, R. L., *The Economic Problem*, Englewood Cliffs, N.J.:
    Prentice-Hall, 1968.
Hobson, H. A., *Work and Wealth*, London: Allen & Son, 1933.
Hook, S., ed., *Human Values and Economic Policy*, New York: New
    York University Press, 1967.
Landes, David S., ed., *The Rise of Capitalism*, New York: Macmillan,
    1966.
Linder, Steffan B., *The Harried Leisure Class*, New York: Columbia
    University Press, 1970.
Olson, Mancur Jr., *The Logic of Collective Action*, New York:
    Schocken Books, 1968.
Reagan, M. D., *The Managed Economy*, New York: Oxford University
    Press, 1963.
Schumpeter, Joseph A., *Capitalism, Socialism, and Democracy*,
    New York: Harper & Row, 1942.
Shonfeld, Andrew, *Modern Capitalism: The Changing Balance of Public
    and Private Power*, New York: Oxford University Press, 1966.
Sombert, W., *The Quintessence of Capitalism*, New York: Howard
    Fertig, 1967.
Tawney, R. H., *The Acquisitive Society*, New York: Harcourt Brace
    Jovanovich, 1924.
Tawney, R. H., *Religion and the Rise of Capitalism*, London:
    Murray, 1936.
Tsuru, S., ed., *Has Capitalism Changed? An International Symposium
    on the Nature of Contemporary Capitalism*, Tokyo: Iwanami
    Shoten, 1961.
Veblen, Thorstein, *The Engineers and the Price System*, New York:
    Viking, 1921.

PART III:
THE MARXIAN THEORY OF
SOCIALISM AND COMMUNISM

4. Marx: his philosophy and interpretation of history

To most of the world Karl Marx and his theories were and have remained an enigma. Although their tremendous influence on human thought appears indisputable, many consider the man and his theories fanatical. And although discussions on Marxism have engaged millions of participants throughout the world, relatively few have read, and fewer still have in any measure understood, Marxian writings. Accepted by some as religious dogma, they are condemned by others as the products of a crackbrained fool; whereas they are sometimes considered so idealistic as to be worthless, they are also damned as crass materialism. Some have held that their significance is limited to certain epochs and places; others have found in Marxism the basic and universal explanations of all important historical events. In some sections of the modern world, students are forbidden the study of Marx's works since there they are considered the very antithesis of truth, while in other parts all else but Marxism is considered heresy. Marx has been interpreted, reinterpreted, added to, and subtracted from by his "followers," who have never come to a complete agreement as to what he meant. Even while he wrote, Marx and his close collaborator Engels repudiated as unorthodox many doctrines their adherents ostensibly gleaned from Marxian thought. Only death saves Marx from the pains he would have experienced as the titular father of the heterodoxy of theories that today are known as Marxism.

THE NATURE OF MARXIAN THEORY

Despite all this, or possibly because of it, the modern student of economic systems must attempt to understand Marxian theory. It forms the theoretical foundations of modern socialism and communism. As has already been hinted, it is by no means an easy task to grasp Marxian theory. To make the confusion created by his interpreters still more confusing, Marx himself was ambiguous and vague in his writings. Some key points in his theories were left undeveloped while he took excursions into pet ramifications of the main stem of his reasoning. In no single work did Marx set forth an organized, consistent, and comprehensive statement of his system of thought. The "Communist Manifesto," which he and Engels prepared as the program of the League of Communists, outlines the broad sweep of his conclusions on the nature and future of the capitalist economy, but it does not reveal the close reasoning a careful student seeks in support of such assertions. Although apparently Marx intended to include such an exposition in his *Capital*, this work leaves much to be desired. Only one of the proposed three volumes was completed before Marx died, leaving Engels to write two additional volumes from Marx's notes. Abstruseness, labyrinthian reasoning, and some inconsistencies characterize *Capital*. In hybrid fashion, the work combines masses of deductive reasoning with extended surveys of current and historical data that Marx considered empirical support for his conclusions.

Although much that is accepted today as orthodox Marxism bears only a stepchild relationship to Marx, there is a certain body of theory that represents the thread of Marxian thought. This will be summarized in succeeding paragraphs. After a preliminary glimpse at the biographical facts of Marx's life, we will note the general nature of his approach by studying the Marxian dialectical method and the economic interpretation of history. We will then proceed through Marx's analysis of the origins of the capitalist system to his description of the chief processes and phenomena that characterize capitalist production. We will review his theory of commodity values and his theory of wages, which, taken together, support the theoretical existence of "surplus value." These two theories are extended into explanations of the formation and accumulation of capital. We will then examine the numerous consequences that, according to Marx flow from these capitalist processes and will culminate in the destruction of capitalism. There will follow a résumé of the steps in social evolution: establishment of the dictatorship of the proletariat, socialism, and then full communism. The place of the proletariat and the Communist Party in these developments will be noted. Completing the analysis of Marxian theory, we will consider its strength and weakness.

THE LIFE OF KARL MARX

The *Encyclopaedia of the Social Sciences* characterizes Karl Marx, who lived from 1818 to 1883, as "social philosopher, revolutionary leader and founder of the chief current in modern socialism." The principal biographical facts concerning the setting of his life may be noted briefly. Marx was born in southwestern Germany of Jewish parents. His father was a lawyer, his paternal grandfather a German rabbi, and his mother a descendant of a Dutch rabbi. His father had "acquired a respectable practice" but had "never learnt the art of making money."[1] When Marx was very young his family turned from the Jewish faith to Christianity.

After completing his early schooling in his native German town, Marx spent one year at the University of Bonn and about four years at Berlin University, receiving a Doctor of Philosophy degree. After remaining in Germany for several years, he moved to Paris. In 1845 he was forced by the Prussian government to leave France, and he moved to Brussels, where he lived for three years. The Belgian government, fearing his revolutionary propensities, forced him to remove to Paris. Later in the same year he returned to Germany, thence back to Paris, and finally, in 1849, he took up residence in London, where he remained.

Marx as a Journalist

This constant moving about during the decade of the 1840s was largely involuntary. Marx's revolutionary doctrines were feared by the European governments during those unsettled years, and on several occasions he found himself an unwelcome resident of his native country or an equally unwelcome alien in a foreign country. During these years the chief source of Marx's meager living was his journalistic activities. The high mortality rate of these projects was due to the opposition of the established regimes and the financial weakness of the journals with which he was connected.

Immediately after receiving his doctorate, Marx did free-lance work for various journals. His work attracted the attention of the editors of a liberal newspaper in the Rhine provinces, and at the age of 24 he became its editor. Voluntarily retiring from this post a year later, he became edi-

[1]M. Beer, *The Life and Teaching of Karl Marx*, London: Parsons, 1921, p. 31.

tor of the *Franco-German Year Books*, to be published in Paris as an organ
for the expression of criticism of social institutions. The project failed to
produce more than one issue, in which was included an article by Friedrich
Engels, who was later to become Marx's close collaborator.[2] After an
intervening period of study and writing, Marx became editor of another
Rhenish paper with an opposition policy. After a year this failed financially,
and Marx's outstanding bills exhausted his limited resources. Throughout
these years and later, Marx carried on many additional sporadic journalistic
activities. In addition to writing for European journals, he was for a time
European correspondent for the *New York Tribune*.

These endeavors yielded Marx neither a large nor a stable income.
Several years after leaving Berlin University, he married the daughter of a
privy counselor residing in his native city. His wife, who came from a
middle-class family, and the three of their children who grew to maturity shared Marx's financial insecurity, which at times approached poverty. The pawnshop was used regularly to tide the family over the worst
crises in its fortunes. It is said that at one time Marx pawned his only
coat to pay for paper needed for a manuscript in preparation. During
the latter portion of his life, which was spent in London, Marx was in
better economic circumstances. This was due to his friends rather than
his own efforts. He was given a legacy by a friend who thought well of
his work, and for a substantial period he received an annual stipend from
his collaborator Engels, who owned a prosperous family business.

Marx as a Student

In addition to the journalistic, two threads weave themselves through
Marx's life; he was a student and a revoluntionary leader. Always and
everywhere Marx was a student. As a youth of 17 he entered the Univer-

[2]"Engels, Friedrich (1820–1895), social theorist and revolutionist. Engels shares
with Marx the distinction of being the founder of scientific socialism. He was born in
Barmen, Germany, of a prosperous commercial family. Although reared in an intensely pietistic Protestant atmosphere he soon broke completely with his religious
traditions. . . . In 1842 he left Germany to take a position with a firm in Manches-
ter, England, in which his father had shares; there he acquired a knowledge of *laissez-
faire* economics. . . . He also wrote at this time for Chartist and Owenite papers. In
the fall of 1844, when in Paris on his way to Germany, Engels met Marx, whom he
had previously known in 1842, and their lifelong friendship and intimate collaboration began. . . . The years from 1845 to 1850 he spent in France, Germany and Belgium, organizing the underground revolutionary groups and collaborating with Marx
on various publications including the Communist Manifesto. . . . After 1850, when
hope of immediate revolution in Europe faded, he reluctantly returned to England to
engage in business and from his income he was able to provide for Marx while the
latter was engaged in writing *Das Kapital*. He retired from business in 1869 and devoted the rest of his life to literary and practical revolutionary activity. He was a
member of the General Council of the First International and played an important
part in the early years of the Second International. In this period he developed the
philosophy and sociology of Marxism, and after Marx's death edited the second and
third volumes of *Das Kapital* from rough drafts and notes left by Marx." Sidney
Hook, in *Encyclopaedia of the Social Sciences*, vol. V, pp. 540–541.

sity of Bonn to study law, a career more the choice of the father than the son. After one year Marx transferred to Berlin University, where he broadened his studies to include philosophy, literature, history, and art. During these years he increasingly lost interest in legal study and was drawn irresistibly to philosophy. This, together with his withdrawal from all university activities except the intellectual, brought censure from his father, who recommended that his son follow the example of his fellow students. He advised as follows:

> Indeed these young men sleep quite peacefully except when they now and then devote the whole or part of a night to pleasure, whereas my clever and gifted son Karl passes wretched sleepless nights, wearying body and mind with cheerless study, forbearing all pleasures with the sole object of applying himself to abstruse studies; but what he builds today he destroys again tomorrow, and in the end he finds that he has destroyed what he already had, without having gained anything from other people. At last the body begins to ail and the mind gets confused, whilst these ordinary folk steal along in easy marches, and attain their goal if not better at least more comfortably than those who contemn youthful pleasures and undermine their health in order to snatch at the ghost of erudition, which they could probably have exercised more successfully in an hour spent in the society of competent men—with social enjoyment into the bargain![3]

Apparently this parental advice fell on deaf ears, for Marx continued to be exclusively an intellectual during his university days. He spent much time in the realm of philosophy, outlining for himself whole systems of thought and taking his principal interest in the philosophy of Hegel. A "Graduates Club" at the university afforded him the desired opportunity for intellectual companionship and controversy. In fact, at this time Marx hoped to follow an academic career. After receiving his doctorate, he applied for a lectureship at the University of Bonn. It was only after he failed to secure this because of his nonconformist thinking that he turned to journalism.

Although Marx remained an intense student throughout his life, these early studies, particularly in the realm of philosophy, were his most important. In accepting basically a Hegelian philosophy, he adopted certain positions, assumptions, and points of view that vitally influenced all his further studies. It is true that he did not accept these philosophical conceptions hastily. Only through the most laborious and searching studies of philosophical systems did he arrive at the one that to him seemed adequate. However, it is also true that, once having adopted the theses of this philosophy, he retained them substantially unchanged throughout his life. Although he continued to be an omnivorous student of human affairs, whatever the conclusions his later studies dictated they were always fitted

---

[3]Beer, p. 39.

into the mold of these early-adopted philosophical concepts. It would be interesting to speculate on whether these candidly accepted philosophical principles made Marx a less scientific and more biased student of human affairs than others of his time and since have been, or whether he merely adopted his bias or his philosophy more systematically and more openly than have others. At least Marx reveals fully the philosophical positions from which his analysis starts; there is no subtle concealment of assumptions.

In the decade immediately following his early philosophical study, Marx studied contemporary socialist literature, largely French and English. During the middle years of the nineteenth century there was a great volume of writing criticizing existing social institutions. Through these influences Marx became a socialist, although not in the utopian sense. Early in these studies he was convinced that socialism was to come only through the operations of social processes whose working he must understand.

During his decade of shifting residence, Marx took every opportunity to study local economic phenomena and to fit his findings into his philosophical scheme. In Brussels he used the extensive library of his friend Engels. After moving to London, and prior to the publication of *Capital*, Marx is reported to have spent some ten years of incessant study in the British Museum. He stayed from the opening to the closing hour, searching out masses of detailed descriptions of economic processes and institutions prevailing throughout the centuries.

Marx appears considerably more striking in the role of student than as a journalist. Most of the energy of his life went into the youthful formulation of his philosophical skeleton and the later avid study of the economic aspects of human life from which he filled out the body of Marxian theory.

Marx as a Revolutionist

Marx the revolutionary leader is less well known than Marx the journalist or Marx the student. While a relatively small portion of his efforts went directly into it, the organization of the working classes was the ultimate objective of his life. Although he felt deeply the necessity and the desire to engage in the active struggle to free workers from their bondage, Marx's abilities along this line appear to have been meager. As a student in Berlin, Marx, who was given to writing poems and short stories, penned what was probaly a deeply felt desire:

> Let us not in base subjection
> Brood away our fearful life,
> When with deed and aspiration
> We might enter in the strife.[4]

[4]Quoted by Harry W. Laidler, *A History of Socialist Thought*, New York: T. Y. Crowell, 1927, p. 153.

During his movements about Europe in the 1840s, Marx kept in contact with groups of dissatisfied workingmen who desired comprehensive and fundamental changes in the economic and political spheres. These groups usually were composed of workingmen who had emigrated from Germany. They maintained a loose international organization, known as the "League of the Just," through which local observations were communicated from group to group. During his residence in Brussels, this organization got in contact with Marx, and, at a conference held late in 1847, Marx (who was 29 years old) and Engels (who was 27), were requested to prepare a program for the League. This organization later was known as the "League of Communists," and the program prepared by Marx and Engels was the "Communist Manifesto." The term communist was chosen to distinguish the League and its program from various utopian and social reformist groups that were known as socialists and for whose doctrines Marx had no respect.

Coincidental with the appearance of the "Communist Manifesto" was the French Revolution of 1848. There were outbursts shortly thereafter in Vienna, Italy, and the German provinces, while in Switzerland and England there were demands for drastic governmental changes. These disturbances led the established governments to crush all signs of revolutionary working-class activity. The leaders of the Communist League were imprisoned and the organization dissolved.

For many years after this brief contact with a working-class organization, Marx devoted himself to study and writing in London, where in 1864 he represented German workingmen at an international conference. Here was organized the "International Workingmen's Association," commonly referred to as the "First International." During the same year Marx delivered several addresses and communications to the International and drew up a statement of its principles. The International was composed of various factions holding different views as to how working-class interests could best be promoted, and for a time the group led by Marx controlled its policies. Through the International he gave advice (which was not followed) to the French workers during their revolt in 1871. After the fall of the Paris Commune in that year, Marx, who was then general secretary of the International, moved the headquarters of the organization to New York City. Controversies within the organization and the failure of revolutionary activities in France had so weakened the International that it expired in 1876.

Thus it appears that Marx, while sensing the interrelationship between organized revolutionary activities and doctrines, and demonstrating a readiness to throw his energies into the promotion of such activities, was unable to breast the counteracting forces at work in the worlds of action and of thought. The experiences and contracts of these years played an important part in the formulation of his theories. However, just as his journalistic activities failed to result in any enduring working-class organ

of propaganda, so his organizational efforts and leadership failed to create any lasting working-class agencies of revolution. We are thus left
with Marx the student and writer. These aspects of Marx's work have en-
dured and exercised worldwide influence. We therefore turn to a somewhat
extended account of Marxian theory.[5]

THE PHILOSOPHY OF MARX

The Hegelian Basis

The philosophical bases of Marx's thought were laid early and remained
unchanged throughout his life. As a student, Marx accepted the philosophy of Hegel as the only sound and adequate explanation of the universe. According to this philosophy, "the only immutable thing is the
abstraction of movement."[6] The one universal phenomenon is change,
and the only universal form of this phenomenon is its complete abstraction. Thus, Hegel accepted as real only that which existed in the mind.
Objective phenomena and events were of no consequence; only the conceptions of them possessed by human minds were real. Ideas, not ob-
jects, were the stuff of which the universe was made. The universe and
all events therein existed and took place only in the mind, and any change
was a change in ideas. Therefore, to account for these changes in ideas
was to account for change in the universe.

In the Hegelian philosophy no idea could exist without an opposite.
Thus, the idea of light could not exist unless there were an idea of darkness, nor truth without falsity, nor high without low. If an idea were labeled
a thesis, its opposite would be its antithesis. Consequently, in this realm
of the mind within which the universe had its only real existence, innumerable theses and antitheses existed. Struggle or conflict was the en-
evitable fact in such a universe—conflict of the thesis with its antithesis.
In this struggle thesis and antithesis acted and reacted on each other, and
a new phenomenon—synthesis—was created. All action or change occurring in the universe was, under the Hegelian philosophy, the product of
thesis, antithesis, and resulting synthesis—all in the realm of ideas, since
objective reality could exist only in that sphere. Since this process was

---

[5]The numerous quotations from Marx, Engels, and Lenin that appear in the
succeeeding exposition of Marxian theory are for the purposes (1) of giving the student some familiarity with the writing styles of these men, and (2) of making sure
that Marxian theory is presented accurately.

[6]Karl Marx, "The Poverty of Philosophy," in *Handbook of Marxism*, p. 355.
The *Handbook of Marxism*, E. Burns, compiler, published by Random House in 1935,
is an excellent collection of excerpts from the writings of Marx, Engels, Lenin, and
Stalin. It presents original text material taken from various books and documents,
with brief notes explaining the significance of each selection. Since this volume
constitutes a most useful book for students who wish to read further in Marxian
theory, page references to the Marxian writings, except for direct references to
Capital, are to the *Handbook*.

universal and never ending, it offered a complete explanation of the causal processes creating all phenomena within the universe.

Modification of Hegelian Philosophy by Marx

The fundamental idea of change occurring as a synthesis of opposing forces Marx accepted as the germ of the universal truth that he, as a philosopher, sought. However, he found unacceptable the Hegelian assumption that these conflicting opposites had realistic existence only in the mind of man. Marx consequently accepted one portion of Hegel's philosophy and rejected the other.

To Marx the thing the mind perceived was realty in itself. Objective existence was exterior to the mind of man, and ideas were the reflections of those exterior phenomena. The phenomena to be explained were therefore the objective events in the universe and not the ideas of those events residing within the mind. It might be said that Marx rejected Hegel's idealism and substituted for it realism. The thesis and antithesis became to Marx actual opposing forces existing in the universe, with synthesis the resulting objective phenomenon that, becoming in its turn thesis or antithesis, played its part in the creation of a new synthetic phenomenon. That this realism constituted a vital modification of the Hegelian system is attested by the numerous clashes Marx had with the followers of the more purely idealistic Hegel. Whereas the latter never departed from the realm of mental images, Marx set out to study the operation of this (to him) universal truth in the everyday events of the world of human affairs. Thus Marx adopted what is usually referred to as the "Marxian dialectic" as the most useful tool wherewith to gain an understanding of the universe.

Limitations of Hegelian Philosophy by Marx

The Marxian dialectic is a universal explanation in two senses. First, it constitutes a philosophical explanation of all categories of realistic phenomena. It could be applied to physical, chemical, astronomical, mathematical, geological, and all other phenomena as a universal explanation of what exists and is occurring in the universe. Second, it includes the mind of man as a part of the universe within which change through thesis, antithesis, and synthesis constitutes the never-ending creative process. Nothing within the dialectic itself excludes any category of phenomena from its scope, nor does anything in it give special place to any particular type of phenomena as occupying a more creative or deterministic position than any other.

Marx placed two limitations on the dialectic as he came to apply it in his studies. First, while admitting that it constituted a universal explanation of all phenomena, he had no interest in applying it outside the field of social institutions and processes. Indeed, it would be impossible for any student to apply a philosophical concept intensively to any but a limited field of phenomena.

Moreover, within the scope of social institutions and processes, Marx contended that one species of phenomena had incomparably greater creative potentalities than any other. These were the economic phenomena, or, to use a Marxian term, the mode of production. According to Marx it was within this economic realm that the basic theses, antitheses, and syntheses existed, and all social institutions were the offshoots of economic forces. Since the basic philosophical assumption from which Marx starts does not include any corollary that makes economic forces superior to any other, this aspect of the Marxian approach must be examined further.

THE MARXIAN INTERPRETATION OF HISTORY

Marx's interpretation of history constitutes an integral part of Marxian doctrine. It was his intent to peer into the future and to determine what historical fate was in store for the capitalist system. Only by understanding the forces that had caused historical events could the forces that would cause future events be envisioned. For this reason Marx sought the ultimate or basic causes of historical events.

To seek out the creative forces in history was somewhat more novel and daring in Marx's day than it is now, when so many historians are vitally interested in studying the causes of historical events. Marx attempted to do something neither historians nor economists had done. Historians had recorded events and economists had explained causes of economic events in specific historical settings without analyzing the creation of those settings. Lenin has summarized as follows the questions Marx felt had to be answered:

> People make their own history; but what determines their motives, that
> is the motives of people in the mass; what gives rise to the clash
> of conflicting ideas and endeavors; what is the sum total of all of these
> clashes among the whole mass of human societies; what are the ob-
> jective conditions for the production of the material means of life that
> form the basis of all the historical activity of man; what is the law of the
> development of these conditions?[7]

If history may be presumed to have a significant economic slant, it might be supposed that the economists would have sought out the laws of historical development, particularly in the field of economic phenomena. Marx found this not to be the case. He expressed this deficiency in "The Poverty of Philosophy" when he wrote: "Economists explain how production takes place in the above-mentioned relations, but what they do

[7]V. I. Lenin, "The Teachings of Karl Marx," in *Handbook of Marxism*, p. 545.

not explain is how the relations themselves are produced, that is, the historical movement which gave them birth."[8]

Marxian Views of Other Interpretations of History

Marx dealt briefly with two theories of history other than his own. These may be referred to as the "idealist" and the "providential." The former held that historical events were the products of human ideas—that these ideas were the original creative stuff from which, in their complex intermingling, historical events flowed. Marx held this explanation to be entirely inadequate. He contended that ideas cannot exist as pure products of a brain, that "the idea is nothing else than the material world reflected by the human mind, and translated into forms of thought."[9]

Engels, repeating the same thought, wrote that "the products of the human brain, being in the last analysis likewise products of nature, do not contradict the rest of nature, but correspond to it."[10] Writing further, he described the idealists as forced to the untenable position "that spirit existed before nature," and since they therefore have no explanation for the greatest of all historical events, the creation of the world, they "*assume* in one way or another that the world was created."[11]

Marx had only scorn for the theory that some providential person or force ruled the universe, creating historical events as mere extensions of its omnipotent will. In "The Poverty of Philosophy," he gave this theory the brief attention he thought it deserved when he wrote: "Providence, providential aim, this is the great word used today to explain the movement of history. In fact, this word means nothing. It is at most a rhetorical form, one of the various ways of paraphrasing facts."[12]

To express his utter contempt for the providential theory, Marx wrote the following paragraph of what he held would be "providential history":

> It is a fact that in Scotland landed property acquired a new value by the development of English industry. This industry opened up new outlets for wool. In order to produce wool on a large scale, arable land had to be transformed into pasturage. To effect this transformation, the estates had to be concentrated. To concentrate the estates, small holdings had first to be abolished, thousands of tenants had to be driven

[8]Marx, "The Poverty of Philosophy," in *Handbook of Marxism*, p. 350.

[9]Author's preface to the second edition of *Capital*, p. 25. The Modern Library (New York, n.d.), edition of vol. I of *Capital* probably is the most convenient and available edition for students. Hence, page references herein are to that edition. Unless otherwise indicated, all references are to vol. I.

[10]Friedrich Engels, "Anti-Dühring," in *Handbook of Marxism*, p. 539.

[11]Friedrich Engels, "Ludwig Feuerbach," in *Handbook of Marxism*, p. 539. Italics ours.

[12]Marx, "The Poverty of Philosophy," in *Handbook of Marxism*, p. 364.

from their native soil and a few shepherds in charge of millions of sheep to be installed in their place. Thus, by successive transformations, landed property in Scotland has resulted in the driving out of men by sheep. Now say that the providential aim of the institution of landed property in Scotland was to have men driven out by sheep, and you will have made providential history.[13]

In the preface to his *Critique of Political Economy*, Marx wrote as follows:

My investigations led to the conclusion that legal relations as well as forms of state could not be understood from themselves, nor from the so-called general development of the human mind, but, on the contrary, are rooted in the material conditions of life . . . that the anatomy of civil society is to be found in political economy. . . . The general conclusion I arrived at—and once reached, it served as the guiding thread in my studies—can be briefly formulated as follows: In the social production of their means of existence men enter into definite, necessary relations which are independent of their will, productive relationships which correspond to a definite stage of development of their material productive forces. The aggregate of these productive relationships constitutes the economic structure of society, the real basis on which a juridical and political superstructure arises, and to which definite forms of social consciousness correspond. *The mode of production of the material means of existence conditions the whole process of social, political, and intellectual life.*[14]

Marx's collaborator Engels has closely paraphrased Marx in his "Anti-Dühring." There he describes the economic interpretation of history as follows:

According to this conception, the ultimate causes of all social changes and political revolutions are to be sought, not in the minds of men, in their increasing insight into eternal truth and justice, but in changes in the mode of production and exchange; they are to be sought not in the *philosophy* but in the *economics* of the epoch concerned.[15]

Many modern writers have sought to summarize lucidly this theory of history. Few, if any, have been able to improve upon the attempts of Marx and Engels. Harry W. Laidler, in his *A History of Socialist Thought*, gives a concise summary of the theory as follows:

The materialist or economic interpretation of history . . . means that in any given epoch the economic relations of society, the means whereby men and women provide for the sustenance, produce, exchange, and distribute the things they regard as necessary for the satisfaction of their

13*Ibid.*
14*Ibid.*, pp. 371–372. Italics ours.
15Engels, "Anti-Dühring," in *Handbook of Marxism*, p. 279.

needs exert a preponderating influence in shaping the progress of society and in molding political, social, intellectual and ethical relationships.[16]

Professor Bober, who has devoted an entire volume to *Karl Marx's Interpretation of History*, summarizes the theory as follows: ". . . Production is the alpha and omega of history, all else is a vexatious parenthetical digression. Except for slight modifications, retardations or accelerations brought about by other agencies, the mode of production is the prime cause of history, the sole cause."[17]

Scientific Nature of the Interpretation of History

It is clear that Marx and Engels considered economic forces as operating with the inevitability of natural law. Two brief statements emphasize this:

> It is a question of the laws themselves, of these tendencies working with iron necessity toward inevitable results. The country that is more developed industrially only shows, to the less developed, the image of its own future.[18]

> The forces working in society work exactly like the forces operating in nature; blindly, violently, destructively, so long as we do not understand them and take them into account.[19]

Marx and Engels thought of the economic interpretation of history as scientific and realistic. There is some justification for their attitude when this theory is compared with others of their day. In a joint work, "German Ideology," Marx and Engels press this point as follows:

> In direct contrast to German philosophy, which descends from heaven to earth, here the ascent is made from earth to heaven. That is to say, we do not start from what men say, imagine, conceive, nor from men as described, thought of, imagined, and conceived, in order thence and thereby to reach corporeal men; we start from real, active men, and from their life-processes also show the development of the ideological reflexes and echoes of this life-process.[20]

In more absolute terms, Engels refers to the Marxian method as "positive science":

---

[16]Laidler, p. 199.
[17]M. M. Bober, *Karl Marx's Interpretation of History*, Cambridge, Mass.: Harvard University Press, 1948, p. 274. Quotations from this book are used by permission of the President and Fellows of Harvard College.
[18]Marx, *Capital*, p. 13.
[19]Engels, "Anti-Dühring," in *Handbook of Marxism*, p. 294.
[20]Karl Marx and Friedrich Engels, "German Ideology," in *Handbook of Marxism*, p. 212.

If we deduce the world schematism not from our minds, but only *through* our minds from the real world, deducing the basic principles of being from what is, we need no philosophy for this purpose, but positive knowledge of the world and of what happens in it; and what this yields is also not philosophy, but positive science.[21]

Mode of Production

The economic interpretation of history has sometimes been made to appear absurd by a too narrow interpretation of the phrase *mode of production*. If this were taken to mean merely the technique of production—that is, the kind of tools and machinery used—it would be ridiculous to argue that all social institutions take their form and content from such a narrow base. There is plenty of evidence in Marxian writings that mode of production means something much broader than the technique of production. Professor Bober, a severe critic of the Marxian theory of history, holds that labor and land are just as much a part of Marx's concept of mode of production as is the technique of production.[22] "Thus the general nature of the laborer and the grouping of the workers in a scheme of division and of cooperation of labor characterize a mode of production and exert a powerful influence on it."[23] A change in the productiveness of the workers may exert powerful influences on the nature of production. The organization of workers is similarly important. The characteristics of the available natural resources—for instance, the abundance or lack of a certain type of power such as wind or water, or the presence or absence of raw materials of good or poor quality—must be included in the Marxian mode of production. Moreover, each of these varying characteristics of technique, labor, and land reacts on the other so that the existing mode of production includes elements that are the results of interactions of the basic agents of production.

Engels, in summarizing his conception of the economic interpretation of history, made "changes in the mode of production and *exchange*"[24] the basis of change in social institutions and processes. The fact that Engels read to Marx the entire manuscript from which this quotation is taken is proof of Marx's approval of this extension of the "mode of production." Marx himself referred to an "aggregate of production relationships" as constituting the "economic structure of society, the real basis upon which a juridical and political superstructure arises, and to which definite forms of social consciousness correspond."[25]

---

[21]Engels, "Anti-Dühring," in *Handbook of Marxism*, p. 234.
[22]Bober, chap. 2.
[23]*Ibid.*, p. 17. The remainder of this paragraph merely paraphrases Professor Bober.
[24]Italics ours.
[25]Karl Marx, "Critique of Political Economy," in *Handbook of Marxism*, pp. 371–372.

It is not far from the original Marxian thought to phrase the economic interpretation of history as follows: In a given situation in which certain natural resources, human resources, and technical knowledge of processes prevail, the economic processes of production, exchange, distribution, and consumption will come to be organized into certain institutions primarily of a social sort, since they involve relationships among men. The totality of these relationships, including of course innumerable interactions among them, constitute as a whole the mode of production, which sets the form and content of all other social institutions. Changes in any one or more of the elements included within this mode of production will be reflected in changes in social institutions and processes; thus all historical events find their basic or prime causes in changes in the mode of production.

In passing, it should be noted that, as G. D. H. Cole has pointed out,[26] this interpretation of history explains events only within a civilization. Engels refers to this theory as applicable to "a given historical period."[27] Thus the economic intepretation of history does not hold *all* history to be a continuous process dominated by changes in the mode of production. It does not, for instance, necessarily account for the historical change from ancient civilizations to modern on the basis of economic forces. It purports only to account for a continuity of historical events occurring within an historical era. It is a universal explanation of history only within these limitations.[28]

It is exceedingly important to realize the comprehensiveness of the influence of the mode of production. Not just a portion of the social organization but all of it is held to be determined by these economic relationships. Numerous passages from Marxian literature indicate that this was clearly Marx's intent. For instance, he wrote: "In acquiring new productive forces men change their mode of production; and in changing their mode of production they change their way of earning their living—they change *all their social relations*."[29] Engels emphasized this aspect of the economic interpretation of history in the following passage: ". . . The economic structure of society always furnishes the real basis, *the whole super-structure* of juridical and political institutions as well as of the religious, philosophical, and other ideas of a given historical period."[30]

Other references could be cited to show that Marx and Engels meant fully what they appear to say. Not only social institutions but man's ideas and ideals spring from economic foundations. A few representative statements may be noted:

[26]G. D. H. Cole, *What Marx Really Meant*, New York: Knopf, 1934, pp. 35–36.

[27]Quoted by Bober, p. 283.

[28]However, neither Marx nor Engels clearly defined what he meant by "historical epoch" or "historical period."

[29]Marx, "The Poverty of Philosophy," in *Handbook of Marxism*, p. 335. Italics ours.

[30]Quoted by Bober, p. 283. Italics ours.

Your very ideas are but the outgrowth of the conditions of your
bourgeois production and bourgeois property, just as your jurisprudence
is but the will of your class made into a law for all, a will whose essential character and direction are determined by the economical conditions of existence of your class.[31]

My standpoint, from which the evolution of the economic formation
of society is viewed as a process of natural history, can less than any
other make the individual responsible for relations whose creature
he socially remains, however much he may subjectively raise himself
above them.[32]

We maintain . . . that all former moral theories are the product, in the
last analysis, of the economic stage which society had reached at that
particular epoch.[33]

What else does the history of ideas prove than that intellectual production changes its character in proportion as material production
is changed.[34]

But during this long period from Descartes to Hegel and from Hobbes to
Feuerbach, the philosophers were by no means impelled, as they
thought they were, solely by force of pure reason. On the contrary.
What really pushed them forward was the powerful and ever more rapidly
onrushing progress of natural science and industry.[35]

Relation of Economic Forces to Other Forces

Students of Marxian theory have long been troubled by the question of
whether Marx intended to make economic forces the sole determinants
of historical events or merely the most important within a totality of
heterogeneous forces. Marx's intention is clear: He will not be satisfied
with any causal explanation of history except that it be a prime, original, or ultimate cause. It was in this sense that the "relations of production" or mode of production became the ultimate factor in his interpretation of history. To modify Marxian theory so as to weaken this tenet is to
destroy that concept of history which is essential to consistency within the
Marxian system as a whole.

And yet such fatally weakening interpretations of Marx are constantly being made. For instance, G. D. H. Cole, in discussing the point
already noted—that man's ideas are the product of economic forces—
interprets Marx to mean that "the situation acts as a stimulus; for it sug-

---

[31]Karl Marx and Friedrich Engels, "Communist Manifesto," in *Handbook of
Marxism*, p. 41.
[32]Marx, *Capital*, p. 15.
[33]Engels, "Anti-Dühring," in *Handbook of Marxism*, p. 249.
[34]Marx and Engels, "Communist Manifesto," in *Handbook of Marxism*, p 44.
[35]Engels, "Ludwig Feuerbach," in *Handbook of Marxism*, p 218.

gests the starting from which we can alone work out the ultimate explanation of problems, and arouses the sense of need. But a stimulus does not necessitate a response. The universe is full of abortive stimuli."[36] This would appear to be a complete negation of the Marxian theory, for Cole implies that some noneconomic force may determine which stimuli in the environment will induce a response and which will not. If on the other hand, we assume that economic forces determine which stimuli will be effective and which will not, the "situation," presumably economic in Cole's meaning, acts not only as a stimulus but also as the determinant of the idea. Either Cole rejects entirely the Marxian thesis of the origin of ideas in economic forces in this statement, or he admits it, merely choosing to state the thesis in more palatable phrases. In either case he adds no legitimate interpretation to the Marxian contention.

Indirect Operation of Economic Forces

The unwillingness of certain students of Marx to admit that he means what he says concerning the place of economic forces in history may arise from their failure to realize that this causal relationship between the mode of production and social institutions and processes need not, in Marx's opinion, be either immediate, direct, or generally understood. Marx emphasized the evolutionary nature of social institutions and processes, and it is an inherent feature of evolutionary change that it takes place gradually, in a sense indirectly, and certainly unconsciously in that the ultimate sources and ends of the evolutionary processes are not observed by onlookers at any one stage of the process.

The operations of economic forces have inherent in them an indirectness and an imperceptibility that Marx's economic interpretation of history comprehends. For instance, it would not be consistent with the economic interpretation of history to expect a new invention to be followed immediately by the full-blown economic relations that may eventually result from it. The invention takes place within an environment that consists of institutions— moral, legal, political, and others—all of which, Marx contends, change slowly. Therefore it is perfectly consistent with Marxian theory to argue these noneconomic social institutions may have considerable bearing on the time lag with which the changes ultimately to come from the invention are created. Thus noneconomic factors may be operative in a time sense without affecting the vital causal connection between a change in the mode of production and the ensuing changes in social institutions and processes.

In another sense noneconomic institutions may be operative without affecting the Marxian theory of history. There is nothing in this theory to deny the contention that, once noneconomic institutions have crystal-

[36]Cole, p. 97.

lized from basic economic forces, they operate as independent forces modifying the mode of production. Reverting to the realm of ideas, for instance, Engels points out that the very idea of equality is the product of historical development in which economic forces played the prime role.[37] However, once an idea of equality takes a certain place in man's mind, it may modify the result of some change in the mode of production. An idea of equality—itself the product of economic forces—may substantially modify the manner in which the inventor or the society uses a given invention. But note that in this case economic forces are still the prime forces, working indirectly by creating ideas, which in turn modify the operations of economic forces in determining social institutions and processes. When one allows for the almost infinite variety of interdependent relationships and reactions between existing institutions—formerly created directly or indirectly by economic forces—and changes in the mode of production, it becomes obvious that students of Marx may confuse the indirection of the effect of economic forces with the existence of what they believe to be independent noneconomic prime causal forces.

Engels has stated this point so clearly and authoritatively that a quotation from his writings is pertinent:

> According to the materialistic conception of history, the production and reproduction of real life constitutes in the *last instance* the determining factor of history. Neither Marx nor I ever maintained more. Now, when someone comes along and distorts this to mean that the economic factor is the *sole* determining factor, he is converting the former proposition into a meaningless, abstract, and absurd phrase. The economic situation is the basis. But the various factors of the superstructure—the political forms of the class struggles and their results, i.e., constitutions, etc., established by victorious classes after hard-won battles, legal forms, and even the reflexes of all these real struggles in the brain of the participants, political, jural, philosophical theories, religious conceptions which have been developed into systematic dogmas—all these exercise an influence upon the course of historical struggles, and in many cases determine for the most part their form. There is a reciprocity between all these factors in which, finally, through the endless array of contingencies (i.e., of things and events whose inner connection with one another is so remote, or so incapable of proof, that we may neglect it, regarding it as nonexistent), the economic movement asserts itself as necessary. Were this not the case the application of the theory to any given historical period would be easier than the solution of a simple equation of the first degree.[38]

Similar confusion arises from the fact that the evolution of social institutions and processes takes place by imperceptible stages with imperceptible causal relationships. For instance, several writers have pointed

[37]Engels, "Anti-Dühring," in *Handbook of Marxism*, p. 254.
[38]Quoted in Sidney Hook, *Towards the Understanding of Karl Marx*, New York: Day, 1933, p. 179.

out how the rise of Protestantism may have been a response in the field of religious institutions to economic forces at work in the world of that day. It is obvious that if such causal relations did exist, they were not perceived by the participants in this struggle. To them the religious issues were exclusive and the change was merely the self-evolution of an institution to meet a higher need than the one it was serving. Yet the fact that this historical event may have been so overlaid with certain mental images conceived in terms of the institution itself as to make the real prime causes of the change imperceptible does not change the basic nature of the causal forces.

QUESTIONS FOR CLASS DISCUSSION

1. Why should a student of modern economic movements and systems be familiar with Marxian theory?

2. The inclusiveness of the term *Marxian theory* is somewhat uncertain. In what sense and why?

3. Would you say that Marx was a man of restricted or broad training? of wide or limited experience with the day-to-day affairs of the world? of a scientific or unscientific turn of mind?

4. From what basic assumption or position do all of Marx's doctrines spring? Was this assumption an original contribution of Marx?

5. What is meant by an interpretation of history? Did Marx hold that there was just one interpretation of history or that there could be many? Would you agree?

6. What meaning did Marx attach to the phrase *mode of production*, and how was this related to his interpretation of history?

7. Did Marx contend that his was an interpretation of history for an indefinite number of centuries into the past?

8. In what sense was Marx's interpretation of history also a theory of the origins of institutions? In his mind was it a theory of the origins of *all* institutions?

9. Did the basic causes of historical events, according to Marx, always operate directly and perceptibly? Of what significance is this in relation to come common misunderstandings of the Marxian interpretation of history?

10. Why is the Marxian interpretation of history sometimes referred to as materialistic?

11. How would Marx apply his interpretation of history to those important historical events known as wars? Illustrate from your knowledge of the circumstances surrounding some specific war.

5. The Marxian theory of value and wages

Having studied Marx as a philosopher and traced his dialectic and his economic interpretation of history, we may now consider him as an economist analyzing the processes at work in the capitalistic economy of his day. How good an economist he was, or whether he should be called an economist at all, has often been questioned. Some commentators have argued that Marx's philosophy or revolutionary purpose and his economic theory cannot be separated because they are component parts of a whole.[1] Marx

[1]Sidney Hook, *Towards the Understanding of Karl Marx*, New York: Day, 1933, p. 223; G. D. H. Cole, *What Marx Really Meant*, New York: Knopf, 1934, p. 206.

to them was not a scientific economist, seeking the true explanations of economic phenomena regardless of results or consequences. He was rather a revolutionist, explaining economic phenomena in such a manner as to induce his fellows to hate the economic system and overthrow it.

Moreover, Marx is often said to be a poor economist because his explanations of economic phenomena are in some respects (to be considered later) invalid in the light of more recent developments of economic theory. But if this were the test, the names of such eminent pioneers of economic science as Smith, Mill, Malthus, and possibly even Marshall would have to be read out of the profession.

Despite these doubts, Marx has established himself in purpose and method as an economist. A mere reading of Marxian theory discloses his attempt at a valid explanation of economic phenomena, particularly those of value, price, and profit. When Marx dealt with economic phenomena, his purpose quite apparently was the same as that of the modern economist—to find an objective, valid explanation of economic phenomena and their causal relationships as they exist within some historical era Marx sought to explain what actually determined exchange values and wage rates, just as modern economists do in presenting value and wage theories. Indeed, the close deductive reasoning and scattered inductive data presented by Marx in his theories of value, wages, and profits bear a striking resemblance to modern economic theory as far as presentation is concerned.

Marx felt, moreover, that the valid explanations of economic phenomena lay deep beneath their surface manifestations. In discussing his explanation of value, he remarks that "the same difference holds that holds in respect to all phenomena and their hidden substratum. The former [that is, the phenomena] appear directly and spontaneously as current modes of thought; the latter must first be discovered by science."[2] Such were Marx's purposes in analyzing economic phenomena, and such he thought were his accomplishments.

In several other respects Marx has earned the title of economist. First, he spent many years on two types of study that are quite orthodox within the profession. His decade of study of economic data in the British Museum has been mentioned. He also studied intensively the leading economists of his day. His writings show that he was thoroughly acquainted with the works of such English economists as Petty, Smith, and Ricardo, and the French Sismondi.[3] Second—and this may be surprising to new students of Marx—when considered in the light of the economic science of his time, Marx was an orthodox economist. The

2Karl Marx, *Capital*, New York: Modern Library, n.d., p. 594.
3See Harry W. Laidler, *A History of Socialist Thought*, New York: T. Y. Crowell, 1927, p. 204.

bases of his theories of value and wages were, in fact, lifted bodily from contemporary orthodox schools of economic thought. The replacement of these partially correct and one-sided theories by more accurate, comprehensive, and well-balanced explanations of economic phenomena no more keeps Marx from being an economist of standing than the modern development of the half-truths of early natural sciences prevents their discoverers from being included in the ranks of scientists.

THEORY OF VALUE

Use Value, Exchange Value, and Price

In analyzing the value-determining forces at work in the capitalist economy, Marx distinguishes clearly between two kinds of value: "use value" and "exchange value." The former means the usefulness a thing has to its possessor, its utility, or the pleasure or satisfaction derived by its possessor from its utilization. Use value is a purely subjective thing, an abstraction that can exist quantitatively only in the mind of the user or prospective user of the thing, and then only as a plus or minus quantity relative to the similarly realized use value of some other thing. By *exchange value* Marx means the power of a thing to command all other things in exchange for itself, or "the proportional quantities in which it exchanges with all other commodities."[4] Since it is only exchange value that he seeks to analyze, he commonly drops that prefix and uses just *value*. By *value* Marx means precisely the same thing the orthodox economist of today means when he uses that term in economics textbooks.

Marx points out that use value and exchange value are obviously vitally related, since no exchange value can exist unless some use value is present. Only in very primitive forms of economy could a thing have use value without having exchange value. If little specialization prevailed and little exchange took place, most things would have use value and yet no exchange value. Since Marx is analyzing the determinants of value in a capitalist economy characterized by specialization and intricate exchange processes, the masses of things commonly produced are destined to be exchanged by their producers for other things and therefore have not only use value but exchange value as well. Things having both of these values he terms *commodities*. It is the determination of the exchange value of commodities that he attempts to explain.

Marx uses the term *price*, just as do modern orthodox economists, to mean the power of a commodity to command money in exchange for itself. As he puts it, price is the "money name" of the value of a commodity.

[4]Karl Marx, *Value, Price and Profit*, New York: International Publishers, 1935, p. 29.

Normal Value and Market Value

Marx, like modern economists, points out that there are several kinds of exchange value (from this point on to be called merely "value"). He distinguishes between what he calls "natural" values (and the corresponding natural prices) on the one hand and "market" values (and the corresponding market prices) on the other. By the former, which Marx also calls "real" value, he means the "normal" value in modern economic terms. This is the normal long-run level of the value of a commodity, on the average, about which short-run values of the commodity oscillate. Deviations from normal value or real value, Marx held, were caused by supply and demand forces, while the normal value itself, which became the market value when supply and demand were in perfect equilibrium, was determined by another force to be described presently. He therefore makes numerous references to market value or prices being out of line with normal values or prices.[5] Like modern economists, who devote their principal efforts to explaining the determinants of normal value, Marx was primarily interested in this. "The question is what determines the amount which becomes the amount at which supply and demand are in equilibrium."[6]

Marx phrased this distinction between normal or real value and market value in several clear paragraphs in his *Value, Price and Profit:*

> You will find that the fluctuations of market prices, their deviations from values, their ups and downs, paralyze and compensate each other; so that apart from the effect of monopolies and some other modifications I must now pass by, all descriptions of commodities are, on the average, sold at their respective values or natural prices.[7]

> At the moment when supply and demand equilibrate each other, and therefore cease to act, the market price of a commodity coincides with its real value, with the standard price round which its market prices oscillate. In inquiring into the nature of that value, we have therefore nothing at all to do with the temporary effects on market prices of supply and demand.[8]

It is interesting to note how closely this distinction follows the words of Adam Smith, whom Marx quotes in *Value, Price and Profit* as follows:

> The deviations of market prices from values are continual, but, as Adam Smith says: "The natural price is the central price to which the prices of commodities are continually gravitating. Different accidents may sometimes keep them suspended a good deal above it, and sometimes forces them down even somewhat below it. But whatever may be the

---

[5]For instance, in one place he refers to the "price realized" as possibly being "abnormally above or below the value." Marx, *Capital*, p. 121.

[6]Marx, *Value, Price and Profit*, p. 26.

[7]*Ibid.*, p. 36.

[8]*Ibid.*, p. 26.

obstacles which hinder them from settling in this center of repose and continuance they are constantly tending toward it."[9]

Labor as the Value-Determining Element Common to All Commodities

A basic tenet of Marx and other economists of the "labor-cost" school of that time was that whatever the value-determining force was, it had to be something common to all commodities.[10] This meant that an adequate explanation of value necessitated the discovery of something objective (therefore use value would not be suitable) and common to all commodities, and an analysis of the metamorphosis whereby that common element as it existed in all commodities became value.

Marx accepted labor, or muscular and mental human effort, as the one element common to all commodities. In question-answer form, Marx puts it thus: "What is the common social substance of all commodities? It is labor. To produce a commodity a certain amount of labor must be bestowed upon it, or worked up in it."[11] If labor is the one element common to all commodities and therefore the clue to values, what common element can be found in all labor? Clearly no qualitative characteristic, for labor obviously varies much from one specialized occupation to another. The common element must be quantitative, and the only element in this category found in all labor is time. Thus, labor time becomes the value-creating and value determining element in all commodities. Marx follows this line of reasoning in a concise summary in *Capital*:

> A use value, or useful article, therefore has value only because human labor in the abstract has been embodied or materialized in it. How, then, is the magnitude of this value to be measured? Plainly, by the quantity of the value-creating substance, the labor, contained in the article. The quantity of labor, however, is measured by its duration, and labor time in its turn finds its standard in weeks, days, and hours.[12]

Summaries of the Marxian Theory of Value

Before we take up certain separate portions of this theory of value for further study, it will be helpful to note several of the most concise of its numerous summaries:

> But what is the value of a commodity? The objective form of the social labor expended in its production. And how do we measure the quantity of this value? By the quantity of the labor contained in it.[13]

[9]*Ibid.*, p. 36.
[10]Recall that a commodity is anything that has both use value and exchange value.
[11]Marx, *Value, Price and Profit*, p. 30.
[12]Marx, *Capital*, p. 45.
[13]*Ibid.*, p. 586.

A commodity has a value because it is a crystallization of social
labor. The greatness of its value, or its relative value, depends upon the
greater or less amount of that social substance contained in it; that is to
say, on the relative mass of labor necessary for its production. The
relative values of commodities are, therefore, determined by the respective quantities or amounts of labor, worked up, realized, fixed in them.[14]

In this sense every commodity is a symbol, since, in so far as it
is value, it is only the material envelope of the human labor spent
upon it.[15]

Theory of Value Includes Past and Current Labor

A complete understanding of this theory of value requires that several
points be noted with particular care. Marx makes it clear that by the
amount of labor embodied in a commodity he means not only the labor
at the *final* stage of the process, or at that point where the commodity
takes on the final characteristics essential to its exchangeability. He emphasizes that the value-determining labor content of a commodity includes
all the labor at *all* stages in its production back through the production
of the necessary raw materials, power, and machinery. The labor required
to restore whatever portions of the machinery are worn away in the production of a commodity is part of the labor content of that commodity.
Similarly, if the raw materials entering a commodity are machine-made,
the labor necessary to restore any part of that machinery worn out in
producing the materials for that commodity is part of the labor content
of that commodity. Thus each commodity becomes the "material envelope"
of the human labor that went into it, despite the fact that the component
parts of this labor are scattered over many separate uses, producing units,
and periods of time. Marx summaries this portion of his theory of value
and illustrates it as follows:

> In calculating the exchangeable value of a commodity we must add
> to the quantity of labor last employed the quantity of labor previously
> worked up in the raw material of the commodity, and the labor be-
> stowed on the implements, tools, machinery, and buildings, with which
> such labor is assisted.[16]

> The labor required for the production of the cotton, the raw material
> of the yarn, is part of the labor necessary to produce the yarn, and
> is therefore contained in the yarn. The same applies to the labor em-
> bodied in the spindle, without whose wear and tear the cotton could not
> be spun.
>   Hence, in determining the value of the yarn, or the labor time re-
> quired for its production, all the especial processes carried on at

[14] Marx, *Value, Price and Profit.* p. 31.
[15] Marx, *Capital*, p. 103.
[16] Marx, *Value, Price and Profit*, p. 32.

various times and in different places, which were necessary, first to produce the cotton and the wasted portion of the spindle, and then with
the cotton and spindle to spin the yarn, may together be looked on
as different and successive phases of one and the same process. The whole
of the labor in the yarn is past labor; and it is a matter of no importance
that the operations necessary for the production of its constituent
elements were carried on at times which, referred to the present, are
more remote than the final operation of spinning. If a definite quantity
of labor, say thirty days, is requisite to build a house, the total amount
of labor incorporated in it is not altered by the fact that the work of
the last day is done twenty-nine days later than that of the first. Therefore, the labor contained in the raw material and the instruments of
labor can be treated just as if it were labor expended in an earlier
stage of the spinning process, before the labor of actual spinning
commenced.[17]

Only Socially Necessary Labor Is Value Determining

This theory of values does not imply that labor in itself creates value, no
matter what the end product of that labor may be and no matter how
inefficient it may be. Marx never argued that the more labor is embodied
in a product the more value that product possesses. It is only "socially
necessary" labor that is value determining. "In saying that the value of a
commodity is determined by the quantity of labor worked up or crystallized in it, we mean the quantity of labor necessary for its production in
a given state of society, under certain social average conditions of production, with a given social average intensity, and average skill of the labor
employed."[18]

Thus if one firm were to turn out a product with greater or lesser
efficiency, in terms of labor time embodied in it, than characterized the
preponderant run of the firms producing that product, the normal value
of that firm's product would be determined not by *its* labor time but by
that of the *bulk* of the producers. Any unusual conditions experienced
by one producer, affecting the labor time embodied in his product but
not "socially necessary" to the production of that product, are not value
determining. Marx illustrates this point as follows: "Though the capitalist
have a hobby, and use a gold instead of a steel spindle, yet the only labor
that counts for anything in the value of the yarn is that which would be
required to produce a steel spindle, because no more is necessary under
the given social conditions."[19]

It thus follows that the normal value of an existing stock of durable
commodities changes in accordance with changes in the socially necessary labor time required to produce identical commodities. Marx logically

[17]Marx, *Capital*, p. 209.
[18]Marx, *Value, Price and Profit*, p. 33.
[19]Marx, *Capital*, p.210.

holds that the quantities of past labor embodied in existing commodities of a certain kind no longer determine the normal values of those commodities if the socially necessary labor required to reproduce them has changed. In illustrating the determination of the normal value of cotton, he contends that

> if the time socially necessary for the production of any commodity alters—and a given weight of cotton represents, after a bad harvest, more labor than after a good one—all previously existing commodities of the same class are affected, because they are, as it were, only individuals of the species, and their value at any given time is measured by the labor socially necessary, i.e., by the labor necessary for their production under the then existing social conditions.[20]

In Marx's theory there are no limits to what may cause a change in the amount of labor socially necessary to produce a given commodity. He makes it a function of the entire environment within which production takes place; consequently, a change in any element in that environment may be the cause of an increase or decrease in the labor time necessary to produce that commodity.

Time Lags in Value Changes

Marx pictures the forces that change the socially necessary labor time to produce any given commodity as working imperfectly and with time lags. Thus if only one firm were to acquire a machine that would shorten the total labor time required in its plant to produce a certain product, that firm for the time being would derive a benefit from the fact that the value of its commodity on the open market (determined by the socially necessary labor time generally required to produce it) has not changed, while its individual value in this limited sphere (determined by the labor time necessary to produce it in this particular plant) has declined.[21] However, Marx further points out that in such a case there would be a downward pull on the commodity's normal value and that the rapidity of its fall would be determined by the degree of competition prevailing among the firms producing this product, while this in turn might be substantially affected by the ability of the originating firm to keep its invention a secret.

Exchange Proves the Presence of Use Value

The injection of the "socially necessary" element into the theory that labor time determines value serves to show that unless a thing has use value, labor spent on it cannot create exchange value. The determination

[20]*Ibid.*, pp. 233–234.
[21]See Marx, *Capital*, pp. 443–444.

of whether a given quantity of labor time has or has not created use value occurs within the exchange process. Marx holds that "whether that labor is useful for others and its product consequently capable of satisfying the wants of others, can be proved only by the act of exchange.[22] Thus the final determination of whether labor is socially useful or not is made by the buyers of the articles in which labor is embodied as they encounter them and react to them in their exchange activities.

There is still another ramification of the "socially useful" idea. According to Marx, it is possible for the social usefulness of a given quantity of labor to be diminished by applying it to some line of production when buyers of commodities would rather have it devoted to some other line of production. This, of course, is merely different in degree from the possibility just cited, in which it is conceivable that labor may be put into the formation of things that have *no* use value—the labor thus used becoming socially unnecessary and therefore not value creating. This subtle meaning of the term *socially necessary* is brought out by Marx in the following illustration:

> Lastly, suppose that every piece of linen in the market contains no
> more labor time than is socially necessary. [That is, no more than is
> necessary to make it physically.] In spite of this, all these pieces taken
> as a whole, may have had superfluous labor time spent upon them. If the
> market cannot stomach the whole quantity at the normal price [that
> is, at the value corresponding to the amount of labor socially necessary
> to produce the physical linen], . . . this proves that too great a portion
> of the total labor of the community has been expended in the form of
> weaving. The effect is the same as if each individual weaver had ex-
> pended more labor time upon his particular product than is socially
> necessary.[23]

The fact that society was demanding another allocation of its total labor time to the various channels of production thus would become evident through market value or price at a particular time being higher or lower than normal or "natural" value or price. In Marxian theory extra surpluses or losses resulting from these discrepancies would stimulate reallotment of labor time to its respective uses, thus reestablishing the dominance of normal value as determined by the content of socially necessary labor time.

Labor Content In Time Units Determines Value

In relation to value determination, qualities of labor have no significance—only quantities measured in time units are effective value determinants.

---

[22]*Ibid.*, p. 98.
[23]*Ibid.*, p. 120.

It is the quantity of labor required for its production, not the realized form of that labor, by which the amount of the value of a commodity is determined.[24]

While, therefore, with reference to use value, the labor contained in a commodity counts only qualitatively, with reference to value it counts only quantitatively, and must first be reduced to human labor pure and simple.[25]

Skilled labor counts only as simple labor intensified or, rather, as multiplied simple labor, a given quantity of skilled being considered equal to a greater quantity of simple labor.[26]

Marx was vague as to just what "human labor pure and simple" meant. Professor Bober concludes that he meant "homogeneous, abstract, unskilled labor."[27]

Marx conceived of all kinds and degrees of occupational skill as being reducible to standard time units of unskilled labor. Thus, to illustrate, a skilled machinist in one clock hour might contribute to production four of these standard time units of unskilled labor. If an average unskilled-labor hour were the standard unit, the skilled machinist would then embody in the commodity on which he working four hours of socially necessary (assuming standard efficiency of equipment, etc.) labor time per clock hour worked, while the unskilled laborer would embody in the commodity only one hour of socially necessary labor time per clock hour worked. Since hours of socially necessary labor time, rather than clock hours, are held to be the determinants of value, a commodity produced by the skilled machinist (assuming, to make the case simple, that he was unassisted by other workers or machinery or materials) in one clock hour would have a normal value equal to that of the product produced by the unskilled laborer (assuming he also was unassisted) in four clock hours. In other words, the normal values of commodities bear to each other exchange ratios directly proportional to the number of socially necessary standard time units of unskilled labor used up in the production of each.

Marx was extremely vague in explaining what determines the number of units of unskilled labor time to which a certain clock time spent by a skilled laborer will be equivalent. It is obvious that the number of ratios necessary to convert all the socially necessary labor in a commodity into a quantity of these hours of unskilled labor time would be not only exceedingly numerous but very complicated in a system characterized by much specialization and multitudinous categories of skill. The conversion of skilled into unskilled units of labor therefore cannot be

[24]Ibid., p. 588.
[25]Ibid., pp. 52–53.
[26]Ibid., p. 51.
[27]M. M. Bober, Karl Marx's Interpretation of History, Cambridge, Mass.: Harvard University Press, 1927, p. 203.

done by one who might wish to study the production of a given product and make such a calculation. According to Marx, "the different proportions in which different sorts of labor are reduced to unskilled labor as their standard, are established by a social process that goes on behind the backs of the producers, and, consequently, appear to be fixed by custom."[28] In a later reference to the problem of converting units of skilled into unskilled labor, he contends that "whenever, by an exchange, we equate as values our different products, by that very act, we also equate, as human labor, the different kinds of labor expended upon them."[29] Marx apparently felt that the impossibility of objectively calculating these relationships or segregating the forces that act in the markets to determine them does not diminish the reality of their independent existence.

Value Is Inherent in the Commodity

Despite certain limitations already noted, Marx finds it possible to contend that value thus becomes something inherent in the commodity. "It becomes plain, that it is not the exchange value of commodities which regulates the magnitude of their value; but, on the contrary, that it is the magnitude of their value which controls their exchange proportions."[30] As Professor Bober points out, it was in this regard that Marx departed from Ricardo's labor theory of value. "Ricardo had constantly in mind exchange value, relative value. To him, value is the power of one product to command others in exchange. To Marx value is exchange value; but it is also an intrinsic entity incarnated in a commodity, and the substance of this entity is congealed labor."[31] It is in this regard that Marx may have involved his theory of value in some internal inconsistencies (to be discussed later) and come nearest to making his theory of value merely a part of his philosophy rather than an objective explanation of what happens in the exchange processes of a capitalist economy.

Relationship of Man-Made and
Nature-Made Instruments to Value Determination

Of course, if value is always merely "congealed" socially necessary labor, neither the man-made nor the nature-made instruments used in production can play any *direct* part in value determination. As previously noted, Marx considered man-made tools and machinery merely the products of labor, so they became indirectly value determining, in that whatever socially necessary labor had gone into tools and machinery actually used

[28]Marx, *Capital*, p. 52.
[29]*Ibid.*, p. 85.
[30]*Ibid.*, p. 73.
[31]Bober, p. 203.

up in the production of a commodity were considered part of the socially necessary labor embodied in that commodity. As far as nature or nature-made instruments are concerned, Marx flatly denies (although there are some minor contradictory statements) that the part they may play in production enters in any way into the value determination of the commodities produced: "Since exchange value is a definite social manner of expressing the amount of labor bestowed upon an object, Nature has no more to do with it, than it has in fixing the course of exchange."[32] "So far no chemist has ever discovered exchange value either in a pearl or a diamond."[33] That is, in the purely natural state they are not commodities, because they have no exchange value. Whatever exchange value they may acquire comes only after the application of labor to the natural materials or in anticipation of the possibility of adding human labor to the natural materials. If labor could not be applied, any such exchange value would immediately vanish. Nature merely furnishes the environment. Exchange values are in no sense a function of the environment. They exist only when labor time has joined itself with nature, and consequently they are the exclusive product of labor time. So runs the Marxian theory.

Labor Content Determines Value of Money

Marx considered price to be merely the "money name" of value. Whatever the chosen money metal might be, its value was determined by exactly the same forces that determined the values of other commodities—the socially necessary labor time embodied in it. "The value of gold or silver, like that of all other commodities, is regulated by the quantity of labor necessary for getting them."[34] Thus each commodity tended to exchange for the number of dollars or pounds containing the amount of gold or silver that embodied an amount of socially necessary labor equal to that embodied in the commodity. "The value, or in other words the quantity of human labor contained in a ton of iron, is expressed in imagination by such a quantity of the money commodity as contains the same amount of labor as the iron."[35] Money thus becomes a common measure of values, whereas money prices merely express relationships between values—that is, between the respective labor contents of commodities on the one hand and of quantities of the monetary metal on the other.

Significance of Monetary Expression of Value

Although Marx held that money prices were mere reflections of values, he attached much significance to the fact that values were so expressed.

[32]Marx, *Capital*, p. 94.
[33]*Ibid.*, p. 95.
[34]Marx, *Value, Price and Profit*, p. 35.
[35]Marx, *Capital*, p. 108.

The real stuff of which values are composed—that is, labor—thus loses its human aspects and is converted into a sort of inanimate abstraction. "When they assume this money shape, commodities strip off every trace of their natural use value, and of the particular kind of labor to which they owe their creation, in order to transform themselves into the uniform, socially recognized incarnation of homogeneous human labor."[36] In discussing this point Lenin held that "money masks the social character of individual labor, and hides the social tie between the various producers who come together in the market."[37]

Modifications of Theory of Value by Marx

Thus far the Marxian theory of value appears to be clear and simple. But from this point on, abstruseness and apparent contradictions feature the theory or theories of value propounded in Volume III of *Capital*. In pursuing his thought, Marx apparently became involved in certain difficulties arising out of his "socially necessary labor" theory of value. This theory appeared to him to fall somewhat short of explaining actual price phenomena as they prevailed in markets. A modified theory of value appears in his later writings. Students have disagreed heartily over whether this modified theory is or is not consistent with the original value theory expounded earlier.

For the purposes of this discussion and for an understanding of the basic features of Marxian thought, it is not necessary to trace these modifications and their ramifications in detail. The earlier value theory, which has been outlined, holds that *each* commodity tends to sell for a value or price determined by *its* content of socially necessary labor. In his later work Marx injected a concept of averages into this theory. Lenin has interpreted Marx on this point as follows: "Naturally, therefore in a society made up of separate producers of commodities, linked solely through the market, conformity to law can only be an average, a general manifestation, as mass phenomenon, with individual and mutually compensating deviations to one side and the other."[38]

Thus, the socially necessary total labor going to produce all commodities determines their total values in terms of each other, or the average socially necessary labor content determines the average value. Professor Bober interprets Marx as holding that "only the total volume of commodities produced in all industries can be said to sell according to the mass of socially necessary labor incorporated in it. In individual cases, commodities in one branch of production will sell at less, and in another at more, than

[36] *Ibid.*, p. 123.
[37] V. I. Lenin, "The Teachings of Karl Marx," in *Handbook of Marxism*, E. Burns, comp., New York: Random House, 1935, p. 549.
[38] *Ibid.*, p. 556.

the value according to the labor theory. But these deviations compensate each other, as we should expect, since the deviations of the items from their average will always cancel out. . . ."[39]

As will appear later, in the discussion of "surplus value," Marx was interested primarily in mass or aggregate phenomena. His whole system deals with the sweep of evolutionary change in social phenomena. It is evident that he considered value theory more pertinent and meaningful when stated in terms of averages or masses than when expressed in terms of individual commodities. "He does not claim that the two theories are identical, but he urges that the first is still the heart and soul of the second, and that therefore the labor theory enunciated in the first volume is not abandoned in the third."[40]

THEORY OF WAGES

Labor Power Is a Commodity

Marx's theory of wages is merely an extension of his general theory of value to a specific category of prices. In the Marxian sense, a wage is a price paid for labor power, not for labor. "By labor power or capacity for labor is to be understood the aggregate of those mental and physical capabilities existing in a human being, which he exercises whenever he produces a use value of any description."[41] "Labor power" is the thing that enters the labor market, being sold by the laborer and purchased by the capitalist employer. Thus, "labor power" is a commodity having exchange value, since the laborer can alienate it from his person as he sells to the capitalist the right to use his use value or labor. It is only this right that can be alienated, and consequently "labor is the substance, and the immanent measure of value, but *has itself no value*" (that is, no exchange value).[42]

In other words, Marx holds that the thing the worker sells to the employer is the right to put him as a worker to work. It is not the productivity of the worker that is sold; it is merely the right to make the worker exert himself. However, since the use value of the productivity of the worker cannot be severed from his *power* to release this use value or productivity, the employer *buys* the labor power but *gets* the use value of that labor power, or the labor itself. Thus, while it may appear that the use value of the worker, or the labor itself, is the subject of the wage contract and is paid for, the fact is that only the labor power is paid for, while the actual use of that labor power is a thing separate and distinct from it. In any event, it is the *labor power* that is paid for, and the *value*

[39]Bober, pp. 212–213.
[40]*Ibid.*, p. 214.
[41]Marx, *Capital*, p. 186.
[42]*Ibid.*, p. 588.

of this labor power is the wage. At this point this distinction is noted only as a part of the Marxian theory of wages. Its significance will be evident in the discussion of surplus value in the next chapter.

To Marx a wage can exist only in a situation in which (1) the worker is free to sell his labor power and (2) he cannot by himself make use of it in producing some commodity for sale.

> Labor power can appear upon the market as a commodity only
> if, and so far as, its possessor, the individual whose labor power it is,
> offers it for sale, or sells it, as a commodity. In order that he may be able
> to do this, he must have it at his disposal, must be the untrammeled
> owner of his capacity for labor, i.e., of his person. . . . The second es-
> sential condition to the owner of money finding labor power in the
> market as a commodity is this—that the laborer, instead of being in the
> position to sell commodities in which his labor is incorporated, must
> be obliged to offer for sale as a commodity that very labor power, which
> exists only in his living self.[43]

Normal Wage and Market Wage

Paralleling his distinction between normal values and market values, Marx notes that the wage actually paid a given worker or group of workers may be temporarily above or below the normal wage. Supply and demand forces only cause oscillations above and below a "certain mean." The mean is the "natural price . . . determined independently of demand and supply."[44] Marx sought to answer these questions. What determines the height of this mean? What forces establish the "natural" or the equilibrium wage toward which actual market wages are incessantly drawn despite their temporary departures therefrom? "On the basis of the present system labor is only a commodity like others. It must, therefore pass through the same fluctuations to fetch an average price corresponding to its value."[45] Marx makes numerous references to situations in which labor power ac- tually sells for more or less than its "value."[46] These deviations mutually cancel each other, leaving the "normal wage" as the selling price of labor power received by workers over a period of time.

Labor Content Determines Value of Labor Power

Like other commodity values, the value of labor power is determined by its content of socially necessary labor time. "Therefore the labor time requisite for the production of labor power reduces itself to that neces- sary for the production of those means of subsistence; in other words,

---

[43]*Ibid.*, pp. 186–187.
[44]*Ibid.*, p. 589.
[45]Marx, *Value, Price and Profit*, p. 55.
[46]See, for instance, Marx, *Capital*, pp. 569, 572, 573, 657, 680.

the value of labor power is the value of the means of subsistence necessary
for the maintenance of the laborer."[47] Numerous concise statements of
this theory of wages are found in Marxian literature. Many of them—as,
for instance, the following—emphasize the physical side of the concept
subsistence:

> The value of laboring power is determined by the value of the
> necessaries required to produce, develop, maintain, and perpetuate the
> laboring power.[48]

> In exchange he [the worker] receives just as much, and no more,
> of the necessaries of life as is required to keep up the repetition of the
> same bargain every day.[49]

> The average price of wage labor is the minimum wage, i.e., the
> quantum of the means of subsistence which is absolutely requisite to keep
> the laborer in bare existence as a laborer.[50]

> Hence, the cost of production of a workman is restricted, almost
> entirely, to the means of subsistence that he requires for his maintenance,
> and for the propagation of his race.[51]

> The value of labor power is determined, as in the case of every
> commodity, by the labor-time necessary for the production, and conse-
> quently also the reproduction, of this special article.[52]

> As with all other commodities, so with labor, its *market price*
> will, in the long run, adapt itself to its value; that, therefore, despite all
> the ups and downs, and do what he may, the working man will, on
> the average, only receive the value of his labor, which resolves into the
> value of his laboring power, which is determined by the value of the
> necessaries required for its maintenance and reproduction, which
> value of necessaries finally is regulated by the quantum of labor needed
> to produce them.[53]

The Normal Price of Labor Power

Expressed in money terms, the normal price of a day's labor power therefore is that quantity of the standard money containing the amount of metal
that could be produced in the same socially necessary labor time as could

[47]*Ibid.*, pp. 189–190.
[48]Marx, *Value, Price and Profit*, p. 40.
[49]Friedrich Engels, "The British Labor Movement," in *Handbook of Marxism*,
p. 199.
[50]Karl Marx and Friedrich Engels, "Communist Manifesto," in *Handbook of
Marxism*, p. 39.
[51]*Ibid.*, p. 30.
[52]Marx, *Capital*, p. 189.
[53]Marx, *Value, Price and Profit*, pp. 56–57.

the necessaries comprising one day's subsistence for the laborer. Marx illustrates this principle as follows:

> Suppose that in this mass of commodities requisite for the average day there are embodied six hours of social labor, then [assuming that a standard length of the working day is twelve hours] there is incorporated daily in labor power half a day's average social labor; in other words, half a day's labor is requisite for the daily production of labor power. This quantity of labor forms the value of a day's labor power or the value of the labor power daily reproduced. If half a day's average social labor is incorporated in three shillings, then three shillings is the price corresponding to the value of a day's labor power.[54]

In elaborating on this theory of wages, Marx placed it on a family rather than an individual basis. "The value of labor power was determined, not only by the labor time necessary to maintain the individual adult laborer, but also by that necessary to maintain his family."[55] "Hence the sum of the means of subsistence necessary for the production of labor power must include the means necessary for the laborer's substitutes, i.e., his children, in order that this race of peculiar commodity-owners may perpetuate its appearance in the market."[56] When family wage and family subsistence are tied together in this manner, Marx goes on to contend that "machinery, by throwing every member of the family on to the labor market, spreads the value of the man's labor over his whole family. It thus depreciates his labor power."[57]

Wage Differential for Grade of Skill

Starting with this theory, wage differentials between grades of skill were also accounted for on the basis of differences in the cost of producing various categories of skill. If a period of training were prerequisite to attaining a given degree of skill, the production of that skill would use up a larger amount of socially necessary labor time, and the labor power of such a skilled laborer would have an equivalently greater value. "As different kinds of laboring power have different values, or require different quantities of labor for their production, they must fetch different prices in the labor market."[58]

This apparently modifies *subsistence* into meaning the subsistence of skill. Each particular grade of skill thus would normally receive a wage sufficient to reproduce its kind. In the following summary Marx implies

[54]Marx, *Capital*, pp. 191–192.
[55]*Ibid.*, p. 431.
[56]*Ibid.*, p. 191.
[57]*Ibid.*, p. 431.
[58]Marx, *Value, Price and Profit*, p. 39.

that education and training are the most important additional costs in the
production of skilled labor power.

> In order to modify the human organism, so that it may acquire skill
> and handiness in a given branch of industry, and become labor power of
> a special kind, a special education or training is requisite, and this,
> on its part, costs an equivalent in commodities of a greater or less
> amount. This amount varies according to the more or less complicated
> character of the labor power. The expenses of this education (ex-
> cessively small in the case of ordinary labor power) enter *pro tanto*
> into the total value spent in its production.[59]

Meaning of Subsistence

In applying his theory of wages to the analysis of economic phenomena,
Marx found himself between two difficulties. If, on the one hand, the
normal wage, or cost of producing the labor, was to be considered an
amount necessary to the worker's bare *physical subsistence*, the theory
not only ran counter to certain easily observable wage facts but also
proved ineffectual all attempts to raise wages under the capitalist system.
If, however, the cost of production of labor power were thought of as
capable of being extended by new desires on the part of workers, it would
appear possible to raise wages through the workers' own efforts under the
capitalist system. Since Marx refused to accept completely either of these
corollaries of his wage theory, his treatment of wages wavers between the
two positions. In certain connections, he appears to accept the mere physical subsistence concept of wage-determining cost of labor power. In other
portions of his analysis, he uses the more elastic interpretation of the concept *subsistence*.

In fact, one can find in Marxian writings passages indicating that
almost nothing was ruled out of "subsistence," provided the worker wanted
it badly enough to think and act as though that thing were a necessary part
of his living. The scope of the items that in one connection or another Marx
and Engels included in "subsistence" may be noted from the following
passages (italics ours):

> The value of labor power is determined by the value of the necessaries
> of life *habitually required* by the average laborer.[60]

> His means of subsistence must therefore be sufficient to maintain him
> in his *normal state* as a laboring individual.[61]

> In contradistinction therefore to the case of other commodities,

59Marx, *Capital*, p. 191.
60Marx, *Capital*, p. 568.
61*Ibid.*, p. 190.

there enters into the determination of the value of labor power a *historical and moral* element.[62]

A fair day's wage, under normal conditions, is the sum required to procure to the laborer the means of existence necessary, according to the *standard of life of his station and country*, to keep himself in working order and to propagate his race.[63]

But where a particular rate of piece wage has for a long time been fixed by *tradition*, and its lowering, therefore, presented especial difficulties, the masters, in such exceptional cases, sometimes had recourse to its compulsory transformation into time wages.[64]

Besides this mere physical element, the value of labor is in every country determined by a *traditional standard of life*. It is *not mere physical life*, but it is the satisfaction of *certain wants springing from the social conditions* in which people are placed and reared up. . . . The important part which *historical tradition* and *social habitude* play in this respect, you may learn from Mr. Thornton's work on *Overpopulation*. . . . This *historical or social element*, entering into the value of labor, may be *expanded*, or *contracted*, or altogether extinguished, so that nothing remains but the physical limit. . . .By comparing the standard wages or values of labor in different countries, and by comparing them in value of labor itself is *not a fixed but a variable magnitude*. . . .[65]

Thus while the Marxian theory of wages in its purely abstract form is clear enough, it becomes blurred by all the concessions Marx made when he found it necessary to define the items comprising the "subsistence" of labor power. At one time subsistence appears to mean only those things vital to the maintenance of physical health; at another, it is enlarged to include items that have come to be wanted by workers because of their social or historical environment.

Physical Subsistence Is Emphasized

However, when Marxian theory is considered as a whole, it clearly holds that wages are bound closely to a physical subsistence level. If there are any tendencies acting counter to this pull of physical subsistence, they are either temporary or so slow in their operation that they may be neglected in analyzing the basic forces at work under capitalism. In various other portions of his thought (to be considered later in another connection), Marx pointed out what he considered to be powerful forces that under capitalism effectively resisted any tendency for wages to rise significantly above a physical subsistence level. Certain modifications that Marx made

[62]*Ibid.*, p. 190.
[63]Engels, "The British Labor Movement," in *Handbook of Marxism*, p. 198.
[64]Marx, *Capital*, p. 607.
[65]Marx, *Value, Price and Profit*, pp. 57–58.

in his theory of value (by way of injecting a concept of averages into it) did not prevent him from holding to the original theory as the "heart" of value determination. Similarly in the case of his wage theory, despite the numerous concessions and modifications apparently made in the subsistence concept, Marx still retained physical subsistence as the heart of the wage-determining cost of producing labor power.

QUESTIONS FOR CLASS DISCUSSION

1. It is often suggested that Marx was either no economist at all or, at best, a very poor one. Do you agree? Why or why not?

2. What evidence is there that Marx set forth what he believed to be the correct theory of value and wages?

3. Define each of the following terms as it was used by Marx *use value; exchange value; price; market value; normal value.*

4. When Marx set out to explain the forces determining value, which of the kinds of value mentioned in Question 3 did he have in mind?

5. By what line of reasoning did Marx support his contention that labor was the value-determining element in commodities?

6. When Marx refers to labor as value determining, does he mean manual or mental labor or both?

7. What difference is there between saying that the labor content of a commodity determines its value and saying that the socially necessary labor time embodied in a commodity determines its value?

8. Does the Marxian theory of value exclude the cost of the machinery used in the production of a commodity from the forces determining the value of that commodity?

9. Did Marx contend that the mere use of labor to form some object gives that object value?

10. Is labor time essentially a homogenous or a heterogenous phenomenon? How did Marx overcome the difficulty created by this fact?

11. Of what significance is it, according to Marx, that in modern societies values are expressed in terms of money?

12. Did Marx think of a wage as being paid for labor or for labor power? What is the significance of this distinction?

13. In what sense could Marx's theory of wages be said to be merely part of his theory of value?

14. How did Marx use the concept of subsistence in his theory of wages? As he used it, was this concept clear-cut? Give examples.

6. The Marxian theory of surplus value and accumulation of capital

THEORY OF SURPLUS VALUE

It was a simple matter for Marx to derive his theory of surplus value by putting together his theory of value and his theory of wages. In skeleton form the theory of surplus value runs as follows: Since the socially necessary labor time embodied in a commodity determines its value, the total of all values produced during a day's labor time will be the total exchange values of all commodities produced by that day's effort. The value of the day's labor power itself will be determined by the socially necessary labor time embodied in the commodities necessary to maintain the worker for a day. However, there is no necessity that wage workers should work only the number of hours socially necessary to produce their own subsistence. When the worker sells a day's labor power to the capitalist employer, the latter specifies the length of the working day. If capitalist employers set the length of the working day at a greater number of hours than the number required to produce labor's subsistence, then the wage the employer must pay the worker, being determined by the latter number of hours, will be less than the total value of commodities produced in such a day, the total value produced depending on the total number of hours worked. Marx held that under capitalism the working day must be longer than the number of hours of average labor required to produce the worker's subsistence (or the amount he gets as a wage). The values produced during these excess hours constitute "surplus value"—that is, values produced by the workers but that they do not get, since their wages are equal to the value of their subsistence.

Theory of Surplus Value as a Formula

This theory can be simplified into the formula $A - B = C$. If A represents the total of commodities produced in the working day and B the total of commodities necessary to subsistence, then C represents the total commodities whose value is surplus value. If A represents the total value produced during the standard working day and B the value of a day's subsistence for the worker, then C represents surplus value. If A represents the length of the working day in hours and B the number of socially necessary hours required to produce a day's subsistence, then C represents the hours during which the worker is producing surplus value. If A represents the total value produced by a day's labor effort and B the value paid back as a wage to the worker, then C represents the value also produced by labor but appropriated by the capitalist employer. If A represents the standard labor day and B the portion of this required to produce the worker's subsistence, then C represents the uncompensated portion of the workday. Or, depending on the angle from which the phenomena are viewed, C may represent the exploited portion of the worker's labor power, or the hours during which the worker labors for the capitalist rather than for himself. From still another point of view, if A represents all the values of commodities put into exchange, then B represents the portion of these commodities that continues to circulate among workers because this much must be paid them as wages, and C represents the commodities that are drawn out of the exchange process by the capitalist employer who uses them partially for his own consumption and partially as further advances (a fund circulating capital) wherewith he again hire workers to produce more surplus value.

Distinction Between Labor Power and Labor

Marx lays the basis for this theory of surplus value when he distinguishes between the exchange value of labor as a commodity and its use value (or between buying labor power and buying labor). The capitalist employer buys labor power but gets labor; he pays out the value of the labor power (subsistence) as a wage, but he gets the use value of the labor as his own to utilize in whatever way he can. The exchange value of the labor power (or the wage) is determined by the cost of producing it (its subsistence), whereas the use value of the labor to the employer, who after the hiring owns it, is determined by what use he can make of it.

Although there are a number of ways in which the employer can make the use value of the labor in creating exchange values greater than the exchange value he paid for it, the most obvious way is to make the laborer work more hours than enough to create exchange values equal to those laid out by the employer as a wage. This capitalist employers will do—they would obviously be fools if they didn't—and so arises surplus value.

Marx constructed the following illustration of surplus value for a workingmen's organization:

> Now suppose that the average amount of the daily necessaries of a laboring man require *six hours of average labor* for their production. Suppose, moreover, six hours of average labor to be also realized in a quantity of gold equal to 3s. Then 3s would be the *Price*, or the monetary expression of the *Daily Value* of that man's *Laboring Power*. If he worked daily six hours he would daily produce a value sufficient to buy the average amount of his daily necessaries, or to maintain himself as a laboring man.
>
> But our man is a wages laborer. He must, therefore, sell his laboring power to a capitalist. If he sells it as 3s daily, or 18s weekly, he sells it at its value. Suppose him to be a spinner. If he works six hours daily he will add to the cotton a value of 3s daily. This value, daily added by him, would be an exact equivalent for the wages, or the price of his laboring power, received daily. But in that case no *surplus value* or *surplus produce* whatever would go to the capitalist. Here, then, we come to the rub.
>
> In buying the laboring power of the workman, and paying its value, the capitalist, like every other purchaser, has acquired the right to consume or use the commodity bought. You consume or use the laboring power of a man by making him work, as you consume or use a machine by making it run. By paying the daily or weekly value of the laboring power of the workman, the capitalist has, therefore, acquired the right to use or make that laboring power work during the *whole day or week*. The working day or the working week has, of course, certain limits, but those we shall afterwards look more closely at.
>
> For the present I want to turn your attention to one decisive point.
>
> The *value* of the laboring power is determined by the quantity of labor necessary to maintain or reproduce it, but the *use* of that laboring power is only limited by the active energies and physical strength of the laborer. The daily or weekly *value* of the laboring power is quite distinct from the daily or weekly exercise of that power, the same as the food a horse wants and the time it can carry the horseman are quite distinct. The quantity of labor by which the *value* of the workman's laboring power is limited forms by no means a limit to

the quantity of labor which his laboring power is apt to perform. Take the example of our spinner. We have seen that, to daily reproduce his laboring power, he must daily reproduce a value of three shillings, which he will do by working six hours daily. But this does not disable him from working ten or twelve or more hours a day. But by paying the daily or weekly *value* of the spinner's laboring power the capitalist has acquired the right of using that laboring power during the *whole day or week*. He will, therefore, make him work daily, say, *twelve* hours. *Over and above* the six hours required to replace his wages, or the value of his laboring power, he will, therefore, have to work *six other hours*, which I shall call hours of *surplus labor*, which surplus labor will realize itself in a *surplus value* and a *surplus produce*. If our spinner, for example, by his daily labor of six hours, added three shillings' value to the cotton, a value forming an exact equivalent to his wages, he will, in twelve hours, add six shillings' worth to the cotton, and produce a *proportional surplus of yarn*. As he has sold his laboring power to the capitalist, the whole value or produce created by him belongs to the capitalist, the owner pro tem of his laboring power. By advancing three shillings, the capitalist will, therefore, realize a value of six shillings, because, advancing a value in which six hours of labor are crystallized, he will receive in return a value in which twelve hours of labor are crystallized. By repeating this same process daily, the capitalist will daily advance three shillings and daily pocket six shillings, one half of which will go to pay wages anew, and the other half of which will form the *surplus value*, for which the capitalist pays no equivalent. It is this *sort of exchange between capital and labor* upon which capitalistic production, or the wages system, is founded, and which must constantly result in reproducing the working man as a working man, and the capitalist as a capitalist.[1]

Surplus Value Is Inevitable Under Capitalism

Marx thus makes surplus value the inevitable accompaniment of a capitalist economy. In a system in which commodity values and wages are determined as they are, and in which the worker is free to and must sell his labor power as a commodity to a capitalist employer, surplus value must arise. It is no more created by the grasping of the capitalist than it can be eliminated by the opposition of the workers. Within the framework of a capitalist order, surplus value would disappear only if capitalist employers were to refrain from making the working day longer than the hours required to produce the worker's means of subsistence, or if the workers were to force their wages up enough to absorb surplus value. The former, Marx held, could not happen because it would be suicidal for the capitalist employers to give up the sole source of their livelihood. Nor could the latter happen, because economic principles operating in a capitalist system prevent wages from rising above a subsistence level.

[1]Karl Marx, *Value, Price and Profit*, New York: International Publishers, 1935, pp. 40–42.

Surplus Value—The Driving Force in Capitalism

Not only was surplus value inevitable under the capitalist system, but to Marx it was the heart and soul of that system. The capitalist employer occupied a key position. During earlier historical stages of capitalism, he exercised personal initiative in the organization of production, and he continued even in the mature stages of capitalism to hire others to do the directing while he retained the passive role of the immediate supplier of funds to pay labor. The attempt to acquire surplus value acts as a key incentive to the production of commodities in the capitalism system.

> Our capitalist has two objects in view; in the first place, he wants to produce a use value that has a value in exchange, . . . and secondly, he desires to produce a commodity whose value shall be greater than the sum of the values of the commodities used in its production. . . .
> His aim is to produce not a use value, but a commodity also; not only use value, but value; not only value, but at the same time surplus value.[2]

Thus the existence of surplus value is so inextricably tied up with the forces of production in a capitalist order that if production is to take place surplus value must be realizable. Since surplus value cannot be severed from the machinery of a capitalist order, its ethical justness cannot be considered separately from that of the entire system of which it is an inherent part.

The Degree of Exploitation Under Capitalism

The absolute amount of surplus value realized by the capitalist employer represents his absolute exploitation or robbery of the worker. Marx sought the most accurate way of expressing surplus value as a percentage so that the degree of exploitation of the worker could be calculated in individual instances as well as in society as a whole. Although the details of these calculations are not essential to an understanding of the theory of surplus value, it is interesting to note that Marx felt that the customary way of expressing profits as a percentage of all the funds owned by the capitalist was very misleading and yielded an understatement of the degree of exploitation. Marx divides the capital used in production into two parts. One consists of all funds going into the purchase of fixed equipment and raw materials, the other of funds used as wages to pay for labor power. The former he calls "constant" capital and the latter "variable" capital. He then argues that the only fair way to compute the percentage of surplus value realized is to compare it with the amount of variable capital. This relationship, he holds, will represent "the real degree of exploitation

[2]Karl Marx, *Capital*, New York: Modern Library, n.d., p. 207.

of labor" by the capitalist employer because it is this "which shows you the real ratio between paid and unpaid labor."[3]

Rent, Interest, and Profit Under Capitalism

To Marx, surplus value was a heterogeneous fund. Despite its homogeneous entrance into the coffers of the capitalist employer, it comes to be split into a number of kinds of individual income. "Rent, interest [to the money-lending capitalist as distinguished from the more active capitalist employer], and industrial profit [left in the hands of the capitalist employer] are only different names for different parts of the surplus value of the commodity, or the unpaid labor realized in it, and they are equally derived from this source, and from this source alone."[4] In another connection Marx refers to "all surplus value, whatever particular form (profit, interest or rent) it may subsequently crystallize into," as "in substance the materialization of unpaid labor."[5] Thus, recipients of rent, interest, and profits, and subsidiary classes drawing their incomes from them, are all in effect acquiring unearned surpluses; they are beneficiaries of the capitalist processes of labor exploitation. In such a society Marx and Engels, indulging in some exaggeration, hold that "those of its members who work acquire nothing, and those who acquire anything do not work."[6]

Normal Values and Normal Wages
Permit Surplus Value Under Capitalism

It is important to note that surplus value arises neither from selling commodities at prices above their real values nor from buying labor power at less than its real value. On this point Marx was insistent. Departures of prices and wages from their norms might cause temporary additions to or subtractions from profit, but the surplus value he was describing was permanent and normal in itself. Surplus value was created for the capitalist employer even when he sold his commodity at its true or normal value and purchased labor at its full normal value.

> The value of a commodity is determined by the *total quantity of labor*
> contained in it. But part of that quantity of labor is realized in a
> value for which an equivalent has been paid in the form of wages; part
> of it is realized in a value for which *no* equivalent has been paid. Part
> of the labor contained in the commodity is *paid* labor; part is *unpaid*
> labor. By selling, therefore, the commodity at its value, that is, as the

[3]Marx, *Value, Price and Profit*, pp. 47–48.
[4]*Ibid.*, p. 45.
[5]Marx, *Capital*, p. 585.
[6]Karl Marx and Friedrich Engels, "Communist Manifesto," in *Handbook of Marxism*, E. Burns, comp., New York: Random House, 1935, p. 41.

crystallization of the *total quantity of labor* bestowed upon it, the capitalist must necessarily sell it at a profit. He sells not only what has cost him an equivalent, but he sells also what has cost him nothing, although it has cost the labor of his workmen. The cost of the commodity to the capitalist and its real cost are different things. I repeat, therefore, that normal and average profits are made by selling commodities not *above* but *at their real values.*[7]

Surplus Value Is Created by Capitalist Production

Thus, surplus value arises out of neither the dishonesty nor the bad intent of the capitalist employer. He cannot will it into existence. As a phenomenon it is created by the nature of the economy under which he and the worker live. Surplus value is not grasped by the capitalist employer; it is something left in his hands by the operation of forces over which he as an individual has no control. "Suppose that the capitalist pays for a day's labor power at its value; then the right to use that power for a day belongs to him, just as much as the right to use any other commodity, such as a horse that he has hired for the day."[8] It is out of the legitimate exercise of the rights the capitalist system bestows upon the capitalist employer that he becomes the possessor of surplus value.

Relationship of Surplus Value
to Lengthening of the Workday

Although the capitalist employer is in no sense individually responsible for the phenomenon of surplus value, he does have a great deal to do with the determination of its amount. As has been noted, every extension in the length of the standard workday past the number of hours socially necessary to produce labor's subsistence adds to the surplus value acquired by the capitalist employer because it extends the unpaid portion of the workday; it keeps the worker at work for a longer time after he has produced enough value to repay the capitalist employer for the wage he must pay the worker. This is the most direct, most obvious, and in Marx's day most widely used device to increase the degree of exploitation of the worker by the capitalist employer. Marx refers to its possibilities in many portions of his writings, and he reviews in minute detail the practical attempts of employers of his day to stretch out labor hours and thus increase surplus value. Marx argued that only drastic legal limitations on the length of the workday could set limits to this type of exploitation. The following quotation from *Capital* hints at the prevailing length of the workday in Marx's time and also discloses the vivid style in which he portrayed these conditions:

[7]Marx, *Value, Price and Profit*, pp. 44–45.
[8]Marx, *Capital*, p. 206.

In the last week of June, 1863, all the London daily papers published a paragraph with the "sensational" heading "Death from simple over-work." It dealt with the death of the milliner, Mary Ann Walkley, 20 years of age, employed in a highly respectable dressmaking establishment, exploited by a lady with the pleasant name of Elise. The old, often-told story was once more recounted. This girl worked, on an average, 16½ hours, during the season often 30 hours, without a break; whilst her failing labor power was revived by occasional supplies of sherry, port, or coffee. It was just now the height of the season. It was necessary to conjure up in the twinkling of an eye the gorgeous dresses for the noble ladies bidden to the ball in honor of the newly imported Princess of Wales. Mary Ann Walkley had worked without intermission for 26½ hours, with 60 other girls, 30 in one room, that only af-forded ⅓ of the cubic feet of air required for them. At night, they slept in pairs in one of the stifling holes into which the bedroom was di-vided by partitions of board. And this was one of the best millinery establishments in London. Mary Anne Walkley fell ill one Friday, died on Sunday, without, to the astonishment of Madame Elise, having previously completed the work in hand. The doctor, Mr. Keys, called too late to the deathbed, duly bore witness before the coroner's jury that "Mary Anne Walkley had died from long hours of work in an over-crowded workroom, and a too small and badly ventilated bedroom." In order to give the doctor a lesson in good manners, the coroner's jury thereupon brought in a verdict that "the deceased had died of apoplexy, but there was reason to fear that her death had been accelerated by overwork in an overcrowded workroom, etc." "Our white slaves," cried the *Morning Star*, the organ of the free-traders, Cobden and Bright, "our white slaves, who are toiled into the grave, for the most part silently pine and die."

It is not in dressmakers' rooms that working to death is the order of the day, but in a thousand other places; in every place I had almost said, where "a thriving business" has to be done. . . . We will take the blacksmith as a type. If the poets were true, there is no man so hearty, so merry, as the blacksmith; he rises early and strikes his sparks before the sun; he eats and drinks and sleeps as no other man. Working in moderation, he is, in fact, in one of the best human positions, physically speaking. But we follow him into the city or town, and we see the stress of work on that strong man, and what then is his po-sition in the death rate of his country. In Marylebone, blacksmiths die at the rate of 31 per thousand per annum, or 11 above the mean of the male adults of the country in its entirety. The occupation, instinctive almost as a portion of human art, unobjectionable as a branch of human industry, is made by mere excess of work, the destroyer of the man. He can strike so many blows per day, walk so many steps, breathe so many breaths, produce so much work, and live an average, say, of fifty years; he is made to strike so many more blows, to walk so many more steps, to breathe so many more breaths per day, and to increase altogether a fourth of his life. He meets the effort; the re-sult is, that producing for a limited time a fourth more work, he dies at 37 for 50.[9]

[9]*Ibid.*, pp. 280–282.

Relationship of Surplus Value to Use of Machinery

The use of machinery, Marx held, would merely stimulate the capitalist employer to make the workday still longer.

> Machinery sweeps away every moral and natural restriction on the length of the working day. Hence, too, the economical paradox, that the most powerful instrument for shortening labor time, becomes the most unfailing means for placing every moment of the laborer's time and that of his family, at the disposal of the capitalist for the purpose of expanding the value of his capital.[10]

The attempt to get the most out of the machine would drive its owner to keep it in operation for the greatest possible portion of the potential working time. This necessarily stretches out the hours of its human tender. Moreover, since the absolute amount of surplus value realized by the capitalist employer depends in part on the number of workers he hires, and since the use of machinery will decrease this number, Marx argues that the employer will attempt to compensate himself for the absolute loss in surplus value due to the decreased number of employees by stretching out the day of each employee and thus making a greater portion of the day of each worker unpaid labor time.[11]

Relationship of Surplus Value to Technological Progress

Moreover, anything that occurred or that the capitalist employer might do to decrease the labor content of commodities constituting labor's subsistence would thereby decrease the amount of time socially necessary to produce this subsistence. As long as the length of the working day remained constant, such improvements in processes or machinery as brought this result would automatically increase surplus value by cutting the portion of the total produced value that the employer had to pay to the worker as a wage—in other words, increasing the unpaid-for portion of the working day. The increasing use of machinery and improvements in machinery and processes would all work toward this end.[12]

Relationship of Surplus Value to Speeding Up the Worker

The same net results in terms of increased surplus value could be achieved by intensifying and speeding up the worker's movements. The more product the worker turned out in a given time, the amount required for sub-

[10]Ibid., p. 445.
[11]Ibid., p. 445.
[12]Ibid., pp. 345, 350, 352, 356–357, 405.

sistence remaining unchanged, the greater would be the surplus value. Marx argued that as hours came to be limited by law, the employer turned to the practice of speeding up his labor. He pointed to machinery and "piece wages" as the two chief devices the employer used to this end. "As soon as that shortening [of the workday] becomes compulsory, machinery becomes in the hands of capital the objective means, systematically employed for squeezing out more labor in a given time. This is effected in two ways: by increasing the speed of the machinery, and by giving the workman more machinery to tend."[13]

Piece wages were useful devices to the employer in speeding up his workers because "they furnish to the capitalist an exact measure for the intensity of labor."[14] Marx thus found that "piece wages is the form of wages most in harmony with the capitalist mode of production"[15] and that "in the workshops under the Factory Acts, piece wages become the general rule, because capital can there only increase the efficacy of the working day by intensifying labor."[16]

Relationship of Surplus Value to Cooperative Use of Labor

In still another manner the capitalist employer by his own efforts could increase surplus value. Marx pointed out that when workers engaged in production as cooperating members of a factory unit, their cooperative endeavors are more productive than the aggregate of their efforts would be if they applied them individually. This added labor power is unpaid for, since the capitalist employer buys his labor by separate units. The product of this uncompensated labor power goes to expand surplus value.[17] Likewise, anything the capitalist employer does to increase the efficiency and smoothness of this cooperation among the units of labor power he has purchased accrues to the recipients of surplus value. Moreover, "because this power costs capital nothing, and because, on the other hand, the laborer himself does not develop it before his labor belongs to capital, it appears as a power with which capital is endowed by Nature—a productive power that is immanent in capital."[18]

Marx concludes that, with wages tied to subsistence, all the improvements in production, the increasing efficiency of industry, and the very increases in productivity of labor itself will go to enhance the surplus-value incomes of capitalist employers, lending capitalists, and landowners.

13*Ibid.*, p. 450.
14*Ibid.*, p. 605.
15*Ibid.*, p. 608.
16*Ibid.*, p. 609.
17*Ibid.*, pp. 361, 365, 366.
18*Ibid.*, pp. 365–366.

Such is the exploitation of workers by owners under the capitalist system of economic organization.

Modern Exploitation of Labor
Compared with Historical Exploitation

Exploitation of labor did not begin with the capitalist system, however. Engels found three historical forms of exploitation: "Slavery is the first form of exploitation, the form proper to the world of antiquity; it was followed by serfdom in the Middle Ages, and wage labor in the more recent period. These are the three great forms of subjection, characteristic of the three great epochs of civilization. . . ."[19]

Similarly, Marx held that the wage worker in modern society was in reality a slave: "The essential difference between the various economic forms of society, between, for instance, a society based on slave labor, and one based on wage labor, lies only in the mode in which this surplus labor is in each case exacted from the actual producer, the laborer."[20]

Marx, however, pictured modern "wage slavery" as more subtle and concealed than the older forms of slavery. In the first period to which Engels referred, it was quite clear that *none* of the labor of the slave appeared to be paid for. He was kept alive by his owner, who could demand all the slave's time for his service. Under serfdom, the portion of the serf's labor that was uncompensated for was also clearly marked off. He owed his lord a certain portion of his time; the rest was his own. If the service to the lord was analogous to surplus value, it at least was not a hidden surplus. In contrast, the slavery of the modern wage worker is concealed. Ostensibly, he is a free agent contracting to sell his services to an employer. He is not required to render any services except those he agrees to sell. Thus all the labor time he puts in appears to be paid for. But if the amount the worker can get per day is limited by the amount his family needs for its subsistence, and if the length of the working day is specified by the employer, who also may issue rules concerning how rapidly the employee must work during those hours, then, Marx contends, compensation is not proportionate to labor performed, and a concealed portion of the workday is not paid for.

> The wage form thus extinguishes every trace of the division of the
> working day into necessary labor and surplus labor, into paid and unpaid
> labor. All labor appears as paid labor. . . . In slave labor, even that
> part of the working day in which the slave is only replacing the value
> of his own means of existence, in which, therefore, in fact, he works
> for himself alone, appears as labor for his master. All the slave's labor

[19]Friedrich Engels, "The Origin of the Family, Private Property and the State," in *Handbook of Marxism*, p. 335.
[20]Marx, *Capital*, p. 241.

appears as unpaid labor. In wage labor, on the contrary, even surplus labor, or unpaid labor, appears as paid. There the property relation
conceals the labor of the slave for himself; here the money relation
conceals the unrequited labor of the wage laborer.[21]

The Roman slave was held by fetters: the wage laborer is bound to his
owner by invisible threads. The apearance of independence is kept
up by means of a constant change of employers, and by the *fictio juris*
of a contract.[22]

THE ACCUMULATION OF CAPITAL

The Origin of Surplus Value—Primitive Accumulation

Marx realized that a complete explanation of the processes at work in
the capitalist economy had to account for the beginning of that system.
His theories of value, wages, and surplus value simply explained the
system as a going affair and analyzed phenomena that were parts of a
complex set of processes and institutions already existing. Where did the
first capitalist employers come from? Where did they get their surplus
funds to hire the first workers on a contractual wage basis? How did free
laborers with the power to sell their own services arise from an environment characterized by the feudal system of serfdom?

Once the processes of capitalism were set in motion, according to
Marxian theory, capitalist employers used surplus value to enlarge the
funds they used to hire labor. But where did the first surplus value come
from, and of what did this original fund consist?

It therefore seems likely that the capitalist, once upon a time, became
possessed of money, by some accumulation that took place independently
of the unpaid labor of others, and that this was, therefore, how he
was enabled to frequent the market as a buyer of labor power.[23]

He, who before was the money owner, now strides in front as capitalist;
the possessor of labor power follows as his labor.[24]

Once such a fund of money existed, and concurrently there were
workers not only free but under pressure to sell their labor power for
money, the two essential ingredients of the capitalist system prevailed. Its
evolution from that point on could be a self-contained thing, since capital
funds accumulated from surplus value.

Marx contended that the capitalist system had its origin in some
historical events that, consistent with his economic interpretation of history,

[21]*Ibid.*, p. 591.
[22]*Ibid.*, p. 628.
[23]*Ibid.*, p. 623.
[24]*Ibid.*, p. 196.

were caused by changes in the mode of production. Such events he found in the England of the late fifteenth and early sixteenth centuries, and in other European countries at various times before the advent of capitalism. These years he refers to as a period of "primitive accumulation." "Primitive accumulation creates, at the one pole, the 'free' proletariat; at the other, the owner of money, the capitalist"[25]—that is, the original proletarians and the original capitalist employers.

> The expropriation of the agricultural producer, of the peasant, from the
> soil, is the basis of the whole process. The history of this expropriation,
> in different countries, assumes different aspects, and runs through its
> various phases in different orders of succession, and at different
> periods. In England alone . . . has it the classic form.[26]

The processes of "expropriation" during those centuries were traced in detail[27] by Marx, who pointed out how, through the intermingling of economic developments and the ruthless use of force by those in power, the old feudal relationships were broken and a peasant agricultural economy was uprooted. The rights of lords to receive services were transformed into money payments, while the rights of peasants to use certain lands were abolished and the land was transferred to uses that had come to be more profitable, notably raising sheep. The elements in this transition are summarized by Marx as follows:

> The spoliation of the church's property, the fraudulent alienation
> of the state domains, the robbery of the common lands, the usurpation
> of feudal and clan property, and its transformation into modern private
> property under circumstances of reckless terrorism, were just so many
> idyllic methods of primitive accumulation. They conquered the field
> for capitalistic agriculture, made the soil part and parcel of capital, and
> created for the town industries the necessary supply of a "free" and
> outlawed proletariat. [28]

Herein were the sources of the original capital funds in the form of money and of the original free proletariat, who, having no rights to land on which they might produce for themselves, could live only by selling their labor power to those possessing money funds. The origins of capitalism, according to Marx, were "the expropriation of the immediate producers, i.e., the dissolution of private property based on the labor of its owner"[29] or "a series of historical processes, resulting in a decomposition of the original union existing between the laboring man and his means of

---

[25]V. I. Lenin, "The Teachings of Karl Marx," in *Handbook of Marxism*, p. 553.

[26]Marx, *Capital*, p. 787.

[27]See the early chapters of part VIII in *Capital*.

[28]Marx, *Capital*, p. 805.

[29]*Ibid.*, p. 834.

labor."[30] This newer form of economic relationship "has no natural basis, neither is its social basis one that is common to all historical periods. It is clearly the result of a past historical development, the product of many economical revolutions, of the extinction of a whole series of older forms of social production."[31]

Capital Accumulation Proceeds from Surplus Value

Once the period of primitive accumulation is past, capital accumulation proceeds by accretions from surplus value. All surplus value realized becomes the property of the capitalist. Portions of this surplus are used for his personal consumption; others are used to hire labor to engage in further production for the further acquisition of surplus value. All funds advanced to labor Marx calls capital, distinguishing funds put into tangible equipment ("constant capital") from those going to pay labor's current wages ("variable capital"). Since it is obvious that such a use of surplus value for capital purposes will not be undertaken unless the capitalist expects to get back more than he has laid out, and since the value processes of a capitalist economy work inevitably to that end, surplus value results from these outlays of capital in production. From these surpluses over and above the original outlays, still more capital is put into the next productive operation, and so on under capitalism in a never-ending spiral of capital accumulation from surplus value. Marx points out emphatically that "by the side of the newly formed capital, the original capital continues to reproduce itself, and to produce surplus value, and that this is also true of all accumulated capital, and the additional capital engendered by it."[32]

After the process of capital accumulation is set in motion, it is "the laborers' own labor, realized as a product, which is advanced to him by the capitalist";[33] "the produce of the labor of those who do work gets unavoidably accumulated in the hands of those who do not work and becomes in their hands the most powerful means to enslave the very men who produced it."[34] "Employing surplus value as capital, reconverting it into capital, is called accumulation of capital."[35]

Abstinence Is Not the True Source of Capital

Marx was aware of the claims of political economists that, in using funds they acquired to hire more labor in the productive process, capitalists

[30]Marx, *Value, Price and Profit*, p. 39.
[31]Marx, *Capital*, p. 188.
[32]*Ibid.*, p. 637.
[33]*Ibid.*, p. 622.
[34]Friedrich Engels, "The British Labor Movement," in *Handbook of Marxism*, p. 200.
[35]Marx, *Capital*, p. 634.

were "abstaining" or "saving." Economists contended that capital accumulation could not take place without such abstinence, which thereby became just as essential to further production as labor power and therefore just as deserving of reward. To this Marx issued a double reply. First, as has been noted, he contended that the original capital funds were merely taken by force from expropriated peasant workers. Second, the funds "saved" by modern capitalists were also stolen, but in a different manner, since they came from surplus value. Marx proposes the question, Should anyone be compensated for saving rather than consuming funds that in any event he has stolen? In the following satirical passage, Marx suggests that since the capitalist finds it a hardship to save what he has stolen, he be freed from this burden by being kept from stealing:

> The simple dictates of humanity therefore plainly enjoin the release of
> the capitalist from this martyrdom and temptation, in the same way
> that the Georgian slave owner was lately delivered, by the abolition of
> slavery, from the painful dilemma, whether to squander the surplus
> product lashed out of his niggers, entirely in champagne, or whether
> to reconvert a part of it, into more niggers and more land.[36]

Exploitation of Labor Inherent in Capitalism

To Marx the essence of the workings of the capitalist system is embodied in the value and wage-determining processes and in the accumulation of capital. These he did not condemn. They were part and parcel of the entire capitalist order. As inseparable parts of it they could not stand alone, nor could the capitalist order exist without them. They were not immortal in themselves but only because they, as inherent parts of an entire economic system, yielded results that Marx held to be contrary to human welfare and internally inconsistent. We will now turn to an examination of the consequences Marx held to be the inevitable outcome of the economic processes at work in capitalism.

QUESTIONS FOR CLASS DISCUSSION
1. In what sense is Marx's theory of surplus value merely a logical combination of his theory of value and his theory of wages?
2. How is the contention that the capitalist employer buys labor power but gets labor related to the theory of surplus value?
3. Does Marx contend that since surplus value is ethically wrong, it ought to be eliminated from our economic system?
4. Would it be correct to say that although Marx objected to incomes consisting of surplus value, he had no similar objections to interest and land rent?

[36]*Ibid.*, p. 655.

5. Would it be correct to say that Marx held surplus value to result from capitalist employers' overcharging for their commodities and underpaying their workers?

6. Could surplus value be done away with by reducing the length of the workday? Did Marx believe that this might take place?

7. As Marx analyzed the situation, did capitalist employers get *all* the benefits arising from the increasing use of machinery and improvement in technical processes?

8. Did Marx contend that modern wage slavery was just like the older types of human slavery?

9. What did Marx mean by a period of primitive accumulation? How did he relate it to the accumulation of capital?

10. Would Marx agree with economists who contend that all society's existing capital equipment has come from a process of saving?

7. The consequences of capitalist production

The most obvious consequence of the value processes at work under capitalism, and of their culmination in surplus value, is the division of modern society into two great classes between which there exists an irreconcilable clash of economic interests. The existence of classes with conflicting interests Marx held to be a universal historical phenomenon. He and Engels wrote into the "Communist Manifesto" that "the history of all hitherto existing society is the history of class struggles."[1] The Marxian

[1]Karl Marx and Friedrich Engels, "Communist Manifesto," in *Handbook of Marxism*, E. Burns, comp., New York: Random House, 1935, p. 22.

dialectic of thesis, antithesis, and synthesis, and the Marxian economic interpretation of history jointly support this conclusion, which continues:

> In the earlier epochs of history, we find almost everywhere a complicated arrangement of society into various orders, a manifold gradation of social rank. In Ancient Rome we have patricians, knights, plebeians, slaves; in the Middle Ages, feudal lord, vassals, guildmasters, journeymen, apprentices, serfs; in almost all of these classes, again, subordinate gradations.
>
>   The modern bourgeois society that has sprouted from the ruins of feudal society has not done away with class antagonisms. It has but established new classes, new conditions of oppression, new forms of struggle in place of the old ones.
>
>   Our epoch, the epoch of the bourgeoisie, possesses, however, this distinctive feature: it has simplified the class antagonisms. Society as a whole is more and more splitting up into two great hostile camps, into two great classes directly facing each other—bourgeoisie and proletariat.[2]

THE CLASS STRUGGLE

The Historical Source of Class Struggle

The dissolution of the relationships existing in the old feudal society created new group alignments. The period of primitive accumulation caused a marking off of two economic groups—those who had the money funds to hire others, and those who, having the personal freedom to hire out themselves, had to submit to being hired as the only possible source of a livelihood. With the accumulation of capital in the hands of the former group and their descendents, the continued tendency for workers to get nothing but their subsistence, and the embodiment of capital funds in new and better mechanical devices, these two classes were pushed further and further apart until in Marx's day their interests became so antagonistic that he felt the situation to be obviously that of a life-and-death struggle between them. It was Marx's purpose to instill into the workers a sense of this irreconcilable clash of interests. With their class consciousness developed, class struggle would ensue, and this, necessarily taking a political form, would be the first step in preparation for the overthrow of capitalism and the establishment of a new order.

Surplus Value—The Economic Source of Class Struggle

In attempting to arouse workers to a consciousness of their own exploited position, Marx wove his argument around his theory of surplus value. The surplus was the essence of the clash of interests; so long as it existed and was acquired by those who had the power to take it, there could be no

2*Ibid.*, p. 23.

basic social harmony. So long as the property institutions of capitalism awarded this surplus to one class, leaving the other to acquire nothing but the means of its subsistence, there was an unbridgeable gulf between the two classes. On one side, acquiring the surplus value out of which they accumulated still more capital, stood the owners; on the other, exhausting their wages in their own reproduction, were the workers. Marx labeled the former the bourgeoisie, the latter the proletariat. So long as capitalism prevailed, surplus value would be generated and would go to the bourgeoisie, and so long as this took place, the proletariat could never change its economic status—it could merely continue to exist.

The Composition of the Bourgeoisie

The distinguishing feature of the bourgeoisie is the ownership of property— in money funds, land, and man-made instruments of production. Since Marx makes surplus value the source of the incomes of the moneylender, the landowner, and the capitalist employer, he implies that there are no essential differences in their interests or their positions within the bourgeoisie. Their ability to acquire income follows from their status as owners. "It is not because he is a leader of industry that a man is a capitalist; on the contrary, he is a leader of industry because he is a capitalist."[3]

Certain sections of the bourgeoisie, however, were not closely knit into the fabric of their class. They could not remain members of it indefinitely.

> The lower strata of the middle class—the small tradespeople, shop-
> keepers, and retired tradesman generally, the handicraftmen and
> peasants—all these sink gradually into the proletariat, partly because
> their diminutive capital does not suffice for the scale on which modern
> industry is carried on, and is swamped in the competition with the
> large capitalists, partly because their specialized skill is rendered worth-
> less by new methods of production.[4]

It is also held that as the class struggle "nears the decisive hour," defection will occur for "a portion of the bourgeois ideologists, who have raised themselves to the level of comprehending theoretically the historical movement as a whole."[5]

The Contributions of the Bourgeoisie

The bourgeoisie were far from the conservative class implied by the modern use of that term. Marx and Engels pointed out:

[3]Karl Marx, *Capital*, New York: Modern Library, n.d., p. 365.
[4]Marx and Engels, "Communist Manifesto," in *Handbook of Marxism*, p. 31.
[5]*Ibid.*, p. 34.

> Historically, the bourgeoisie has played a most revolutionary part. The bourgeoisie, wherever it has got the upper hand, has put an end to feudal, patriarchal, idyllic relations. It has pitilessly torn asunder the motley feudal ties that bound man to his "natural superiors," and has left no other nexus between man and man than naked self-interest, than callous "cash payment." It has drowned the most heavenly ecstasies of religious fervor, of chivalrous enthusiasm, of philistine sentimentalism, in the icy water of egotistical calculation. It has resolved personal worth into exchange value, and in place of the numberless indefeasible chartered freedoms, has set up that single unconscionable freedom— Free Trade. In one word, for exploitation, veiled by religious and political illusions, it has substituted naked, shameless, direct brutal exploitation.[6]

In short, the bourgeoisie played the role of innovator in the changes that laid the basis for modern industry. Those arrangements, customs, and institutions which stood in the way of change it promptly dispensed with, oftentimes forcibly and with great human suffering and alienation.

These changes were not without benefit to human society as a whole. They brought the parts of the world into close contact.

> Modern industry has established the world market, for which the discovery of America paved the way. This market has given an immense development to commerce, to navigation, to communication by land.[7]

> The bourgeoisie . . . has been the first to show what man's activity can bring about. It has accomplished wonders far surpassing Egyptian pyramids, Roman aqueducts, and Gothic cathedrals; it has conducted expeditions that put in the shade all former Exoduses of nations and crusades. . . . The bourgeoisie, during its rule of scarce one hundred years, has created more massive and more colossal productive forces than have all preceding generations together. Subjection of nature's forces to man, machinery, application of chemistry to industry, and agriculture, steam navigation, railways, electric telegraphs, clearing of whole continents for cultivation, canalization of rivers, whole populations conjured out of the ground—what earlier century had even a presentiment that such productive forces slumbered in the lap of social labor?[8]

Creation of the Proletariat by the Bourgeoisie

Despite all these accomplishments, the bourgeoisie has set in operation certain forces that will cause its ultimate downfall. In a sense these forces are personified in the proletariat—"a class of laborers who live only so long as they find work, and who find work only so long as their labor increases capital. These laborers, who must sell themselves piece-meal, are

[6]*Ibid.*, p. 25.
[7]*Ibid.*, p. 24.
[8]*Ibid.*, pp. 26, 28.

a commodity, like every other article of commerce, and are consequently exposed to all the vicissitudes of competition, to all the fluctuations of the market."[9] Since the bourgeoisie can exist only if and to the extent that there is a proletariat, the former may be said to have created the latter.

Moreover, in developing modern industrial processes the bourgeoisie often herded large masses of workers together under one roof and in one town. The proletariat was therefore in a much better position to "form combinations (trade unions) against the bourgeois," to "club together in order to keep up the rate of wages," to "found permanent associations in order to make provisions beforehand for these occasional revolts." The proletariat is further strengthened "by the improved means of communication that are created by modern industry, and that place the workers of different localities in contact with one another." Moreover, the bourgeoisie is constantly getting portions of the proletariat to fight its battles for it, battles with antagonistic elements within the bourgeoisie and with foreign bourgeoisie. The bourgeoisie thus "supplies the proletariat with its own elements of political and general education; in other words, it furnishes the proletariat with weapons for fighting the bourgeoisie."[10] Combining all this with the already-noted defections from the bourgeoisie to the proletariat, Marx concludes that "what the bourgeoisie therefore produces, above all, are its own gravediggers. Its fall and the victory of the proletariat are equally inevitable."[11]

THE STATE AS AN AGENCY OF OPPRESSION

Marx contended that in the class struggle the state was an agency or device controlled by the bourgeoisie to advance its own interests. By the state Marx meant nothing synonymous with organized society or government.[12] Sidney Hook holds that in the Marxian sense "we may speak of a state only where a special public power of coercion exists which, in the form of an armed organization, stands over and above the population" In support of this he quotes Marx as saying that "the state presupposes the public power of coercion separated from the aggregate body of its members."[13] Presumably an organized society could exist in the absence of such power (Marx held that it would under full communism), while the government is merely the machinery in which this power resides.

The state in this "power of coercion" sense would have no function

9Ibid., p. 30.
10Ibid., pp. 32–33.
11Ibid., p. 36.
12Except for brief references this theory of the state was not treated by Marx. It was developed by Engels and Lenin. In our treatment their contributions are included as parts of Marxian theory.
13Sidney Hook, *Towards the Understanding of Karl Marx*, New York: Day, 1933, p. 256.

to perform unless there were something or somebody to be subjected to that power.

> The state, therefore, has not existed from all eternity. There have been societies which managed without it, which had no conception of the state and state power. At a certain stage of economic development, which was necessarily bound up with the cleavage of society into classes, the state became a necessity owing to this cleavage.[14]

> The state is the product and the manifestation of the irreconcilability of class antagonisms. The state arises when, where, and to the extent that the class antagonisms cannot be objectively reconciled. And, conversely, the existence of the state proves that the class antagonisms are irreconcilable.[15]

> Political power, properly so called, is merely the organized power of one class for oppressing another.[16]

During each period in history, therefore, the state is in the possession of the class dominant at that particular time.

> Former society, moving in class antagonisms, had need of the state, that is, an organization of the exploiting class at each period for the maintenance of external conditions of production; that is, therefore, for the forcible holding down of the exploited class in the conditions of oppression (slavery, villeinage or serfdom, wage labor) determined by the existing mode of production. The state was the official representative of society as a whole, its embodiment in a visible corporation; but it was this only in so far as it was the state of that class which itself, in its epoch, represented society as a whole; in ancient times, the state of the slave-owning citizens; in the Middle Ages, of the feudal nobility; in our epoch, of the bourgeoisie.[17]

Thus a state can be nothing else than a dictatorship—a dictatorship of one class over one or more other classes.[18]

The Bourgeois State

Such is the abstract nature of the state as an institution. Its particular evolutionary forms are determined by the changing modes of production. Therefore, the same forces that brought into existence the original capitalist employer and the original wage worker created what Marx, Engels, and Lenin have called the bourgeois state. As the power of the owning class

---

[14]Friedrich Engels, "The Origin of Family, Private Property and the State," in *Handbook of Marxism*, p. 332.
[15]V. I. Lenin, "The State and Revolution," in *Handbook of Marxism*, p. 724.
[16]Marx and Engels, "Communist Manifesto," in *Handbook of Marxism*, p. 46.
[17]Friedrich Engels, "Anti Dühring," in *Handbook of Marxism*, p. 295.
[18]Hook, p. 300.

has developed with the accumulation of capital, the power of the bourgeois state has increased concurrently until it "is nothing but the organized
collective power of the possessing classes, the landowners and the capitalists as against the exploited classes, the peasants and the workers. What
the individual capitalists (and it is here only a question of these because in
this matter the landowner who is also concerned acts primarily as a capitalist) do not want, their state also does not want."[19] The officials who
"now stand as organs of society *above* society" are "but a committee for
managing the common affairs of the whole bourgeoisie."[20] "Moreover,
this power, which is the essence of the state and is wielded by the bourgeoisie, grows stronger in proportion as the class antagonisms within the
state grow sharper. . . ."[21]

Democracy in the Bourgeois State

The state whose function is thus portrayed in Marxian theory is not
necessarily a monarchical state, although at certain times it has been that.
Engels takes particular care to point out that the *"modern representative
state* is the instrument of the exploitation of wage labor by capital. . . . The
highest form of state, the democratic republic, which in our modern social
relations is becoming more and more an unavoidable necessity, and is the
form of state in which alone the last decisive battle between proletariat and
bourgeoisie can be fought out—the democratic republic no longer has any
official cognizance of property differences. In it, wealth wields its power
indirectly, but *all the more effectively.*"[22] These "indirect" controls, to Engels, exist "on the one hand in the form of direct corruption of the officials—America is the classic example of this; on the other hand in the
form of an alliance between the government and the stock exchange,
which comes about all the more easily the more the public debt increases
and the more share companies concentrate in their hands not only transport but even production, and in turn find their own center of gravity in
the stock exchange."[23]

Still more subtly, "the possessing class rules directly by means of
universal suffrage. So long as the oppressed class, that is, in our case, the
proletariat, is not yet ripe for self-liberation, so long will it, that is, the
majority, regard the existing social order as the only possible one, and be
politically the tail of the capitalist class, its extreme left wing."[24]

[19]Friedrich Engels, "The Housing Question," in *Handbook of Marxism*, p. 347.
[20]Engels, "The Origin of the Family, Private Property and the State," in
Handbook of Marxism, pp. 329–330; Marx and Engels "The Communist Manifesto,"
in *Handbook of Marxism*, p. 25.
[21]Engels, "The Origin of the Family, Private Property and the State," in *Handbook of Marxism*, p. 329.
[22]*Ibid.*, pp. 330–331. Italics ours.
[23]*Ibid.*, p. 331.
[24]*Ibid.*, p. 332.

Lenin contributes a more detailed catalog of devices whereby the bourgeoisie controls the votes of the proletariat in a "democracy." He holds:

> Both in the . . . so-called petty details of the suffrage (residential qualification, exclusion of women, etc.), and in the technique of the representative institutions, in the actual obstacles to the right of assembly (public buildings are not for "beggars"!), in the purely capitalist organization of the daily Press, etc., etc.—on all sides we see restriction after restriction upon democracy. These restrictions, exceptions, exclusions, obstacles for the poor, seem slight, especially in the eyes of one who has himself never known want and has never been in close contact with the oppressed classes in their mass life . . . but in their sum total these restrictions exclude and squeeze out the poor from politics and from an active share in democracy. Marx splendidly grasped this essence of capitalist democracy, when, in analyzing the experience of the Commune, he said that the oppressed were allowed, once every few years, to decide which particular representatives of the oppressing class should be in parliament to represent and oppress them.[25]

Lenin concludes not only that the so-called democratic state under capitalism oppresses the proletariat but also "a democratic republic is the best possible political shell for capitalism, and therefore, once capital has gained control . . . of this very best shell, it establishes its power so securely, so firmly, that *no* change, either of persons, or institutions, or parties in the bourgeois republic can shake it."[26] Thus, in all but the most exceptional cases—"periods when the warring classes so nearly attain equilibrium that the state power, ostensibly appearing as a mediator, assumes for the moment a certain independence relative to both"—state power in a modern "democratic" capitalist society remains an agency of oppression wielded by the bourgeoisie against the proletariat.[27]

From this it follows that "the working men have no country."[28] The machinery of state cannot be counted upon to alleviate any but the most trivial of the woes of the proletariat—it is by no means an instrumentality through which effective gradual steps toward socialism can be taken. The state, rooted by its very nature in class struggle, can never be anything but an agency of oppression until class struggle disappears, and the class struggle between bourgeoisie and proletariat cannot disappear until capitalism itself is supplanted by communism.

THE INCREASING MISERY OF THE PROLETARIAT

Contradictions Within Capitalism

Neither the class struggle nor the use of the political state as an agency of oppression in themselves would destroy the capitalist system. Capital-

---

[25]Lenin, "The State and Revolution," in *Handbook of Marxism*, p. 744.
[26]*Ibid.*, p. 731.
[27]Engels, "The Origin of the Family," in *Handbook of Marxism*, p. 330.
[28]Marx and Engels, "Communist Manifesto," in *Handbook of Marxism*, p. 43.

ism, including these two phenomena, could exist indefinitely were it not for what Marx held to be certain "contradictions" that develop automatically and inevitably within the capitalist order. Capitalism and the bourgeois state are unable to cope with these difficulties, which seal the eventual doom of the system. A capitalist society "that has conjured up such gigantic means of production and of exchange is like the sorcerer who is no longer able to control the powers of the nether world whom he has called up by his spells."[29]

While capital accumulates, workers are pressed into deeper and deeper misery. Despite this, the rate of profits realized by capitalist employers falls. With the increasing misery of workers, their purchasing power declines and they are unable to absorb their accustomed fractional part of the output of industry. Cyclical fluctuations of industrial activity are generated by the resulting overproduction. Surpluses of goods on markets and declining rates of profit increase the intensity of competition among capitalist business units. This competition, reaching cutthroat proportions, leads to the killing off of the smaller industrial units and the concentration and centralization of the control of industry in fewer and fewer hands.

The formation of monopolies engenders control by a group of financial overlords during a stage of "finance capital." Accompanying these domestic consequences of overproduction are the attempts of capitalist employers to find foreign markets for their surplus products. Pressing the power of the state which they control—into their service, they create "capitalist imperialism." These contradictions, which have fatally weakened the foundations of capitalism by the time the period of "finance capital" arrives, will reach the peak of their development during an imperialistic war. A "revolution" will occur and the proletariat, if properly prepared and organized under the leadership of the Communist Party, will pick up the reins of control and carry on.

Although Marxian theory is not pieced together with the precision this résumé implies, it emphasizes the automatic nature of the inherent contradictions that develop within the system and carry it from stage to stage, ending in a complete economic collapse. We will now review briefly the most important of these inherent contradictions within the capitalist system as they have been analyzed by Marx and his closest followers.

Surplus Value and Increasing Misery. In discussing the Marxian theory of surplus value, it was noted that every increase in the productivity of labor or the efficiency of industry would accrue to the recipients of surplus value, since it would act to decrease the socially necessary labor time required to produce labor's subsistence. Thus the proportionate share of the total product realized by labor would constantly decline as long as the efficiency of production was increasing.

[29]*Ibid.*, p. 29.

The Reserve of Labor. Marx viewed the forces at work in the capitalist system as operating in still other ways to press the proletariat into deeper and deeper "misery." He argued that since, as capitalism developed, the demand for labor would not develop proportionately to the accumulation of capital, a "reserve of labor" or "overpopulation" would be created, and this in turn would beat down wages through increased competition for the available jobs.

Machinery and the Reserve. This labor reserve is due primarily to the fact that as the total amount of capital increases a larger and larger portion of it goes into instruments of production (constant capital), leaving a smaller and smaller portion available for hiring labor directly (variable capital). Marx held that the "demand for labor is determined . . . by its variable constituent alone."[30] This is just another way of saying that as more machinery is used, workers will be set free from their old jobs more rapidly than new jobs develop. The reason for this is that the increased eficiency due to the expansion of machinery does not create mass purchasing power because it goes into surplus value rather than into expanded wages. In modern terms, Marx was contending that accumulating technological unemployment would create a larger and larger army of unemployed workers. This condition would press wages downward in a number of ways. "The pressure of the unemployed compels those who are employed to furnish more labor, and therefore makes the supply of labor, to a certain extent, independent of the supply of laborers."[31] This surplus labor also "floods all the more easily accessible branches of industry, swamps the labor market, and sinks the price of labor below its value."[32] Finally, "a surplus working population, which is compelled to submit to the dictation of capital," would be less inclined to resist decreases in wages or increases in hours proposed by capitalist employers.[33]

The Business Cycle and the Reserve. In like manner, the movements of the business cycle create temporary reserves of labor. During times of prosperity these surpluses may be reabsorbed into industry, cushioning demand and keeping wages from showing the strength they might otherwise display, while during times of depression the competition among these reserve laborers for jobs beats down the current wage rates. In Marx's words, "The industrial reserve army, during periods of stagnation and average prosperity, weighs down the active labor army; during the periods of overproduction and paroxysm, it holds its pretentions in check."[34]

Concentration of Capital and the Reserve. Still a third set of forces as-

[30]Marx, *Capital*, p. 690.
[31]*Ibid.*, p. 702.
[32]*Ibid.*, p. 470.
[33]*Ibid.*, p. 445.
[34]*Ibid.*, p. 701.

sists in the creation of the reserve army of labor that characterizes the capitalist system. Marx holds that there is a continuing tendency for industry to become concentrated into fewer and fewer large units. The expanding scale of production in each industrial unit increases pressure for the substitution of machinery for hand labor, thus further enlarging the labor reserve.[35]

THE DECLINING RATE OF PROFITS

Although surplus value is inherent in capitalism and increases as a portion of the total product of industry, and although the reserve army of workers and its effects on wages under capitalism increase still further the misery of the workers, nevertheless the *rate* of profits tends to decline as capitalist production develops and capital accumulates.

Marx's line of reasoning on this point is concise. As capital accumulates in a capitalist society, proportionately more of the total will consist of machinery and tools (constant capital) and proportionately less of it will go into the payment of current wages (variable capital). Only the latter can yield surplus value, however, since only labor creates value. Thus, since a smaller portion of the total outlay of capital goes into uses in which surplus value is created, the surplus value realized will tend to be a smaller and smaller percentage of the total (constant and variable) capital as that total increases.[36]

Resistance to the Decline

The only practicable way whereby the capitalist employer can try to resist this tendency is to increase the degree of his exploitation of labor so that a given expenditure of variable capital yields in itself a sufficiently higher percentage of surplus value to cause the rate of profit on the total capital to remain constant or to increase. The theory of the declining rate of profit is merely another slant on the contradictions and antagonisms Marx holds to be inherent in the capitalist system. The tendency for the misery of the workers to increase and the tendency for the rate of profits to fall bear an inverse relationship to each other. If workers can successfully resist the attempts of capitalist employers to increase the degree of exploitation, the rate of profits must decline; if they cannot, the rate of profits may remain constant or even decrease.

THE BUSINESS CYCLE

Even if it were assumed that workers could effectively resist the capitalists' attempts to exploit them more intensively, and even if the rate of

---

[35]*Ibid.*, p. 689.

[36]See Karl Marx, "Excerpts from *Capital, Vol. III*," in *Handbook of Marxism*, p. 495.

profits were assumed to remain fairly constant, the adherence of wages to subsistence and the existence of surplus value would generate still another contradiction within the capitalist system. The "crisis"—or, in modern terms, depression—is an inevitable product of forces inherent in the capitalist economy. Crises arise, according to Marx and Engels, from "the fact that the social organization of production within the factory has developed to the point at which it has become incompatible with the anarchy of production in society which exists alongside it and above it."[37] The capitalist employer is under constant competitive pressure to install new and better machinery and to increase the output of his industrial unit. Because he is the sole decision maker for his unit, he can and does add new machinery, change labor about, and coordinate the entire process *within* his plant to the end that its products are turned out in greater volume. Since each capitalist employer is subjected to the same pressure, each follows the same policy. While this, when examined from the standpoint of the single plant, appears to be an orderly and logical procedure, from the standpoint of *industry as a whole* the situation becomes "anarchy," for there is no planned coordination of the total output to the total market purchasing power.

Capitalist Overproduction as the Underlying Cause of Crises

Indeed, since the incomes of the masses of workers are limited to their subsistence, and since surplus value, which accounts for the remainder of the values produced, flows off to a limited number of owners who already have relatively high incomes, there is no adequate force at work expanding mass purchasing power as industry expands its output. Only one thing can happen: After a time, capitalist employers find unsalable stocks of commodities on their hands; overproduction has occurred, and industry must slow down to enable these surplus stocks to be liquidated. After an intervening period of liquidation—accompanied, of course, by severe human costs and the creation of a "reserve" of labor—industry revives and the cycle is repeated.[38]

Marx carefully points out that the underlying cause of crises is overproduction in a "capitalist" sense and not in the sense of more being produced that can be consumed.

It is not a fact that too many necessities of life are produced in proportion to the existing population. The reverse is true. Not enough is produced to satisfy the wants of the great mass decently and humanely.

[37]Engels, "Anti-Dühring," in *Handbook of Marxism*, p. 290.
[38]See Engels, "Anti-Duhring," in *Handbook of Marxism*, pp. 289–291; Marx and Engels, "The Communist Manifesto," in *Handbook of Marxism*, pp. 29–30; Marx, "Excerpts from *Capital, Vol. III*," in *Handbook of Marxism*, pp. 524–527.

... Too many commodities are produced to permit of a realization of the value and surplus value contained in them under the conditions of distribution and consumption *peculiar to capitalist production,* that is, too many to permit of the continuation of this process without ever-recurring explosions.[39]

Severity of Crises Increases

Uncertainty and instability thus become quite normal in the modern capitalist society. But more than this, industrial crises are constantly becoming more and more severe. They return periodically and "each time more threateningly."[40] The continually developing productive powers of mechanical devices are subjecting the capitalist employers to ever-greater pressure to modernize their equipment. The increases in surplus value, while wages cling to subsistence, make the domestic market unable to absorb current output, thus causing the accumulation of surpluses of commodities. The exploitation of foreign markets as outlets for these surpluses has a limit that, when reached, will cause overproduction to be more concentrated on domestic markets, and crises therefore will be more severe. These contradictions inherent in capitalist production, appearing as increasingly severe industrial crises, in Marxian theory constitute one of the major causes of the ultimate downfall of the capitalist system.

CONCENTRATION AND CENTRALIZATION OF CAPITAL

Increasing Intensity of Competition

The tendency for the rate of profits to decline, the cyclical periods of overproduction, and the tendency for commodities to become cheaper as more machinery is used and labor productivity increases combine to create an intensely competitive situation.

The fall in the rate of profit connected with accumulation necessarily creates a comprehensive struggle. . . . The same thing is seen in the overproduction of commodities, the overstocking of markets. Since the aim of capital is not to minister to certain wants, but to produce profits, and since it accomplishes this purpose by methods which adapt the mass of production to the scale of production, not vice versa, conflict must continually ensue between the limited conditions of consumption on a capitalist basis and a production which forever tends to exceed its immanent barriers.[41]

The battle of competition is fought by cheapening of commodities.[42]

[39]*Ibid.,* pp. 525–526. Italics ours.
[40]Marx and Engels, "Communist Manifesto," in *Handbook of Marxism,* p. 29.
[41]Marx, "Excerpts from *Capital, Vol. III,*" in *Handbook of Marxism,* p. 524.
[42]Marx, *Capital,* p. 686.

As capitalist production develops, each individual capitalist employer finds himself in a life-and-death struggle with his rivals. The development of credit facilities places an additional competitive weapon in the hands of capitalists who are able to command them. In fact, "competition and credit . . . develop in proportion as capitalist production and accumulation do."[43] The smaller capitalist employer finds his position fatally weak. He drops out of the competitive struggle, or rather, is swallowed by the larger industrial units. "This is a new form of expropriation. One capitalist expropriates, 'decapitalizes' another. 'One capitalist kills many.' Under the stress and strain of the contest capitals finally abandon their old positions and amalgamate into a few powerful hands."[44]

Concentration of Capital

Thus there is generated within the capitalist system of production a two-sided concentration of capital. The very nature of the productive process is conducive to this development, since "concentration of large masses of the means of production in the hands of individual capitalists is a material condition for the cooperation of wage laborers."[45] Marx distinguishes between two phases of this concentration of capital. One he refers to as "concentration" proper. This takes the form of new accumulations of capital gravitating to the hands of relatively few capitalists, where they are transformed into large-scale industrial units.

Centralization of Capital

The other aspect Marx calls the "centralization" of capital. This may take place whether or not capital accumulation is occurring, since it "is concentration of capitals already formed, destruction of their individual independence, expropriation of capitalist by capitalist, transformation of many small into few large capitals. . . . Capital grows in one place to a huge mass in a single hand, because it has in another place been lost by many."[46] This centralization is the consequence of competition in which "the larger capital beat the smaller . . . The smaller capitals, therefore, crowd into spheres of production which modern industry has only sporadically or incompletely got hold of. Here competition rages in proportion to the number, and in inverse proportion to the magnitudes, of the antagonistic capitals. It always ends in the ruin of many small capitalists, whose capitals partly pass into the hand of their conquerors, partly vanish."[47] Meanwhile credit "becomes a new or formidable weapon in the competitive struggle,

---

[43]*Ibid.*, p. 687.
[44]M. M. Bober, *Karl Marx's Interpretation of History*, Cambridge, Mass.: Harvard University Press, 1927, p. 219.
[45]Marx, *Capital*, p. 362.
[46]*Ibid.*, p. 688.
[47]*Ibid.*, pp. 686–687.

and finally transforms itself into an immense social mechanism for the centralization of capitals."[48]

Concentration and Centralization Are Self-Perpetuating

Once concentration and centralization of capital begin, they perpetuate and strengthen themselves, since "the cheapness of commodities depends on the productiveness of labor, and this again on the scale of production."[49] Also, the use of large-scale methods of production, involving as they do proportionately more machinery and less hand labor than small-scale methods, sets in motion further forces tending to decrease the rate of profits. The cheapening of commodities and the decreasing rate of profit both further intensify competition, thereby causing further centralization of capital.

FINANCE CAPITAL AND CAPITALIST IMPERIALSM

Marx implied that the spiral of ever-intensified competition among capitalist industrial units would culminate in "finance capital" and "capitalistic imperialism." In Marx's tracing of the "historical tendency of capitalist accumulation," "the monopoly of capital becomes a fetter upon the whole of production."[50] Moreover, "hand in hand with this centralization or this expropriation of many capitalists by the few," Marx foresaw "the entanglement of all peoples in the net of the world market" and the creation of the "international character of the capitalistic régimé."[51]

Monopolistic Nature of Finance Capital

To Lenin, who expounded upon this portion of Marxian theory in some detail, the stage of capitalist development that he termed "finance capital" is characterized by the evolution of two sets of circumstances:

1. The concentration of production and capital, developed to such a high stage that it has created monopolies which play a decisive rôle in economic life.
2. The merging of bank capital with industrial capital and the creation, on the basis of this "finance capital," of a financial oligarchy.[52]

Thus "capitalist monopolies" would replace "capitalist free competition."

---

[48]*Ibid.*, p. 687.
[49]*Ibid.*, p. 686.
[50]*Ibid.*, p. 837.
[51]*Ibid.*, p. 836.
[52]V. I. Lenin, "Imperialism: The Highest State of Capitalism," in *Handbook of Marxism*, p. 690.

Monopoly is the direct opposition of free competition; but we have seen the latter being transformed into monopoly before our very eyes, creating large-scale production and squeezing out small-scale production, replacing large-scale by larger-scale production, finally leading to such a concentration of production and capital that monopoly has been and is the result; cartels, syndicates and trusts, and, merging with them, the capital of a dozen or so banks manipulating thousands of millions.[53]

In such a stage of capitalist production, the capitalist himself reaches the highest possible degree of parasitic existence. The control over production resides in liquid funds of money and credit. These are manipulated through monopolistic industrial units to squeeze out of the capitalist processes of production not only surplus value but *monopolistic* surplus value. The capitalist and the control he exercises in the stage of finance capital have lost the last vestiges of any functional connection with the actual production of goods possessing use value.

Transition to Capitalistic Imperialism

Finance capital reaching out beyond the boundaries of a single capitalist country becomes "capitalistic imperialism." Lenin suggests the following as steps in this transition:

> The export of capital, as distinguished from the export of commodities, becomes of particularly great importance.
> International monopoly combines of capitalists are formed which divide up the world.
> The territorial division of the world by the greatest capitalist powers is completed.[54]

The stage of capitalistic imperialism cannot exist until finance capital becomes dominant domestically—that is, until capital comes to assume the money or credit forms in which it can easily transfer its residence from one country to another. Although capitalistic imperialism "undoubtedly represents a special stage in the development of capitalism, . . . it would be absurd to dispute . . . over the year or decade in which imperialism became 'definitely' established."[55] In fact, the stages of finance capital and capitalistic imperialism may well arrive in various nations at various times, "for under capitalism there cannot be an *equal* development of different undertakings, trusts, branches of industry or countries."[56]

[53]*Ibid.*, p. 689.
[54]*Ibid.*, p. 690.
[55]*Ibid.*, pp. 690–691.
[56]*Ibid.*, p. 718.

Capitalistic Imperialism—The Highest Stage of Capitalism

Despite the uncertainties and irregularities in the development of this stage of capitalist production, featuring an imperialistic struggle for markets and opportunities for profitable investment of finance capital, Lenin felt that it had arrived in some countries when he wrote in 1916, "We see a few imperialist powers fighting amongst themselves for the right to share in this monopoly, and this struggle is characteristic of the whole period of the beginning of the twentieth century."[57]

A year later Lenin described World War I in a similar but more vigorous tone when he wrote, "The belligerent powers, the belligerent groups of capitalists, the 'masters' of the capitalist system, and the slave-drivers of a capitalist slavery, have been shackled to each other by the war with chains of iron. *One bloody lump*, that is the sociopolitical life of the historic period through which we are now passing."[58]

To Lenin, capitalistic imperialism is the "highest stage" of capitalism because it is the last. In finance capital and capitalistic imperialism, all the contradictions developed within the capitalist system of production arrive at their ultimate and collective climax. The mutually antagonistic interests nurtured by the capitalist system finally rise to such a pitch that they are self-destructive, the system itself being destroyed in the final clash. The monopolies that evolved from capitalist processes are essentially parasitic. Under finance capital "the stimulus to technical, and consequently to all other progress, to advance, tends to disappear. . . ." This puts monopoly, which "exists in the general capitalist environment of commodity production and competition, in permanent and insoluble contradiction to this general environment."[59] The capitalist system cannot continue without production, but the stage of monopoly or finance capital, which capitalist production itself breeds, is essentially destructive of productive forces. Thus, in Marx's words, capitalist production begets with the inexorability of a law of nature its own negation. It sets in operation monopolistic forces that "at last reach a point where they become incompatible with their capitalist integument. This integument is burst asunder. The knell of capitalist private property sounds."[60]

Imperialist Warfare

Capitalistic imperialism exists when the contradictions created by capitalist production play upon the world instead of a nation. Finance capital and

---

[57]*Ibid.*, p. 709.

[58]V. I. Lenin, "Letters from Afar," in *Handbook of Marxism*, p. 763.

[59]Lenin, "Imperialism: The Highest Stage of Capitalism," in *Handbook of Marxism*, p. 700.

[60]Marx, *Capital*, p. 837.

monopoly, extending beyond national boundaries, "introduce everywhere the striving for domination, not for freedom. . . . Particularly acute also becomes national oppression and the striving for annexation, i.e., the violation of national independence."[61] Imperialistic colonization discloses the true nature of the capitalist system. "The profound hypocrisy and inherent barbarism of bourgeois civilization lies unveiled before our eyes, turning from its home, where it assumes respectable forms, to the colonies, where it goes naked."[62]

Alliances in a stage of capitalistic imperialism, "whether of one imperialist coalition against another or of a general alliance of *all* the imperialist powers, *inevitably* can be only 'breathing spells' between wars. Peaceful alliances prepare the ground for wars and in their turn grow out of wars."[63] These international antagonisms are destructive. Eventually, according to Marxian theory, imperialist war or wars will generate sufficient destructive force to rend the capitalist system of production, which is, at once, the environment within which capitalistic imperialism exists and its creator.

We have examined the contradictions or antagonisms that under Marxian theory are rooted in the valuation processes of a capitalist economy, are nurtured by it, and ultimately will destroy it. The fate of capitalism is thus inevitable, since it is sealed by the very processes that the system itself inherently generates. Marxian theory includes an analysis of the institutions and processes that may succeed capitalist production. To these we now turn our attention.

QUESTIONS FOR CLASS DISCUSSION

1. What did Marx mean by "class" in his doctrine of "class struggle"? On what basis could the "proletariat" be distinguished from the "bourgeoisie" in modern society?

2. In what respect was the class struggle under capitalism distinctly different from class struggles that had preceded the advent of capitalism?

3. Would Marx have agreed that if there is a class struggle under capitalism every effort should be made to reconcile the interests of the struggling classes?

4. Is the Marxian theory of class struggle in any way connected with the theory of surplus value?

5. What thesis did Marx put forth concerning the great middle class to which present-day speakers and writers so often refer?

---

[61]Lenin, "Imperialism: The Highest Stage of Capitalism," in *Handbook of Marxism*, pp. 719–720.

[62]Karl Marx, "India," in *Handbook of Marxism*, p. 193.

[63]Lenin, "Imperialism: The Highest Stage of Capitalism," in *Handbook of Marxism*, p. 718.

6. In what sense did Marx hold that the bourgeoisie "produces, above all, its own gravediggers"?

7. Did Marx use the word *state* as synonymous with *government* or *organized society*?

8. What part did Marx contend the state plays in a society featured by capitalism? Would this be true even of a democratic state?

9. What forces did Marx find working in a capitalist system to increase the misery of the workers?

10. Was it not inconsistent for Marx to argue that while workers were being forced into increasing misery the rate of profits was declining?

11. Did Marx favor the smoothing out of the cyclical fluctuations in business activity under a capitalist economy?

12. Distinguish between the "concentration" and the "centralization" of capital. Toward what end did Marx consider both of them to be working?

13. In what sense was capitalistic imperialism held to be the highest stage of capitalism?

14. Did Marx believe the capitalist system would fall even though no revolutionary groups sought its overthrow?

8. Capitalism's successors —socialism and communism

Marx held that the culmination of the internal contradictions generated by capitalist production would be the breaking up of the entire capitalist system and its adjunct, the political state. The proletariat could seize power, establish its own state, crush all capitalist employers and their class ideology, and subject all economic processes to the proletarian state machinery. This would be *socialism*, or the *first stage of communism*. With the liquidation of capitalist property, institutions, and surplus value, there would develop a new socialized or communized psychology, permitting the gradual liquidation of the proletarian state and its agencies of oppression, which had been directed against the former capitalists. Each person then would be motivated to work in accord with his full capacity and to consume from the common product merely in accord with his needs. The era of *full communism* would be ushered in. This latter Marx held to be the best possible form of economic society. And, since economic institutions give the tone to all institutions, society would have reached its highest possible state of perfection.

TRANSITION BY REVOLUTION

What degree of force and violence will accompany the fall of capitalist production and the assumption of economic and political power by the proletariat? Can the change be accomplished by peaceful, evolutionary, parliamentary methods, or is a revolutionary coup accompanied by substantial measures of violence inherent in such a change? Students of Marxian theory have waged wordy battles over these matters, and international working-class movements have been wrecked again and again by disagreements among their adherents as to what transitional pattern is implicit in Marxian theory.

In several respects Marxian theory bearing upon this point is unmistakably clear. State power in a capitalist system is possessed by the owning class and used to support and defend that system. This means, according to Marxian theory, that the proletariat cannot acquire power over the economic system without gaining possession of the political state. As Lenin put it, "Every economic fight of necessity turns into a political fight, and social democracy must indissolubly combine the economic with the political fight into a united class struggle of the proletariat."[1] Unquestionably, Marx held that the proletariat should seize political power when the "death knell" of capitalism sounded.

Moreover, Marxian theory places much stress on the role force has played in history. Capitalist private property and the accumulation of capital are rooted in that forceful disruption of institutions and relationships Marx called primitive accumulation. Engels criticized Dühring (a German philosopher and political scientist, contemporary of Marx and Engels) for holding that "force is the absolute evil" and "the original sin."

> That force, however, plays another role in history, a revolutionary
> role; that, in the words of Marx, it is the midwife of every old society
> which is pregnant with the new, that it is the instrument by the aid
> of which social movement forces its way through and shatters the dead,
> fossilized, political forms—of this there is not a word in Herr Dühring.
> . . . And this in spite of the immense moral and spiritual impetus which
> has resulted from every victorious revolution![2]

[1] V. I. Lenin, "Our Program," in *Handbook of Marxism*, E. Burns, comp., New York: Random House, 1935, p. 575.
[2] Friedrich Engels, "Anti-Dühring," in *Handbook of Marxism*, p. 278.

The writings of Marx and Engels give ample basis for Lenin's contention that "the replacement of the bourgeois state is impossible without a violent revolution."[3] A number of the more concise statements of this revolutionary doctrine may be noted:

> He [Marx] certainly never forgot to add that he hardly expected the English ruling classes to submit, without a "pro-slavery rebellion," to this peaceful and legal revolution.[4]

> With us it is not a matter of reforming private property, but of abolishing it; not of hushing up the class antagonism, but of abolishing the classes; not of ameliorating the existing society, but of establishing a new one.[5]

> The arming of the whole proletariat with rifles, guns, and ammunition must be carried out at once; we must prevent the revival of the old bourgeois militia, which has always been directed against the workers. Where the latter measure cannot be carried out, the workers must try to organize themselves into an independent guard, with their own chiefs and general staff, to put themselves under the order, not of the government, but of the revolutionary authorities set up by the workers. Where workers are employed in state service they must arm and organize in special corps, with chiefs chosen by themselves, or form part of the proletarian guard. Under no pretext must they give up their arms and equipment, and any attempt at disarmament must be forcibly resisted.[6]

> In short, the communists everywhere support every revolutionary movement against the existing social and political order of things. . . . The communists disdain to conceal their views and aims. They openly declare that their ends can be attained only by the forcible overthrow of all existing social conditions. Let the ruling class tremble at the communist revolution. The proletarians have nothing to lose but their chains. They have a world to win. Working men of all countries, unite![7]

> It is to force that in due time the workers will have to appeal if the dominion of labor is at long last to be established.[8]

These tenets of course do not make the revolution inevitable. As Sidney Hook points out, Marxian theory logically permits chaos to be the successor to and the result of the breakup of capitalist production—provided

---

[3] V. I. Lenin, "The State and Revolution," in *Handbook of Marxism*, p. 739.

[4] Friedrich Engels' preface to Karl Marx, *Capital*, New York: Modern Library, n.d., p. 32.

[5] Karl Marx, "Address to the Communist League," in *Handbook of Marxism*, p. 64.

[6] *Ibid.*, p. 67.

[7] Karl Marx and Friedrich Engels, "Communist Manifesto," in *Handbook of Marxism*, p. 59.

[8] Karl Marx, quoted in Sidney Hook, *Towards the Understanding of Karl Marx*, New York: Day, 1933, p. 289.

the proletariat is not organized and equipped to take over the reins of political and economic control.[9] Short of this, however, if organized society is to continue to exist, the change must be revolutionary, accompanied by organized force and probably by violent acts.

This does not mean that the revolution must follow some standardized course in every country at the same time. Marx and Engels admitted that the specifiic revolutionary tactics and weapons of combat would have to fit the time and place of revolutionary activity.[10] Nor could the revolution be successful unless certain objective conditions prevailed. The transition to a new society "becomes realizable not through the perception that the existence of classes is in contradiction with justice, equality, etc., not through the mere will to abolish these classes, but through certain new economic conditions."[11] Sidney Hook has summarized these conditions to include, first, "the breakdown of the forces of production and distribution" in the capitalist system; second, "lack of immediate political homogeneity on the part of the ruling classes," such as would be brought about by a crisis, a war, some natural calamity, or disagreement among the bourgeoisie over policy, any of which might cause a substantial loss of bourgeois prestige; and third, "spontaneous manifestations of class consciousness and struggle" such as strikes, riots, or mass demonstrations.[12]

When such conditions developed, they were expected to be obvious to Marxians, although their actual discernibility becomes doubtful when one recalls that Engels, writing about England in 1886, felt that "we can almost calculate the moment when the unemployed, losing patience, will take their own fate into their own hands"[13] and that the "Communist Manifesto" referred to Germany as being "on the eve of a bourgeois revolution" that "will be but the prelude to an immediately following proletarian revolution."[14]

To initiate a revolution at a time or in a place lacking these objective prerequisites to its success, rather than to await their creation, was to engage in "mad adventurism" rather than a true communist revolution.[15] Nor was the ultimate necessity for revolution to prevent the cooperation of those who saw its necessity with social reformers who did not. The "Communist Manifesto" called upon communists to "labor everywhere for the union and agreement of the democratic parties of all countries."[16] Such cooperation would strengthen and better organize the proletariat for its postrevolutionary tasks.

[9]*Ibid.*, p. 110.
[10]See Harry W. Laidler, *A History of Socialist Thought, New York*: T. Y. Crowell, 1927, pp. 182–194.
[11]Engels, "Anti-Dühring," in *Handbook of Marxism*, p. 296.
[12]Hook, p. 276.
[13]Engels' preface to Marx, *Capital*, pp. 31–32.
[14]Marx and Engels, "Communist Manifesto," in *Handbook of Marxism*, p. 59.
[15]Hook, pp. 273–274.
[16]Marx and Engels, "Communist Manifesto," in *Handbook of Marxism*, p. 59.

Shift of Emphasis to Nonrevolutionary Change

In contrast with the "odes to physical violence" noted previously is the following much-quoted passage from Marx:

> But we do not assert that the way to reach this goal it the same every-
> where. We know that the institutions, the manners and the customs of
> the various countries must be considered, and we do not deny that
> there are countries like England and America, and, if I understood your
> arrangements better, I might even add Holland, where the worker
> may attain his object by peaceful means. But not in all countries is this
> the case.[17]

In the later writings of Marx and Engels, other statements, less direct but nonetheless meaningful, disclose a certain shift of emphasis from revolutionary to evolutionary processes of social change. Marx and Engels appeared to rely less on the inevitable necessity of revolutionary transformation and to place more hope in social-reform measures as means to the end of ultimate control by the proletariat.

Professor Bober, while admitting that "it is hard to tell" why Marx and Engels made this shift, ventures some "suggestions":

> In the early period [prior to 1848–1851] they were fiery men in their
> thirties, smarting in exile, fresh with the memories of abuses dealt
> out to them by various governments, while, later, older age brought a
> cooler attitude and a calmer way of looking at things. There were
> doctrines of evolution before and throughout the first half of the nine-
> teenth century, but Darwin's *Origin of Species* in 1859 impressed
> people's minds with the idea of gradual development; and Marx and
> Engels were eager followers of the achievements of science. Actual
> experience of the uprisings of '48 and later convinced them that a few
> enthusiasts cannot prevail against bullets and cannon balls directed
> by skilled hands. Again, in the 1840's, and for a while afterward, the
> plight of the workers appeared to be serious. There were no effective
> factory laws and no public opinion favoring the laborer to any consid-
> erable extent. He was helpless. It was a time when so judicious a
> person as John Stuart Mill was pessimistic about capitalism, doubted
> whether all the inventions lightened human toil, and wondered at
> times whether socialism held better promise. A brutal conflict seemed to
> Marx and Engels the inevitable means of emancipation. But later,
> when the worker gained dignity, power, and suffrage, they began to see
> hope in other expedients.[18]

Marxian Theory Is Basically Revolutionary

What can be concluded as to the place of revolution in Marxian theory? If one tries to strike a balance between the portions of the theory empha-

[17]Quoted from Marx's speech at the Hague Convention of the First International in 1872. Laidler, p. 194.

[18]M. M. Bober, *Karl Marx's Interpretation of History*, Cambridge, Mass.: Harvard University Press, 1927, pp. 252–253.

sizing the inevitability of revolutionary change and those implying an evolutionary and parliamentary transition to socialism, the former appear more weighty. Marxian theory is saturated with reasoning that can lead to no other conclusion than a violent death for capitalist production. To interpret Marx as really expecting or urging anything other than this would actually necessitate rewriting to the point of inanity a large portion of Marxian thought. Suggestions in Marx that imply the possibility of effective nonrevolutionary change from capitalism to something better are found to be cursory, superficial, and hastily formulated when compared with the basic fabric of Marxism. The latter is wholly revolutionary and, to say the least, not unsuspecting of the necessity of violence as a phase of the coming revolution.

The existence of statements contradicting the revolutionary thesis must be accounted for by the piecemeal way in which Marx and Engels often wrote, the temporary and passing uses (notably, various speeches and newspaper articles) to which they thought much of their writing would be put, and the pressure of somewhat inconsistent but surface influences the events of the time brought to bear on them. No comprehensive nonrevolutionary interpretation of Marx has stood the test of consistency that careful students of Marxian theory impose upon it; in all likelihood none ever will.

THE DICTATORSHIP OF THE PROLETARIAT AND SOCIALISM

The Proletarian State

Portions of what has come to be called Marxian theory are the development of what were potent but much abbreviated statements by Marx and Engels. Such is the theory that outlines the nature and functions of the political and economic machinery to be set up immediately upon the destruction of capitalism. This machinery is known collectively as the dictatorship of the proletariat. Marx's brief reference to the necessity for such a transitional stage along the way to full communism was made in his criticism of the Gotha Program, a program of social reforms: "Between the capitalist and the communist systems of society lies the period of the revolutionary transformation of the one into the other. This corresponds to a political transition period, whose state can be nothing else but the revolutionary dictatorship of the proletariat."[19]

As amplified by Lenin, the state during the dictatorship of the proletariat would be—as a state by its very nature must always be—an agency of oppression. In this particular setting it would be possessed by the proletariat (in power after the downfall of the capitalist system) and used by them to oppress the capitalist class—in fact, to destroy capitalists completely—"for there is no one else and no other way to break the resistance

[19]Quoted by Laidler, p. 195.

of the capitalist exploiters."[20] In terms of political power, the classes have merely changed places. The bourgeoisie have lost possession of the state power and the proletariat have acquired it, the ruled have become the rulers, the expropriators have had their political power expropriated.

Democracy in the Dictatorship of the Proletariat

But this dictatorship embodies more real democracy than did the preceding bourgeois state, even though that may have been called a democracy. Democracy in the Marxian sense means the absence of restrictions on liberty. Whereas this form of democracy formerly prevailed for the capitalists (the few) and not for the workers (the many), it now prevails for the workers (the many) and not for the lingering capitalists (the few). The latter must be crushed "in order to free humanity from wage slavery; their resistance must be broken by force; it is clear that where there is suppression there is also violence, there is no liberty, no democracy. . . . Democracy for the vast majority of the people, and suppression by force, i.e., exclusion from democracy, of the exploiters and oppressors of the people—this is the modification of democracy during the *transition* from capitalism to communism."[21]

The Proletarian Economy: Socialism

Certain economic features of the dictatorship of the proletariat will be strikingly similar to those of capitalist production. The external appearance of industry will have changed very little. There will have been no major changes in the industrial equipment or the technical processes of production. The one all-important change is that the capitalists' property will have been appropriated by the proletariat acting through what will then be *their* state.

> The means of production are no longer the private property of individuals. The means of production belong to the whole society.[22]

> All citizens are here transformed into hired employees of the state, which is made up of the armed workers. All citizens become employees of one national state "syndicate." [The] scientifically educated staffs of engineers, agronomists, and so on [who have been] obeying the capitalists . . . will work even better tomorrow, obeying the armed workers.[23]

Wages Under Socialism

Laborers will work for wages, each worker receiving "for an equal quantity of labor an equal quantity of products," and "he who does not work, shall

[20]Lenin, "The State and Revolution," in *Handbook of Marxism*, p. 744.
[21]*Ibid.*, p. 745.
[22]*Ibid.*, p. 748.
[23]*Ibid.*, p. 757.

not eat."[24] Since, as will be recalled from the Marxian theory of wages, an hour of skilled labor is the equivalent of some multiple of an hour of unskilled labor, daily wages will not be equal, but "every worker, therefore, receives from society as much as he has given it."[25] "The first phase of communism, therefore, still cannot produce justice and equality; differences, and unjust differences, in wealth will still exist, but the exploitation of man by man will have become impossible, because it will be impossible to seize as private property the *means of production*, the factories, machines, land, and so on."[26] This society is "one which is just emerging from *capitalist* society, and which therefore in all respects—economic, moral and intellectual—still bears the birthmarks of the old society from whose womb it sprung."[27]

Preparation for the Next Stage

When such an economy, dominated by the proletarian state, has gotten into smooth operation, nonconformity by an individual will be "a rare exception, and will probably be accompanied by such swift and severe punishment (for the armed workers are men of practical life, not sentimental individuals, and they will scarcely allow anyone to trifle with them), that very soon the *necessity* of observing the simple, fundamental rules of everyday social life in common will have become a habit. The door will then be open for the transition from the first phase of communist society to its higher phase. . . ."[28]

FULL COMMUNISM—THE ULTIMATE GOAL

The transition from capitalism to the ideal society does not end with the ownership and operation of industry by a proletarian state—that is, with socialism. Marx referred to and Lenin developed the details of a full communistic society that was expected to evolve out of the socialistic dictatorship of the proletariat. Apparently Marx and Engels envisioned such a society when they wrote in the "Communist Manifesto" that if the proletariat successfully "sweeps away by force the old conditions of production, then it will, along with those conditions, have swept away the conditions for the existence of class antagonisms and of classes generally, and will thereby have abolished its own supremacy as a class. In place of the old bourgeois society, with its classes and class antagonisms, we shall have an association in which the free development of each is the condition for the free develop-

[24]*Ibid.*, p. 751.
[25]*Ibid.*, p. 749.
[26]*Ibid.*, p. 749.
[27]Lenin quoting Marx, *ibid.*, p. 748.
[28]*Ibid.*, p. 759.

ment of all."[29] More specifically, Marx has described this full communism as follows:

> In a higher phase of communist society, when the enslaving sub-ordination of individuals in the division of labor has disappeared, and with it also the antagonism, between mental and physical labor; when labor has become not only a means of living, but itself the first necessity of life; when, along with the all-around development of individuals, the productive forces too have grown, and all the springs of social wealth are flowing more freely—it is only at that stage that it will be possible to pass *completely* beyond the horizon of bourgeois rights, and for society to inscribe on its banners: from each according to his ability: to each according to his needs![30]

However, the transition from socialism to full communism is not inevitable in the same way that the internal contradictions of the capitalist system lead to its inevitable destruction. Referring to critics who held full communism to be an unobtainable utopia, Lenin pointed out that their position was one of "ignorance—for it has never entered the head of any socialist to 'promise' that the highest phase of communism will arrive. . . ."[31] He further pointed out that full communism cannot be "introduced" and that "by what stages, by means of what practical measures humanity will proceed to this higher aim—this we do not and cannot know."[32]

Conditions Necessary to Attainment of Full Communism

Only if the proletariat is prepared to accept its responsibilities under the socialistic dictatorship of the proletariat and to use its power to develop the objective and psychological conditions essential to full communism will the highest stage of communism be ushered in. Marx hinted at the nature of these conditions in the statement just quoted. Lenin summarized them as being "both a productivity of labor unlike the present and a person not like the present man in the street, capable of spoiling without reflection . . . the stores of social wealth, and of demanding the impossible."[33] He contended that when we note how "incredibly" capitalism retards productive forces, "we have a right to say, with the fullest confidence, that the expropriation of the capitalists will inevitably result in a gigantic development of the productive forces of human society."[34]

Thus the organized proletariat after the downfall of the capitalist system was to work for the establishment of state-owned and operated in-

[29]Marx and Engels, "Communist Manifesto," in *Handbook of Marxism*, p. 47.
[30]Lenin quoting Marx in "The State and Revolution," in *Handbook of Marxism*, pp. 751–752. Italics ours.
[31]*Ibid.*, p. 753.
[32]*Ibid.*, p. 754, 756.
[33]*Ibid.*, p. 753.
[34]*Ibid.*, p. 752.

dustry, the tremendous expansion of production by freeing it from capitalist restrictions, and the creation of a new psychology in which each would *want* to perform his social function. All capitalist ideology would be crushed, and all antagonistic differentiation between manual and mental labor (and therefore between town and country and between degrees of skill) would cease.

As the proletariat gradually accomplishes these goals, the state—the political weapon of the proletariat during its dictatorship—correspondingly ceases to exist; it "withers away." Since the Marxian theory of the state holds it to be merely an agency of class oppression, as class distinctions and antagonisms disappear there gradually come to be fewer and fewer functions for the state to perform, and it therefore atrophies.[35] The state is not "abolished"; it disappears by the operation of processes that are entirely automatic, since they are generated by changes in the mode of production.

As these forces work to their ultimate conclusion, which "must obviously be a rather lengthy process."[36] the state ceases to exist in any degree. Classes have entirely disappeared; there is no class to be oppressed and consequently no function for a political state. Whatever economic functions of control the state formerly performed will have been absorbed either by the operation of the individuals' communized psychologies, which now direct them to do what the proletarian state has previously ordered them to do, or by voluntary cooperative agreements among citizen workers (as, for instance, on the length of the workday). Lenin has pictured this political aspect of the highest phase of communism in several remarkable passages.

> Only in communist society, when the resistance of the capitalists has been completely broken, when the capitalists have disappeared, when there are no classes (i.e., there is no difference between the members of society in their relation to the social means of production), *only then* "the state ceases to exist," and "*it becomes possible to speak of freedom.*" Only then a really full democracy, a democracy without any exceptions, will be possible and will be realized. And only then will democracy itself begin to *wither away* due to the simple fact that, freed from capitalist slavery, from the untold horrors, savagery, absurdities and infamies of capitalist exploitation, people will gradually *become accustomed* to the observation of the elementary rules of social life that have been known for centuries and repeated for thousands of years in all school books; they will become accustomed to observing them without force, without compulsion, without subordination, without the *special apparatus* for compulsion which is called the state.[37]

Finally, only communism renders the state absolutely unnecessary, for

[35]See Friedrich Engels and Karl Marx in *Handbook of Marxism*, pp. 564, 733, 734, 735.
[36]Lenin, "The State and Revolution," in *Handbook of Marxism*, p. 740.
[37]*Ibid.*, p. 745.

there is *no one* to be suppressed—"no one" in the sense of a *class*, in the sense of a systematic struggle with a definite section of the population. We are not Utopians, and we do not in the least deny the possibility and inevitability of excesses on the part of *individual persons*, nor the need to suppress such *excesses*. But, in the first place, no special machinery, no special apparatus or repression is needed for this; this will be done by the armed people itself, as simply and as readily as any crowd of civilized people, even in modern society, parts a pair of combatants or does not allow a woman to be outraged. And, secondly, we know that the fundamental social cause of excesses which consists in violating the rules of social life is the exploitation of the masses, their want and their poverty. With the removal of this chief cause, excesses will inevitably begin to "wither away." We do not know how quickly and in what succession, but we know that they will wither away. With their withering away, the state will also wither away.[38]

Economic Aspects of Full Communism

The chief economic features of full communism may be summarized briefly. Society, now composed entirely of workers except for those who are physically or mentally incapacitated, owns in common the natural and man-made instruments of production. Although differences in personal tastes and many individual idiosyncrasies remain, society is classless because the former owning class has been partly destroyed and partly absorbed into the working class. With surplus value no longer received by anyone, the workers possess the entire product they, assisted by nature and man-made implements, turn out. The more labor *produces*, the more labor *has*. Consequently, each is motivated to perform his part in the cooperative undertakings of production in accordance with his full abilities. The increased productivity of society assures each member of getting what he needs, and each therefore consumes in accordance with these needs. The citizen of such a society is unable to store up private possessions in the form of capital or capital funds and finds it unnecessary to store up private possessions of consumer goods.

Paradoxically, economic life assumes at once both fullness and simplicity, on the one hand affording the material basis for higher forms of pleasure and culture and, on the other, permitting leisure and freedom from economic worries, thereby encouraging the pursuit of higher pleasures. "As soon as this cherished system arrives, antitheses having nothing to feed on, the antagonisms allay and the dialectic ceases in its travail."[39] Truly, this is a *new society* to its very philosophical foundations.

THE FUNCTION OF THE COMMUNIST PARTY

Whether the breakdown of the capitalist system is to be followed by an evolutionary development of full communism or by chaos depends, in

[38]*Ibid.*, p. 747.
[39]Bober, p. 44.

Marxian theory, almost entirely on the ability and willingness of the proletariat to grasp power at the opportune time and to choose tactics suitable to the situation and the task to be performed. Marx hints that these tactics are not to be discovered by fine theorizing. "A class in which the revolutionary interests of society are concentrated, so soon as it has risen up, finds directly in its own situation the content and the material of its revolutionary activity: foes to be laid low; measures, dictated by the needs of the struggle, to be taken; the consequences of its own deeds to drive it on. It makes no theoretical inquiries into its own task."[40]

Nevertheless, as Marx looked about him he found the proletariat unorganized, unconscious of its common interests, politically ignorant, and mentally subservient to prevailing bourgeois ideology. Should it remain so, the breakdown of capitalism would merely bring chaos. Exploitation in itself would not necessarily create class consciousness; understanding and emotional arousal were needed. In short, the proletariat had to have leadership.

To Provide Leadership

In such terms Marx conceived of the functions of the Communist Party— a new, thoroughly revolutionary party to lead the proletariat. Stalin must have precisely paraphrased Marx's thoughts when he remarked that "a working class without a revolutionary party is like an army without a general staff. The party is the military staff of the proletariat."[41]

> The communists are distinguished from the other working-class parties by this only: (1) In the national struggles of the proletarians of the different countries, they point out and bring to the front the common interests of the entire proletariat, independently of all nationality. (2) In the various stages of development which the struggle of the working class against the bourgeoisie has to pass through, they always and everywhere represent the interests of the movement as a whole. [The communists are to form the] most advanced and resolute section of the working-class parties of every country [since] they have over the great mass of the proletariat the advantage of clearly understanding the line of march, the conditions, and the ultimate general results of the proletarian movement.[42]

The Aim of the Communist Party

"The immediate aim of the communists is . . . the formation of the proletariat into a class, overthrow of the bourgeois supremacy, conquest of political power by the proletariat."[43] Forming the proletariat into a "class"

[40]Karl Marx, "The Class Struggles in France," in *Handbook of Marxism*, p. 105.
[41]J. V. Stalin, "Foundations of Leninism," in *Handbook of Marxism*, p. 843.
[42]Marx and Engels, "Communist Manifesto," in *Handbook of Marxism*, p. 37.
[43]*Ibid.*, p. 37.

means, in Marxian terms, the development of class consciousness—that is, a full realization that the capitalist employers are exploiting the workers and that this exploitation is an inherent part of the capitalist system. Educated economically and politically so that they understood this in all its ramifications, and with the Communist Party as the center of a class solidarity, the proletariat would rise up (with the advent of the necessary objective conditions) and seize possession of the political machinery and the ownership of capital. Once this was accomplished, the Communist Party would dominate the governmental machinery of the dictatorship of the proletariat in the establishment of socialism, the first stage of communism.

The party would direct the strategy of the dictatorship of the proletariat to the complete liquidation of capitalists and capitalist ideology, the fusion of all classes into one, the withering away of the state, and finally, complete communism. When this mission had been fulfilled, the Communist Party presumably either would cease to exist or would experience a substantial change in nature and function, since the repressive state whose pilot the Communist Party had been would no longer exist. Certain educational, cultural, and cooperative economic activities would, no doubt, then be centered in the Communist Party.

THE UNION OF INEVITABILITY AND PURPOSE ACTION

The revolutionary overthrow of capitalism and the establishment of socialism and then communism were in no sense an automatic, inevitable procedure to Marx, Engels, and Lenin. Certain objective conditions causing capitalism to fall would be created by capitalist production itself, but aside from this there were no predestined consequences. The seizure of power by the proletariat—the only alternative to complete chaos—and the development to full communism could occur only if the proletariat were prepared to play its role effectively. To this end, Marx was intensely interested in and gave much energy to the creation of a revolutionary Communist Party. In this sense Marx the revolutionist was in the end dominant over Marx the theorist.

QUESTIONS FOR CLASS DISCUSSION
1. What is meant by the statement that "every economic fight of necessity turns into a political fight"? Is this consistent with the Marxian theory of the state?

2. Did Marx hold that the seizure of power by the proletariat would be sudden or gradual? evolutionary or revolutionary? peaceful or violent? Was Marx's position on these matters always consistent?

3. Did Marx hold that political power would automatically be vested in the proletariat after the collapse of capitalism?

4. Did Marx contend that the organized proletariat should engage in active revolutionary tactics whenever any opportunity for them arose?

5. In what sense of the word is the rule of the proletariat immediately after a successful revolution to be a dictatorship?

6. Would the proletarian state after the revolution differ in its basic nature from the bourgeois state it replaced?

7. Is there any possibility that the proletarian state existing during the dictatorship of the proletariat would be more democratic than the bourgeois state had been?

8. What would be the chief features of the economic system during the dictatorship of the proletariat? In what major respect would it differ from the economy that had preceded it?

9. In what major respects would the economy under full communism differ from the socialist economy existing during the dictatorship of the proletariat?

10. What changes would have occurred in the nature of the state by the time full communism was achieved?

11. Was it inevitable that full communism would develop from socialism?

12. What did Marx picture as the major functions of the Communist Party (a) before the revolution and (b) after the revolution?

9. An evaluation of Marxian theory

There are numerous tests to which Marxian theory might be subjected. Are the purely theoretical parts of the analysis correct and sound? Are they adequately substantiated by inductive data? Are there logical fallacies within the system of Marxian thought? Has it continued as the belief of substantial groups of thinkers? Have its predictions of future events been wholly or partially correct? Has it led to any action to remedy the ills it dwells upon? Did it lay a substantial basis for later theorizing and action? Does it supplement other analyses of our society and thereby assist us to a more rounded understanding of it? Did it contribute any *original* thought to our social theories? Are its conclusions those of scientific analysis, or are they the outgrowth of prejudiced hypotheses?

These are all legitimate and pertinent questions, but few of them can be treated here.

Marxian theory may be evaluated in terms of its success or failure in accomplishing what it set out to do. Marx apparently had three major purposes:

1. He wished to set forth an accurate description of the basic processes at work in the capitalist economy. His attempts at this were embodied in his theories of value, wages, and surplus value.
2. He sought to find a simple basic set of causal forces at work in the world that would enable him to interpret past events and predict those of the future. His fundamental philosophy and economic interpretation of history yielded him this basis for portraying the future of the capital order.
3. He hoped to establish foundations for the organization of a class-conscious proletariat that would both constitute the intellectual center of and generate the action necessary for the development of full communism.

Marxian theory should be judged primarily, if not exclusively, in terms of these objectives, to which we now turn our attention.

THEORIES OF VALUE, WAGES, SURPLUS VALUE

Failure to Recognize the Part
Played by Demand in Value Determination

Marx was correct, although not original, in assigning the leading role in the economic drama to value. He saw clearly the crucial function values performed and how they penetrated every cranny of the capitalist economy. What he did not see was the true nature of value determination in the sort of economy he tried to describe—that is, one characterized by the private ownership and operation of competing industrial units for private profit. His theory that, assuming a commodity has use value, the amount of socially necessary labor embodied in it determines its exchange value is untenable, despite all the efforts of his interpreters and modifiers to make it conform with present-day theories of value. The fact that Marx's value theory was in part the orthodox and accepted theory of his time may excuse him for using it, but that does not justify its later use or the conclusions based on it. Marx failed to note that normal value is no less a result of demand than of supply and that supply is affected by the commodity's embodied content of other factors of production no less than labor time.

While Marx had some insight into the role of demand in value determination, he ruled it out as insignificant. In admitting that use value was a prerequisite to exchange value, he touched upon the inadequacy of labor cost as the sole determinant of value. If *some* use value is necessary to the existence of exchange value, the *amount* of use value apparently has some relation to the *amount* of exchange value. This use value, affecting consumer bids for commodities, constitutes the pressure to apply the scarce productive agents to the production of respective commodities. The intensity with which the agents are applied has much to do with their physical productivity, with their worth in a society in which they are privately owned, and consequently, with the long-run cost of producing commodities.

This reflection of demand on cost and thus on normal long-run value Marx, along with others of his time, failed to comprehend. His theory of value fails to allow for the fact that as the demand for a commodity increases more pressure is put on, say, land to produce that commodity. As more pressure is put on land, diminishing returns may increase the cost and the normal long-run value of this commodity.

It is the same in the case of capital equipment. Even if one were to grant Marx's contention that capital comes from "stolen" funds, demand for goods puts pressure on income receivers to save and thus helps produce capital equipment that can be used in the production of those goods. As long as it is more pleasant to spend for immediate consumption than to save, saving must be rewarded, the value of the saving thus becoming one element in cost that the long-run normal price must cover.

In short, Marx failed to realize that, just as labor is valuable in the capitalist economy only because of demand for the products of labor, so the value of land and capital is reflected from the demand for products they help to produce. The cost of producing these agents—even labor— has no *inherent* right to be covered by the selling prices of products. It will be met only if these agents produce commodities in quantities that demand will absorb at a price equal to the full cost of producing them. Long-run normal value is an equilibrium value determined by the opposing forces of consumers' bids for commodities, on the one hand, and on the other, the scarcities of the productive agents. There appears to be no reason for believing that in a capitalist economy the mere *amount* of any *one* of these agents of production plays an exclusive or even dominant part in determining exchange values. Hence, the Marxian theory of value does not account accurately for the real values at which commodities exchange for each other in a capitalist economy.

Failure to Recognize the Place
of Demand in Wage Determination

The same error permeated Marx's theory of wages. There is no more reason to believe that labor power has value because it is brought into existence by the expenditure of a certain amount of sustenance than there is to believe that a finely carved wooden automobile tire would have value because of the effort expended on its construction. Nor is the *amount of value* represented by labor or power (the wage) any more determined by the *amount of sustenance* that went into it than is the value of the wooden tire determined by the *amount* of effort that went into its production. Labor power, a scarce thing, has value because of the pressure of demand for the commodities labor produces. The greater the demand for the commodities and the more limited the quantity of labor suitable for use in their production, the greater the value of that labor—regardless of what that labor power cost to produce. The values of inborn talents, or the wages paid for their use, are neither greater nor smaller than the values of like talents acquired by training. The cost of producing the talents has nothing to do with the value of such talent except as it constitutes one type of resistance (for instance, natural scarcity) and is just as much a determinant of value as is this cost of producing labor power.

Indeed, Marx seemed to sense this point when he dealt with the translation of units of skilled labor into standard homogeneous time units of unskilled labor. He admitted that the skilled was valued in terms of the unskilled and vice versa *by the market processes* through which buyers bid for the products of these various skilled categories of labor. However, except for this one implication, which is not carried to its logical conclusion, Marx's theory of wages failed to recognize the demand element in the determination of wages.

Inadequate Definition of Subsistence

From still another angle, the Marxian theory of wages is very unsatisfactory. Subsistence, as the cost of producing labor power and therefore the basis of the wage, became an indeterminant quantity in Marx's writings. Whereas on certain occasions he used the term to include only the commodities necessary to physical health, on others he extended it to include consumption items dictated by the mere desires of workers or by some mysteriously originating social habit or custom that placed the item within their minimum-subsistence living standard. Marx never expained how a subsistence living standard could *expand* to include conventional items during the very time when, according to him, wages were tied down to subsistence living standards *without* such items.

Although his emphasis on surplus value forced Marx generally to use a purely *physical* concept of subsistence, he did not adhere consistently to it. Only with rigorous acceptance of physical subsistence could the theory of surplus value have been valid at all. But universal adherence to the physical concept of subsistence was impossible, for, even as Marx admitted, normal wages in certain places and times rose above a physical subsistence level. Moreover, the consistent use of the physical concept would have forced Marx to admit that wages could never rise above their existing level. Thus the organization of labor for immediate wage-raising purposes would have been proved ineffectual and could not have been used as the starting point of the organization of a class-conscious proletariat.

On the other hand, as soon as Marx admitted that his subsistence level of wages (the cost of producing labor power) *could* come to include certain conventional items not previously included, he destroyed completely the theoretical base he had established for surplus value. If wages could rise to include items of merely *conventional necessity*, then why could they not rise to include so many such items that all of what Marx called "surplus value" would be absorbed in a wage high enough to permit such subsistence? Thus the adoption of a conventional subsistence living standard as the determinant of the wage level permitted wages *under capitalism* to rise to indefinite heights—theoretically high enough to absorb all surplus value. This destroys the Marxian thesis that surplus value is an inevitable accompaniment of capitalist production. For the sake of theoretical consistency of his arguments with the theses they were to support, Marx was forced to adopt the physical concept of subsistence. However, his numerous references to existing wage levels and to the possibilities of workers' forcing wages up under capitalism indicate that on occasion he sacrificed theoretical consistency to the facts and to his desire to stimulate workers to organize.

The Problem of Flexible Versus Inflexible Wages

Indeed, if subsistence were to include items not necessary to physical health, wages would have such flexiblity that, under the pressure of certain forces, they would tend to rise so as to absorb all surplus value. These forces were the intense competitive struggles pictured by Marx himself under capitalism. Assuming wages to be flexible, it could be argued that competition among capitalist employers for employees would force surplus value to be paid out as wages. As long as the labor of any employee yielded to *his* capitalist employer a surplus of the type Marx described, it would pay *some other* capitalist employer to try to hire him by offering a slightly higher wage. If this competitive situation prevailed on an extensive and intensive scale, the struggle among employers to add to their individual labor staffs in order to increase their individually realized surpluses presumably would bid wages up to a point at which *no* capitalist employer any longer found any surplus attached to the labor of any worker employed by *another* employer. This type of competition would cease only when wages had absorbed all surplus values formerly going to capitalist employers. Marx assumed keen competition among capitalist employers in the sale of their products but failed to show why there was no similar competition in buying the labor power to which these attractive surpluses were attached. Assuming wages to be flexible and competition among capitalist employers to exist, forces inherent in the situation would tend to cause surplus value to be squeezed out of owners' incomes and into wages.

It appears that the Marxian theory of surplus value becomes logically untenable unless it is based on a physical subsistence theory of wages; on the other hand, that basis is untenable because wages are known to rise above physical subsistence levels.

Theory of Surplus Value Lacks Theoretical Support

If neither the Marxian theory of value nor the Marxian theory of wages can be accepted, and if these theories are the dual support of the theory of surplus value, what happens to that theory? It is impossible to find in the capitalist system any fund of value possessing the theoretical characteristics and coming from the theoretical origins Marx pictured as those of surplus value. Under the capitalist order the values of commodities are not determined *solely* by their labor content, nor is the value of labor— its wage—determined by the *physical* necessities of existence. What Marx pictured as surplus value under the capitalist system could just as well be absorbed by wages as by the profit of the capitalist employer or the interest of the lender or the rent of the landowner—or all three. There can be no inherent surplus value such as Marx described, unalterably directed under capitalist production into the pockets of the owners.

Unearned Incomes Are the Surplus Value of Capitalism

Thus it would appear that the Marxian theoretical system of value, wages, and surplus value is broken down by its own internal inconsistencies and that the Marxian conclusions hang in midair without support. However, such a conclusion is unwarranted. It is quite possible that if Marx were writing today with the assistance of modern value theory he would describe the value-determining processes much differently and would establish quite different theoretical bases for his surplus value or exploitation thesis.

If Marx should write that in a capitalist society dominated by the private ownership and inheritance of nature-made and man-made productive instruments there will necessarily be some owning-class persons who will gain incomes that are unearned, his thesis would merit further consideration. It may be significant that he ended the first volume of *Capital* with the statement that "the capitalist mode of production and accumulation, and therefore capitalist private property, have for their fundamental conditions the annihilation of self-earned private property; in other words, the expropriation of the laborer."[1] Was this the essence of Marx's theory of surplus value?

If one were to grant the assumption that the capitalist system could not prevail without the private ownership of *nature-made* as well as *man-*

[1]Karl Marx, *Capital*, New York: Modern Library, n.d., p. 848.

made instruments or without the ownership of *inherited* property as well as property arising from *personal productivity*, it would be possible to find inherent in the capitalist order certain personal incomes that come substantially close to being what Marx called surplus value. The owner of land or natural resources, purely as an owner, collects what the economist calls economic rent. This is his payment for the use of his land by someone else, or a surplus arising out of his own use of the land over all other expenses of production. The owner has not made the land; its productivity is created by nature; but the economic worth of those scarce productive properties that collectively are called land currently flows to the owner.

This income is used by its recipient either for consumption purposes or as a source of capital funds, much as Marx pictured surplus-value funds as being used. If it is used to purchase consumption commodities, these are a portion of the total national income in whose production labor has played its part. There is a surplus in the sense that the owner performs no personal productive effort in return for the real income. Since whatever he uses must have some labor embodied in it, and since he, the owner, furnishes no labor to society, it might be said that he "exploits" the labor of others and that the implement of exploitation is the private ownership of land.

Moreover, the recipient of land rent appears to be in that increasingly fortunate position Marx held was occupied by the recipient of a constantly increasing surplus value. Since land is the only agent of production whose quantity cannot be increased by man's efforts, its owners possess something that grows increasingly scarce relative to expanding population. As people increase in number and natural resources remain constant, more intense competition for the scarce natural agent creates a long-run upward trend in land rents. This trend has no counteracting influence in the form of an increased supply of land induced by the increase in rents. The upward movement of land rents relative to other values, recalls the Marxian theory that all increased productivity of labor goes to swell surplus value.

The owner of inherited capital occupies a similar position relative to the receipt of unearned income. Even if interest on capital funds is called compensation for willingness to save, the heir who receives interest on inherited funds nevertheless cannot be said to have incurred the irksome efforts for which it is paid. He gains title to social product without adding his personal productive effort to the economic process.

It is only in terms of unearned incomes of this nature, rather than in the theoretical trappings Marx gave it, that anything similar to his surplus value can be inherent in the capitalist economy. Certain modernizers of Marx come very close to revamping his theory of surplus value in terms of what is here called unearned income.[2]

[2]See, for instance, G. D. H. Cole, *What Marx Really Meant*, New York: Knopf, 1934, p. 275.

Certain Deductions of Marxian Theory are Unsound

Certain deductions that Marx drew from his theories of value, wages, and surplus value are, along with their theoretical bases, unsound. The proletariat has not experienced the increasing misery Marx deduced to be its lot. Although there might well be some question as to how workers relative to owners have shared in the increasing national incomes under capitalism, in absolute terms their misery has been alleviated rather than deepened. If wages are not linked rigidly to physical subsistence, the dire consequences for the proletariat Marx drew from his theoretical reasoning cannot be *inherent* in the capitalist system. Machinery, as the creator of labor reserve pressing wages downward, may seem at times to act its Marxian role, but its force is neither so completely nor so persistently in that direction as Marx's theorizing led him to believe. Although technological unemployment from time to time has been a major problem, our modern economy has experienced certain recurring and long-run transformations of machine efficiency into lower unit costs and lower prices, thus creating new demand for labor that has been more potent and durable than Marx admitted.

The rate of profits has not followed the decline that Marx felt the value processes, coupled with the growth of machinery, would bring. Nor have fluctuations in economic activity turned out to be as completely an overproduction phenomenon as Marx made them. Careful studies indicate that a number of forces, wholly outside his simple overproduction (because of surplus value) theory, are important factors in their causation. Moreover, there is a question as to whether business booms and recessions have tended to become more serious, despite the severe depression of the 1930s.

The class consciousness of the proletariat and the homogeneity of the owning class under capitalism have not congealed as firmly as Marx believed they would. The proletariat—at least in the United States—can still sire labor organizations that defend actively all the basic institutions of capitalism. Whole sections of the unorganized proletariat in the white-collar and service categories remain desperately sure that their interests are closely linked with those of their capitalist employers. This they demonstrate by a refusal to be led into the dangerous paths of "radical" thinking, acting, and voting. The "bourgeoisie" today includes—again, at least in the United States—such heterogeneous and sometimes opposing interests as those of the small merchant, the chain-store owner, the large industrialist, the small-scale farmer, and the powerful banker. The last named—personifying, in Marxian theory, finance capital—probably has not achieved the domination Marx pictured as thrust upon him by inevitable forces at work under capitalism. Professional classes of lawyers, physicians, ministers, and teachers, aside from the ever-present exceptional individual and minority group, show little tendency to look for their ideals and chief source of support to other than the customary bourgeois sources. The industrial technicians—chemists, engineers, industrial managers, and the like

—still react in a bourgeois fashion to political programs, strikes, and "radical" movements.

The tendency for the inherent forces of capitalism constantly to push certain portions of the bourgeoisie into the proletariat and to induce other portions to merge their interests with it has not worked so powerfully as Marx suggested it would. If such a trend has existed in specific sections of the bourgeoisie, there have been counteracting movements in other portions, such as the creation of a large group of owners of independent restaurants, motels, and service facilities at the very time the chain stores and supermarkets have been transforming many small-scale independent bourgeois merchants into hired employees. While competition and the advantages of large-scale production have been concentrating economic control in certain lines of production, modern corporate securities, the development of insurance, changing techniques, and new products have been spreading ownership and creating a new "petit bourgeoisie" that attaches its strength with no mean loyalty to the central bourgeois owning interests.

There is no question that the inaccuracies and inadequacies of Marx's theoretical analysis led him into certain deductions concerning the consequences of capitalist production that, once their theoretical bases are proved fallacious, seem to be left without theoretical support and unproved by empirical observation of the post-Marx capitalist world. The inevitability of the forces inherent in capitalism that would eventually destroy it was a *theoretical* inevitably. The inductive study of data in the social sciences was wholly undeveloped in Marx's day and even today is entirely inadequate to act comprehensively as either support or refutation of a theoretical system as extensive as that Marx constructed. Marx cited voluminously from factual material in the realm of economic phenomena, but practically all these citations constitute illustrative rather than inductive quantified support for his theoretical points, and none of them meets modern tests of statistical adequacy.

Possible Elements of Truth in Marx's Prophecies

Despite all this, we cannot hastily dispose of Marxian conclusions and predictions by considering them a mere superstructure built on inadequate and inaccurate theoretical foundations. We have already noted the probability that unearned incomes are inherent in a capitalist society, and the possibility that these, in their essence but not their theoretical source, may be like Marx's surplus value.

Likewise, it is clear that many of the consequences of capitalism that Marx derived from his theoretical reasoning have plagued our capitalist system. Technological unemployment has recurred ever since the capitalist system developed substantial maturity, and it would be foolish to dispose of it on purely theoretical grounds.

The holding company and similar devices have made the *control* of industry more important than its *ownership* in relation to sharing its benefits. This control has reached monopoly proportions in some important industrial fields, and those who control the credit agencies make many of the basic decisions.

The wages of the masses of workers appear to have risen slowly when the tremendous technical advances in productive methods and instruments are considered. Although excess production—that is, more output than can be sold at cost—is far from being the sole causal factor of business depressions, excess productive capacity in a particular industry may be contributory. Common observation discloses the ills that have often spread cumulatively throughout our economy in the wake of excess production in some industry or group of industries. Government excursions into the restriction of many agricultural crops during recent decades may not demonstrate the theoretical inevitability of general overproduction in a capitalist order, but they do mark it as a major problem at times demanding the closest attention of government.

Finally, what can we make of Marx's prediction that capitalism would end in collapse? On first thought this may seem ridiculous. However, we should seriously ponder events since 1929. In the early 1930s capitalism in the United States did collapse, and financial calamity ushered in a prolonged and desperate economic crisis. Although the outcome of the Great Depression was not the socialism Marx predicted, capitalism today differs from capitalism in 1929. It is highly probable that only the massive arms expenditures of 1941–1945 managed to pull capitalism, at least in the United States, out of the depression of the 1930s. Furthermore, it is often persuasively argued that the postwar resurgence of capitalism in the United States and Western Europe (especially since European recovery was for a long period dependent upon the aid of the United States) has been continuously underwritten by large governmental defense expenditures. In the absence of World War II and postwar arms spending, what would have occurred? Can it be categorically denied that capitalism might have followed trends similar to those Marx described? Orthodox Marxians, of course, insist that history has not yet passed final judgment on the events of our century.

The Dilemma of Marxian Theory

We return to the question, What of the validity of the Marxian theories of value, wages, and surplus value, and the deductions made therefrom by Marx? This becomes a most difficult question to answer. The theoretical validity and consistency of the Marxian reasoning cannot be defended. The errors in the theoretical portion of Marxian thought are so serious and so basic that they cannot be corrected by interpreting or modernizing Marx, nor can they be considered superficial.

This, however, does not destroy the value of Marxian theory. It has been noted that through this theoretical analysis Marx somehow or other discerned the aspects of capitalism that cause defenders of that system their greatest concern—the concentration of industrial control, monopoly, occasional excess production, technological unemployment, fluctuations in industrial activity, unearned incomes, and the relatively low incomes of unskilled workers. The problem is perplexing: How could Marx draw correct or enlightening conclusions from unsound theoretical analysis? This has remained the dilemma of the numerous students of Marx who have found his theoretical reasoning imperfect and unsatisfactory but who nevertheless feel that they have been led, at least here and there, to a more complete understanding of the process at work within capitalism by viewing them, in part but not exclusively, through Marxian concepts.

THE MARXIAN VIEW OF HISTORY

In a sense a person's philosophy cannot be evaluated. It can be subjected neither to any empirical examination nor to any test of its logical consistency with external phenomena. It is part of its possessor, his way of looking at things, his approach to an understanding of the universe, his basic assumptions, and his prejudices. It comes to him or upon him from the totality of his reactions to external stimuli—both mental and physical.

There is but one test that can legitimately be applied to a person's philosophy. This involves an examination of the breadth and depth of his contact with other philosophies and with objective phenomena in the formulation of his own philosophy. In this sense a person's philosophy is of his own making, for he can either consciously and deliberately place himself in wide and open contact with the philosophies and objective phenomena of the universe, or he can shut himself up in his own closet and in its darkness spin out his own philosophy.

Evaluation of Marx's Philosophy

Needless to say, philosophies formulated under the latter circumstances are suspect. They lack the very stuff of which adequate philosophies must be made—contact with the thoughts of others and with the world as it is. In this respect no criticism can be leveled at Marx. Searching study of philosophies occupied the early years of his life. He struggled to the point of literal exhaustion over the conflicting philosophical systems he encountered. It was only after the most careful examination of the philosophical ideas of his day and of the past that he accepted the essence of Hegelian philosophy.

Although his contacts with the outside world were limited during his early years, he was projected from his student life directly into the midst of a most active life in the world of reality. His numerous journalistic endeavors, his contacts with workingmen's groups, and his years of study in the British Museum gave him an extensive and intimate knowledge of the world in which he had lived. Although his philosophy is in a sense chiefly the product of his philosophical studies, it nevertheless must have been conditioned and matured by these worldly contacts. By these tests, Marx's basic philosophy stands above criticism.

This, of course, does not mean that Marx necessarily found the one ultimate, absolute truth in the universe. It is just as meaningless to say that the Marxian philosophy was right and other philosophies were and are wrong as it is to say that tall men are better than short men or blue eyes better than brown without specifying arbitrarily some standard whereby they are to be judged. From the standpoint of its inherent quality, Marx's philosophy was no better than others that have been formulated out of equally sincere, comprehensive, and deep contact with ideas and events. Conversely, it could be innately worse than others only in the sense of having been fabricated out of shallow and less searching thought and experience than other philosophies have been. Judged in this manner, the Marxian philosophy is quite adequate to justify its becoming, unchallenged, the philosophical starting point from which anyone who wishes to accept it may launch his attempts to understand the forces at work in the universe.

Application of Marxian Philosophy to an Interpretation of History

Other matters are involved, however, when one seeks to evaluate the application of this philosophy to an interpretation of history. A man's philosophy by its very nature may not be susceptible to evaluation. The same cannot be said for the manner in which he uses that philosophy or applies it to an ostensibly objective interpretation of specific events in the world in which he lives. Here certain rules of observation, logic, and consistency enter the picture as standards of evaluation. As a philosophical abstraction, one might see fit to assume that all human action is dominated by selfish motives. As an abstraction, such a philosophy except for the tests of worth suggested earlier, could not be challenged. Yet the possessor of that philosophy could legitimately be challenged if he were to interpret every human act as actuated by desire for the greatest *economic* gain for himself. In this case either there are aspects of selfishness other than the economic, or the economic aspect is made so all-inclusive as to become meaningless. Failure to apply the basic philosophy so as to respect this point would merit criticism.

Indeed, it is just that sort of application of his philosophy for which Marx has been criticized. His basic philosophical assumption that all objective phenomena are syntheses resulting from theses and antitheses at work in the world cannot be challenged, for reasons already noted. However, he may well be criticized when, in applying this philosophy to the specific explanation of just what has happened and will happen in the world, he either neglects all categories of these antitheses except the economic or so defines the economic as to include all others, thereby making it meaningless as a limited homogeneous category. He has a perfect right to his basic philosophy because of the comprehension and depth of the thought and experiences out of which it grew, but his *use* of this philosophy violates commonly accepted rules of logic and consistency to such a degree that the practical worth of his economic interpretation of history may legitimately be questioned.

In passing, it should be noted that some modern adherents to Marxian theory refuse to make any distinction between Marx's philosophy and his economic interpretation of history. In a narrowly orthodox sense, they accept all of Marx and insist that it be all or nothing. His basic philosophy appears to them adequate, and once this is accepted they hold that all interpretations of historical events and prophecies of future events that *he* arrived at in the application of his philosophy must be accepted in minute detail. G. D. H. Cole has referred to this attitude as "the opium of the socialist orthodox" and to its adherents as "those who seek to save themselves the pain of mental building by inhabiting dead men's minds."[3]

Thus, although students of Marxian thought have seldom challenged his basic philosophy, they have been most critical of his application of that philosophy to a specific interpretation of historical events. It will be recalled that Marx found only *economic* theses and antitheses as the basic forces at work in the world. All other forces were derivatives of the economic which he termed, collectively and relative to any given point in time, the mode of production. This is held to be a one-sided interpretation of history since, it is claimed, Marx has merely assumed without demonstration that the mode of production sets the content of all social institutions and processes, and that changes in this mode of production generate and determine the course of changes in all social institutions. Marx's critics have been quite voluble in pointing out forces they hold to be noneconomic but nonetheless deserving of inclusion among the independent and original forces that collectively determine the nature of existing and future social institutions and processes.

Professor M. M. Bober, for instance, devotes a detailed discussion to this weakness in the economic interpretation of history.[4] In fact, he concludes that "Marx's theory is impotent to account for historical processes, and the reason is that he failed to ascribe sufficient weight to the many noneconomic agencies in history."[5] Although Marx admitted the existence of noneconomic forces, "he regarded them as emanations from the economic subsoil, and granted them the subordinate function of only accelerating or retarding or slightly modifying the workings of the mode of produc-

---

[3]Cole, p. 42.
[4]M. M. Bober, *Karl Marx's Interpretation of History,* Cambridge, Mass.: Harvard University Press, 1927.
[5]*Ibid.,* p. 290.

tion."[6] Professor Bober contends that the factors emphasized by Marx as all-important are, in fact, plainly secondary to other factors. "The geographical environment and man, with his intelligence and other traits, are the primary and basic factors of history. The mode of production cannot rank with them, because it is a derived phenomenon."[7] Professor Bober admits that Marx recognizes the geographic factor but contends that he accords it insufficient influence of an economic character and neglects entirely its noneconomic effects.

Contributions of the Marxian Theory of History

If the Marxian theory of history and the predictions based on it are a one-sided oversimplification of the actual forces shaping the processes and institutions of society, it nevertheless has contributed substantially to human thought and understanding. It has offered a more realistic interpretation of history than certain other, also unbalanced theories that preceded and followed it. In comprehension and depth of understanding it is incomparably superior, for instance, to the "great man" theory of history, which holds that an institution is the lengthened shadow of one man. It emphasizes the continuity of history and, by searching for the causes of *all* historical events, it has challenged the concept of history as a collection of mere chaotic or chance happenings. It stresses the dynamic nature of human institutions, processes, and ideas. Although it is, of course, impossible to judge precisely how much of the modern historian's increasing interest in economic causation was inspired by Marx, without question his interpretation of history played a substantial part in creating this trend. Although Marx cannot be credited with originating the idea of evolution in social institutions, in its use he reached a level of effectiveness sufficiently high to stimulate emulation on the part of many others. He showed what a comprehensive monistic theory of history would be like if one could be found. In these ways, at least, the Marxian economic interpretation of history has contributed to an understanding of the sources of the economic world in which we live, of the closeness of the relationship between the economic and the other aspects of that world, and of the nature of historical processes.

THE BASIS OF REVOLUTIONARY PROLETARIAN ORGANIZATION

Although the Marxian theories of value, wages, and surplus value can be proved to be basically unsound, they have nevertheless remained alive, and powerful in their impact on current thought, in all sorts of modified and interpreted forms. And although Marx's theory of history

[6] *Ibid.*, p. 289.
[7] *Ibid.*, p. 300.

was too unbalanced to do effectively what he intended it to do, it has been accepted by many as the most adequate available explanation of history. In both of these spheres Marx, despite the defects and inadequacies of his work, left influences that have substantially affected the thinking of hundreds of millions of people and the economic and political systems of much of the modern world. It is, however, in the realm where Marx appeared least effective while he lived that his most concrete contribution was made. He and his collaborator Engels unquestionably established the basis of all organized proletarian revolutionary activity that has occurred since they wrote.

A pre-Marxian brand of socialist thought—and even action—played its part in the world of its day and in the establishment of the modern movements of socialism and communism. It was, however, unfitted to cope with the realities of the modern world. It hoped to create a new order without dealing with the world that existed; men were to be transplanted from the world in which they lived into a new one without experiencing the difficult sacrifices necessary to accomplish a transition from the one to the other.

With Marx, this type of utopian socialism lost its hold on the minds of men and was replaced by what has come to be called "scientific socialism" or, perhaps better, "realistic socialism." Post-Marxian socialism thoroughly absorbed the Marxian position that if socialism, and finally full communism, were to be achieved, the proletariat had to come to grips with the realities of the world. There was no easy road to the new society. Its internal contradictions would destroy capitalism as a form of economic organization, bourgeois democracy falling with it. The proletariat had to face these realities, organize itself, and otherwise prepare to take over the economic and political reins upon the collapse of capitalism. Only if this were done would chaos be avoided. Organization became the central necessity among the proletariat.

The history of the international socialistic and communistic organizations of workers during the past century is the history of action for which Marxian theory laid the foundations. Despite the disagreements among these organizations, their numerous internal factions, and their failures, they have continued to live and to act, finding their roots in Marxian theory. Despite the apparent failure of the revolutionary organizations with whom he personally was connected, Marx possibly achieved his supreme purpose in laying the basis for international proletarian organization.

MARX AND KEYNES

In terminating our formal study of Marxism, we will examine an issue that has drawn attention over the past three decades. What is the relationship between Marxian and Keynesian economics—the latter now generally accepted by Western economists? As is often found in studying economic institutions, there are no clear-cut answers. The theories of John Maynard Keynes seem to be neither "socialism-Marxism," as one group in the United States would have us believe, nor the purely "non-Marxian manifesto" that some defenders of Keynes categorically claim. In fact, there are areas of both similarity and conflict in the two schools of thought.

Similarities

From the beginnings of their careers, both Marx and Keynes showed heterodox tendencies with respect to accepted economic doctrines of their times. Both were appalled by the inability of accepted doctrines to explain serious problems of the real capitalist world in which they lived. Hence, each attempted to formulate an economic theory fitting the way the economy actually functions. Marx violently rejected the abstract "vulgar economics" of Ricardo, Nassau Senior, and John Stuart Mill, for he felt that these "classical economists" did little to explain the harsh *reality* of industrial capitalism during the period 1840–1880. Keynes felt that the bases of the later neoclassical economics, which was accepted with little question before 1929, "happen not to be those of the economic society in which we actually live, with the result that its teaching is misleading and disastrous if we attempt to apply it to the facts of experience."[8]

The common ground between the two schools goes further. Both explicitly repudiate one special classical assumption, embodied in "Say's law of markets"—that aggregate production (supply) equals aggregate income (demand) and that as a result there can be no sustained lack of overall demand for the output of the entire economy, since production itself automatically creates demand. An increase in output supposedly always generates a sufficient increase in income, purchasing power, and spending to clear the market of the extra goods. Before Marx, little heed was paid to Malthus' warnings of "ineffectual demand" and a "general overproduction glut"—Say's law had proved that to be "impossible." Marx pointedly noted the "childish" reasoning of Say's "dogma that . . . the circulation of commodities necessarily implies an equilibrium of sales and purchases," and claimed that "if the split between the sale and the purchase becomes too pronounced, [this] . . . asserts itself by producing—a crisis."[9] Keynes also built his theories on a refutation of Say's law as being "not the true law relating the aggregate demand and supply func-

---

[8]J. M. Keynes, *The General Theory of Employment Interest and Money*, New York: Harcourt Brace Jovanovich, 1936, p. 3.

[9]Marx, *Capital*, vol. I, pp. 127–128. Even earlier Marx had sharply attacked "the view adopted by Ricardo from the inane Say . . . that no *overproduction*, or at any rate *no general glut of the market*, is possible." *Theories of Surplus Value*, New York: International Publishers, 1952, pp. 369–372.

tions. . . ."[10] Both men, in rejecting Say's law, firmly established explanations for the existence of recession and crisis in the capitalist system. Instead of the "equilibrium" situations of stable production and full employment that the neoclassicists in particular postulated after 1870, Marx and Keynes envisioned a capitalist system whose *norm* was *instability*. This might take the form of dynamic growth cycles of prosperity and crisis, raising national product over the long run but bringing about the ultimate collapse of the system through a final breakdown (Marx), or of a tendency toward irregular patterns of growth, slump, or even stagnation, depending chiefly on the level of private capital investment (Keynes). But regardless of the precise sort of instability, the mere emphasis on instability as a fact led both men to reject the optimistic view that free market capitalism naturally brings about a harmony of all economic forces and an automatic adjustment ensuring long-run stability and full employment. Neither Marxists nor Western Keynesian economists in general accept such preestablished harmony as normal under laissez-faire capitalism.

Why did rejection of Say's law carry with it such assumptions of capitalist instability? The main reason is that if aggregate demand and supply are not in balance, and if there are no automatic forces in a capitalist economy to right the balance, then there can be cases of aggregate error. One result might be market gluts, if overall demand is insufficient to take up all goods supplied. Another might be aggregate money demand in excess of production, leading to inflation. Both Marx and Keynes hold that capitalism has an *inherent tendency* to develop the first kind of crisis—overproduction stemming from lack of effective demand. Marx wrote that lack of purchasing power resulted from exploitation of the working masses by capitalists, who paid laborers only subsistence wages. Keynes believed that lack of effective demand would be caused principally by the inability of private investment to absorb growing quantities of savings produced by highly developed capitalist economies.

Finally, the arena in which Marx and Keynes saw these developments taking shape was far removed from the classical microeconomics of price, value, and individual firms. They look at the capitalist system essentially as an aggregative *whole*, one that calls for the study of the total social product, its composition, and the forces determining it (Marx) or of the determination of national income and its components of consumption, savings, and investment (Keynes). Thus, along with the idea that capitalism would not automatically gravitate toward an "ideal" equilibrium, the modern concern with the aggregate level of economic performance, or macroeconomics, is a legacy of both schools.[11]

[10]Keynes, p. 26.
[11]On macroreproduction schemes in Marx and Keynes, see the appendix by Shigeto Tsuru in Paul M. Sweezy, *The Theory of Capitalist Development*, New York: Monthly Review, 1956, and Lawrence R. Klein, *The Keynesian Revolution*, New York: Macmillan, 1947, pp. 130–134.

Differences

On the simplest level, the economics of the Marxian and Keynesian theories are wholly different. Marx adopted many of the accepted mid-nineteenth-century classical economics tools, such as the labor theory of value and the subsistence wage, to deduce drastically new conclusions regarding capitalism as a system. Keynes thought little of such tools. His own analysis owes much to the post-1870 neoclassical school; he wrote that "if our central controls succeed in establishing an aggregate volume of output corresponding to full employment as nearly as is practicable, the [neo] classical theory comes into its own from that point onwards.[12] To Marx such hope would have seemed futile.

However, the more important differences are broader in scope. Keynes was motivated by the desire to preserve capitalism insofar as possible, and to this end he formulated a theory that he hoped might be used to construct a reformed, "liberal" capitalism. He was a conservative who desired to extend the life of capitalism rather than to replace it by another economic system. The contrast with Marx is striking. Marx wrote works that were passionate, bitterly critical, and destructive. His sole interest was to prove how capitalism had already fulfilled its historical mission and had consequently outlived its usefulness. For Marx, all thought of reform was either pointless or at worst reactionary, since capitalism was doomed by the progressive forces of history. In short, "Keynes wanted to apologize and conserve, while Marx wanted to criticize and destroy."[13]

It is true that Keynesian theories regarding the weaknesses of capitalism have been used by socialists to promote their own cause. This must be regarded as somewhat ironic, because Keynes made his personal distaste for socialism quite clear. That he was strongly opposed to widespread nationalization of industry, to collectivism, and to the economic system of the Soviet Union was well known. Perhaps only his often-stated low opinion of Karl Marx surpassed his dislike of any alternative prospect to capitalism. In his *General Theory* Keynes even relegated Marx to the "underworld" of economics, along with such minor and forgotten figures as Silvio Gesell and Major Douglas.[14] The future predicted by Marx filled Keynes with consternation; he had no desire to live in a society dominated by "the boorish proletariat."[15]

Another difference just as great exists in the social bases of the two schools. The Keynesian system, despite its desire to preserve capitalism, is socially indifferent in its analytical structure. Its aggregate variables can be used to study economic activity in any country at all, whatever its eco-

[12]J. M. Keynes, "The Balance of Payments of the United States," *Economic Journal,* June 1946, p. 186.
[13]Klein, p. 77; see also Dudley Dillard, *The Economics of John Maynard Keynes,* Englewood Cliffs, N.J.: Prentice-Hall, 1948, pp. 318–326.
[14]Keynes, *The General Theory of Employment Interest and Money,* p. 32.
[15]J. M. Keynes, *Essays in Persuasion,* New York: Norton, 1963, p. 300.

nomic institutions. In the eyes of Marxian economists, "The Keynesians
tear the economic system out of its social context and treat it as though
it were a machine to be sent to the repair shop, there to be overhauled by
an engineer state."[16] For Marx, economic systems cannot be separated
from the social, cultural, political, and psychological institutions to be
found with them at any given stage of history. He believed that economic
theory cannot be treated apart and alone, as Keynes, the neoclassicists,
or the classicists do. Marxism purports to be a *complete* historical system that explains *all* material phenomena, not only the economic.

QUESTIONS FOR CLASS DISCUSSION

1. Before anything can be evaluated, tests of its value must be
established. What do you think these tests should be in the case of
Marxian theory?

2. What is the major weakness in Marx's theory of value? How
does this affect his theory of surplus value?

3. Does the same weakness appear in his theory of wages?

4. Why was it essential for Marx to maintain consistently either that
wages are flexible or that they are inflexible? Why did he not do so?

5. What inconsistencies can be found in Marx's handling of his
subsistence theory of wages?

6. How do the inaccuracies in Marxian wage theory affect his theory
of surplus value?

7. Does a proof that there is no sound theoretical support for
Marx's theory of surplus value also disprove his contention that under
capitalism workers are exploited by capitalist employers?

8. If one rejects the theory of surplus value but accepts as a fact
some exploitation in a capitalist economy, can that exploitation be
removed without destroying capitalism? Compare your answer with Marx's
analysis of the possibility of removing surplus value from the capitalist
system.

9. Marx made specific predictions of certain developments that
would occur under the capitalist system. Have these predictions proved
correct?

10. Is it merely difficult or is it practically impossible to evaluate
Marx's basic philosophical tenets? Does this mean that we must accept
Marx's philosophy?

11. In what sense can the Marxian theory of history be said to be
one-sided? Is this equivalent to saying that it has no value?

12. Is it legitimate to evaluate Marxian doctrines, regardless of their
theoretical soundness, on the basis of their influence on world thought?
What can be concluded when this test is applied?

[16]Sweezy, p. 349.

13. What similarities and contrasts are there between Marxian and Keynesian thought?

SUGGESTED SUBJECTS FOR STUDENT REPORTS FOR PART III

1. The degree to which the Paris Commune of 1871 carried out Marxian ideas.

2. The degree to which the Internationals followed Marxian doctrines.

3. The history of one or more of the Internationals.

4. The contrast between Marxian and Hegelian philosophy.

5. The place of noneconomic institutions in Marxian theory.

6. Marx's influence on the present-day writing and teaching of history.

7. The sources of Marx's theories of value and wages.

8. Marxian doctrines in recent political platforms of Socialist and Communist parties.

9. The Marxian theory of capitalist imperialism compared with historians' analyses of the causes of World War I and World War II.

10. The story of the "enclosures" in England.

11. Are business depressions becoming more severe?

12. The concentration of control of industry in the United States.

13. The role of Marxian theory in the Soviet Union today.

14. The relationship of recent technological change to Marxian theory.

15. A detailed comparison of Keynesian with Marxian theory.

16. The degree and manner in which Marxian ideas may have played a role in the development of the American labor movement.

17. The degree and manner in which Marxian doctrines may have affected American student movements.

18. An assessment of the degree to which Marxian doctrines influence political movements in Central and South America.

19. The reasons for and against American colleges and universities giving Marxism more attention in the curricula of their social sciences, philosophy, and history departments.

20. An assessment of the role Marxian doctrines may have played in racial disturbances in the United States during the 1960s.

SUGGESTIONS FOR FURTHER READING FOR PART III

Apthecker, H., ed., *Marxism and Democracy*, New York: Humanities, 1965.

Bell, D., *Marxian Socialism in the United States*, Princeton, N.J.: Princeton University Press, 1967.

Berlin, I., *Karl Marx, His Life and Environment*, New York: Oxford University Press, 1963.

Bober, M. M., *Karl Marx's Interpretation of History*, Cambridge, Mass.: Harvard University Press, 1948.

Browder, E. R., *Marx and America: A Study of the Doctrine of Impoverishment*, New York: McKay, 1958.

Caute D., ed., *Essential Writings of Karl Marx*, New York: Macmillan, 1968.

Chang, S. H. M., *The Marxian Theory of the State*, New York: Russell & Russell, 1965.

Drachovitch, M. M., ed., *Marxist Ideology in the Contemporary World— Its Appeals and Paradoxes*, New York: Praeger, 1966.

Hook, S., *From Hegel to Marx*, Ann Arbor: University of Michigan Press, 1962.

Lachs, J., *Marxist Philosophy*, Chapel Hill: University of North Carolina Press, 1967.

Lobkowicz, N., ed., *Marx and the Western World*, South Bend, Ind.: University of Notre Dame Press, 1967.

Mandel, Ernest, *Marxian Economic Theory* (two volumes), New York: Monthly Review Press, 1968.

Marx, K., *Capital*, vol. 1: *Capitalist Production*; vol. 2: *Circulation of Capital*; vol. 3. *Capitalist Production as a Whole*, London: Lawrence & Wishart, 1960.

Marx, K., *Value, Price and Profit*, New York: International Publishers, 1935.

Marx, K. and F. Engels, *Communist Manifesto*, Chicago: Great Books Foundation, 1952.

Robinson, J., *An Essay in Marxian Economics*, London: Macmillan, 1947.

Rossiter, C., *Marxism: The View from America*, New York: Harcourt Brace Jovanovich, 1960.

Sweezy, P., *The Theory of Capitalist Development*, New York: Monthly Review Press, 1956.

Wolfe, B. D., *Marxism: 100 Years in the Life of a Doctrine*, New York: Dial, 1965.

Wolfson, Murray, *A Reappraisal of Marxian Economics*, Baltimore: Penguin, 1968.

Zeitlin, I. M., *Marxism: A Reexamination*, Princeton, N. J.: Van Nostrand Reinhold, 1967.

PART IV: THEORETICAL SOCIALISM

10. Democratic socialism

Analyzing an unfamiliar ideology is a difficult mental task because one's own ideology unconsciously gets in the way. *Socialism*, like other emotionally charged words, means different things to different people. For some it is a utopian panacea; for others it is a catchword for whatever economic and social doctrines they find personally repugnant. The multifaceted scope of socialism is pointed out in the following statement of its nature:

> It is both abstract and concrete, theoretical and practical, idealist and materialist, very old and entirely modern; it ranges from a mere sentiment to a precise program of action; different advocates present

it as a philosophy of life, a sort of religion, an ethical code, an economic system, a historical category, a judicial principle. . . .[1]

Concern here necessarily centers on the economic aspects of socialism, but we also consider the ideological pattern of beliefs and values
underlying the concept. Our working definition of socialism refers to *the
movement that aims to vest in society as a whole, rather than in individuals, the ownership and management of all capital goods used in large-scale
production to the end of increasing national income and distributing it
more equally without materially destroying the individual's economic motivation or his freedom of occupational and consumer choice.*

The mainstream of modern non-Marxian socialism—"social democracy" or "democratic socialism"—is unmistakably allied with the growth
of democratic institutions in Western Europe and the United States. In a
sense, it both precedes and outlives Marxian socialist doctrine, which
placed scant faith in the possibility of socialism evolving out of a capitalist system whose basic institutions it held existed to protect the owners
of the means of production. In general, social democrats believe that the
existing parliamentary process is an avenue through which the working
class can achieve socialism by voting itself into power; this was the strategy of political movements that first appeared in Western Europe during
the late nineteenth century. Modern socialists claim that capitalism has
proved itself incapable of creating real freedom without gross inequalities
and class differences, at the very moment in history when, they believe,
science and technology are making such freedom attainable.

THE ECONOMIC CORE OF SOCIALISM

The heart of socialism is *economic*. When the definition presented before
and its implications are examined, the central issues are found to be property rights in capital goods, decisions relative to using those goods, and
distribution of the real income produced when labor is combined with
them. The periphery of political, social, religious, and other concerns should
not be confused with the central problem of how society wishes its production, distribution, and consumption of economic goods to be organized.

The multitude of social-welfare services such as old-age pensions,
unemployment compensation, health services, and factory and wage legislation also fall outside our definition of socialism. Although they are frequently attacked as socialistic, these measures are better understood as
efforts on the part of industrialized nations to adapt private-property rights
to changes in technology and industrial organization and in corresponding human needs. These programs are open to criticism, but using the
slogan "creeping socialism" is not an adequate substitute for judging the

[1]A. Shadwell, "Socialism—Its Origin and Meaning," *Quarterly Review*, July
1924, p. 2.

merits and shortcomings of each case. Such laws are essentially capitalist because they bring about no basic shifts in the ownership of capital goods. Welfare programs may be advocated by the socialist, but he regards them as inadequate without the shift of power from individuals to society as a prerequisite to any satisfactory operation of the economy.

Nor is the socialist satisfied with isolated instances of government ownership. Americans seldom regard the post office or the municipal water works as unwarranted socialism; in some nations the telephone system or the broadcasting industry likewise falls into the category of government-owned enterprises. Each nation draws up its own list of natural governmental functions; to the socialist these are token adjustments to the capitalist system, not the transformation of society *as a whole* which socialism seeks.

More significantly, in recent years a somewhat similar relationship between government and private capitalism has developed in the form of government contracts, purchases, and subsidies to industries under private ownership and management. The beginning of such practices in the United States dates back to the nineteenth century, when laws (tariffs, patent protection, rights of corporations) and outright grants of funds and land (to railroads, farmers, and educational institutions) created profit opportunities for specific sectors of the population. Most of these types of government aid have continued to exist, but since 1940 they have been dwarfed by the rise of armaments expenditures and research subsidies. Such contracts cannot be considered socialistic, since the government uses general tax revenues to purchase goods from, and to support, industries owned and controlled by *private* interests. No socialist considers them to be socialist oriented; indeed, the symbiotic relationship between the modern defense industry and government is regarded by many socialists as a basic flaw in the capitalist system.

Alternative Forms of Socialism

If our definition of socialism includes the main connotations of the term, what can serve as a modern definition of communism? Certainly not the far-off full communism of orthodox Marxism, in which each contributes according to his ability and receives according to his needs; no modern nation remotely approaches this utopian ideal. In fact, the economic system of the nations that we refer to as the communist bloc are in general conformity with our definition of socialism. Thus it seems clear that our use of the term *communism* is a reference to political and psychological conditions rather than a fundamental dichotomy of economic systems. The term, as used in the West, implies one-party rule, intolerance of opposition, and the use of economic power to advance political aims.

A more important economic distinction can be drawn between socialist systems that rely primarily on market forces to allocate resources and those that centralize decision making in a command type of economy. The following chapter will elaborate on the economic consequences of each form. It is relevant at this point, however, that there is no invariant connection between the political structure of a socialist nation and the mixture of market and command institutions by which its economy operates. A major thrust of the economic reforms occurring in the nations of Eastern Europe over the past decade has been the greater reliance on market incentives as the task of centralized economic planning has become larger and more complex.

THE SOCIALIST ATTACK ON CAPITALISM

Unrelenting criticism of capitalism has been one of the most salient characteristics of the socialist movement. Concentrating on the deficiencies discussed in Part II as shortcomings of capitalism, the socialist contends that these are sufficiently serious and irremediable to render the capitalist system not only no longer useful but in fact dangerously outmoded. He considers these criticisms generally consistent with the Marxist attack on capitalism, although he balks at accepting all portions of the Marxian economic analysis and its belief in the ultimate necessity of revolutionary action. Both Marxists and democratic socialists insist that capitalism suffers from an incurable *basic contradiction*: The technological and economic forces of capitalist production are *social* in nature, while control of this process and the resulting profits remain in private hands.

From this alleged basic dilemma of capitalist society, the socialist proceeds to indicate features that he feels logically and inevitably generate grave problems. Although we are by now familiar with them, the specific areas of the socialist argument may profitably be examined more closely, since it is from these alleged failures of capitalism that many of the goals of modern socialism are derived.

Failure to Create Sufficient Aggregate Demand

Modern macroeconomic theory tells us that national product is analogous to the total purchasing power in the hands of consumers, businessmen, and government agencies. Aggregate demand and purchasing power have a direct link to the overall level of employment of resources; when national product rises, employment also tends to rise, and vice versa. The socialist points to the Great Depression of the 1930s, when as much as one-fourth of the labor force was involuntarily unemployed, as evidence that there is no *automatic* mechanism in free-market capitalism to ensure that the national product will be of sufficient magnitude to employ all resources. If left to itself, the free market *might* generate sufficient aggregate demand to achieve full employment, but the possibility exists that it might not. To the socialist these possibilities are gambles that cannot be tolerated because they involve the fate of millions of human beings. Widespread unemployment involves atrophy of skills and human demoralization, which are judged intolerable in an advanced industrial society.

Those who would ward off socialism often answer this criticism by invoking the same Keynesian theories. They point out that, even without socialization of the means of production, the government can take steps to compensate for any lack of aggregate demand by means of appropriate fiscal and monetary policies. Full employment of resources can be achieved with government purchases or tax policies filling any gap that would otherwise exist in demand by the private sector. Socialists do not necessarily deny this (although some claim that these policies become ultimately impossible in the face of corporate capitalist power) so much as they deplore cyclical instability and the subsequent use of Keynesian remedies to attempt to cure something that should not have been permitted to happen in the first place. They would prefer to change capitalist economic institutions so as to eliminate such fluctuations at their source. Moreover, they would never accept what they deem to be a situation in which the basic decision-making powers with regard to resource utilization, technology, and industrial location remain in private hands, while the government can do little better than *react* to the use or misuse of private economic power.

Maldistribution of Wealth and Income

Socialists hold that extreme concentration of property and income are inevitable features of capitalism. "The free market will almost always, immediately and cumulatively, produce greater inequality than the minimum necessary to get human capacities exercised. . . . Uncorrected by deliberate social decisions, natural economic forces in a laissez-faire regime would today and in the future, as in the past, generate ever greater inequality."[2] The result is seen to be the negation of many of the benefits of political equality and heightened tensions among social classes.

Another injurious effect of maldistribution of income, in the eyes of the socialist, is that it destroys consumer sovereignty in lower-income groups. The array of goods reflects the "dollar votes" of the more affluent, and an index of social and human welfare based on decent standards of living for all suffers accordingly. Moreover, the danger of a subculture of poverty in which cultural values and life-style make it extremely difficult for future generations to escape the demoralizing cycle of limited income may be created.

Chronic Shortages of Public Goods

The socialist believes that one result of the inequality of income that draws resources toward the satisfaction of luxury desires is the lopsided contrast

[2]Douglas Jay, *Socialism in the New Society*, New York: McKay, 1962, pp. 11, 30.

of "private opulence and public squalor."[3] The free reign given to the private sector, the persuasive power of advertising, and the natural un-willingness of individuals to contribute fully to services from which others will also benefit create a relative economic bias against public goods such as transportation facilities, schools, parks, and pollution-control devices.

A corollary to shortages of public goods, claims the socialist, is a built-in tendency for the capitalist system to misjudge present consump-tion needs at the expense of the future. This might include failing to adequately maintain the social-overhead capital (such as public health, ed-ucation, and recreation facilities) needed for a growing population and depleting, at perilous rates, irreplaceable stocks of natural resources. It is contended that a socialist planning board could make more rational choices to coordinate social categories that capitalism ignores in the pur-suit of immediate profit opportunities.

Degeneration of Aesthetic and Qualitative Values

In what is acknowledged to be a matter of value judgment, socialists have argued (with increasing intensity in recent years) that the quality of capi-talist society undergoes progressive deterioration. It is claimed that sci-entific advances and artistic efforts are systematically perverted to the simple ends of profit making. The resulting cultural chaos is seen in the opulent standards of private consumption maintained while urban blight continues unchecked; "vulgar" advertising and sadistic violence fill the air-waves; cultural and educational institutions desperately search for funds; military hardware expenditures are politically sacred, but programs to con-front human needs are too expensive; the communication gap between races, between classes, and between generations atomizes society. These, socialists insist, are some areas that reveal the extent to which capitalism debases man. The nature of these charges, the question of whether ob-served defects follow inalterably from the inherent character of capital-ism, and the obviously subjective nature of human judgments make this one of the fiercest points of controversy between socialists and defenders of the system they attack.

GOALS OF DEMOCRATIC SOCIALISM

From these basic contradictions and specific attacks, many of the goals of socialism can be inferred. It would be a mistake to conclude that so-cialist thought consists only of a negative view of capitalism; it is also an idealistic vision of what the socialist regards as a better society, based on both eliminating the shortcomings of capitalism and building on its

---

[3]J. K. Galbraith's *The Affluent Society*, Boston: Houghton Mifflin, 1958, has developed the economics of this argument, which was always implicit in socialist thought.

acknowledged successes. Along with Marxists, modern socialists believe that capitalism in the West has created extraordinary powers of technology and production, necessary as a "material base upon which socialism can be built." Capitalism creates impressive levels of productive capacity, but at the same time it allegedly renders itself obsolete by generating the morass of problems identified as its inherent faults. Consequently, capitalism becomes ripe for replacement by a system the socialist feels can go further in constructing a truly humane society.

Nationalization and Public Ownership

Socialism has traditionally stood for the public ownership of at least the strategically important industries; capital goods used in large-scale production and requiring the employment of significant quantities of hired labor must be controlled by society as a whole. Since property breeds such power over crucial economic decisions, its use must be rendered accountable to the masses of individuals inevitably affected by it. The only way to accomplish this, according to the socialist, is to transfer such property and its power attributes to public agencies.

Modern socialists do not usually anticipate socialization of the entire range of producers' goods in the economy. Priorities are given to industries that are heavily capitalized and highly concentrated in terms of output and employment, thereby making them bastions of economic power. It matters not that there may be no desire on the part of the capitalist owners to use this power for antisocial purposes; the mere fact of the *existence* and *potential use* of economic power is enough to qualify an industry as a candidate for nationalization according to the socialists' criteria.

Undoubtedly, the financial sector stands near the top of the socialization list. Since the banking system is the agency supplying the funds that make production possible, it controls the very lifeblood of productive activity. It would be unthinkable to the socialist that society should take over industry without also controlling the power to grant or withhold credit. The socialist also advocates the early takeover of the public-utility industries. Utilities often cannot be operated on other than a monopoly basis, and this factor, together with the public-welfare aspects involved in many utilities, makes transportation, electric and gas companies, broadcasting, and similar industries prime targets for public ownership.

Possibly the next chronological group to be socialized would be the natural-resource industries—coal, timber, metallic minerals, petroleum, and similar products (but excluding agriculture). The large-scale manufacturing industries would probably follow. Roughly speaking, those that used the most capital-intensive techniques and produced standardized products for mass consumption would receive earliest attention.

This would leave agriculture and small-scale handicraft and distributive activities as the only substantial economic sectors outside the socialized orbit. Socialist opinion differs on their fate, but most socialists feel that these sectors could remain in private hands without seriously compromising the operation of the socialized industries. Some part of these sectors possibly would assume unique forms of cooperative organization.

Economic Planning

Modern socialism insists on comprehensive economic planning to link together the mass of separate aims and programs contained within it. The term *economic planning* has been so grossly misused that we must specify what it means in the present case. Economic planning means a shaping of all economic activities into "group-defined spheres of action which are rationally mapped out and fitted, as parts of a mosaic, into a coordinated whole, for the purpose of achieving certain rationally conceived and socially comprehensive goals."[4] The unique connotation that the socialist ascribes to this definition is his insistence that only under a socialized economy can real economic planning take place. Plans can be drawn up by agencies lacking economic power, but unless they coincide with what the real decision makers already wish to do (in which case no "plan" would be necessary), they serve roughly the same purpose as stamping one's foot in the airport to make the plane come sooner. According to socialists, the necessary prerequisite for planning and control over the disposition of capital goods can arise only within the context of ownership by government.

Socialists believe that economic planning can improve upon the performance of free-market capitalism in two important ways. First, they count on being able to achieve a steady rate of economic growth while smoothing out the capitalist business cycles of boom or bust. In so doing, they hope virtually to banish what is regarded as the most debilitating failure of the capitalist system—the periodic inability to provide steady work for all who wish to be employed. This might be accomplished in several ways: The government could serve as an "employer of last resort," thus guaranteeing everyone a job and creating aggregate demand through the purchasing power of previously unemployed persons; the reduction of excess industrial capacity through coordinated planning would eliminate much of the waste of resources observed in the capitalist economy; the ability to channel resources into the "starved" public sector would stimulate additional output and employment.

The second area of anticipated improvement is in treating certain nonmarket costs and benefits from the standpoint of social welfare. The classic example is smoke, which unavoidably accompanies the operation of a factory; the factory need take no cognizance of the damages its smoke may cause to others because there is generally no legal or market mech-

[4]W. N. Loucks, "Economic Planning," in *Annals of the American Academy of Political and Social Science*, July 1932, p. 114.

anism by which the injured party can be compensated for the cleaning expenses or other costs he incurs. Socialists claim that economic planners would be in a position to weigh the benefits of the factory's output versus the social costs created by the smoke. We will discover later that incorporating social costs into the planning framework involves grave theoretical and practical difficulties, but the desirability of attempting to do so is apparent to anyone who experiences the myriad social interdependencies of an urbanized industrial society.

Reduction of Inequality

As specific socialist goals were in the process of being reached, according to the socialists, social and economic inequality would be progressively diminished. By nationalizing ownership of capital goods and thereby preventing them from being passed on through the capitalist institution of inheritance, the socialist government would be abolishing one major cause of income inequality—widely disparate holdings of income-producing property. Moreover, the achievement of full employment and the creation of meaningful economic opportunity for all, which socialists foresee, would further reduce obstacles in the path of equality.

When the socialist castigates capitalism for creating inequality, he does not mean that under socialism there would be no inequality at all. The goal of socialism is the "minimum of inequality that is workable if human beings are actively to use their talents; not equal shares, but fair shares; not equality, but social justice."[5] In the case of earned incomes, reduction of inequality means the existence of wage and salary differentials big enough only to evoke the necessary productive efforts from individuals by distinguishing among them according to intelligence, effort, and productivity.

Changing Human Attitudes and Behavior

Education is of vital interest to the socialist because he sees little hope that the system will work in the absence of changed human behavior. He reminds himself that the mechanical aspects of socialism—nationalization and planning, especially— will not in and of themselves ensure its success. Part of the process of education would be directed toward providing true equality of occupational opportunities by abolishing class barriers and financial restrictions; attention would also focus on consumer education. Equality of opportunity must be accompanied by an enlightened citizenry.

The broader goal of education in a socialist system is to create an altered mental outlook to heighten the social consciousness of individuals. Mature human behavior is the product of two sets of forces—one inborn,

[5]Jay, p. 9.

the other environmental; the relative importance of each has been debated endlessly. The socialist points out, however, that the institutions of capitalism favor above all the development of self-centered, acquisitive traits. Defenders of capitalism view those same characteristics as the chief motivating factors behind capitalist production. The socialist concludes that a different set of legal and economic institutions could conceivably produce individuals with fewer and milder acquisitive traits without destroying personal economic incentives to engage in productive activity.[6] For anyone raised in a capitalist society, it is an interesting intellectual exercise to question how much of his skepticism about the potential for change in human attitudes under socialism is itself the product of living in a capitalist milieu.

The socialist believes that human beings would have to learn to live and think differently under socialism because the future society would require such change. For the first time the personal rewards of the individual would include betterment of the entire society of which he is an integral part. Qualities of mutual trust, brotherly love and identification of self with the common good, the socialist admits, are absolutely necessary to the success of socialism if it is to escape the fate of capitalism—exaggerated individualism or, "to each according to what he can grab." It would be the goal of the educational system to develop as second nature a public conscience in the individual to complement his personal desires.

We will study the economic aspects of the socialist system more closely before proceeding to a detailed critique of the claims and goals of socialism that we have listed in this chapter.

QUESTIONS FOR CLASS DISCUSSION

1. What are the essential ingredients of an adequate and correct definition of socialism?

2. In what sense is the heart of socialism economic in character?

3. How is socialism sometimes confused with other movements or ideas that are not essentially socialistic? Give examples.

4. How does socialism differ from mere government ownership and operation of industry?

5. How may socialism be distinguished from communism?

6. What is the focus of the attack that socialists make on capitalism?

7. Why do socialists reject the idea that whatever socialism could achieve can be achieved through capitalism by adopting Keynesian methods?

8. What major shift in the current allocation of productive resources in a nation like the United States does socialism advocate?

[6]See David C. McClelland, *The Achieving Society*, New York: Free Press, 1967, for an interesting attempt to study entrepreneurial motivation cross-culturally.

9. Is the socialist concerned about noneconomic aspects of a society in which the economy is capitalistic? Give examples.

10. In what sense does socialism adopt an idealistic vision of the future for Western nations?

11. Do socialists propose a gradual or a sudden changeover from capitalism to socialism? Why?

12. Socialists imply that only in a socialized economy can true and successful economic planning occur. Why?

13. What does it mean to say that a socialist economy would be more cognizant than a capitalist system of the social costs of production?

14. How do the socialists propose to reduce economic inequality?

15. Does the socialist contend that it is possible through socialism to change human psychological traits?

11. The operation of a socialist economy

Any economic system must decide how to approach inevitable economic choices concerning production, technology, and income distribution. This chapter will deal with theoretical models of a socialist economy and with practical problems that an actual regime would be forced to consider. These are vital issues that must be treated before a wide-ranging critique of socialism can be made.

It will be recalled that our discussion of capitalism began with an abstract idealized version in which perfect competition prevailed, in which all prices were flexible, and in which all factors of production were rewarded according to their contribution to the productive process. These conditions have never occurred fully in the real world, but the pure model of capitalism proved useful because it enabled us to see the resulting harmony of the entire system if market prices were given full rein.

The operation of the capitalist model resulted in a set of prices and quantities for each of the product and factor markets in the system. Our goal is to establish a corresponding model for socialism. If, in the process of manipulating prices and quantities under socialism, behavior in each individual market corresponds to that under capitalism, then the abstract socialist model is equally as efficient or optimal as the theoretical model of capitalism.

ECONOMIC MODELS OF SOCIALISM

Price-Directed Socialism

One of the classic disputes in the history of economics centers on the question of whether rational economic choices could conceivably result from the functioning of a socialist economy. Several possible schemes have been developed, the best known of which is often called Lange socialism in honor of its author.[1] Imagine a socialist economy allowing consumer and occupational freedom of choice and possessing the same resource endowment and structure of firms as an equivalent capitalist economy. Since the capitalist model assumes the costless entry and exit of firms in any industry, the socialist model does also. Instead of a free market setting prices, there is a Central Planning Board that establishes the prevailing price for each *commodity* and *factor of production*. These prices serve as guides for consumers and suppliers of labor in freely choosing what to consume and which job to take; they also aid the manager of each socialist firm in deciding which goods to produce and which mix of productive factors (hence, which technology) to use in producing them.

Each socialist manager is an employee of the state, and the state supplies him with a set of rules that he must follow in making decisions concerning his establishment. The rules are threefold: (1) Figure out how to produce each quantity of your product or products as cheaply as possible on the basis of *factor* prices existing at any given moment. (2) Choose to produce the *specific* quantity for which the additional cost of making the last unit just equals the existing price for that *commodity*. (3) Ignore all opportunity for monopoly gains. The first two rules are identical with those the manager of a perfectly competitive capitalist firm uses to maximize his profits. The third makes doubly certain that the distorting effects of monopoly power remain absent.

The Central Planning Board is looking for a set of equilibrium prices that, once established, could continue unchanged until demand patterns or occupation preferences shift. The question is how to achieve a set of consistent equilibrium prices. Lange's answer was that a series of *trial-and-*

[1]Oskar Lange in B. E. Lippincott, ed., *On the Economic Theory of Socialism*, New York: McGraw-Hill, 1964.

error operations by the planning board could approach closer and closer to the ideal pattern. The key indicator in this adjustment would be the level of inventories in each market.

If undesired inventory buildup was observed, a downward adjustment in prices would reduce current output as managers eliminated high-cost production and simultaneously encourage greater current consumption at the more attractive price. On the other hand, higher prices would offset depletion of the inventory pool by turning up the production spigot while partially blocking the consumption drain. An identical procedure would prevail for each type of employment, although a lag between wage changes and the shift of workers into or out of particular occupations would undoubtedly exist.

The Central Planning Board would also be charged with establishing the rental charge for the use of socialized land and the interest charge for the use of money capital by firms to expand their productive capacity. In both cases the object would be the same—to set the price so as to clear the factor market. This calculation is of crucial importance in the capital market, where the short-run decision of disposing of an arbitrarily determined amount of capital gives way in the long run to a choice of how much to set aside for future growth in the economy and how much to allocate for current consumption. This so-called social dividend, consisting of returns to factors of production that would be privately owned in a capitalist system, is what the socialist regards as the main economic benefit of socialism. Part of it would be plowed back into capital investment for future growth, part would be returned to the population in equal per-capita shares, and part would provide for public goods such as the educational system or a symphony orchestra.

The point of this lengthy intellectual exercise is not that Lange socialism would operate easily in the real world. (A change in one market, for instance, would throw the whole system out of equilibrium.) Rather, the claim is that this system, *in theory*, can accomplish everything that the abstract model of capitalism accomplishes *in theory*, with the additional benefit of having the social dividend available to reduce income equality and to ensure the provision of public goods. Lange's system, in short, allows a set of equilibrium prices to achieve socialist goals without reliance on the profit motive as a source of economic incentives.

Critics of Lange generally concede the validity of his claim that it is theoretically possible for rational economic calculation to occur in a socialist economy. They argue, however, that the complexities of market interactions, the problems of data collection, and the human limitations of the members of the planning agency would create insurmountable obstacles to the actual operation of price-directed socialism. The development of modern computers makes that objection somewhat less compelling, although it is interesting to note that no modern socialist nation has actually attempted a planning strategy based entirely on Lange's model. The criticism that efficient social planning is *impractical* must be recognized as a retreat from the original position that such planning is theoretically impossible.

Quantity-Directed Socialism

The institutional arrangements described in the preceding section made it unnecessary for the central pricing agency directly to order correct levels of output in each firm, because the guidelines for managers indicated the proper decisions, once prices were established. An alternative scheme for operating a socialist economy involves the direct determination of physical quantities to be produced in each industry, without major reliance on prices as a planning tool. This is the method of input-output analysis that was developed by Professor Wassily Leontief of Harvard University.[2]

Input-output economics establishes a framework for describing an entire economy and then draws further conclusions from the economic relationships observed. Table 1 shows a four-sector division (agriculture, mining, manufacturing, and services) of the United States economy in 1899; input-output tables with up to 500 sectors have been constructed. The table is a two-way classification of quantities of sales (reading across rows) or quantities of purchases (reading down columns) of each sector when measured in billion-dollar units. Value added is the sum of factor payments—wages, interest, profits—made by each sector; final demand consists of sales to ultimate consumers, who account for the national product of the economy.

Final demand may be thought of as what is "left over" out of total production after the raw materials needed to make goods and services

[2]Wassily Leontief, *Input-Output Economics*, New York: Oxford University Press, 1966.

TABLE 1. U.S. INPUT-OUTPUT TABLE FOR 1899 (in billions of dollars)

		PURCHASES				
		AGRICUL-TURE	MINING	MANU-FACTURING	SERVICES	FINAL DEMAND	TOTAL OUTPUT
Sales	Agriculture	1.39	0.00	1.89	0.03	1.45	4.76
	Mining	0.00	0.04	0.34	0.05	0.18	0.61
	Manufacturing	0.30	0.06	3.63	0.85	6.93	11.77
	Services	0.41	0.06	1.21	2.00	8.21	11.89
	Value Added	2.66	0.45	4.70	8.96	16.77	—
	Total Output	4.76	0.61	11.77	11.89	—	29.03

Based on data in W. G. Whitney, *The Structure of the American Economy in the Late Nineteenth Century* (unpublished doctoral dissertation, Harvard University).

have been set aside. A more interesting problem is created when the situation is viewed the other way around: If one desired the economy to produce a specified level of final-demand goods in each sector, how much total output would satisfy both the final-demand goals and the raw-material requirements for the production process to operate? An answer to this question can be obtained if we make the crucial assumption that the relationship between raw materials and total output observed in each column remains constant for other levels of output—that is, twice as much output requires exactly twice as much in purchases of raw materials from each sector, and so forth. Using this assumption of constant returns to scale, a modern computer is easily programmed to find the required level of total output in each sector to fulfill a desired pattern of final demand; the arithmetic is simply a bigger version of the two equations, two unknowns type of problem solved by students in introductory algebra.

The object of input-output economics is to derive a *consistent* plan, one in which no bottlenecks or superfluous raw materials appear. The materials-balancing planning process used in the Soviet Union has been shown to reach substantially the same results as would be calculated by an input-output model.[3] Input-output planning is carried out in terms of physical quantities as measured by some set of fixed accounting prices. These are not scarcity prices such as operate in the models of purely competitive capitalism and Lange socialism to adjust production to consumer preferences and alter technology in reaction to changes in relative factor prices. Socialist planners assert that individual preferences do not adequately reflect social needs and that opportunities to substitute one factor for another are very limited in the real world. The fact remains that price-directed socialism produces optimal results in theory, while quantity-directed socialism does not.

The application of input-output analysis is not limited to centrally planned economies. Capitalist nations have found it a useful technique to study the possible economic impact of disarmament, trade liberalization, or future population growth. The American business community has come to rely increasingly on input-output projections to estimate marketing opportunities for the products of individual sectors. Such projections have also proved helpful to underdeveloped nations in assuring an adequate supply of raw materials to achieve development targets.

PRACTICAL PROBLEMS OF SOCIALISM

Socialists dare not congratulate themselves on overcoming *theoretical* difficulties, for they know that the application of socialist models to real-

[3]Herbert S. Levin, "Input-Output Analysis and Soviet Planning," *American Economic Review*, May 1962, pp. 127–137.

world circumstances would immediately uncover complex practical problems. Intellectual honesty requires that those who criticize capitalism because it does not conform *in fact* to the ideal of free-market theory be equally willing to submit their ideal economic model to the same test.

The Transition Period

The first problem focuses on the pattern of institutional changes that would prevail in the period between the initial rise to power of a socialist regime and the time when the last vestiges of capitalism disappear so that the new society can be judged entirely on its own merits. The transfer of control of the means of production from individuals to society is the first step in the socialist program, but basic questions appear when one inquires into the way this transfer is to be accomplished.

Should the transition be sudden and comprehensive or gradual and fragmentary? The socialist movement has long been split into two schools of thought on this question. The revolutionary socialists hold that it must be sudden; socialist goals, they claim, involve a complete revamping of patterns of economic behavior. Gradual socialization removes the possibility for coordination of the total economy and creates the danger that industries outside the socialized orbit may be able to sabotage the entire planning effort. The evolutionary socialists argue that the skills necessary to operate a completely socialized economy may be absent in the early stages; selective socialization will create opportunities for planners to develop competence. In addition, it is claimed that initial successes on a limited scale will have a beneficial impact on public opinion, thus creating a more favorable environment in which to expand the boundaries of the public sector.

Socialists who stop short of outright confiscation of private property face delicate questions about the level and nature of compensation for former owners. Should the former owners of producers' goods be compensated for the property shifted to socialized control? Generous provision of nontransferable pensions or long-term bonds means a diversion of funds and the creation of inequality through unearned incomes in a society dedicated to greater equality. Meager compensation, on the other hand, would lead to the alienation of owners who possess vital management skills that could perhaps be utilized by the new regime. The issue of compensation is likely to be settled on the basis of judgments of immediate needs rather than by provoking arbitrary ideological slogans. As such, it will probably involve a compromise position of partial compensation.

The Forms of Social Organization

It is widely believed that title to socialized producers' goods would be vested in the central government and probably in some agency of that government created for the purpose of owning and operating *all* socialized industries. The actual plans of socialism do not warrant this interpretation; ownership by *society as a whole* does not necessarily imply a single agency of society. The specific institutional form of socialized ownership would probably attempt to incorporate the two ideals of efficient operation and responsiveness to public welfare.

The industrial groups could be incorporated directly into the political process, for example, as in the case of the ministry of transportation in a parliamentary government. The minister would be a political official and hence, supposedly, attuned to the political wishes of the electorate. The expression of economic preferences in such a system is a very complex matter of open channels of communication, which often exist more in theory than in practice. In addition, the danger of "meddling" in economic matters for political ends by elected politicians exists when socialized industries are enmeshed with political institutions.

An alternative form of organization for large-scale units closely resembles that of the modern corporation in our present economy. A central management staff of technical experts would be charged with making day-to-day decisions for the industry, free from outside political interference. In the place of a board of directors as a broad *policy-making* body, there would be a committee representing consumer, worker, and technical opinion. This group would formulate policy on major issues, leaving the translation of policy into action to the professional managers.

A third form of organization disperses the control of producing units to cooperative associations of workers or consumers. The basic features of such cooperatives would be the autonomy of decision making by the members themselves and control over proceeds from current operations for future expansion or bonus payments to supplement current income. This form of organization is thought to provide maximum incentives for high productivity at the expense of fragmenting control of the overall direction in which the economy will proceed.

It is apparent from the preceding discussion that no single form of organization can simultaneously achieve all the goals of a socialized economy. The potential conflict between narrow criteria of efficiency and preservation of the consumer's freedom of choice is but one of the problems that must be settled in a less-than-optimal manner.

Labor Incentives

No question is put to the socialist more often than this one: "How would you get people to work under socialism?" The questioner is certain of the impracticability of socialism when he gets this reply: "Much as you do under capitalism." The answer is sincerely given; the modifications proposed by modern socialists would directly affect only a small portion of the gainfully employed population, and the effect on this group would be less than is often supposed. The basic reason for this has already been stated: The socialists do not desire complete economic equality, but instead advocate the degree of inequality necessary to spur individuals to exert their best efforts. This is coupled with the promise that the inequality arising from unearned incomes under capitalism will be abolished.

The socialist prefaces his program by pointing out that an overwhelming portion of the mental and physical effort put into capitalist production is *not* induced by the profit motive. Only the "enterprisers" are so motivated; the wage-worker group extends from the assembly line through the managers and research workers who hold the keys to current and future industrial development. The growing dominance of the large corporate business unit creates a strong tendency for the entrepreneurial function to be centered in a small group of salaried managers.

Socialists contend that the basic stimulus with which capitalism motivates *employees* is fear—fear of declining living standards and, in some cases, of reduced ability to subsist. The socialist would substitute a combination of wage differentials, piecework rates, and bonuses as inducements to productive effort within an environment of reduced economic insecurity.

The socialist places greater reliance on noneconomic incentives than exists under capitalism. In part, this source of motivation would stem from the education of citizens to appreciate social values. However, the socialist also foresees some use for the system of rewards used under capitalism. For example, socialists claim that high executives in private industry are motivated partly by desire for power, by the excitement of "playing the game" of management, or by the desire to acquire honor or prestige. The executive's salary is important in itself, but it also represents a scorecard that measures success. Far-sighted executives, like hard-hitting shortstops and fearless steeplejacks, would still be highly rewarded under socialism because they would still be in limited supply. The point is that noneconomic incentives can conceivably play a large role in bringing forth the creative talents and specialized skills essential for the operation of a socialist economy.

Critics of socialism often imply that a transition from capitalism to socialism would destroy or reduce the existing body of technical knowledge used in the management of industrial firms. Socialists find no reason to believe this is true. The technical expertise required to operate the banking system or steel industry, for instance, would not change appreciably under socialism, and socialists would have every reason to preserve and protect banking experts and steel technicians during a transition to socialism.

Government Under Socialism

Socialism assumes the existence of organized government, and the socialist declares forcefully that he believes in democracy. True political democracy, it is claimed, must begin with *economic democracy*—the social ownership of capital goods. Socialists place major emphasis on the legislative branch of government because in their view true democracy must include not only democratic enactment of laws but also *direct* democratic control over how they are interpreted and carried out.

The reliance on democratic institutions can present interesting problems for a socialist government. Often such governments are elected with members of labor unions providing the most important bloc of political support. Once major industries are socialized, however, the government faces the necessity of reaching labor settlements with the very unions that helped bring the government to power. The dilemma of trying to deny wage increases to workers for economic reasons while asking the same workers what benefits they want their democratic socialist government to provide has comic overtones.

The problem of bureaucracy often arises in discussions of government under socialism. Bureaucracy is inevitable in any organization, if by that term one means the impersonal hierarchy of command and the standardized set of rules and procedures that arise whenever the scale of an institutional arrangement, private or public, exceeds the administrative capacity of a single head. The term *bureaucracy* means little so far as the technical structure of government goes; its antisocial potentials become significant only when powerful public agencies fail to reflect enlightened popular will. The charge of bureaucracy more often is meant to convey an image of low productivity, low morale, and fanatical concern for petty regulations on the part of employees of nonprofit organizations. We will return to the issue of attitudes under socialism in the next chapter; it is sufficient at this point to recognize that the question of incentives provided for high-quality work within government agencies is of crucial importance in a society that plans to make such agencies the center of economic decision making.

The socialization of industry would, of course, automatically eliminate most of the pressure on each individual concern to search for and adopt new technical improvements. The social-planning agency would thus be forced to work out plans for the installation of new processes as an integral part of an industrial plan for the entire economy. The socialist contends that the profit motive in private "oligopolistic" industries freqently leads to the suppression of innovations to protect current profits or capital values; he therefore believes that socialism would be more open to new technology. It is important to note that the research laboratories of large American corporations appear to be a continuing source of economic and scientific innovation despite the prediction of one astute observer that the "routinization" of corporate research in formal organizations would eventually dry up the flow of new discoveries and thus cause the downfall of capitalism.[4] The socialist is confident that the mixture of in-

---

[4] Joseph Schumpeter, *Capitalism, Socialism, and Democracy,* New York: Harper & Row, 1942.

tellectual curiosity and desire for recognition that spurs the scientist could ensure that the stimulation to do research and to invent would not be lacking, despite the absence of the private-profit motive in a socialist economy.

In presenting this list of potential problems to be faced in a socialist economy, we have implicitly suggested that acceptable solutions might not be available. These potential stumbling blocks will be considered in the following chapter in the context of an overall critique of a socialist system.

QUESTIONS FOR CLASS DISCUSSION

1. When the socialist discusses the new socialist economy, does he have an abstract model that is equally as efficient as that of pure capitalism?

2. What line of reasoning is followed by some critics of socialism, who contend that under a fully socialized economy rational choices in the allocation of productive resources would not be possible?

3. How do socialists propose to use a pricing system in the direction of productive activity in a socialist economy?

4. Under such a pricing system, what would be the functions and responsibilities of a Central Planning Board? What would it use to guide the socialist economy to a proper allocation of productive resources among their several uses?

5. Is there any question as to the practical possibility of using a pricing system such as Oskar Lange has proposed? Would its practicability be greater today than it was 50 years ago?

6 Under the Lange proposals, what guides for decision making would be available to managers of socialist industrial enterprises?

7. How does an input-output basis for operating a socialist economy differ from the Lange proposals? Would it be more or less reflective of social needs?

8. How does socialism answer the question of whether a transition from capitalism to socialism should be sudden and full or on a gradual, step-by-step basis?

9. Socialism would involve formerly privately owned producers' goods being transferred in ownership to the government—how do socialists propose to effect this?

10. As the socialist uses the phrase, what does "ownership by society" mean?

11. How does the socialist propose to bring incentives to bear upon the laborer, inducing him to work as hard and as skillfully as possible, in a socialist system?

12. How does the socialist answer charges that socialism would bring debilitating bureaucracy into government and industry?

12. A critique of socialism

Modern socialism has advanced beyond the patchwork of anticapitalist animosities, utopian proposals, and romantic hopes that distinguished early socialist schemes. Probably no other type of economic system, including capitalism and Marxian communism, has constructed for itself a theory that covers such a wide range of social phenomena.

It is toward a critique of socialist theory that this chapter is directed, rather than toward criticism of minute details of some administrative plan or political platform. The socialist blueprint does not extend to the level of detailed programs because, the socialist claims, desirable changes in society are not necessarily hastened by concern over questions of organizational form, which in any case would vary greatly according to the circumstances prevailing when the socialist government assumed power.

The intermediate ground between abstract socialist theory and meticulous operational plans represents a fair arena for considering the validity of socialist claims. If serious defects appear in parts of the theoretical structure, it is unlikely that any degree of administrative juggling could overcome those faults; if, on the other hand, other proposals appear practicable in theory, then the subsequent chapters, which survey the actual operations of socialist economic systems, should give an accurate view of how such factors work in the real world. Before we can get down to a basic analysis of socialism, however, we must dispose of several superficial criticisms.

SUPERFICIAL CRITICISMS

The claim that the advocate of socialism is merely interested in bettering himself at the expense of others who are more successful under capitalism is as flimsy as the parallel contention that all defenders of capitalism are simply protecting their own vested interests. The challenge that the socialist immediately relinquish any personal property he might possess to prove his sincerity is equivalent to testing the sincerity of the ardent Republican or Democrat by his willingness to contribute his personal fortune to the party campaign chest. The only objective proof of the sincerity of the wealthy advocate of socialism is his willingness to accept a reduction in his own standard of living *after* the entire system has been socialized, and there is no way in which this test can be applied before the advent of socialism.

Defenders of capitalism often charge that socialists fail to recognize gains under capitalism that make socialism unnecessary. This sort of criticism is considered superficial, not because its claim to progress under capitalism is unfounded but because it fails to meet the major point of socialism that, *whatever* the record of economic progress under capitalism, the existence of private property and the profit motive inherently limit the potential of capitalism to serve human needs in an adequate way.

Finally, the epithet "un-American" has often been applied to socialism. In its most superficial sense, this criticism means nothing more than that the person making it does not like socialism. Few American institutions, not excepting the major forms of religious observance and our system of common law, lack foreign roots; ideas, like people, deserve to be judged on their intrinsic merits rather than according to their country of origin. Slogans are not an adequate substitute for honest evaluation.

BASIC CRITICISMS

Turning from these superficial arguments against socialism, we can cite several basic criticisms of socialist programs. As with capitalism, there are theoretical problems involved in the operation of a socialist order that go to the heart of the economic process and thus far have not been solved satisfactorily by the proponents of socialism. In attempting to devise solutions for each of these problems, moreover, socialists often become entrapped in basic inconsistencies that prevent the simultaneous attainment of multiple goals.

Difficulties of Pricing

Although the model of Lange socialism operates efficiently in theory, the actual implementation of a socialist economy using centrally established prices for all commodities and factors of production is an overwhelming administrative task. Trial-and-error adjustment of prices in each market would require the planners to know which markets would be most affected by demand shifts in a given portion of the economy. Carried one step further, this knowledge implies the previous existence of a complete mathematical model of the entire economy. The capacity of modern computers is perhaps approaching the point at which such disaggregated models are within the realm of possibility, but the immense flow of high-quality economic data that would be required to create and sustain such a system would undoubtedly divert a substantial share of the work force away from the production of goods and services for final consumers.

Even if a functioning system of prices could be established in a socialist economy, the ability claimed by the socialist to cope with externalities (the smoking factory, for instance) may prove as illusory as it was under capitalism. If central planners assume responsibility for balancing social costs and benefits, they tremendously complicate the planning process; if they order the manager of each firm to take *social* costs into account when determining his own output, the central planners assume that each unit is aware of its own impact on the economic universe. Either way, dealing with externalities destroys, or at least scrambles the economic signals with which price-directed socialism is supposed to guide the allocation of resources.

The pricing process in a socialist economy that does not use scarcity prices is also subject to criticism. In this situation, production targets are determined on the basis of input-output models or other methods of physical planning. Prices still have a place in such an economy, but it is the role of "clearing" a market once the level of output in it has *already* been determined by fiat, rather than the role of pointing out shifts in consumer demand. The socialist planner may congratulate himself on choosing high enough prices to adjust quantity demand to supply available, but he should remember that consumer sovereignty means more than the passive acts of consumers to make the best of an unappealing menu of choices. Economic democracy is not achieved unless consumers' preferences count in determining output in the first place.

Difficulties of Economic Coordination

It has been boasted that socialist planners will have the breadth of vision and the practical means to achieve greater economic coordination than is possible under oligopolistic capitalism. This claim implies a considerable degree of centralization in socialist planning machinery. The ability to view the total situation is achieved, however, only with the sacrifice of some of the flexibility and familiarity with local conditions that come from assigning decision-making powers to those actually on the scene. It is by no means automatic that overall efficiency would be improved by efforts to build coordination of dissimilar activities explicitly into the planning structure.

The achievement of complete centralization of economic planning is impossible in any modern socialist nation; the task becomes manageable only when responsibility is divided according to economic functon or geographical area. This involves not only the loss of overall direction but the danger that the quest for efficiency at lower levels may result in "suboptimization," which is actually detrimental to the total performance of the economy. For instance, the electric industry, in an effort to cut costs, might choose to generate power with coal as fuel rather than to develop potential hydroelectric power, thus limiting the supply of coal to other industrial uses. If the cost difference in power technology were small, the allocation of coal might not be optimal from a social standpoint. Likewise, maximum development of the trucking industry might create underutilized railroad facilities.

It is apparent that socialists have been overoptimistic regarding the ease with which the benefits of economic coordination could be secured under central planning. The administrative compromises that a socialist regime would have to make in order to function at all would hide many of the opportunities for economic integration that capitalism is blamed for overlooking.

Morale and Competence

All of the socialist disclaimers to the contrary cannot erase the critic's suspicion that it could easily bog down in a morass of low morale, inefficiency, and red tape. There is no inherent reason why a sense of pride and professionalism would not be found at all levels of administrative responsibility in a socialist government; indeed, during the transition phase the excitement of building institutions anew and perhaps the existence of a charismatic leader might provide the kind of intellectual ferment that challenges people to put forth their best efforts. The main question, however, concerns the staying power of ideological zeal as a motivating factor. As our New England forefathers discovered, is it difficult to pass a vision on to succeeding generations.

In a technocracy occupational groups may form standards of professional competence, one possible way of establishing norms within the civil service. This requires that government service itself must not be used as a social-welfare program to provide employment for excess workers or as a sinecure for those of mediocre talents. Evidence suggests that both socialist and capitalist bureaucracies face these temptations;[1] the seriousness of poor performance in a socialist bureaucracy is compounded, of course, by the crucial role it plays in the total economy.

THE BASIC INCONSISTENCY
IN THE ECONOMICS OF SOCIALISM

The socialist scheme implicitly suggests that consumers' and workers' choices can be freely and independently made while, at the same time, overall social goals can be imposed by central planners. Whereas in the capitalist economy individual choices are the ultimate variables shaping free-market prices, which direct the economic process, socialism makes the chosen social goals the starting point and sets prices and quantities to achieve those ends. Which set of priorities is better from a strictly ethical point of view is a matter for philosophical debate; the vital distinction is that if comprehensive goals are chosen, individual action must conform to them, whereas if individual actions are left free from the start, no planned social goals will be possible. This is the basic inconsistency in the economics of socialism. The conflict of values is the point of Schumpeter's quip that socialist planners "may still let the comrades choose as they like between peas and beans. They may well hesitate as to milk and whiskey and as to drugs and improvement of housing. And they will not allow comrades to choose between loafing and [building] temples . . ."[2]

Apparently socialists have not fully comprehended this dilemma, or they have tended to avoid discussing it seriously. The socialist rejoinder that neither consumers nor workers are entirely free to make whatever decisions they please under capitalism as it exists confuses the issue by trying to compare the *theory* of socialism with the *practice* of capitalism. The socialist, by his very case, must deal with the *inherent nature* of capitalism in contrast with the *inherent nature* of socialism.

On this plane it becomes clear that capitalism inherently emphasizes individual choices as directing forces in the economy, whereas socialism emphasizes comprehensive goals. If we are to follow the ideas of socialism in this regard, we must expect some deviation from the freedom of individual choice allowed under theoretical capitalism. This freedom, although much qualified in actual life, is apparently highly valued by many

---

[1]Alan Harrington's *Life in the Crystal Palace*, New York: Avon, 1967, presents a startling view of one man's reactions to life in an American corporate bureaucracy.
[2]Joseph Schumpeter, *Capitalism, Socialism, and Democracy,* New York: Harper & Row, p. 184.

toward whom socialist claims are directed. To be consistent, programs of socialism must either cease to promise a continuance and enlargement of individual economic freedom or else successfully demonstrate how that freedom can be preserved in a socialized economy. Modern socialism has, as yet, done neither.

THE GROWING IRRELEVANCE OF NATIONALIZATION

Over the past two decades, democratic socialism has been beset by a dilemma. A significant segment of socialist opinion seems to be deemphasizing the orthodox concern with socializing all large-scale industry in favor of investigating the use of economic power by governmental authorities to achieve comprehensive social controls while preserving the institution of private property.[3]

The reason for this doctrinal shift is twofold. First, and most important, the economic resurgence of basically capitalistic economies in Western Europe has (at least for the time being) disarmed traditional socialist appeals at a time when workers are enjoying rising living standards. Second, actual nationalization in Britain and France have not, for many reasons, yielded the results predicted by their early advocates. Specifically, government-operated industries that incur financial deficits must ultimately be supported by tax revenues. It has thus become an electoral risk for socialists to advocate nationalizations that voters may feel will simply raise their own tax obligations.

The alternatives offered by the "revisionist" socialists are related to the concept of the "mixed economy" in which public and private sectors coexist, with the public sector formulating a plan that includes social controls over private industry and greater attention to public goods consumed by all. The general approach is one of pragmatic reform, with the public takeover of industry proceeding only in selected instances where other avenues of control have been exhausted.

Even such modest aims raise major questions about the minimum boundaries of the nationalized sector and the nature of the social controls exerted over the private sector. It is far from certain that socialists are prepared to face these issues squarely, but the broader scope of topics included under the socialist agenda indicates that nationalization is only the first among many possible forms of economic planning in the modern world.

The organization of Part V gives cognizance to these developments that blur the distinctions between the institutional structures appropriate

[3]See, for instance, Douglas Jay, *Socialism in the New Society*, New York: McKay, 1962, and C. A. R. Crosland, *The Future of Socialism*, London: Cape, 1956.

to capitalist and to socialist economic systems. Economic planning can occur in nations located at all points on the ideological compass.

QUESTIONS FOR CLASS DISCUSSION

1. Why should an evaluation of socialism deal particularly with the ground between abstract socialist theory and meticulous plans put forth by socialists?

2. Why is it valid to dismiss categorically certain commonly expressed criticisms of socialism?

3. What, according to socialists, ultimately limits any economic progress made under capitalism? Why?

4. Do the various theories and proposals of socialists completely avoid inconsistencies? If not, why should anyone seriously consider them?

5. Insofar as socialists propose centrally established prices for all commodities and productive factors, what valid question can be raised about socialism?

6. What specific, detailed problems would arise in an attempt to set such centrally established prices in a socialist economy?

7. If central planners under socialism attempt to have social costs calculated into production costs of goods produced, what problems arise?

8. Under socialism, is there any danger that centrally set prices may fail to reflect shifts in consumer demand? If so, is this a weakness of socialist pricing? How do socialists answer this question?

9. Would a socialist administration face the problem of how centralized or decentralized the pricing of goods should be? In this connection, what is the danger of possible "suboptimization"?

10. Could a socialist economic administration be assisted by professionalization of administrative responsibilities? Give examples. What would be necessary to make this feasible?

11. Does the socialist face a real, or only an apparent, dilemma when he promises both autonomy for consumers' and workers' choices *and* achievement of overall planned goals? Is it adequate for the socialist to point to the fact that autonomy of consumers' and workers' choices is not fully realized under capitalism?

12. Would it be logical for socialists to concede that the benefits of central planning and goal setting would to some degree be offset by impairment of the autonomy of consumer and worker choices in a socialist society?

13. Why has modern democratic socialism placed less emphasis on the nationalization of one industry after another in recent years?

SUGGESTED SUBJECTS FOR STUDENT REPORTS FOR PART IV

1. An evaluation of the most valid and the least valid, socialist attacks on capitalism.

2. How the development of macroeconomics has affected the theory of socialism.

3. How the development of econometrics and mathematical economics has affected pricing as a central problem of theoretical socialism.

4. Utopianism as a forerunner of modern theories of socialism.

5. An assessment of the strengths and weaknesses of current socialist parties in the Western world.

6. A review of the history of the Socialist Party of the United States.

7. The attitude of modern socialist theory on inequality of incomes.

8. An evaluation of the history of the Tennessee Valley Authority relative to socialist theory.

9. Arguments *pro* and *con* the proposition that true economic planning can be successful only in a nation with a predominantly socialist economy.

10. A detailed analysis of one of the pricing systems proposed for a socialist economy.

11. Select some important American industry; assume it is to become owned and operated by the government; outline a specific plan for compensating its private owners.

12. Modern psychology's impact on socialist ideas that non-economic incentives to work should be emphasized more than they are under capitalism.

13. The idea of Joseph Schumpeter on the sources of technological advance and the relation of socialism to it.

SUGGESTIONS FOR FURTHER READING FOR PART IV

Allen, R.V., et al., *Democracy and Communism: Theory and Action,* Princeton, N.J.: Van Nostrand Reinhold, 1967.

Cole, G. D. H., *Socialist Economics,* London: Gollancz, 1950.

Crosland, C. A. R., *The Future of Socialism,* London: Cape, 1956.

Davis, H. B., *Nationalism and Socialism,* New York: Monthly Review Press, 1967.

Dickinson, H. D., *The Economics of Socialism,* London: Oxford University Press, 1939.

Dobb, M., *On Economic Theory and Socialism,* London: Routledge & Kegan Paul, 1955.

Feinstein, C. H., *Socialism, Capitalism and Economic Growth,* London: Cambridge University Press, 1967.

Hall, R. L., *The Economic System in a Socialist State,* New York: Russell & Russell, 1967.

Hayek, F. A., von, ed., *Collectivist Economic Planning,* London: Routledge & Kegan Paul, 1935.

Jay, D., *Socialism in the New Society,* New York: McKay, 1962.

Lerner, A. P., *The Economics of Control,* New York: Macmillan, 1944.

Lippincott, B. E., ed., *On the Economic Theory of Socialism*, New
    York: McGraw-Hill, 1964.
Mises, L. von, *Socialism—An Economic and Sociological Analysis,*
    New Haven, Conn.: Yale University Press, 1951.
Radice, G., *Democratic Socialism*, London: Longmans, 1965.
Schumpeter, J. A., *Capitalism, Socialism and Democracy*, New York:
    Harper & Row, 1942.
Sombart, W., *Socialism and the Social Movement*, New York:
    Augustus M. Kelley, 1968.
Sweezy, P. M., *Socialism*, New York: McGraw-Hill, 1949.
Tugan-Baranouski, M. I., *Modern Socialism in Its Historical Development,*
    New York: Russell & Russell, 1966.
Ward, B. N., *The Socialist Economy—A Study of Organization
    Alternatives*, New York: Random House, 1967.
Wiles, P., *The Political Economy of Communism*, Cambridge, Mass.:
    Harvard University Press, 1962.

PART V:
TYPES OF
ECONOMIC PLANNING

13. British nationalized industry

To understand democratic socialism, it is illuminating to study the practical application of socialist reform in a specific free-enterprise economy. The post-World War II program of nationalization of basic industries carried out by the British government offers an excellent example. Within a relatively few years—1945 to 1951, when the Labour Party was in power—a large and strategically important sector of the British economy was nationalized: central banking, coal, gas, electric power, transportation, communciations, and steel. These industries today employ over 1.25 million workers and account for 10 percent of Britain's gross domestic product. Along with these measures came extensions of welfare schemes such as the National Health Service and economic planning and controls that brought major changes in the British economy and in the daily life of British citizens.

Perhaps the most interesting aspect of these economic experiments is not their drastic nature but rather how quickly they became an integral part of the overall economic system. Through two complete swings of the political pendulum—Labour (1945–1951) to Conservative (1951–1964), back to Labour (1964–1970), and return to Conservative rule in 1970—only the steel industry was a subject for debate over the merits of continued nationalization. There may be shadings of emphasis depending on which party is in power, but to a major extent policy decisions affecting the nationalized sector are today largely outside partisan politics.

The creation of the British Labour Party at the turn of the century was intimately connected with both unionism and socialism. In 1918, the Party formally adopted a socialist-oriented constitution, and public ownership of key industries has remained as a cornerstone of ideology and policy ever since. In the 1930s, comprehensive economic planning was added to the ideological tool kit in order to coordinate nationalized industries and achieve overall economic balance.

Nationalization was only one plank of the election platform that swept the Labour Party to an overwhelming parliamentary victory in 1945. The list of industries meeting the "test of national service" criteria for social ownership was pragmatically arrived at in two senses—it reflected what the electorate would support and what economic planners within the party felt capable of managing.

It is important for students of economic systems to understand just how nationalization of basic industries occurred in Great Britain, why particular industries were selected and others left in private hands, how nationalization affected prices and other economic variables, and how the problems of operating nationalized industries were resolved. Each of the industries presented its own unique difficulties, both for the act of nationalization and for subsequent management and operation. We will discuss five—steel, electricity, railways, coal, and gas—that offer a range of fundamental and enlightening experiences. We will choose several areas in which policy decisions were made and then compare the relevant aspects of particular industries in relation to that policy. Beginning with the economic condition of each prior to government ownership, we will continue through decisions concerning transfer of ownership, management and labor policy, and pricing and investment decisions, and conclude with an overall evaluation of the past performance and future prospects of each.

COMPARISON OF KEY NATIONALIZED INDUSTRIES

Physical Condition Prior to Nationalization

The generally run-down state of the industries acquired through the nationalization program of the postwar Labour government must be considered against a background of twentieth-century decay and slow growth for British industry as a whole. The 1920s were marred by low profits and crippling strikes. Although the Great Depression was not as severe in Britain as in the United States (thanks partly to government spending for housing and other municipal improvements), it nevertheless provided little incentive for modernization or expansion within the industrial sector. Finally, World War II brought both a strain on physical capacity and outright destruction by German air raids. Thus there was at least 20 years of catching up to be accomplished at the end of the war, whether a particular industry came under socialized ownership or not.

For many years preceding nationalization, British coal was a sick industry. Between the wars it deteriorated physically, economically, and in morale: Total annual output and exports declined, equipment was obsolete and run-down, output per man-shift and total employment were falling. Absenteeism and wildcat strikes were chronic problems. A variety of subsidy measures represented a history of government involvement. In 1938 the government purchased all coal in the ground but left the mining companies and their equipment privately owned and operated. During World War II the government took "operative control" over the industry as part of the coordinated war effort.

Problems were less pressing, but not absent, in our other examples. In the electricity and gas industries the dual needs of integrating scattered private and municipal plants into a grid to smooth peak load problems and of investing heavily in new capital equipment to meet demand by residential and industrial users provided a rationale for government planning. The profit outlook was sufficiently rosy to point toward the private financial market as a source for needed funds. As in other nationalized industries, an intricate history of increasingly stringent controls preceded the Labour Party's proposal to nationalize the rail, highway, and inland waterway facilities of Great Britain. Wasteful competition between inefficient railroads and the growing trucking industry aroused hopes that government ownership could coordinate them into a rational policy. Unprofitable rail lines would be closed in order to concentrate desperately needed investment on track and rolling stock for a viable railroad network. The government assumed complete control over all transportation during the war and, despite continued deterioration of equipment, demonstrated that output could be significantly increased through coordinated planning.

The British iron and steel industry merits special consideration because of stiff opposition to nationalization by private owners and the lack of agreement within the Labour cabinet concerning the pace and extent of public ownership. Three principal reasons were given for the decision to nationalize: (1) The government would have to provide a large portion of the funds needed for modernization in any case; (2) some central authority would have to oversee decisions on kinds and location of new plant capacity; (3) a continuation of tariff protection and of price fixing by some central authority would create monopolistic control too powerful to reside in private hands. Representatives of the industry refused to smooth the way for nationalization, preferring to hold out for a compromise that left ultimate control over steel production in private hands.

Details of Nationalization Acts

Coal was the first major industry to be nationalized, and the government was anxious that the transition be accomplished to the satisfaction of former owners and the public at large. On January 1, 1947 the government acquired some 1500 collieries plus company-owned villages, thousands of pit ponies, and several hundred thousand coal cars. The government became the employer of roughly 700,000 miners and 25,000 managerial and clerical workers.

Compensation of former owners was based on a "global" hypothetical market value for the entire industry if it had been sold as a unit on the open market, and then divided up on a regional basis among the individual firms that were acquired. Compensation was in the form of government interest-bearing negotiable bonds; former mining companies could thus remain as conduits for paying dividends to their stockholders from the interest stream or else diversity into other economic undertakings. The $600 million paid out as compensation appears, in retrospect, to be a very generous settlement; higher costs of production were inevitable as existing coal veins were exhausted. The share prices of former coal companies actually rose on the London Stock Exchange following nationalization. This represented a public-opinion victory, but also a costly economic burden, for the Labour program.

Compensation for the electricity and gas industries was considerably less complicated because of the large portion already under public (municipal) ownership. In both industries former private owners were given fixed-interest bonds equal to the market value of their securities traded on the London Stock Exchange; local governments were compensated by the Electricity Authority's simply assuming responsibility for interest and sinking-fund charges on debt incurred in constructing and operating generating facilities. The former owners were satisfied with the terms and, in fact, advised the Minister of Power concerning the best form of organization to establish under nationalization. Railways and canals were also acquired for the average market value of their securities on selected dates; privately owned railway cars and long-distance lorries (trucks) were purchased individually for their estimated market value. The settlement was attacked for failing to maintain the income accruing to former owners; but considering the run-down state of the railroads, dividends could not have been maintained. To an outsider, therefore, the compensation scheme appears equitable relative to what the government got for its money.

The uniqueness of the treatment of steel compared with other nationalization measures should be noted carefully. In merely transferring the securities of individual companies to the Iron and Steel Corporation of Great Britain, the steel companies were left intact as individual corporate entities, each retaining its old name, managers, and internal organization. Although compensation was generally accepted as completely fair, the nationalization of steel was a hotly contested issue. The industry's excellent record of output, labor relations, and technological innovation, compared with that of other candidates for government ownership, created doubts whether the public welfare might not suffer from the effects of nationalization.

Administrative Organization and Labor Relations

The organization of economic decision making within the nationalized sector (we will discuss relations between industries and their associated ministries in the next chapter) follows two major patterns: industry-wide management boards with both planning and day-to-day operations within their control and decentralized schemes such as the British Steel Corporation in which regional groups of firms retain some degree of independence.

The basic concept behind the management of nationalized industries is that they should remain free from outside political interference with their day-to-day operations while at the same time being responsible to elected representatives in the House of Commons and the Prime Minister's cabinet for direction in resolving broad policy issues. At the top of each nationalized industry is a professional management board headed by a director. Supervision of individual units is arranged in a hierarchial structure, usually on a geographical basis, which is supposed to ensure that production is organized efficiently and that the proper output mix is achieved. Other forms of administration have been tried, but they often resulted in the local manager receiving conflicting orders from various divisions at the industry level.

The two key questions are the quality of managerial talent that has been recruited for top positions in the nationalized sector and the ability to make complex policy decisions. In earlier years many managers were former executives of private firms whose commitment to public ownership was lukewarm at best; present obstacles to getting superior managers consist largely in the inferior wage and pension arrangements in government service. It is fair to say that the tradition of dedicated civil service prevailing in the Treasury or Diplomatic Corps has not carried over to careers in industrial management. Questions concerning the location of new plants, the closing of obsolete facilities, or pricing structure among competing users often have political overtones that may swamp the economic logic of the situation. Top industry managers are thus sometimes forced to choose between taking a stand for what they believe is right for their industry and what the minister above them regards as politically expedient.

This is nowhere more evident than in the area of labor relations. The state of labor-management relations in the nationalized sector in recent years may be summarized in one word—*terrible!* Within a recent two-year period, crippling strikes or slowdowns by miners, postal workers, blast-furnace operators, dockers, and railroad employees have created genuine hardships in the form of food shortages, power blackouts, and other disruptions. The thought of enduring British winter weather without coal or electric heat, as millions were forced to do during the miners' strike of January 1972, generates chills of sympathy from any American who has lived in England. In that instance, as in many others, the government settled the strike by increasing the subsidy to the affected nationalized industry.

Britain has a long tradition of wildcat strikes and labor disputes. The Industrial Relations Act of 1971 gave the government power to order essential workers back to their jobs, but it is a politically risky matter to invoke a cooling-off period or other forms of intervention. It remains to be seen how effective the act will be in preventing unofficial strikes and official strikes judged to be the result of unfair industrial practices. Even if it does prevent strikes, the Industrial Relations Act will do little to moderate wage demands in the public sector and their consequent inflationary tendencies.

Pricing and Profit Policy

Profits are an indicator of success in a free-enterprise system because the firm has power both to charge as much as possible for its product and to buy its raw materials and factors of production inexpensively if it can. If either condition is violated in a nationalized industry, the profit criterion loses operational significance.

The initial philosophical problem revolves around what should be the profitability target of individual industries under public ownership. Efficient allocation of resources is achieved under the rule of marginal cost pricing, with the government treasury receiving any residual surplus or making up any deficit. Users of peak load services such as gas or electricity would thus be charged a higher rate to cover extra costs of production. Any deviation from the marginal-cost rule results in the misallocation of resources because a more satisfying bundle of output could have been produced.

There are several grounds on which deviations from economic criteria might serve the public interest at the cost of some loss in overall efficiency. Railroad freight rates, for instance, have been kept artificially low in order to lower the costs of producing goods for export. Coal was judged to be such a vital consumer good in postwar Britain that pricing policy subsidized the consumer. The structure of coal prices on varieties suitable for export, industrial use, and home use pose difficult questions of equity and national priorities. In the absence of a binding incomes policy, the Confederation of British Industries (CBI) agreed to a voluntary effort to hold price increases to under 5 percent annually; the *quid pro quo* from the government was to hold prices in the nationalized sector within those limits. As a result, the British Steel Corporation was unable to raise prices to take advantage of rising demand in the early 1970s.

At the same time that revenues were sacrificed because of constraints on pricing policy, government-owned industries also faced intervention on the cost side. One source was the fact that nationalized industries do business with one another so that pricing policy may affect costs somewhere else. This issue of "cross subsidization" might serve to achieve a global maximization of efficiency, but in practice, it serves primarily to arbitrate political disputes between contending regions and occupations. Thus railroad losses are due partially to indirect subsidies for the cost of transporting coal for use in the nationalized electricity and steel industries. The Central Electricity Board calculated that nuclear energy was cheaper than coal for a new generating plant to be built in the heart of the northeast coal field; the Coal Board vigorously protested that miners would be injured by the decision. It appears that many nationalized steel firms would prefer to import semifinished steel for further processing rather than buying the corresponding products produced by domestic firms also under public ownership. Each direct order from above to violate economic rationality sacrifices some measure of accountability for profits.

The most important instance of imposing costs was probably in the area of wage negotiations, where, as mentioned before, nationalized industries were caught between escalating union demands and parliamentary softness when serious work stoppages occurred. Once the public treasury becomes a source of funds for wage increases, there are few institutional constraints to temper wage demands by public employees (a fact, by the way, that American school teachers, policemen, firemen, and civil servants have increasingly recognized).

The way coal was treated set a pattern. Within 24 hours of the news that the Government was giving the coal industry nearly £200m in various forms of cash and a further £60m in higher prices, the steel industry was letting it be known that its losses were running at £120m this year and called for special treatment too. Within 48 hours, the rail unions had turned down offers from British Rail of 8 per cent and then 10 per cent of their earnings and persisted in their own demand for 16 per cent. This, after the 25 per cent rise that the miners won, acknowleges that the railways are already receiving heavy subsidies (which the coal industry was not, at the time of the miners' strike). But it will be extraordinarily hard now for British Rail to convince the men that the cash will not be there for them in the end.[1]

[1]*The Economist*, March 11, 1972, p. 77.

What a far cry these subsidies are from the profit picture that was originally envisioned for the public sector! The general view was that nationalized industries should be able to cover their operating expenses immediately and all expenses, including amortization of long-term debt, in the long run. Initial grants for postwar modernization were to be made directly from the government budget, but even in this respect it was believed that some industries, such as gas and electricity, were sufficiently viable to be able to borrow competitively on the open market to cover investment needs.

Gradually, one by one, the individual components of the public sector slipped below the break-even point until today government *subsidies* amount to approximately 1 percent of gross national product required to produce the 10 percent of total output arising within publicly owned firms. Sound accounting practices would require that losses incurred from uneconomical activities (such as keeping inefficient mines or rail lines open) should be kept separate; as things stand now it is impossible to know what portion of losses arises from hidden subsidies of this kind and what portion from inefficiency in activities in which needed production occurs without adequate attention to opportunities for cost cutting. With only the gas industry currently in the black and airlines and the post office breaking even, there is probably going to be an increase in conclusions like that of *The Economist*: "A restructuring of the whole policy of nationalization is what the Government should be looking into, if it dared."[2]

Output and Investment Policy

Among the policy decisions concerning nationalized industries that have confronted the British government is the rate of growth to be achieved by each component and the requisite investment for meeting the growth target. As previously indicated, the deteriorated state of the coal and railroad industries at the time they were acquired made massive modernization efforts necessary. A 15-year Plan for Coal, announced in 1950, had exhausted its funds by 1956 owing to inflation and failure to recognize the demand for coal and the magnitude of funds needed to produce it efficiently; in spite of large-scale investment, man-year productivity improved little, if at all, as labor troubles continued to mount. A fresh infusion of government funds in 1956 more than doubled the cost of the original program, but productivity continued to lag. Considering the recent discoveries of oil and natural gas in the North Sea, the Conservatives will probably be increasingly prepared to suffer the political uproar of closing obsolete mines rather than sinking additional funds in what appear to be losing ventures.

The original impetus for nationalization of the transportation sector—

the integration of railroads, trucking, and other modes of transportation —was largely lost when the Conservatives denationalized long-distance trucking in 1953. An impressive modernization of British Rail was carried out in the early 1960s involving both the phasing out of superfluous branch lines and a switch from coal to diesel or electric locomotives and other updating of rolling stock. These measures produced a very efficient passenger service (from an American perspective) and a freight service that performed relatively well given the small size of the freight cars and other historical anomalies built into the rail system. They did not, however, accomplish the reduction in operating losses that had been envisioned. British Rail is currently searching for funds to finance a new generation of fast intercity passenger trains; it may try private capital markets to accelerate implementation if investors can be lured by guarantees that profits from the new venture will not be used to cover losses from other operations.

The gas and electricity industries have suffered from a chronic lag of generating capacity behind demand. The prices of these products are very high relative to British income levels, and power emergencies are not uncommon in cold weather. The shift from manufactured coal gas to utilization of North Sea natural gas will revolutionize the whole energy situation in the nation and will undoubtedly involve a large investment in pipelines and distribution facilities. The pace of exploitation has been slow thus far, but as more and more new discoveries are made it becomes apparent that there are adequate reserves to allow for a massive shift to natural gas as a source of energy for consumers and industry. The level of investment in electricity-generating capacity is higher than for any other nationalized industry, but it has nevertheless suffered from disputes over coal versus atomic power and over design problems in British-made nuclear generating facilities. The costs of generating power will be progressively reduced as an increasing base of large-scale generating plants is built up.

Special Problems of the Steel Industry

It may illuminate some of the problems of democratic socialism to note several additional details of the fate of the British steel industry during the past two decades. Steel was the last industry to be nationalized by the Labour government, in 1949, and firms were not actually acquired until 1951. Later that same year, the Conservative victory made it clear that the Party would carry out its election promise to return the industry to private ownership. Thus the first experience with government ownership of steel ended without confrontation with the problems of coordination and modernization.

The Conservative government, in its 1953 to 1956 denationalization of steel, encountered serious practical difficulties. Just before the original nationalization in 1949, substantial amounts of stock of private steel companies—representing ownership rights—had been acquired by institutional investors like insurance companies and trust funds, solely because on the date when the industry would be nationalized that stock would be converted into Treasury-guaranteed British Iron and Steel Corporation 3½-percent stock. Presumably these institutional investors would not be interested, upon denationalization, in converting this Treasury-guaranteed stock into equity holdings in private steel companies carrying managerial responsibilities and financial risk.

The question of who would buy the steel companies from the government was further complicated by the pre-denationalization announcement by the Labour Party that when it next returned to power the industry would again be nationalized, with private owners being paid no more compensation than they were in the 1949 nationalization. Added to a host of highly technical matters connected with denationalization, these threats created a basic question of exactly who would buy the government-owned steel companies and, if prospective buyers were found, what types and amounts of premium inducements would be required to counterbalance the possibility of renationalization on unfavorable terms.

Fortunately for the Conservative Party, the Steel Nationalization Act had left the corporate structures in the industry basically unchanged. The old privately owned corporate entities, their boards, and their management staffs had been left intact. It appeared to be mere paper work to transfer them back to their former owners. However, this transfer of ownership, involving the world's third-largest steel industry, involved much travail.

In 1953 the Conservative government directed the Iron and Steel Corporation of Great Britain to transfer all its iron and steel company securities to a newly created body, the Iron and Steel Holding and Realization Agency. In this agency was vested the duty of selling these securities back to the public, and it was given wide latitude to devise specific means and procedures to accomplish this. The Holding and Realization Agency was permitted to sell these securities directly through syndicates of investment bankers. Although directly negotiated sales of the smaller companies proceeded one by one very satisfactorily, these accounted for only a minor portion of the steel industry. The real task of the Agency, and the most serious of its problems, lay in the sales of the large companies, where appeal had to be to the investment market rather than to a single buyer.

Two factors favored the Agency's disposal operations. To attract buyers for various issues, the shares' probable future earnings and dividends were indicated, and these were high in comparison with other available opportunities to invest in equity-share securities. Also, there was a general upsurge of prices in the London stock market that added attractiveness to the steel shares being offered by the Agency. These circumstances enabled the Conservative government to keep its pledge to denationalize the industry. With the assistance of fortuitous circumstances, the Agency did dispose of the bulk of the industry to private purchasers without apparent interruption of or interference with the efficiency and development of the steel industry. On the financial side, the entire operation, when concluded, was without any significant financial loss to the government.

However, throughout this denationalization of steel, the Labour party continued to state that if it were returned to power it would renationalize the industry. As has been mentioned, it was returned to power in 1964 by a narrow majority in the House of Commons, and this was enlarged in the 1967 election. Thereupon, a Renationalization Act was passed by the House of Commons. The opposition from the industry itself that had characterized the initial nationalization of steel did not reappear in 1967. The industry leaders cooperated with the government to carry out renationalization with minimal disturbance to the industry's operations and efficiency. It was the Labour government's position that the technology of producing steel, as recently developed, necessitated very large production units that could meet foreign competitive costs for steel per se and for products in which it is an important component. Both the governmental and private interests recognized that this might be achieved only through public ownership of the industry, making possible concentration of production in gigantic units under unified top management at the national level. These considerations, together with the clear fact that Britain, as an exporter of industrial products, needed a large-capacity, most efficient, and low-cost source of steel, helped renationalization go smoothly.

A few details of the transition to renationalization indicate how it was accomplished organizationally. The British Steel Corporation was created by the government. To it were transferred all of the stock shares and evidences of debt of any steel company normally producing more than 475,000 tons of crude steel annually. Thus the 14 largest steel-producing companies, with 30 million tons annual capacity and over 270,000 employees, have been merged into the British Steel Corporation. The private owners were paid for their holdings at the average prices at which these companies' shares sold on the London Stock Exchange during the 61 months preceding April 1966, or an average over the six months before April 1966—whichever was more advantageous to the seller. They were paid with 6½ percent government Treasury stock (bonds). The 14 member companies of the Corporation are grouped into four regional top managerial units. The Corporation does not exercise highly centralized controls over the regional organizations but, rather, acts to coordinate the execution of consistent basic policies throughout the 14 companies.

The technical problems facing the British Steel Corporation and entry into the European Common Market have pretty much scrapped whatever "redenationalization" plans the Tory Party may have had when it returned to power in 1970. Except for splitting off some chemical by-product plants and a possible swap of some facilities with private firms to tidy up operations, the steel industry will stay in the public sector. Whether this will allow the giant "greenfield" steel mill that the Corporation wants to build is doubtful; political expediency points toward additions to existing plants in the interest of preserving jobs in present locations.[3] Continued losses make the Conservative government reluctant to make major outlays in the face of limited prospects for the growth of British steel demand over the next decade. It is reluctant to accept management's excuses of price restraints and obsolete equipment for the unfavorable financial situation.

> The government may not see as big a steel industry for Britain as the corporation would like, but without a fairly steady pace of development the industry will have no market at all, and it is reaching one of those watersheds now where, unless the next stage of development is cleared fairly soon, Britain will be importing raw steel for finishing on outdated mills in the probable boom of 1979–80 just as it did in 1969–70. And after that the import bill for steel would just go on increasing.[4]

Performance and Prospects in the Nationalized Sector

There are real conceptual difficulties inherent in efforts to answer the question, How well have British nationalized industries performed in the post-war era? We will deal with the question at the individual industry level in this concluding section. The next chapter will treat the same topic in the context of the entire economy.

It is appropriate at this point to recall the original rationale for nationalization that the Labour Party relied on during the initial round of public acquisitions:

> The wider social arguments pointed to taking industries over in order of size. And the largest industries were in fact either public utilities (gas, electricity, railways), effective monopolies (coal, steel), basic (coal, transport, steel, electricity) notably inefficient under private enterprise (coal), apparently in need of large scale or central re-organisation (coal, gas), heavy capital users (electricity, steel, transport), or subject to exceptionally bad labour relations (coal).[5]

On these criteria there is a strong likelihood that the government would have had to be involved in the financing, organization, and labor relations of firms that ended up in the public sector. There are several reasons for believing that economic performance would not have been markedly different had nominal ownership remained private. First, the demand situation is largely outside the control of producers: The number of underground coal miners would have fallen by at least 60 percent during the 1960s, for instance, and the 3½ percent rate of growth in demand for steel in the 1970s would not justify an entirely new giant steel complex under any ownership scheme. Second, labor relations have been equally

---

[3]*The Economist*, July 3, 1971.
[4]*The Economist*, May 13, 1972.
[5]C. A. R. Crosland, *The Future of Socialism*, London: Cape, 1956, p. 315.

dreary in both public and private spheres such as automobiles and ship-building; it is unlikely that nationalization is the culprit. Third, the level of managerial talent does not seem markedly inferior to that in the private sector; British society in general accords less status and puts less emphasis on technical managerial skills than is the case on the other side of the Atlantic.

In short, the British government acquired a set of industries that, with the exception of steel, had blighted profit outlooks. It operated them with about the degree of managerial skill that could have been expected from declining industries with pay levels somewhat below the norm. The current profit picture in steel and electricity is particularly discouraging, but blame must be divided between managerial bungling and government price and labor-relations policies.

There are several bright spots in this otherwise bleak discussion. The discovery of large reserves of oil and natural gas in the North Sea could solve Britain's balance-of-payments and energy problems within a few years. For the first time a comprehensive, coordinated energy policy is feasible. Once natural gas is widely distributed and electric power is freed of reliance on coal in favor of cheaper atomic, gas, or fuel-oil generators, the profit position for three nationalized industries—gas, electricity, and coal—should improve. The further loss of mining employment is bound to work hardships, but wage increases recently demanded by the miners' union were granted on the assumption that marginal operations would have to be phased out.

With the government subsidizing the nationalized sector so heavily, the opportunity also arises for using the public sector to effect countercyclical fiscal policy by varying investment to stimulate or retard the economy. Managing boards have previously been pretty much on their own. One can also wish for a little more effectiveness in creating an incomes policy in which the public sector is not a leading contributor to wage-price inflation.

We tend to agree with Crosland's conclusion:

> Ownership as such makes little difference; and a transfer to public ownership will improve efficiency only if either (1) the Government puts in better management, or compels the existing management to take greater long term risks, or (2) if it is able to adapt the structure of industry (e.g. by amalgamations) in a manner obviously required by productive efficiency. Conversely, it will make things worse if it does the opposite.[6]

There are no obvious candidates for further nationalization. Nor is it obvious that any of the currently nationalized industries, including steel, would perform significantly better under private auspices. The status quo appears to be firmly anchored.

[6]*Ibid.*, p. 326.

QUESTIONS FOR CLASS DISCUSSION

1. What were the main reasons given for nationalization of certain industries by the postwar Labour government? How were those industries selected?

2. Why is steel a special case in the nationalization picture?

3. Was compensation "fair"? Does a generous compensation policy provide a good start for the nationalized sector?

4. Should present value or future earnings potential be the basis for compensation? Contrast the advantages of acquiring physical property versus those of acquiring ownership shares.

5. Should each nationalized industry's economic performance be judged by the profits it earns? Should the total nationalized sector be judged by the profit situation? When should profits be sacrificed to the attainment of other goals?

6. What problems of labor relations arose in the nationalized sector? How were they resolved? How should they have been resolved? Are such problems inevitable?

7. Has modernization been accomplished for the nationalized industries? Why were operating losses incurred after modernization had taken place?

8. Can professional managers operate a nationalized industry as efficiently as if it were in private hands? Isn't management a matter of technical skill alone? Aren't most managers salaried?

9. Discuss the impact of North Sea oil and gas on the British economy in general and on the nationalized sector in particular.

10. Should further nationalization occur? Should denationalization occur? If so, in what industries?

14. An evaluation of British nationalization

Except to the doctrinaire, nationalization of industry is not an end in itself. Unless, on balance, its practical application increases efficiency, productivity, stability, and net well-being, it must be regarded as a liability to any nation. Whether or not it is a better alternative to private operation of industry cannot be decided by exact computations of costs and benefits because some of each are intangibles, which are not reflected in the accounting or physical output statistics of an industry. Conceivably, nationalization of one or more industries may have beneficial or deleterious effects on such phenomena as inflation, amount of employment, or rate of growth.

Britain emerged from World War II a militarily victorious but economically bankrupt nation. To a large extent it had lost its national source of economic livelihood. Its round-the-world investments, earnings from which had enabled it to import large amounts of raw materials so that it could produce for domestic consumption and for export, were almost completely dissipated by its war efforts. Some of its domestic industries, such as railways, were physically in a shambles. Some new national policy was needed to give people encouragement and hope that by hard work they could recoup, at least in part, the good life they had known.

In the immediate postwar election, the Labour Party offered nationalization as a new hope—proposed on a gigantic scale—and the British electorate bought it. The subtle psychological effects of the program in operation are not susceptible to concrete measurement. Britain very materially lifted itself out of a slough of postwar physical and psychological misery, and the nationalization program of the Labour Party and government may well have been a major contribution to this end. Moreover, Britain's experience has proved that gigantic industries can be removed from private ownership and placed under government ownership with the attendant problems of the transfer being solved. These achievements stand to the credit of the postwar Labour government and the ingenuity and patient persistence of the British people.

In the years since the transition to sizable nationalized industries was completed in the legal and technical sense, many deep problems have arisen and still exist. The persistence of these does not necessarily prove that British nationalization of key industries was a mistake. They do demonstrate that any extensive program of nationalization of sizable and strategic industries in any democratic nation will encounter hard problems of organizing, operating, and integrating nationalized industries, structurally and operationally, with other sectors of the economy that are on a free-enterprise, profit-motivated basis. Here we seek to point out the nature of some of these problems as experienced by Great Britain.

POLITICAL PROBLEMS OF NATIONALIZATION

Possibly the most basic problem of all is the question of how a program of nationalization of industry is kept attuned to the wishes of a democratic electorate. In more concrete terms, what is to happen if the electorate changes its mind about a certain industry and decides that industry should be returned to private ownership and operation? Britain has had two cases of denationalization—steel and long-distance trucking. Denationalization of neither of these industries was a simple matter, despite the fact that neither was as scrambled as the components of some other nationalized industries are. The specific question is whether once an industry is fully nationalized it is thereby cut off from political democratic processes as far as possible reversal of its nationalization is concerned. The decision of the current government not to denationalize steel a second time around points to limited flexibility in this regard. The British Steel Corporation may be a composite of units that are either too unprofitable for private industry to want or too large or technically advanced for private industry to afford the risks and costs of further development. One of the authors once visited a steel mill in Britain that had installed two modern oxygen furnaces in an otherwise outmoded plant just before the 1967 renationalization; apparently the motive was to render the plant too expensive to abandon, even though cost of production remained high.

Parliamentary Responsibility for Economic Efficiency

In an economy dominated by competition and without much interference from the state, a firm or an industry that cannot make profits reasonably frequently will cease to exist. Thus efficiency is a simple matter demonstrated through cost and price relationships. In the case of nationalized industry, neither these nor other efficiency criteria can be clear-cut. Hence, a fundamental question is what criteria of efficiency may be applied to a nationalized industry. It is self-evident in Britain that there is need for some means of testing the efficiency with which a nationalized industry utilizes scarce productive resources. This need presumably was the basic reason for inserting in each nationalization measure an admonition that costs be covered by receipts from sales of product or service, taking the good years with the poor. However, this precept has not been vigorously applied, and there has been a tendency to accept deficits and subsidization from public funds as normal. The consequence is a substantial lack of reliable bench marks whereby efficiency, or lack of it, in nationalized industries can be determined.

In the administration of the nationalized industries, the British have never faced this problem squarely and apparently have been unable or unwilling to sense its significance. It would be solved, at least in one plausible way, if the nationalized industries were operated as parts of a comprehensive economic plan such as has existed in the Soviet Union. If that were the case, the inputs of physical factors of production would be planned, the production results to be obtained would be specified, and failure to yield the latter would be judged to be inefficiency. But this type of economic planning does not occur with physical output, even on an industry-by-industry basis. If the House of Commons becomes sufficiently interested or worried about matters of efficiency in any nationalized industry, a special committee of inquiry is established to resolve such concern. This committee has to establish its own criteria of efficiency. In making its findings and recommendations, one committee may use tests of efficiency closely related to those pertaining to private industry ("commercial criteria"); another may use criteria dealing more with physical input and output ("engineering criteria"); and another may think of efficiency in terms of how well a nationalized industry serves public needs for its product (regardless of "commercial" or "engineering" results), as the members of that committee conceive of the public need.

The nub of this problem is the need for reliable and adequate standards whereby each nationalized industry may continuously be subjected to a determination of whether or not it is operating with the maximum possible efficiency. Two facts have militated against the establishment of such criteria for the British nationalized industries. The first is that there has been no clear dividing line between costs that a nationalized industry incurs but that should not be entirely recouped in the price for its product because they are costs of serving national needs (as, possibly, *some portion* of freight costs that should not be collected from shippers to ports because of the national advantage of expanding exports as mean of acquiring foreign exchange) and costs that should be recouped from purchasers of the product just as would be expected in a private competitive industry. The second fact is that, when receipts have fallen below costs, government funds have almost automatically been made available to fill the breach. There have been several attempts to meet this problem by specifying in advance how far the government will go in making up deficits. However, it is clear that these limits are regarded as flexible and are breached from time to time by various means. Thus a nationalized industry's purpose is jointly that of serving *broad social needs* and *supplying customers* with products or services—the two objectives being so inextricably mingled that many costs cannot be allocated to either. Hence, no one really knows which costs should be paid by the taxpayer through use of public-fund subsidization and which should be covered by receipts from product sales. This is the reason why a minister, the House of Commons, or an astute economic journal has trouble knowing whether to criticize an industry running a deficit for its inefficiency or to consider the deficit attributable to public service and advocate that it be paid by a grant of tax or loan funds from the Treasury.

Parliamentary Responsibility for Broad Policy Decisions

At the top level of policy making, a problem of utmost importance exists, not only for practical reasons but because it impinges on a fundamental principle of socialism. How are the policies of a nationalized industry to be made subject to the democratically expressed wishes of the citizenry? In the British nationalized industries, the minister is presumed to be the link between the democratically formulated wishes of the House of Commons, representing the citizenry, and the formulation of policies to be implemented in the day-to-day operations of an industry. The minister is empowered by the nationalization acts to issue general directions to any nationalized industry placed under his jurisdiction. These, in effect, are policy instructions to the management board of that industry. The minister, in turn, is responsible to the House of Commons for the policies that are pursued by that nationalized industry. The theory is that the minister will exercise the initiative, judgment, and courage to direct the policies of a nationalized industry and will then stand ready to defend them before the House of Commons. Actually, this responsibility does not focus quite so sharply on the individual minister, since any major policy he formulates for a nationalized industry would be one that had been discussed and approved by the cabinet. In this sense the cabinet bears responsibility for policy formulation for nationalized industries, and it is the cabinet that must be prepared to step down if any major policy for a given industry is not supported by the House of Commons. From these responsibilities and relationships emerge two sets of quite tangible problems: (1) Have the nationalization acts made the individual minister's powers commensurate with the responsibilities he assumes, and have the ministers properly used the powers given them? (2) Has the House of Commons influenced ministers' policies so that they reflect the democratic wishes of the citizenry?

It is clear that the nationalization acts have given the ministers very great powers to give general directions and, when coupled with his power to appoint the members of the board, have obviously given him a large measure of authority to determine what happens in any nationalized industry. The ministers have exercised their powers with a proper sense of the adverse effect on the administrations under them if they interfere extensively in a board's work. There apparently is some confusion over whether the minister should act as the agent of the House of Commons to control policy making in the nationalized industries or as the spokesman to present and defend board actions in parliamentary debate and question periods. In practice, the latter has been the inclination of many ministers.

There are three means whereby the House of Commons can inquire into the conduct of a nationalized industry and thereby make a minister aware of its feelings:

1. The members may ask a minister questions during the regular question periods when ministers or their representatives must appear before the House. There has been great variation in inclination and skill to evade the real points of questions raised. This, coupled with the fact that the ministers generally assume a defensive attitude when answering questions and in many cases give no more information than absolutely necessary, greatly restricts the usefulness of what might appear to be a very effective means of democratic control. The time allotted for questioning is short, and the queries are much inclined toward matters of extreme detail and hence go unanswered. The questions usually do not pertain to the most important aspects of the nationalized industries, such as their plans for capital investment or their personnel policies.

2. Issues of importance are more likely to be thoughtfully discussed

in House of Commons debates. Yet the House of Commons spends much less time in debating the nationalized industries than their importance would seem to demand. Even in debate, both ministers and members of the House have been hesitant to come to grips with basic problems—the members, possibly because of the difficulty of becoming fully informed on complicated issues involving the industries under discussion.

3. Reports and accounts of the nationalized industries are scrutinized by the Public Accounts Committee of the House. For many years this was the only permanent House committee having a measure of direct contact with the nationalized industries as such. However, this committee reviews many accounts other than those of the nationalized industries and has neither the time, the facilities, nor the purpose to inquire into the basic matters of policy and operation on which the House's attention should focus.

Neither separately nor jointly do these three methods of inquiry place the individual nationalized industries in the position of accountability to Parliament that their position of eminence in the economy warrants.

The Conservative government that took office in 1951 was intensely concerned with this problem of accountability to Parliament. The thoughtful public has also been alert to it and inclined to characterize the situation as one in which "Britain's industrial structure is now composed of a large number of private industries over which the state has considerable powers of control and a small number of public industries over which it has no control whatever."[1] The practical alternatives for the Conservative government were (1) to create special committees composed of members drawn from outside the House of Commons that would make extensive periodic investigations of each of the nationalized industries or (2) to create a permanent committee in the House of Commons whose sole function would be to keep continuously informed of the policies and administration of each of the nationalized industries and report back to the House with recommendations for needed action. The Conservative government chose the second alternative, but it was put into effect very slowly.

In 1957, after a number of abortive attempts, the House of Commons established its Select Committee on the Nationalized Industries for the purpose of keeping the House informed on the policies of the respective nationalized industries and recommending such parliamentary action as the Committee deemed appropriate. Although this Committee is self-bound not to investigate details of management decisions or ministerial policy, it is otherwise unfettered in its operations. The Committee has proceeded to

[1]As phrased in *The Economist*, May 19, 1956, p. 688.

investigate and issue an extensive report on each nationalized industry after holding appropriate hearings. Its voluminous reports constitute the most comprehensive and penetrating analyses available of the policies, operations, and problems of the several nationalized industries.

However, it required seven years for the Select Committee to make its first investigatory round of all the nationalized industries. This time span is a fundamental flaw in this means of solving the problem of parliamentary responsibility. If each industry is to be studied only once in seven years, how will the resulting reports assist members of the House of Commons to express views on policies and problems that shape up quickly in the dynamic areas of the British economy occupied by nationalized industries?

It is eminently clear that the Select Committee on the Nationalized Industries, despite its best intentions and some excellent work, is not an adequate or effective answer to the problem of parliamentary responsibility for the nationalized industries. In late 1968 the Select Committee submitted its first comprehensive report on the nationalized industries. Its 1200 pages represent the first extensive effort to evaluate the achievements, problems, and future of each of the industries making up the nationalized sector. One of the report's major proposals was that a new Ministry of Nationalized Industries take over the supervision of all of the nationalized industries now under separate ministries. Clearly, an *organizational* reform of this character, even if adopted (which is by no means certain), could not ensure the solution of the problems of the nationalized industries discussed in this chapter. These are economic, political, and social in nature, and it is vain to hope that organizational changes can contribute materially to their solution.

PROBLEMS OF MANAGEMENT OF NATIONALIZED INDUSTRIES

From the experience with nationalized industries in Great Britain have emerged general problems of management that cut across all of them, differing only in detail from industry to industry. Merely to state the dual objective of efficient operation and response to the public will poses one of the most basic of management problems: Shall a nationalized industry be operated for commercial ends—that is, receipts that cover costs—or shall its operations be directed to serve broad economic and social needs? The nationalization acts allow ministers and boards to exercise judgment with respect to whether and for how long a given industry may permit its revenues to fall below costs in order to permit it to pursue some course considered to be in the public interest or desired by the public. In general, the government ministers and the boards accepted the commercial principle of operation, being concerned about repetition of annual deficits and seeking measures to prevent them. Like them or not, however, massive annual deficits have become a common occurrence in large portions of the socialized sphere. The commercial principle cannot be applied when circumstances call for some measure of price restraint or for costly wage settlements in industry after industry. The challenge of Common Market entry should call for more strict adherence to commercial principles and more inspired leadership from managers of nationalized industries.

Management Personnel

This question is closely related to the problem of the personnel makeup of the respective top management boards of the nationalized industries. Should they be composed of men with experience in private industry, who will approach their management problems from the more strictly private business point of view; should they be men whose broader backgrounds and philosophies lead them in the direction of emphasizing the contribution an industry can make to social need, even though this means operating at a deficit; or should they be drawn principally from the specific nationalized industry itself, with board membership as the reward for efficient managerial service at some lower level? The ministers are responsible for appointing the board, and the nationalization acts give them leeway in their selections. When the nationalization acts were passed, it was Labour's expectation that some essentially new type of top management would come to the fore in industries such as coal and transportation. Indeed, strongly socialist elements in the Labour Party itself always visualized strong labor representation in top management of socialized industries, possibly looking toward complete self-management by the workers in the industry after experience had given them a good grasp of managerial problems. Obviously, nothing approaching such expectations has occurred.

The trend has been for ministers to appoint personnel from top levels of sub-board managerial staffs of nationalized industries. Such appointments are often popular with the public, which feels that the appointee is an expert in this industry, and the House of Commons may well share this view, while management people in the industry are pleased by a promotion from within. However, such choices may be of questionable merit because of the probability that they bring continuance of traditional approaches to managerial problems while failing to bring to the board the stimulating ideas an outsider might contribute. Moreover, the appointment of insiders may make a board more responsive to the ideas of former managerial associates and union representatives, to the neglect of board aspects of the industry's role in the economy or the interests of the nation as a whole. There have been some marked exceptions to this trend that have brought top-level private business leaders to board chairmanships. However, the problem merits much more astute analysis and thought than it has been given by either political party or by the public press.

Shared Ownership

The Conservative victory in the 1970 parliamentary elections did not signal a radical shift toward returning public industries to private ownership, but it did open the way to significant new philosophical approaches to ownership. "As elaborated so far the new Government's policy towards the nationalized industries entails three things: the industries are apparently to be required to shed their peripheral activities; they are to be less subject to ministerial control; and, having been put on a profit-earning basis wherever possible, minority interests in the equity of some will be sold off to the public."[2]

Shared ownership would subject the public sector to commercial criteria of performance while allowing the director of the nationalized industry freedom from direct government interference in management decisions. A beginning was made in this direction when the British Overseas Airways Corporation (BOAC) issued "public dividend capital" to private investors in 1966. Instead of bonds on which interest had to be paid regardless of recent profit levels, public dividend capital payments varied according to how well BOAC (and later British Steel) was doing financially. Unless the industry pays reasonable dividends, of course, private investors will not choose to hold this form of security; thus, the managing board will have to approximate the performance of private industry in order to secure financing for continued modernization and expansion.

A second proposal would actually sell a minority interest in nationalized industries to private investors. Equity financing of this sort would also have to meet the market test of adequate dividend payments in order for share prices to be maintained on the London Stock Exchange. Candidates for this form of shared ownership might include technological innovations in established industries such as high-speed passenger trains or some types of special steel, or the exploitation of new discoveries such as North Sea oil and gas deposits. Since all new investment in nationalized industry is supposed to earn at least a "test discount rate" of 10 percent, existing industries should be able to attract outside capital once the book value of their assets is adjusted to realistic levels.

Both of these innovations are predicated on the necessity of any government intervention in the internal decisions of nationalized firms being accompanied by a subsidy to cover additional costs. The cost of requiring coal-burning electric generators or purchasing domestically produced planes for nationalized airlines, to name two actual examples, would thus show up immediately and become a matter for public discussion. A start has been made by paying a direct grant to British Rail for continuing rail service on loss-producing lines. Once compensation was paid for all costs imposed in the public interest, the government's relationship with the indi-

[2]*The Economist*, October 17, 1970.

vidual nationalized industries would very much resemble its stance toward large oligopolistic private industries: regulation of monopoly elements, enforcing wage and price controls, and occasionally facilitating major reorganizations in order to promote efficiency and realize economies of scale.

> That part of the British economizing market occupied by its nationalized industries is not characterized by invisibility, automaticity, or anonymity. Of necessity, nationalized industry approaches its tasks directly and explicity. Its economizing machinery is uncomplicated and exposed; the kitchen is always open for inspection. Problems are posed and resolved, programs are promulgated, and actions are taken explicitly by identified persons, and reasons or rationalizations are spelled out painfully and in octuplicate. No one can hide behind "flows" and "forces"; these are man made, and their making and their makers are matters of record.[3]

A movement toward shared ownership in the nationalized sector would seem to combine some of the equity and public-welfare advantages of socialization with the efficiency and innovation usually associated with private enterprise.

CONCLUSIONS: THE NATIONALIZED
SECTOR AND THE TOTAL BRITISH ECONOMY

In 1870 Great Britain had the highest per-capita income in the world; a century later it had been surpassed by the United States, by the nations of Scandinavia and Western Europe, and by its former possessions—Canada, Australia, and New Zealand. Japan is rapidly catching up. The gap is widening because Britain has been growing at only roughly half the rate of her leading competitors for the past 20 years.

In this concluding section we will view the nationalized sector in its dual role of contributor to and victim of the sluggishness in the British economy. The leading American authority on British public enterprises groups them into three categories: (1) coal, railways, and steel, which are faced primarily with reorganization and the accompanying social impact; (2) capital-intensive industries such as electricity, gas, and telecommunications, which require rapid growth and hence considerable purchases of capital equipment; and (3) industries on the frontiers of new technology, which directly perform research and development activities—atomic energy and broadcasting.[4]

---

[3]Ben W. Lewis, "British Nationalization and American Private Enterprise: Some Parallels and Contrasts," *American Economic Review*, May 1965, pp. 50–64. Lewis points out that giant American corporations make decisions profoundly affecting the general welfare in secret and without public accountability for the consequences.

William G. Shepherd, "Innovation under Constraint in British Public Enterprises," *Bulletin of the Association for Comparative Economics*, 1970, pp. 1–27.

Employment declined in coal mining and railroads at an annual rate of 3 percent between 1955 and 1968. The task of reorganization under conditions of decreasing output meant the closing of inefficient units and the lack of alternative employment opportunities for those displaced. Physical output per employee was largely a result of destroying the less productive portion of the industry; capital formation proceeded slowly and represented a relatively minor demand linkage to the machinery and engineering industries. Steel production grew at only about the same rate as the total economy, further evidence that the overall rate of investment was low. Despite the construction of two new steel complexes, the slow rate of growth led to an older average age of production facilities in Britain and hence less opportunity to incorporate new technological advances. If steel output grows at 20 percent per year, as it has in Japan, the average plant is less than five years old; no wonder Britain is at a competitive disadvantage in attempting to modernize its steel production.

The picture is much brighter in the public utilities—gas, electricity, and telephone. Rapid growth in demand and the need to replace obsolete equipment combined to generate an annual rate of capital formation of approximately 10 percent in the years after 1955. This represents an important source of demand for the products of the British heavy-machinery industry and is probably the largest single stimulus to the private sector provided by the nationalized industries.

Firms at the frontiers of technology are not usually brought under public ownership, if opportunities for private development exist. It is increasingly the case, however, that the scale of development outlays is so great in areas like supersonic airplanes, atomic energy, and military hardware that the government must become a major participant in research and development activities. The British Atomic Energy Agency led in the development of commercially feasible generators, but in recent years the Central Electricity Generating Board has claimed control over research in this area. At any rate, the economic impact of R&D activities usually shows up in significant magnitude only after a long period.

A visitor to Great Britain is struck by how little awareness of the nationalized sector actually shows up in day-to-day living. Beyond occasional complaints about standards of service for electrical and telephone problems and a vague awareness that the railroads are government-owned, the difference between the United States and Britain is not very evident. This seems to be further evidence that the legal fact of ownership is less important than the technological and economic facts of life with which a given industry must deal. Nationalization was the cornerstone on which early socialist movements were built; those who fought the ideological battles of the nineteenth century would probably be astonished to learn that the managers of public enterprises are neither markedly better nor significantly worse than their counterparts in the private sector. That seems to be the primary lesson of the British experience.

Once nationalization ceases to be a crucial question of economic ideology, attention naturally turns to other policy tools for achieving planned
economic goals. Succeeding chapters will study techniques for influencing
the level of output and employment, controlling inflation, and affecting income distribution and access to vital services such as medical care.

QUESTIONS FOR CLASS DISCUSSION

1. Why was nationalization part of the Labour Party's postwar
program?

2 .How heavily should considerations of general welfare weigh in
the decisions of public enterprises?

3. What has been the position of cabinet ministers in relations
between nationalized industries and Parliament? What should it be?
Why has it been so difficult to exert parliamentary influence on the public
sector?

4. Are engineering criteria an adequate basis for judging economic
performance? Are profit criteria?

5. Should nationalized industries be forced to buy machinery that is
domestically produced? keep plants open in regions of high unemployment?
choose technology that minimizes imports of raw materials? hold down
price rises to reduce inflationary pressures? Why or why not?

6. How much concern should the British Parliament devote to the
operation of public enterprises?

7. What points favor some form of shared ownership for nationalized
industries?

8. How can the permissible amount of annual deficits be decided
upon?

9. Would a large voice of workers in management reduce labor
tensions in the socialized sector?

10. In what ways does nationalized ownership give rise to public
discussion of economic policy decisions?

11. Which nationalized industries boosted Britain's overall economic
growth rate; which industries slowed it down?

12. Why is the existence of the public sector so unapparent to an
American visitor to Great Britain?

15. Macroplanning
—output policies

Nationalization is an extreme form of central economic planning, one in which those charged with formulating economic policy for the nation and those who react at the corporation level are all employees of the state. This chapter deals with less intrusive institutional arrangements to influence the aggregate level of output so that the full utilization of available resources and the potential for future economic growth are maintained.

Our starting point is the Keynesian aggregate-demand model, which provides methodological ground rules for much of modern economic analysis. Economists differ widely when making value judgments about preferred choices among various policies, but the debate is usually conducted within the intellectual framework of the Keynesian system. The classical remedy for recessions was to cut wages, thereby attempting to increase profit margins and stimulate greater output. As Keynes pointed out, however, money wages are not easily reduced because of worker opposition; in addition, reduced payrolls diminish the purchasing power needed to absorb the extra output that the original wage cut supposedly generated. Therefore, argued Keynes, wage reductions are likely to be less effective than expansionary monetary and fiscal policies in achieving a full-employment level of aggregate demand. In recent years, various nations have moved beyond sole reliance on the regulation of the money supply and the manipulation of taxes and government expenditures to more sophisticated efforts to maintain balance among different sectors of their economies. We will use the Dutch and French experiences to illustrate this development.

INNOVATIONS IN FISCAL AND MONETARY POLICY

Some form of fiscal and monetary policy is utilized in every nation in which a large share of productive capital remains in private hands. If there is a central bank, a specific decision concerning the money supply must be made; similarly, the level and composition of taxes and expenditures must be decided by the proper governmental authorities. Desirable as the idea may be, the possibility of a neutral government policy in economic matters is largely impractical in the modern world. Choices must be made, and they will affect individuals differently. Higher interest rates hurt existing bondholders by lowering the prices of bonds; tax relief granted to one group probably means that some other group will have to pay more taxes. Policy choices also advance or hinder the achievement of economic goals. In the following pages we will discuss some of the techniques adopted in various countries to try to keep their economies moving along the full-employment growth path.

Monetary Policies

The goal of monetary policy is to influence the level of interest rates, which in turn affects investment decisions in sectors of the economy that depend on outside borrowing to finance projects. The main instrument of U.S. monetary policy—purchases and sales of government securities in the open market—is not available in most other Western nations because a sufficiently active bond market does not exist; only in the United Kingdom and West Germany does the central bank engage in such transactions to implement policy decisions.[1]

For the most part, private banking in most foreign countries is concentrated in a relatively small number of firms, thus permitting a working

[1]Angus Maddison, *Economic Growth in the West*, New York: Twentieth Century, 1964, p. 123.

relationship between the monetary authorities and the banks; informal gentlemen's agreements or selective credit controls become the channel by which regulation of the money supply operates. The Swiss National Bank, for instance, cooperates with the powerful commercial banks to reduce the liquidity of the banking system by exchanging holdings of foreign currencies for Swiss francs held by private banks. The Bank of Italy actually possesses veto power over large individual loans by private banks to their customers.[2]

An interesting example of the ability of the central bank to influence financial conditions is found in West Germany, where it is traditional for private bankers to be represented on the supervisory boards of individual firms and to participate actively in their financial affairs. The intimate relationship between the German Bundesbank and the largest commercial banks, in turn, means that the central bank has some degree of direct influence on corporate investment policy.

Although the ties between the German business, financial, and governmental sectors are unique in many ways, the relative success of monetary policy there in the postwar period bolsters the generalization that the sensitivity of investment to changes in the availability and price of outside funds is the key element determining the efficacy of instruments of monetary control. The existence of retained earnings in the private sector tends to insulate investment decisions from the immediate pressure of conditions in capital markets. The process of rapid economic growth may allow a sudden shift to internal financing and thus diminish governmental authority over the future course of aggregate demand generated by the private sector of the economy.

Fiscal Policies for Stabilization

Fiscal policies to smooth out business-cycle fluctuations attempt to alter the timing of economic decisions to reduce aggregate demand during booms and to increase it during recessions. Tax rates that vary according to the state of the economy are one means of accomplishing this end.

One widely studied fiscal stabilization measure is the Swedish investment fund policy, which allows firms to set aside 40 percent of profits during boom periods in a tax-free investment reserve. Tax advantages are instituted during periods of economic stagnation to encourage the unfreezing of these reserve funds.[3] The government encouraged the use of investment funds three times in the decade after 1958, when the reserve became an important instrument of fiscal policy. Available evidence indicates that

[2]U.S. Joint Economic Committee, "Comparative Features of Central Banks in Selected Foreign Countries," Paper No. 1 on Economic Policies and Practices, 1963.

[3]Assar Lindbeck, "Theories and Problems in Swedish Economic Policy in the Post-war Period," *American Economic Review*, Supplement, June 1968, pp. 40–44.

firms were quite responsive to these tax incentives, thus smoothing out potential fluctations in the growth record of the Swedish economy.

A similar device may be evolving in the United States. When business investment failed to revive adequately after the relative slack of the late 1950s, an investment tax credit involving a reduction of 7 percent in tax rates for expenditures on new machinery was instituted in 1962. Four years later the economic situation was reversed, and the tax credit was suspended by Congress. Although the investment tax credit was only one element in the total economic picture, it is clear that the impact of the credit and its subsequent removal was helpful in influencing the timing of investment.

One difficulty of relying on changing tax rates for fiscal-policy purposes is the possibility that legislative action will be sluggish because of political factors or bureaucratic inertia. President Kennedy suggested that the Chief Executive be granted discretionary power to adjust personal income tax rates within certain limits for the coming year. The economic logic of his proposal was swept aside in the rush to guard congressional prerogatives in the field of taxation.

Fiscal Policies for Growth

Full employment is a worthwhile goal in itself, but the mix of aggregate demand that permits full employment of resources is important as well. Generally speaking, the larger the share of investment demand relative to personal consumption and government expenditures, the more the productive capacity of the economy will be expanded in the subsequent period. The increase in productive capacity is the primary factor determining the possible rate of economic growth. Many nations use tax incentives to promote investment by private firms. We will briefly discuss accelerated-depreciation schemes, special tax exemptions, and promotion of business savings.[4]

Depreciation is an accounting estimate of costs arising from the wear and obsolescence of machinery used in producing goods over a given period. Government permission to depreciate machinery more rapidly during the first years of use overstates costs and therefore understates current profits. In countries where a corporate-profit tax is levied, this means deferring taxes; since the money saved can be used productively until the taxes fall due, a net advantage to the firm results. Almost every industrialized private-enterprise economy has adopted such allowances in order to make investment more worthwhile by including a tax gain in addition to the rate of return for the project itself.

Tax policy is sometimes used to favor some industries over others.

---

[4]These topics are discussed in much greater detail in National Bureau of Economic Research, *Foreign Tax Policies for Economic Growth*, New York: Columbia University Press, 1966.

The German government granted special concessions to basic industries like steel, coal, and shipbuilding in the postwar recovery period and also encouraged residential construction. Japanese policy favors export industries, and in Great Britain a tax on employment in service industries is designed to shift resources into sectors exhibiting higher productivity.

Differential treatment of personal income received in the form of capital gains from the sale of assets that have risen in price over time results in a situation that encourages the accumulation of retained earnings by private firms. Stockholders are more willing to forgo dividends if capital gains are taxed at a lower rate. Since internal funds are usually considered a low-cost source of finance relative to outside borrowing, the ability to reinvest retained earnings must be considered a stimulus to business investment.

DUTCH ECONOMETRIC PLANNING

The particular aspect of economic planning to be studied in this section is the work of the Central Planning Bureau (CPB) in the Netherlands. This agency has developed complex models of Dutch economy, which it uses in advising the government on economic policy matters. Thus its function goes beyond passive *forecasting* of future trends to the more active role of *simulating* different economic situations resulting from alternative policy decisions. Professor Jan Tinbergen, the founding director of the CPB, was the first economist to use statistical techniques to fit national income data into the Keynesian aggregate-demand theory. The resulting equations estimate future economic patterns on the basis of past regularities observed between the variables making up the model.

In simple terms, these models break down aggregate demand into subcomponents of consumption, investment, government purchases, and exports, and then estimate each type of demand on the basis of other variables that appear to have influence (investment, for instance, will probably be sensitive to interest rates). Additional equations relate the production needed to fulfill a given level of aggregate demand to demand for factors of production and to prices and wages that will result under those particular market conditions. The economic variables are so interrelated (wages are both a factor payment and a source of consumer demand, for example) that the equations must be solved simultaneously by computer to yield final results. Once constructed, the reaction of the total model to changes in any variable or to shifts in underlying relationships can be calculated.[5]

The supplying of expert opinion on economic policy by the Central Planning Bureau revolves around a short-term econometric forecasting model consisting of roughly 30 equations. The importance of international

---

[5]See Lawrence R. Klein, *The Keynesian Revolution* (2nd ed.), New York: Macmillan, 1966, chap. IX, for a brief explanation of econometric models. Professor Klein is the leading expert on econometric models of the American economy.

trade in the Dutch economy is reflected in the importance attached to the equations predicting exports and imports within the model. The CPB provides technical advice to the Minister of Economic Affairs and to the committee of cabinet ministers actually charged with setting economic policy. Preliminary versions of the annual plan are submitted to two different groups that include representatives of labor and management organizations.

The resulting document is both a forecast and a plan, since it incorporates the policy decisions to which the government is committed for the coming year. When it is finally published, it has undergone exposure before a series of consultative bodies both inside and outside the government and therefore represents, to some extent, a consensus on short-term goals by major economic interest groups.

The Central Planning Bureau also prepares annual forecasts of the anticipated growth of output in major industrial sectors by means of a crude input-output model, as well as occasional long-term plans charting the effects of population growth and capital accumulation on the ability to achieve economic policy targets. In all of these activities it has gained a worldwide reputation among economists for the imagination and care devoted to its advisory function.

> There is, unfortunately, no simple way of testing the influence of Dutch
> annual plans on the economic fortune of the Netherlands. However,
> it is tempting to point to the great stability of the Dutch economy as
> proof of planning efficiency. In spite of war damages and of the post-
> war loss of Indonesian holdings and expulsion of Dutch citizens from
> Indonesia, the Netherlands has enjoyed full employment and has had
> relatively few balance-of-payments difficulties. Other European coun-
> tries fared less well, though their problems were easier to handle.[6]

This statement holds, in general, for subsequent years, except for rises in wage rates and overall price levels between 1953 and 1965 that were the highest of any European nation.[7] The rapid rise in manufacturing productivity that undoubtedly contributed to keeping Dutch export prices competitive in world markets and the remarkable record of full-capacity utilization of productive resources are positive factors for which the Central Planning Bureau can claim some measure of credit.

Cost-push inflation is a threat to continued reliance on econometric techniques. Dutch productivity growth is the most rapid in Europe, but with wages rising over 10 percent per year it is inevitable that inflation will result. This, in turn, puts pressure on export earnings and domestic profits. Investment from retained earnings is the backbone of future productivity growth. Holland's competitive position in the world economy will suffer unless this impasse is broken.

[6]Stanislaw Wellisz, "Economic Planning in the Netherlands, France and Italy," *Journal of Political Economy*, June 1960, p. 266.
[7]*The Economist*, October 28, 1967, p. 414.

The increasing capacity of computers and the accumulated experience of econometric-model builders points to the continued development of more sophisticated aggregate economic models. A group of economists has already developed a model with well over 100 equations for the United States economy that provides quarterly estimates to increase the reaction speed of policy makers to changing conditions.[8] It is likely that the Dutch experience will serve as a prototype of efforts to make economic policy formation a more scientific pursuit.

FRENCH INDICATIVE PLANNING

So far, we have discussed several means of utilizing the traditional tools of fiscal and monetary policy. Even in the Dutch case the object is to control only the economic variables over which the government has some degree of authority so that its decisions, plus the independent choices made in the private sector, result in the simultaneous attainment of specific economic goals.

The French have gone one step further—how big a step is a matter of considerable dispute—in attempting to achieve better balance between various sectors of the economy. The process is termed "indicative" planning to distinguish its claim of voluntary compliance by private economic units from the "command" type of central direction. Ardent supporters view it as an ideal compromise, one that grafts the anticipated benefits of coordinated central planning onto an economic system retaining the fundamental liberties of political democracy and private property.

The ascendency of worldwide interest in the French experiment with noncoercive planning covered the decade after 1958, beginning with the economic reforms that followed the balance-of-payments crises and change of government occurring in that year and ending with the economic strains following the riots and demonstrations by students and workers in the spring of 1968. It is not entirely coincidental that this period was generally one of rapid and steady economic growth during which France, under De Gaulle, became a world power once again in economic and political matters; this raises the vital question of the extent to which prosperity was due to the specific institutional form of economic planning.

Origins of French Planning

The French planning experience began in 1946 with the government's decision to initiate a modernization and equipment plan under a new government agency, the *Commissariat Général du Plan,* which was to organize

---

[8]J. Duesenberry, G. Fromm, L. R. Klein, and E. Kuh, eds., *The Brookings Quarterly Econometric Model of the U.S. Economy,* Skokie, Ill.: Rand McNally, 1965.

the work of drafting the plan, administering it, and forming a group of professional economists and technicians to sustain it as an institution. The objective was to obtain from limited means of production the rehabilitation of the retardative basic sectors of the French economy. The universally recognized need to recoup wartime economic losses brought general acceptance of this innovation; the choice was between modernization, with the possibility of rapid growth, and economic decadence.

The outgrowth was the adoption of the First Plan (1947–1953). The main personality in the plan was M. Jean Monnet, who possessed significant economic power based largely on his control of funds made available by the United States under the Marshall Aid Program. In a frontal effort to overcome the long history of economic stagnation in France, six key target areas were established. These were construction, cement and concrete, agricultural machinery, transportation equipment, steel, and electricity.

In the Second Plan (1954–1957) the scope of planning was extended. In fact, the Second Plan became the first really comprehensive national plan in France. New sectors such as agriculture, housing, and general manufacturing were embraced for the first time. The general theme of the Plan was to raise the "quantity and quality" of private industrial output. National income accounting was also improved, giving the planners more reliable instruments for undertaking complex measurements and forecasts for the French economy. By 1957 all output goals had been surpassed, especially in private manufacturing and private-profit levels. In the ensuing thrust forward, a serious imbalance in international payments developed, and full employment kindled mounting pressures for wage and price increases.

The Third Plan (1958–1961) continued the emphasis on general manufacturing. It also encountered difficulties, even though mixed measures of restraint and currency devaluation sought to avert them. Policies for austerity and fiscal discipline restricted the rate of economic growth. During 1958–1959 gross national product rose at the reduced annual rate of 2.5 percent.[9] By 1960 economic indicators showed more favorable signs of rapid improvement, and by the end of 1961 most of the planned targets had been achieved.

In the Fourth Plan (1962–1965) the scope of planning was broadened to "economic horizons"—20-year goals of regional development and balanced rural-urban shifts in population and industrial concentration. The Plan further sought to increase aggregate production by 24 percent, or an annual average of 5.5 percent. This was a higher rate than most realized growth rates in Europe and in the United States, and somewhat higher than the average rate of growth in France since 1945.

The Fifth Plan (1966–1970) reflected France's Fourth Plan experience with inflation in the early years and an economic slump in 1965. The

[9]Some of this slowdown can also be attributed to the political crisis and change of government that took place in 1958.

Fifth Plan called for a slightly lower annual increment of 5 percent in production and attempted to utilize price controls for key sectors and wage restraint in the nationalized industries in order to dampen inflationary tendencies. Emphasis was on investment, with industrial investment to increase by 55 percent and house building by 35 percent over the five years as a whole. This meant a slight reduction in the planned consumer share of national product in order to achieve rapid growth combined with stability.

As France has become more integrated with the total European and world economies, the ability of *le plan* to operate apart from outside forces has been progressively reduced. Fiscal policy thus has become the main instrument of plan implementation. The Sixth Plan's targeted growth rate of slightly less than 6 percent is to be achieved by keeping needed government spending on housing and education under strict control in order to avoid harming industrial modernization. For the first time, a computer model of the economy is being used to trace the impact of plan policies on prices and the balance of payments.

Features of French Planning

Two principal features form the core of French economic planning. One is the element of cooperation to be achieved, it is hoped, through group agreement on objectives established by consultation among business firms, unions, and government agencies. The other is the cohesiveness of the overall approach and the stimulus provided to private firms for expanding output or making investments in the direction and magnitude indicated by the Plan.

The institutions ensuring mutual accommodation and full and free discussion in the French planning process are novel. The *Commissariat Général du Plan* was and is small, numbering less than 200 employees of all types; this means that much of the work of planning is shared with groups in industry, confining the role of the Commissariat inside the government machinery to *proposing, advising*, and *estimating*. It takes the initiative in discussing economic problems and programs, and provides neutral ground to resolve potential conflicts between various economic interest groups, including the government and its various agencies.

Detailed consultations between private economic interests and the Commissariat take place through the Modernization Commissions, each consisting of 30 to 50 members who serve voluntarily and without pay. The Commissions are organized either "vertically" by economic sector (mining, chemicals, steel, and so forth) or "horizontally" to deal with broad problems (such as manpower, finance, or regional location). The membership of each commission, typically consisting of executives of firms and trade associations, union representatives, government officials, and academic experts, then considers the implications of the national plan for their area of the economy.

Through these planning bodies, psychological factors are expected to favor the successful implementation of plans. Members of the Modernization Commissions should feel some attachment to making *their* plan work, and since this group includes officials from major firms in each sector, the power to advance that goal is also present.

The internal consistency of the plan is the second major feature that encourages compliance with planned roles by industrial sectors and by individual firms. If each firm plans its own output on the assumption that projected outputs in other sectors will actually materialize, the plan takes on the nature of a self-fulfilling prophecy because each firm, by acting in its own self-interest, will be doing its part to maintain the planned quantities. Those who exceed indicated production norms will find inadequate market outlets, which will make them more eager to follow the plan next time. To illustrate with a simple example: If each new automobile requires five new tires, an accurate projection of automobile output will create a situation in which production of either more or less than five times that number of tires will probably turn out unprofitably for the tire manufacturers. This is the same kind of consistency provided by the input-output approach to economic planning, and the information provided to individual firms by such a plan is valuable because it reduces the risk of economic loss through inaccurate estimation of market demand. Likewise, the addition of new productive capacity within an industry can proceed in an orderly way, with individual firms recognizing the folly of each attempting to grab all the incremental demand for their product by overinvesting in additional plant and equipment.

In France, as in many other democratic countries, the government possesses fairly extensive regulatory powers so that the economic carrot of self-interest is matched, at least implicitly, by the economic stick of governmental sanctions, existing primarily in the form of positive incentives rather than punitive actions. Illustrative of these incentives are reduced tax rates on earnings from new investments that conform to the plan, access to the capital market under especially favorable terms, and outright subsidies for research and development. The selective implementation of such incentives substantially complements the "indicative" nature of French economic planning.

Beyond these incentives, the government holds considerable control over the level of domestic investment. Roughly one-fourth of gross domestic investment is made in the public sector, comprising government agencies, the heavily subsidized housing industry, and a nationalized sector that includes railways, utilities, and the largest automobile enterprise. Another one-fourth of domestic investment is carried out through financial intermediaries either owned or regulated by the government. When the potential influence of price controls, tax allowances, and purchases by nationalized industries on the private sector is added, it can easily be seen that the government is scarcely a passive agent in the French economy.

The Planning Process

The initial stage of planning consists of an attempt to arrive at the maximum rate of economic growth over the plan period that is consistent with balance-of-payments equilibrium and relative price stability. This key variable, determined after the consideration of alternative rates, receives legislative approval as the official target rate of growth. Implicit in this target are estimates of final demand in the last year of the plan; these are derived from an analysis of consumers' expenditures and assumptions about international trade and domestic investment. Input-output relationships between sectors then serve as a basis for projections of sales and purchases at a disaggregated level.

At this stage the Commissariat staff holds consultative talks with representatives of industry and other interest groups in the Modernization Commissions. This is what gives the plan its "indicative" flavor. The Commissions check the planners' assumptions regarding the potential technological advance, new investment, and expansion of output in the several industry sectors. Finally, after ironing out conflicts and inconsistencies, the Commission submits its report to the central planning body, where it is synthesized with other reports to verify the planners' own assessment of the pattern of total consumption, investment, and trade implied by the basic growth target. The final step is formal approval of the complete plan by the French Chamber of Deputies.

Summary Evaluation of French Planning

Economic planning is considered by some to be the major source of the remarkable growth of the French economy in the postwar period; critics take the more skeptical view that growth would have occurred anyway.[10] The measurements required to settle this debate are lacking, and much depends on one's own definition of successful planning.

> In some ways, the development of French planning in the 1950's can be viewed as an act of voluntary collusion between senior civil servants and the senior managers of big business. The politicians and the representatives of organized labour were both largely passed by. The conspiracy in the public interest between big business and big officialdom worked, largely because both sides found it convenient. Since the Government had a substantial part of the nation's economic activity under its direct control and exerted an indirect, though powerful, influence on a great deal more, it was not too difficult to convince private business that its decisions would be more intelligently

[10]See John Hackett and Anne-Marie Hackett, *Economic Planning in France*, Cambridge, Mass.: Harvard University Press, 1963; John Sheahan, *Promotion and Control of Industry in Postwar France*, Cambridge, Mass.: Harvard University Press, 1963; Vera Lutz, *French Planning*, Washington, D.C.: American Enterprise Institute, 1965.

made, over a wider range of industry, if they were made in unison with the public authorities.[11]

If this view is correct, a large part of the decreased commitment of French businessmen to the Plan in the 1960s can be traced to the increased availability of internal funds for financing private investment. When the government controlled the purse strings by monitoring the flow of credit, it was a bold act to "violate" the Plan; the presence of retained earnings, especially under inflationary conditions that penalized a firm postponing an investment project, make it neither necessary nor always advantageous for the private sector to conform.

The statement just quoted also downgrades the participation of workers or their representatives in the indicative-planning scheme. The revitalization of the French economy after 1958 was achieved in part by a severe curb on wages, and the fact that French wage costs per unit of output increased less than in other European nations strengthened her position in international trade. "The objectives of the [Fifth] plan could be met only by not giving in to labor demands."[12] These demands focused less on compensation per se than on the right to share in decisions on income distribution, working conditions, and the direction of proposed economic change.

Increased attention to labor demands since the worker (and student) uprisings of 1968 requires a very delicate balance between wage levels and productivity if inflation is to be avoided. The government has placed its faith in contracts with public employees allowing cost-of-living raises if inflation gets out of control; thus the spiral of wage and price increases can be broken for a significant portion of the labor force once inflation is initially controlled. A related move toward monthly wage guarantees and increased fringe benefits is aimed at providing more job security and increased status for French workers.

Thus French planning is threatened from at least two directions. The first is the danger that contingencies such as labor unrest or inflation will prevent adherence to the long-term goals of the Plan; alternatively, the government may come to exercise so little effective control over business behavior that the Plan will become a mere forecasting exercise without actually being able to influence the course of events. Even if these pitfalls are avoided, there remain the problems of participation of all relevant interest groups in plan formulation, finding effective and flexible noncoercive methods of expressing the government's viewpoint, and finally, coping with the dual issues of income distribution and price movements. Our next chapter is devoted to this last problem.

[11] Andrew Shonfield, *Modern Capitalism: The Changing Balance of Public and Private Power*, New York: Oxford University Press, 1965, pp. 128–129.

[12] Sanche de Gramont, "A Bas—Everything!" *New York Times Magazine*, June 2, 1968, p. 23.

QUESTIONS FOR CLASS DISCUSSION

1. Why is a neutral government policy in economic matters regarded as impractical in capitalist countries?

2. Why are most foreign banking systems more amenable to use for economic planning purposes than is that of the United States?

3. What is the inherent and vital element in fiscal policies used for economic stabilization? Give examples by reference to Swedish experience.

4. What is meant by the "mix" of aggregate demand, and what is its relevance to economic planning?

5. Why is the economic planning of the Netherlands called "econometric planning"?

6. To what extent and in what manner does a Dutch economic plan incorporate groups having different economic interests?

7. What is the function of the Central Planning Bureau in Dutch economic planning?

8. What is the evidence on the degree of success Dutch economic planning has experienced?

9. What is the significance of the term *indicative* as used to refer to French economic planning?

10. What is the specific role of the *Commissariat Général du Plan* in French economic planning?

11. In what sense has French economic planning involved free discussion by interested parties?

12. Specifically, what is the role of Modernization Commissions in French economic planning? May this role appear somewhat different in practice than in theory?

13. What self-serving reasons may cause a French private industrial enterprise to conform voluntarily with plan goals?

14. What affirmative incentives are offered French private economic interests to conform with planned goals?

15. Why are there differences in various overall evaluations of the success French economic planning has experienced?

16. Macroplanning — guideposts and incomes policies

Even the most carefully drawn plans (to paraphrase Robert Burns) often go astray; when modern economic plans go astray, they veer most often in the direction of inflation. Inflation, by which we mean simply a chronic rise in the general price level, has proved a distressingly persistent occurrence in Western Europe and North America during the past two decades. Compared with 1963 figures, consumer prices had increased by approximately 50 percent by 1971 in the Netherlands, Britain, and Japan, followed by 38 percent in France, 33 percent in Italy and the United States, and 29 percent in Canada. West Germany's 26 percent over eight years still represents an inflationary rate of 3 percent annually, or a doubling of prices in 25 years.[1] For the typical American worker, inflation meant that the real purchasing power of his or her take-home pay was no greater in 1971 than it had been in 1965.

THE PROBLEM OF INFLATION

Economists who take pride in the belief that economic science has helped create institutions to avoid excessive unemployment in the total economy should ponder the record of inflation just cited. Perhaps we have merely exchanged one problem for another. Although unemployment, especially unemployment comparable to that experienced during the Great Depression in the United States, represents an appalling waste of human resources and a potential threat to social stability, the debilitating effects of persistent inflation, though more subtle, cannot be overlooked.

If the income of each individual kept pace with the ascending price level, inflation would not be such a vital matter for social concern. But this is hardly the case in the real world; while some people may be able to increase their real incomes during inflationary periods, individuals in groups with relatively fixed income positions will watch their purchasing power erode away. The erosion is cumulative over long periods and works a special hardship on those trying to provide for future economic needs. Many of the traditional forms of low-risk savings such as insurance policies, bank accounts, and government bonds are not inflation-proof. Assets such as real estate or common stocks that can be expected to rise in value when inflation occurs necessarily involve a higher degree of risk than the moderate-income individual may be prepared to assume.

The probability that those lacking wealth and political power will generally have fewer avenues of escape from the detrimental effects of inflation than those already well situated means that the income-redistribution effects of inflation may actually operate in the direction of greater economic inequality. That is why inflation is sometimes described as "the cruelest tax."

Inflation also complicates the economic decision-making process, impairing the quest for efficiency at the corporation level and in the economy as a whole. Every calculation must include a margin for anticipated price rises, thus increasing interest rates and the prices of contractual services. Producers attempt to hoard raw materials or choose to build new factories in anticipation of future demand, thereby perpetuating the inflationary pressure of excess aggregate demand. Throughout the economy there is a temptation to skimp on quality or customer services as a cost-cutting measure. Exporters find their products being priced out of international markets, and the nation may encounter a balance-of-payments crisis.

This melancholy roster should serve as evidence that inflation is a serious economic problem; the question is whether it can be avoided while

[1]U.S. Council of Economic Advisers, *Economic Report of the President, 1972*, Washington, D.C., 1968, p. 304.

achieving the equally laudable goals of full employment and sustained economic growth. The obvious recourse is to the fiscal and monetary policy tools described in Chapter 15. If inflation is the opposite of unemployment, the argument runs, then the prescribed increase in aggregate demand to cure the latter suggests a decrease in aggregate demand to cure the former. Anti-inflationary measures would include some combination of tighter monetary policy to raise interest rates, higher taxes levied on individuals and corporations, and reductions in governmental expenditures.

Recent experience in the United States, however, has created doubts concerning the efficacy of relying solely on the aggregate-demand approach to securing a full-employment economy in which the price level remains relatively stable. Congressional willingness to *reduce* taxes to stimulate the economy, first demonstrated in 1964, is no guarantee of a parallel willingness to *increase* taxes to avoid inflationary overheating. Congress balked for two years before passing the tax rise of 1968, while prices increased at roughly 3 percent each year. Monetary policy during inflationary periods is likely to be a blunt instrument; the "credit squeeze" of 1966 sent the housing industry into a tailspin in an effort to restrain the whole economy. The goal of restrictive fiscal and monetary policies is to reduce, directly or indirectly, the level of investment in new equipment or of expenditures on "human capital" programs of education, job retraining, and public health. Since new technology and skills are embodied in such expenditures, the danger exists that, in attempting to achieve short-term stability by fiscal and monetary means, the long-term growth potential of the economy may be jeopardized.

Moreover, the historical record shows that the price level may begin to rise while substantial aggregate unemployment remains, a finding that leads to the gloomy possibility that the elimination of inflation may be achievable only by depressing the economy *well below* the full-employment point. If this framework is correct, the manipulation of aggregate demand in an attempt to achieve full employment and price stability simultaneously is both futile and self-defeating.

In recent years some economists have put forth the view that the unpleasant choice between some inflation and some unemployment might be avoided if greater attention is devoted to a different set of economic relations—the connection between wages and prices. Keynes himself anticipated that wage rates could be an inflationary force in an expanding economy. "These points, where a further increase in effective demand in terms of money is liable to cause a discontinuous rise in the wage-unit, might be deemed, from a certain point of view, to be positions of semi-inflation, having some analogy to the absolute inflation which ensues on an increase in effective demand in circumstances of full employment."[2] It is in this intermediate range that most of the industrialized nations of the Western world

[2] J. M. Keynes, *The General Theory of Employment, Interest and Money*, New York: Harcourt Brace Jovanovich, 1936, p. 301.

operate most of the time. The Keynesian remedies of fiscal and monetary policy presumedly are capable of avoiding the extremes of massive unemployment and galloping inflation. The search by these nations for some institutional form of an incomes policy, which we will describe in the following pages, is more of a fine-tuning device, geared toward the suppression of a less serious, but still bothersome, gradual upward drift of the general price level over time.

The structure of an economy in which wage-price interactions are a vital element is vastly different from that in which the model of perfect competition holds sway. Labor unions are assumed to exist as mature economic institutions possessing both political influence and effective bargaining power in negotiating wage rates and other conditions of employment. Employers are assumed to be oligopolistic corporations exercising a degree of control over the market prices of their products and competing against other firms in their industry primarily in nonprice areas. Thus the stage is set on which the "wage-price spiral" can operate, with wage increases passed on to consumers in the form of price rises that at least cover the increased wage costs and, more likely, serve as an opportunity to push up profit levels as well. It is apparent that the effectiveness of fiscal and monetary policy moves to combat inflation may be seriously compromised if unions can offset personal tax increases at the bargaining table and corporations can shift higher interest costs or tax rates to the consumer in the form of price rises. If the government sector is large enough so that its fiscal policy decisions can affect the entire economy, it is probably also, for better or worse, in a position to influence other economic variables, including wages and prices.

Opinions will differ concerning the validity of these assumptions, but few will deny that there is some correspondence between them and the conditions observed in the present-day American economy. A firmer basis for judgment can be gained by looking at a simple model of wage-price inflation. The easily comprehended approach of Professor Sidney Weintraub, a pioneer in this area of economic theory, will enhance the subsequent discussion of policy issues.[3]

A WAGE-PRICE MODEL

Following Weintraub,[4] the total money value of all goods and services sold in an economy can be denoted as the product of the average price level (P) multiplied by the quantity of physical output (Q). This revenue is then apportioned as income in the form of wage payments and returns to other

---

[3]Sidney Weintraub, *Classical Keynesianism, Monetary Theory, and the Price Level*, Philadelphia: Chilton, 1961, is the book perhaps best suited for undergraduate use.

[4]*Ibid.*, chap. 3.

factors of production; thus, total sales receipts equal some multiple (k) of the total wage bill that results when the average money wage (w) is paid to each of the total number of workers (N). Stated algebraically,

$$PQ = k(wN) \qquad (1)$$

The equation holds because we assign k a value that makes it balance. (For instance, if the wage bill is $\frac{1}{2}$ of all sales revenue, then $k = 2$; if $\frac{2}{3}$, then $k = \frac{3}{2}$; if $\frac{4}{5}$, then $k = \frac{5}{4}$; and so forth.) Dividing both sides of the previous equation by Q yields

$$P = k \ \frac{wN}{Q} \qquad (2)$$

If k remains relatively constant, as is usually observed to be the case over short periods (actually k changes very slowly over longer periods as well), then the price level will rise or fall depending on whether unit labor costs, defined as the wage bill per unit of physical output, rise or fall. A rising money wage rate thus becomes a potential source of inflationary pressure in the economy. A final bit of algebra focuses the key role of wages more sharply:

$$P = k \ \frac{w}{Q/N} = k \ \frac{w}{A} \qquad (3)$$

where average productivity (A) equals output (Q) divided by the number of workers (N).

Average productivity depends on several factors, including the quantity of capital goods available for use, the education and skill of the work force, and the level of managerial efficiency prevailing in the economy. Improvements in the quantity and quality of human and physical capital over time should allow average productivity to grow, thus providing an environment in which wage increases can occur without inflationary consequences.

A ratio of one number to another is unchanged if both parts increase by the same percentage. The importance of the third equation, therefore, lies in the key conclusion that *prices need not increase so long as the percentage change in the average wage level does not exceed the rate of average productivity increase.* This is a guidepost rule for wage determination in an economy committed to the goal of price stability.

An important corollary of the guidepost rule is that if wages and productivity move together the distribution of income will be constant. The residual left over for nonwage incomes goes up proportionately also, leaving the relative position of each group unchanged. Economic interest groups following the guidepost rule would thereby sacrifice the possibility of short-term gains at the expense of competing groups in order to share in the fruits of long-term economic progress without fear of losses due to inflation.

The preceding pages have outlined a theory of the wage-price spiral in abstract terms. There are no heroes or villains in the abstract model—it doesn't much matter whether the motivating force is corporate policy that marks up wage costs to set product prices, unions bent on securing a bigger slice of the income-distribution pie, or simply the path of least resistance in a complex economic system. Nor does it matter that no precise designation of the sources of productivity advance is possible. If a firm political decision to eradicate creeping inflation is made, however, new institutional forms for dealing with the inevitable conflicts that arise under an incomes policy must be devised. We will discuss the efforts of the United States in this area in some detail before moving on to the experiences of other industrialized nations.

WAGE-PRICE GUIDEPOSTS IN THE UNITED STATES

The rate of economic growth in the United States lagged over the latter half of the decade of the 1950s, and unemployment amounting to over 4 percent of the labor force persisted. A strange phenomenon was noted at that time: Prices continued to inch upward, even though the economy was supposedly depressed. When the stagnation continued into 1961, the government undertook a policy of economic expansion to close the gap between the actual level of output and the full-employment potential of the economy. In this setting, the fear was expressed that the price drift might accelerate under the pressure of more rapid economic growth.

Accordingly, the 1962 *Economic Report of the President* enunciated, for the first time, guidelines on noninflationary wage and price behavior.

> The general guide for noninflationary wage behavior is that the rate of increase in wage rates (including fringe benefits) in each industry be equal to the trend rate of over-all productivity increase. General acceptance of this guide would maintain stability of labor cost per unit of output for the economy as a whole—although not of course for individual industries.
>
> The general guide for noninflationary price behavior calls for price reductions if the industry's rate of productivity increase exceeds the over-all rate—for this would mean declining unit labor costs; it calls for an appropriate increase in price if the opposite relationship prevails; and it calls for stable prices if the two rates of productivity increase are equal.[5]

[5]U.S. Council of Economic Advisers, *Economic Report of the President, 1962*, Washington, D.C. 1962, p. 189.

Upward modifications in the guidelines were permitted in cases in which industries were attempting to attract additional labor, additional profits were needed to finance expansion in capacity, or wage rates were below those for similar types of work in other industries. In general, however, it was hoped that the guideposts would be followed, accepted by both unions and management as vastly preferable to the unpleasant alternatives of government price fixing, compulsory arbitration, or direct participation by government in wage negotiations as a means of holding the wage-price spiral in check.

There are two points in the preceding quotation that deserve special emphasis. First, it is *overall*, economy-wide productivity that establishes the standard in *all* industries. If each industry were to raise wages in line with productivity gains in its own industry, there would soon be wide disparities in wage rates *between* industries for workers filling similar jobs. Second, high-productivity industries cannot merely hold prices steady— there would have to be price cuts to balance the rises in low-productivity sectors for the general price level to remain unaffected. If industries in which lower prices were indicated failed to act, their fattened profit margins, resulting from lower unit wage costs, would be a bitter pill for unions abiding by the guidepost criterion.

The initial guidepost proposal encountered mixed reactions. Some dismissed it as a "jawbone" policy relying on persuasion rather than enforceable sanctions; others feared that the guideposts would prove to be the entering wedge to much more radical federal involvement in economic affairs. For the first time, the possible connection between individual wage and price decisions in the private sector and inflation in the total economy became a matter for public concern and debate.

The guidepost concept is still evolving as a policy tool in the United States, but it seems accurate to characterize its present status as a presidential touchstone for public statements and for behind-the-scenes conversations with business and labor groups on the subject of inflation. Public awareness of the existence of the guidepost policy has been concentrated on a few episodes, especially the confrontations with the steel industry in 1962, 1966, and 1968. In each case a price increase by the leading steel firms was criticised by the President or his Council of Economic Advisers, and in all but the 1966 instance, a partial rollback of the original price changes took place. Steel is crucial to the price level in the United States because it is an important cost element in other products, especially automobiles. Some economists believe that the wage-price guideposts were originally developed with the steel industry primarily in mind.

The executive branch of government has several avenues of persuasion available, such as limiting defense purchases from industries involved in inflationary wage or price moves and reducing strategic stockpiles to exert downward pressure on prices. In general, however, the full prestige and force of the presidential office has not been applied in specific instances. The guideposts were broken to settle the 1966 airline machinists' strike that grounded most flights, and the inflation ensuing from heavy military involvement in Vietnam made it impractical to hope for management or union compliance in the face of general price rises.

President Nixon's New Economic Policy

Most economic studies ascribe some credit to guideposts in stabilizing unit labor costs between 1961 and 1965, when the return to a full-employment economy was achieved under Presidents Kennedy and Johnson.[6] It remained for a Republican president, who previously had often voiced opposition to direct controls over wages and prices, to transform the guidepost concept into a set of temporary institutions for dealing with inflationary pressures. On August 15, 1971 President Nixon announced a New Economic Policy (an ironic title to students of the Soviet economy) consisting of a 90-day freeze on prices, rents, wages, and salaries; this was followed by Phase II, which established an administrative apparatus to regulate wages and prices on a semipermanent basis. Phase II lasted from November 1971 until January 1973, when Phase III, a system of quasi-voluntary controls, was instituted.

The economic conditions that provoked such drastic measures were the familiar lineup of sluggish growth in output and employment coupled with persistent price and wage inflation, and balance-of-payments difficulties. For the first time in the twentieth century, the United States was importing more goods and services than it was exporting. Overseas holders of dollars, fearing devaluation, were shifting to gold or other currencies. British "stagflation" had arrived in the United States!

The initial freeze on wages and prices was aimed at breaking the spiral of psychological expectations that boosted wage demands, speeded up construction and inventory accumulation, and perhaps accelerated consumer purchases in anticipation of future inflation. It was believed that once the shock effect had registered, the way could be paved for moderate increases to take account of productivity gains and to mitigate the misallocations and inequities that a permanent freeze would surely create. A temporary tariff surcharge and suspension of dollar convertibility into gold (a de facto devaluation of 12 percent) were to provide a temporary fillip to the balance of payments and thus stimulate domestic output.

In its *1972 Economic Report*, the Council of Economic Advisers concluded that the initial 90-day freeze had been an "unqualified success" and cited the slowing of the rate of increase in consumer prices, industrial wholesale prices, and average hourly earnings as proof. Perhaps equally important, moreover, was the relative absence of strong protests from economists, labor leaders, or businessmen amid the general sentiment that more forceful policies were needed. Whether inflationary expectations had

---

[6] J. Sheahan, *The Wage-Price Guideposts*, Washington, D.C.: Brookings, 1967.

indeed been exorcised or merely stifled for a brief period was a major question to be answered during Phase II, as the sequel of the August 15 program was called.

The Phase II Cost of Living Council's administrative structure was embodied in a Price Commission and a Pay Board with members originally divided equally among business, labor, and public representatives. Among the first acts of these bodies, which became operational in November 1971, was to announce targets of no more than a 2½ percent annual increase in prices and a 5½ percent rate for wages. These goals were to be achieved through review of key industrial prices and union settlements, with the power to roll back increases judged to be out of line. This soon alienated four labor representatives on the Pay Board, who resigned to protest what they regarded as an unfair cutback imposed on labor-contract pay levels. The President responded by abolishing the categories of membership on the Pay Board.

An assessment of the Phase II is hindered by the failure of other variables to remain constant. President Nixon, facing a reelection campaign, proposed a 1972 budget calling for a deficit of more than $35 billion. In addition, prices outside the purview of the Price Commission, especially for meat and fresh produce, shot up. Phase III, which was announced early in 1973, abolished mandatory wage and price controls and the agencies that enforced them. In their place an appeal for voluntary compliance by labor and management was made by President Nixon, backed by threats of selective controls for violators. Thus the institutional apparatus continues to evolve.

Inflation cannot be halted by any control mechanism if fiscal and monetary conditions continue to provide excessive stimulation to the economy. If restraint can be exercised in these areas, however, there is some evidence that the United States has considerable latitude for administering an effective guidepost policy: The importance of prices in key sectors, such as steel and autos, is recognized; there is widespread sentiment to give controls a try among the business community and rank-and-file workers who are tired of inflation; and the Pay Board and Price Commission did not initially appear to be pawns in the game of partisan politics. Guideposts are successful only to the extent that they shift the Phillips Curve relationship between historically observed rates of unemployment and inflation. That is a long-term proposition, with business and union leaders eventually accepting the new status quo of moderation in pressing their wage and price claims. This appears to be one of those rare times when economic analysts get a second look at the results of significant changes in economic policy.

INCOMES POLICIES IN OTHER COUNTRIES

Three nations serve to illustrate possible institutional forms of incomes policies. They are Sweden, the Netherlands, and the United Kingdom. It

is no coincidence that all three are heavily dependent on international trade
to sustain highly developed economies; the sensitivity of the balance of
payments to inflationary pressures is so great in such cases that opposing
economic interest groups participate more readily in programs if they recognize the necessity of keeping exports competitive in world markets.

Sweden

The unique feature of Swedish wage policy is the central wage bargain
that is drawn up, without direct government intervention, between the organization of trade unions (LO) and an association of employers (SAF).

> Usually, since 1952, the SAF and LO have met at intervals of one or
> two years to thrash out the differences of all the LO members who
> are employed by SAF members, which means more than eight hundred
> thousand jobs or more than one fifth of the entire labor force. When
> the negotiating bodies of the SAF and the LO reach some sort of
> compromise they draw up a recommendation, a preliminary agreement,
> which acts as a guideline for their affiliated organizations. The national
> unions and their opposite numbers then sit down to work out detailed
> industry-wide agreements within the framework of the central agreement.
> If they run into snags, they can refer them to the central federations
> for mediation. None of the agreements becomes final, however, until
> all the organizations are ready to sign.[7]

The result has been full employment and an excellent record of strike
avoidance, but not, unfortunately, a very impressive example of noninflationary wage policy. The problem is centered in the supplemental wage
increases requested by the LO for industries in which earnings have lagged,
usually the less prosperous industries such as textiles. The result of this
practice of wage solidarity is to place deliberate pressure on the less efficient firms in an industry, perhaps even forcing them out of business.[8] The
most important impact of the Swedish system thus seems to be the promotion of economic efficiency by encouraging modern methods of production
and by shifting labor out of low-productivity sectors, rather than the adherence to any wage policy per se. Wage bargains far in excess of productivity advances have in fact prevailed, and they must be cited as a major
element of rapid inflation over the past decade.

The Swedish pattern of central wage negotiation is possible only because of the cohesiveness and power of each of the contracting parties.
This fact, combined with a mutual distrust of government involvement at
the bargaining table, allows some accommodation to be reached on the
issue of relative wages in different industries. The degree of cooperation

---

[7]Frederic Fleisher, *The New Sweden: The Challenge of a Disciplined Democracy,* New York: McKay, 1967, pp. 88–89.

[8]Andrew Shonfield, *Modern Capitalism: The Changing Balance of Public and
Private Power,* London: Oxford University Press, 1965, pp. 207–209.

between labor unions and employers in Sweden would seem to constitute the ideal setting for a broad social view of the inflationary consequences of privately determined wage bargains. That sufficient self-discipline is not forthcoming to maintain wages within the bounds of productivity growth is evidence that a voluntary incomes policy is unlikely to succeed elsewhere. Indeed, the Swedish government may eventually be forced to play a larger role in this area, stating its views on wages more forcefully and perhaps acting to restrain supplemental increases above the basic agreement.

The Netherlands

Unlike Sweden, the Netherlands has adopted direct wage and price controls in an attempt to restrain inflationary pressures. The optimal range of wage and price movements is calculated by the Central Planning Bureau, which uses input-output analysis and econometric models to predict trends in output, prices, and the balance of payments under alternative policy decisions.

During the period of severe restraint from 1947 to 1953, real wages failed to increase at all, with labor unions apparently willing to hold the line on wages for fear of mass unemployment if the Dutch position in international trade was not strengthened by price stability. As the full-employment point was reached at the end of the decade of the 1950s, employers began to grow restive, along with the unions, because of the difficulty of recruiting labor under the system of controls; the practice of paying "black" wages beyond legally permitted rates became widespread. Finally, in 1959, industry productivity advances were permitted to enter as a factor in wage negotiations, a change that led to highly dubious statistical manipulations by the industries involved and to a rapid rise in the overall wage level. The government responded by invoking price controls to keep firms in line and a temporary freeze in 1966 to halt runaway wages. It seems apparent that a cooperative attitude of unions and employers toward wage and price regulations is a thing of the past. So is the competitive advantage achieved for Dutch products during the early period when such controls were effective. The Netherlands, despite its arsenal of governmental regulations, has not shown that it is markedly superior to Sweden in limiting the inflationary impact of wage and price decisions under conditions of full employment; in fact, the tendency seems to be away from government intervention in this area of the economy.

It appears that the guidelines policy machinery has degenerated into an ad hoc review of wage settlements with some residual central power to rescind individual agreements judged too far out of line.

The United Kingdom

The British economy in the postwar period has exhibited an interesting mixture of economic phenomena—slow growth of output, full employment, limited productivity advance, and a very delicate balance-of-payments position. Money wages have risen less than in other industrial nations, but when the inadequate record of productivity growth is taken into account, wages nevertheless become a potential source of inflationary pressure.

Government efforts to moderate wage pressures date from 1961 and 1962, when a "pay pause" was instituted in an attempt to hold the line and the newly formed National Economic Development Council (NEDDY) sought to link questions of short-term stabilization and long-term growth. The Labour government was elected in 1964 on a platform that included a promise to halt the "Tory stop-go" policy of alternate stimulation and restraint of the economy, but in succeeding years the deteriorating balance-of-payments situation has severely constricted its freedom of action. The 1966 decision to freeze wages completely for a period of one year and the subsequent retention of the power to delay proposed wage and price increases could not prevent the need to devalue the currency late in 1967. The National Board for Prices and Incomes, which is charged with the review of increases in those areas, appears to doubt its own effectiveness because of the pressure from other government agencies to avoid strikes in export industries.[9]

The epidemic of strikes by workers in key sectors (among them, railway employees, coal miners, postal workers, and longshoremen) in recent years demonstrates how vulnerable the British economy has become. To demand restraint of public-service unions has proved difficult during prolonged strikes, and each round of increases in the public sector makes it all the more difficult to restrain unions in the private sector.

The first British experiment with a statutory incomes policy ended in 1968. More recently an informal agreement between the Conservative government and the Confederation of British Industry (CBI) placed a ceiling on price increases in the private sector of 5 percent annually. The same limit was also to be applied to nationalized industries.

In spite of some success on the price front, wages continued to rise by over 8 percent each year throughout 1972. This intolerable situation resulted in the renewed imposition of strict curbs on prices, wages, dividends, and rents in late 1972 and in 1973. These measures came about after union leaders refused to support a program of voluntary guidelines. Prime Minister Heath patterned the British controls on America's Phase II administration by a Pay Board and a Price Commission.

In summary, it appears that an incomes policy will finally be given a rigorous trial in the United Kingdom. The Trades Union Council seemingly refuses to accept any strict productivity criteria as the basis for wage negotiations, and in the light of the productivity experience one can scarcely blame them. The modernization of techniques of production and the evolution of a cooperative approach toward noninflationary wage and

[9]*The Economist*, July 27–August 2, 1968, p. 42.

price movements can occur only when a longer-range perspective has been achieved. In the meantime, strict controls have replaced voluntary cooperation, over the continued opposition of the Trades Union Council.

LESSONS FROM RECENT EXPERIENCE

From the preceding pages the conclusion emerges that an incomes policy, if it is to be successful, must avoid several of the defects demonstrated by the policies discussed. An effective structure would have to cope with the persistent "wage drift" that results from the upgrading of employees to higher job categories and the expansion of fringe benefits as a means of avoiding wage controls. Some means must be found for dealing with "exceptional cases" of inequity between labor categories without creating a general clamor for individual permission to exceed general guidelines. Also, a conscious decision on whether to allow the downward course of low-productivity industries to be accelerated by maintaining their wage levels in line with economy-wide productivity advances must be faced. The greatest obstacle, however, is likely to be the issue of income distribution.

> What a fully fledged "incomes policy" really implies is the equivalent of a new Social Contract: it presupposes a society in which the different interest groups have marked out a sufficient area of agreement about the present distribution of wealth to deny themselves the right to try, in the future, to obtain certain advantages at each other's expense. Without this, one or another will surely find sooner or later a tactical opportunity for redistributing some of the existing wealth, and exploit it—even if it results in inflation. The common interest in avoiding the erosion of money values will not, by itself, be an overriding argument against making such an attempt. All this is another way of saying that a practical approach to a more rational wages policy must be deliberately and extensively political.[10]

To preview the final chapter, it is our view that new forms of cooperation between economic interest groups are essential if the American capitalistic system is to survive and prosper. If this is the case, the question of income distribution must eventually come into the orbit of rational economic policy rather than being settled by a survival-of-the-fittest struggle in a world of continual inflation. The wage-price guideposts or some variant that recognizes the role of productivity trends and money wages in the economic process seems a logical starting point.

The political nature of a workable incomes policy is demonstrated by the kinds of economic sanctions it requires. A wide variety of presidential actions are potentially available to discourage violators of guidepost regulations, ranging from shifts in government purchases to surveillance by regulatory agencies to actions in the area of antitrust and union recognition

[10]Shonfield, p. 219.

policies.[11] These are unpleasant to consider, but so is continual inflation; economic policy choices are almost never easy. The hope is for an eventual recognition of the mutual stake in long-term price stability among all economic interest groups. "The only valid and noninflationary standard for wage advances is the productivity principle. If price stability is eventually to be restored and maintained in a high-employment U.S. economy, wage settlements must once again conform to that standard."[12] An effective incomes policy may one day take its place beside fiscal and monetary actions as a fundamental means of achieving full employment without inflation.

QUESTIONS FOR CLASS DISCUSSION

1. Why is persistent inflation characterized as "distressing" in the Western nations?

2. Has the emergence of Keynesian theories met the problem of controlling inflation in nations where private enterprise is a major factor in economic operations?

3. In what ways does inflation affect the decision-making at the level of the individual firm?

4. Why do so many current economic issues in the Western world involve the dichotomy between full employment and stable value of the monetary unit?

5. Why does it appear that in the United States there is a grave doubt as to whether we can continue to rely on an aggregate-demand approach to the resolution of this dichotomy?

6. To what extent does the problem of persistent inflation in the United States find its source in the fact that our economy has departed from a situation of truly effective competition?

7. Why is there now a real question as to whether fiscal and monetary measures can in fact yield concurrently high levels of employment and stable prices?

8. Given technological advances and improved managerial skills in industry, is there any reason why we should not contrive some way to share the benefits of these advances fairly and yet avoid inflation?

9. Has the experience of the United States with wage-price guideposts been successful?

10. Why must overall, economy-wide advances in productivity be the criterion by which wage and price movements are limited?

11. Has the experience of Sweden demonstrated that voluntary wage and price restraint can be successful in avoiding inflation? Insofar as it has shown any success, what special circumstances may have been responsible?

[11]Sidney Weintraub, "In Defense of Wage-Price Guidelines . . . Plus," unpublished paper, 1966.
[12]U.S. Council of Economic Advisers, *Economic Report of the President, 1968*, Washington, D.C., 1968, p. 126.

12. What would be a fair evaluation of the success of the Netherlands in avoiding inflation while encouraging economic growth?

13. Insofar as Great Britain has to some degree limited her wage-price spiral, what has been the cost of doing so in terms of firm governmental limitation of private decision making?

14. If the United States is to effectively seek both relatively full employment and relative price stability, why are new forms of cooperation between economic interest groups necessary?

17. The welfare state— the scope of social services

Paralleling the increased concern for new institutional forms of aggregate economic planning in recent years is the inclusion of questions of social policy within the framework of economic decision making. Social programs have become a major feature of every modern industrialized nation; therefore they are not the exclusive province of any narrowly defined category among possible economic systems. At some point the scope and level of communally provided social services becomes sufficiently great, however, that we can begin to deal with the concept of the welfare state.

A "welfare state" is a state in which organized power is deliberately used (through politics and administration) in an effort to modify the play of market forces in at least three dimensions—first, by guaranteeing individuals and families a minimum income irrespective of the market value of their work or their property; second, by narrowing the extent of insecurity by enabling individuals and families to meet certain "social contingencies" (for example, sickness, old age and unemployment) which would lead otherwise to individual and family crisis; and third, by ensuring that all citizens without distinction of status or class are offered the best standards available in relation to a certain agreed range of social services.[1]

The humanitarian motives behind the welfare state are apparent from this definition, but there is an economic rationale as well. In every area of life subject to a large degree of uncertainty, insurance schemes are likely to be found also. Insurance allows a group that is subject to an event for which the total probability of occurrence is known to pool their funds so that the individuals actually affected can be compensated; a certain level of premium payments guards against the uncertainty of possible catastrophic economic loss. In the annuity form of insurance, a lump-sum premium guarantees yearly payments for the lifetime of the beneficiary in order to guard against the contingency of outliving a fixed amount of savings.

If insurance is capable of providing security against catastrophic events, the question arises of why state-supported schemes should ever be needed to supplant the freedom of private individuals to choose and the ability of private enterprises to supply the varieties of insurance coverage desired. A partial answer comes from an understanding of the nature of the actuarial calculations on which insurance premiums are based. Risks, for instance, may be too great to be insured against at a rate people can reasonably afford. Thus earthquake insurance in a city straddling a fault line or burglary insurance in a crime-ridden area might be judged matters for social concern and action in the form of subsidized rates.

There is an understandable tendency for insurers to search out subcategories of low-risk clients in order to offer them policies at especially attractive rates. Health insurance is cheaper if older people are denied covage, and automobile insurance is available at reduced cost from a company that does not insure teen-age drivers. When exclusion of risky groups creates serious social consequences, it may be desirable, on grounds of equity or need, to require some type of all-inclusive compulsory insurance. The case for such programs is strengthened if there are also economies of scale to be gained from organization and administration on a comprehensive basis. Finally, economies of scale may exist.

Private charity and private insurance alone, it is believed, are likely to prove less than adequate in meeting expectations of citizens in economically advanced nations. Purely economic considerations of specific welfare pro-

[1]Asa Briggs, "The Welfare State in Historical Perspective," in Mayer N. Zeld, ed., *Social Welfare Institutions*, New York: Wiley, 1965, p. 43.

grams quickly give way to normative questions of what services a society ought to provide to advance the general well-being of the population. The definition cited previously includes consideration of standards of minimum quantity and uniform quality of services as possible justifications for creating the welfare state.

A discussion of the scope of welfare activities in any nation should include some mention of the spirit in which the programs are administered. Cultural values play a large role within any society in determining attitudes of dominant groups toward those outside the economic mainstream. Each country is free to choose whether selected areas of human behavior such as the nutrition of children, the treatment of mental illness, or the provision of dentures should be a matter of governmental rather than strictly private responsibility. Modern nations have included a wide variety of social-welfare programs among the basic rights of citizenship; we should beware of the xenophobic fallacy of considering measures that are foreign to our own experience to be inherently undesirable under any circumstances.

Each nation also has considerable latitude in choosing what distribution of income among groups within the society is preferred; thus, the potential importance of welfare programs in determining final consumption patterns should be noted. Just as a progressive income tax theoretically reduces inequality by *taking* proportionately more from the wealthy than from the poor, a welfare program that *gives* benefits on an equal per-capita basis or is weighted toward low-income groups serves to even out the standard of living among different sectors of the population. Differing value judgments concerning an equitable division of economic rewards may be a very delicate political issue, and actual adjustments to changing situations can perhaps occur most readily under the guise of comprehensive social benefits such as universal education or subsidized public transportation. The juxtaposition of Federalist Paper Number 10 and a current daily newspaper will reaffirm the crucial and timeless nature of these issues for a democratic society.[2]

WELFARE PROGRAMS IN THE UNITED STATES

Comprehensive programs of social insurance in the United States date from the New Deal legislation of the 1930s. The severe depression of that decade made it painfully evident that the ability of an individual to meet the economic risks of unemployment, sickness, and old age was constricted in an economy subject to prolonged periods of high aggregate unemployment. Present programs are for the most part extensions of the Social Security Act of 1935; coverage has also been expanded, with virtually all employed workers except transient farm and domestic workers protected

[2]Alexander Hamilton, James Madison, and John Jay, *The Federalist*. The Tenth Paper, written by Madison, served as the starting point for Charles A. Beard's famous book, *An Economic Interpretation of the Constitution of the United States*, New York: Macmillan, 1913.

by the basic social-security measures or by similar provisions for government and railroad employees. A brief survey of the major areas of assistance will give an overview of the general nature of welfare programs in the United States.[3] Such a survey also provides a point of departure for the subsequent discussion of welfare measures in other countries.

Social Security

The best-known legislation is the Social Security program, which provides cash benefits when earnings are cut off by old age, total disability, or death. It is an annuity scheme with benefits varying according to the amount of social-security taxes collected from the individual and his employer; however, congressional action raising both benefits and taxes to compensate for persistent inflation has partially modified the annuity program into one involving transfer payments from the currently employed to retired and disabled workers. More than nine-tenths of all citizens reaching age 65 are now eligible for monthly cash benefits under Social Security; a similar number of children and mothers would be eligible for payments if the male head of the family died. Benefits are a right rather than a matter of charity, so a retired worker can qualify even if he also has a private pension or some other form of personal savings. Since 1966, health insurance for the aged, popularly known as Medicare, has been included in the package of retirement benefits. The long and sometimes bitter debate over whether this area was properly one for governmental involvement illustrates the political element underlying the choice of social-welfare activities in any society.

Unemployment Insurance

Unemployment insurance is an element in the system of social security that is administered by the individual states but is subject to federal standards. The programs are financed by a payroll tax levied on employers; the rate varies according to the past unemployment experience of the individual firm. Workers who become involuntarily unemployed are eligible to receive roughly half of their weekly income for up to six months. Recipients must be willing to work if an appropriate job is available; in recent years retraining programs have been established to enable the unemployed to qualify for new jobs requiring different skills from those they have.

Workmen's Compensation

The workmen's compensation program to assist those injured on the job was the first form of social insurance to gain wide acceptance in America; most states passed legislation in this area before 1920. The injured worker

---

[3]Most of the information in this section is condensed from the pamphlet of the U.S. Social Security Administration entitled *Social Security Programs in the United States*, Washington, D.C., 1966.

receives cash payments and free medical care while recovering. The employer pays the cost of liability insurance, which is often secured through a private insurance firm.

Public Assistance

The final, and most controversial, area of social-security coverage is public assistance. Unlike the retirement, unemployment, and workmen's compensation plans, in which eligibility is related to employment, public assistance is allocated on the basis of need. Federal grants to states allow them to establish services for the aged, the blind, the disabled, and the dependent children of low-income families who are not adequately covered by other welfare programs. Each state imposes criteria for eligibility and determines the level of benefits, but the major financial share is federal in origin. In most instances the level of payments is far below the amount recognized as needed to provide a comfortable standard of living for those affected. The specific program that is growing most rapidly, whether measured by numbers covered or by total cost, is aid to families of dependent children. In recent years the question has been raised as to whether this program, which excludes children living in households containing an employed male, may not contribute inadvertently in some instances to the weakening of family ties.

The activities carried out by the Social Security Administration constitute only a limited share of the total network of welfare services provided at all levels of government. Veterans' benefits, public-health programs of immunizations or child and maternal health, recreation facilities, educational loans, public housing, and subsidized homeownership at favorable mortgage rates are also widespread. It might be thought that the United States has entered every conceivable area of welfare services. The next section will show that this is not the case; other nations have entered new fields or have created new institutional forms for treating old problems.

FROM CRADLE TO GRAVE IN OTHER COUNTRIES

It is useful to investigate the range of welfare services in economically advanced nations, although it goes without saying that the brief space devoted to this topic means a superficial glance at a complex set of philosophical, institutional, and administrative issues. To prove that the supporters and detractors who speak of "cradle to grave" welfare programs have a valid point, the discussion ranges over the entire human life cycle.[4]

[4]Further information on welfare services can be found in various publications of the International Labour Office in Geneva and the United Nations. See especially the country studies of the U.N. Department of Economic and Social Affairs under the title *Organization and Administration of Social Welfare Programmes*. The initial surveys in 1967 covered Canada, Norway, the United Arab Republic, United Kingdom, and U.S.S.R.

Birth and Childhood

Many nations include special maternity provisions within their welfare programs. Prenatal and postnatal care is one of the benefits in all countries with "socialized" health schemes; some social-security programs, including those of France, Denmark, and the Soviet Union, offset wages lost by working mothers during their pregnancies. Cash grants or free baby equipment may be provided to the families; in Sweden low-income families receive a monetary grant, layette items, and supplemental food if needed.

The claim has been made that the United States is the only industrialized nation in the Western world without a "family allowance" based on the number of minor children in each household.[5] In underpopulated nations this may be viewed as a spur to population growth, although there is no conclusive evidence on this interesting point. The Canadian program, to take a typical instance, provides monthly payments to the mother of each child under 16 years of age, and such allowances are not taxable. The question of whether the costs of child raising should be subsidized by public funds raises fundamental issues of social ethics, such as whether a relatively overpopulated nation should penalize large families by eliminating their family-allowance benefits. Discussion of the pros and cons of family allowances has become more frequent in the United States in recent years

Education is one form of child support that is so ubiquitous throughout the world that it is generally not even discussed as part of the social-welfare program. In many nations competitive examinations at various stages determine who will continue to advance to the next stage in the educational hierarchy. The financial subsidy is usually limited to direct educational expenses, although in the Soviet Union virtually every college student receives living expenses as well. In Britain most college students receive a grant for full or partial support that is administered by local governmental units; in the Netherlands the benefits extend to subsidized housing and cultural activities as well.

Medical Care

The issue of free medical care is so widely disputed in the United States that we will devote the entire next chapter to a detailed investigation of one such plan, the British National Health Service. However, it should be mentioned here that several other countries, among them Australia, Sweden, West Germany, and New Zealand, allow free medical care, either for all residents or for the employed and their dependents.

The area of medical services serves to accentuate the theoretical questions raised at the beginning of this chapter. No one doubts that maintaining a healthy population benefits both the individual citizen and the nation

---

[5]Philip Wogaman, *Guaranteed Annual Income: The Moral Issues*, Nashville, Tenn.: Abingdon, 1968.

as a whole. Yet there is no intrinsic reason why a system of private medical practice, combined with some form of private health insurance available to all, cannot provide high-quality care in an economy where most people are relatively affluent. The historical background, the ability of an existing system to keep up with changing medical needs, and the expectations of citizens expressed through the political process all converge to determine the extent of social involvement in providing health services in each specific instance. One thing is certain—health care is too vital a human concern to be viewed merely as one consumer good among many.

Employment Benefits

In the area of employment benefits the American system most nearly approaches the comprehensiveness of the social services in other industrialized nations. Pension schemes, payments to cover expenses and loss of income arising from employment-related injuries, and unemployment benefits are nearly universal elements in social-welfare systems throughout the world, although the level and duration of the payments vary greatly. Sick-leave provisions, which are often part of generous fringe-benefit packages for employees in the United States, are more often included among social-security benefits in foreign countries.

Old-age pensions in most countries may be considered essentially an employment benefit because they are usually based on credits accumulated from the payment of employment taxes. Sweden also makes housing for the elderly a basic part of retirement benefits, a concern made more urgent by the severe housing shortage there.[6]

Funeral Costs

Just for completeness, it is true that several nations allow payments upon the death of a citizen. Even critics of the cradle-to-grave welfare state must concede that it is thorough.

GUARANTEED ANNUAL INCOME

Social-welfare programs have the goal of providing those affected by the contingencies of modern life with some measure of income maintenance, albeit in a rather piecemeal and uncoordinated way. Recent proposals have been advanced that focus on setting a floor below which individual income would not be permitted to fall for any reason whatsoever. This guaranteed annual income would be a fundamental right of citizenship, a sign that a wealthy economy can afford to spare every citizen from abject poverty if it chooses to do so.

[6]Frederic Fleisher, *The New Sweden: The Challenge of a Disciplined Democracy*, New York: McKay, 1967.

The case for a guaranteed annual income can be made from divergent ideological perspectives. Robert Theobald foresees the arrival of an automated society where only a small portion of the potential work force is needed to produce an abundant quantity of goods and services; therefore, he argues, some income-redistribution scheme will be required to supply adequate purchasing power and to provide a sense of personal worth and social status apart from the identity now provided by occupational categories. Milton Friedman, another advocate, backs an income floor as a means by which a society can fulfill its humanitarian responsibilities toward the disadvantaged without creating an expensive welfare bureaucracy in which myriad regulations infringe upon the freedom of those who are assisted. He proposes a negative income tax incorporating incentives to earn as the simplest and most equitable form of payment.[7]

Rugged individualism is a dominant strain in our national past, and the idea of a guaranteed annual income clashes with deeply ingrained American cultural values. There is strong sentiment against the inherent right to income without work; those who receive charity are expected to be humble and grateful for their good fortune. The fear is expressed that the income would be spent unwisely unless there were close supervision and that an "underclass" of the dependent would be perpetuated from generation to generation.

The position in support of the guaranteed annual income cannot be developed fully here. However, it is significant to note that the individualism of the prosperous, historically and currently, proves upon close investigation to encompass several instances of socially provided access to education and other forms of economic opportunity. Also, present welfare programs have disincentive features similar to those mentioned in connection with income-maintenance schemes, in addition to exacting a toll in terms of human dignity and control over personal destiny.

The costs of income-maintenance schemes obviously depend on the level of benefits, but several estimates place the net outlay required to lift everyone above the poverty level of $3,000 (annual income, for a family of four) in the range of $20 to $30 billion per year.[8] This large amount represents less than half of either the annual increment in the U.S. gross national product or the annual outlay for military purposes. As concern has grown about the long-range prospects of a society in which the lowest fifth of the population subsists in dramatic contrast to the material comforts of the other four-fifths, more leaders from the business and academic communities have announced in favor of a guaranteed annual income, and a small experimental test of it was begun in several New Jersey communities in 1968. Dispassionate study of all facets of the proposal is obviously indicated in years to come.

[7]Robert Theobald, *Free Men and Free Markets*, Garden City, N.Y.: Doubleday, 1963; Milton Friedman, *Capitalism and Freedom*, *Chicago*: Phoenix, 1962.
[8]Wogaman, p. 20.

WHO PAYS THE BILL?

Welfare programs are expensive, whether the cost is measured in absolute terms or in the opportunity costs of alternative projects forgone. The ultimate fact that someone has to pay the bill becomes apparent over time; with comprehensive welfare programs that require earmarking a discernible share of a nation's resources to this end, it is apparent that the burden cannot entirely be shifted to someone else—the tax bite must start far down the income-distribution curve.

Greater efficiency means lower costs, but why should efficiency be greater? Will economies of scale be offset by the red tape of an overcentralized bureaucracy? Can high morale continue among members of professions that must fit into a civil-service framework? Can programs instituted during prosperous times maintain quality and momentum when the economy levels off?

There is no shortage of points to criticize or doubts to raise. At some stage, however, hard economic analysis gives way to ethical considerations. The questions of what a good society is and how it can be achieved cannot be avoided because, in part, problems spring from the same sources as the benefits enjoyed. The Marxist criticism accused capitalists of blindness to the fact that the plight of the workers derived inexorably from the system of production itself; it would be ironic if modern-day beneficiaries of capitalistic abundance should become so inured to the social realities arising in part from the complexities of modern existence that they would risk upsetting the entire system by giving traditional responses to new problems. What is required is some sort of humane pragmatism that approaches social issues openly and compassionately.

It seems likely that the guaranteed annual income will be adopted in the United States under the guise of "welfare reform." President Nixon outlined an income-maintenance scheme during his first term in office, and his unsuccessful opponent during the 1972 Presidential campaign, George McGovern, countered with a proposal of his own. Nixon's program provides for an income guarantee of $2400 for a family of four up to a maximum of $3600 for eight or more; able-bodied adults, except mothers of young children, would have to register for acceptable employment; an incentive scale would allow some outside earnings to be retained until family earnings reached $4140. The McGovern program set a higher floor—$4000 for a family of four, including some portion in food-stamp benefits; work requirements and retained earnings would probably be somewhat more lenient than the Nixon alternative. Both programs allowed for the creation of public-service jobs—200,000 in the Nixon plan and one million in McGovern's—and for expanded coverage and benefit levels under the Social Security program. Cost estimates range from approximately $6 billion initially for the Nixon package to $15 billion for the expanded coverage envisioned by the Democratic challenger.

Thus far it appears that income-maintenance schemes have negative political appeal in the United States. The McGovern trial balloon of a $1000 social-dividend payment for every American citizen was met with extreme hostility. Congressional debate on the Nixon proposal, which the President has pushed only halfheartedly, is vulnerable to any hint that employable adults might receive benefits. The saving in administrative costs to be achieved and the advantage of increased spending power for every impoverished American would appear to make some form of guaranteed annual income a worthy cause for economists and consumer lobby groups. At present, however, it remains an idea whose time has not quite come.

QUESTIONS FOR CLASS DISCUSSION

1. Specifically what may be regarded as a welfare-state form of economic planning?

2. Are advocates of welfare-state programs necessarily motivated solely by humanitarian concerns?

3. Why cannot all welfare-state arrangements for caring for the risks of human existence be provided by privately owned and operated insurance companies supplemented by private charity?

4. How are welfare-state measures related to the distribution of real incomes in our society?

5. How can one account for the beginning of comprehensive social insurance in the United States?

6. In what sense has the Social Security program come to involve some "transfer payments from the currently employed to retired and disabled workers"? Does this aspect subject it to valid criticism?

7. What is the basic difference between programs of social insurance and programs of public assistance?

8. Is it possible for a program of public assistance pertaining to some specific human need to have adverse effects on one or more of our basic institutions? Might there be socially beneficial offsets to this?

9. What is meant by saying that the proper extent of welfare programs involves philosophical, institutional, and administrative issues?

10. What is meant by a family allowance as a welfare measure? How many nations in the Western world provide for such an allowance?

11. Why is free or nearly free medical care supplied through public funds generally one of the most controversial of all welfare programs?

12. As a social-welfare program, what, in general, is the proposal for a guaranteed annual income? Why is this usually considered highly controversial?

13. With respect to the United States, is a program of guaranteed incomes clearly infeasible because of its overall cost?

14. In considering various welfare programs, why might one say that at some stage "hard economic analysis gives way to ethical considerations"?

18. The welfare state—the British National Health Service

The National Health Service segment of the 1945–1951 Labour government program probably has been discussed more widely in the United States than any other part. A great deal of misinformation about it has been popularized, and proponents and opponents quickly dismiss the program with a nod of approval or a head-shaking opprobrium wholly unwarranted in the light of its extremely complex nature. It is our aim to explain what the scheme is, how its complex parts operate, and what some of its current problems are, without attempting to pass final judgment on it.

BACKGROUND AND PURPOSES

The British National Health Service is a nationalization project only in the sense that nearly all the hospitals formerly operated by voluntary organizations and by local governments are now owned and operated by the national government. The National Health Service is, in effect, a communization of the nation's health facilities. The stated purpose of the National Health Service Act, which was passed in 1946 and became fully operative in 1948, is to establish a comprehensive health service to improve the physical and mental health of the people and to prevent, diagnose, and treat illness free of charge.[1] In practice, this has meant to every resident of Britain the free provision of the following services and facilities: the services of general medical practitioners, dentists, oculists, medical specialists, and midwives; hospitalization; surgery; X-rays; physical therapy; mental health services; hearing aids; artificial limbs; wigs (when needed because of an accident or pathological condition); home nursing; ambulance service; blood transfusions; and a host of minor supplementary services. In addition, spectacles, dentures, and pharmaceutical prescriptions have been provided for nominal or small fees. Some 80 percent of the cost of these services and facilities has been paid for directly from the national Treasury, about 2 or 3 percent from local taxation to support certain local health services, and about 10 percent from the National Insurance Fund, which regularly makes appropriations to the National Health Service.[2] The remaining 5 percent or so has come from the nominal or small charges to users of the Service. Every resident of Great Britain, including a foreign visitor who is there for more than a short time, is eligible for all of these services. As aptly expressed by a representative of the government, the National Health Service "is a governmental expenditure in just the way road maintenance is and every resident is eligible without any test [i.e., without proving inability to pay]."[3]

Before the passage of the National Health Service Act, the national and local governments had long been undertaking more and more extensive health improvement measures. Local governments had developed hospital facilities, home nursing services, medical and dental care for schoolchildren, and other services open to use on the basis of need rather than ability to pay. In 1911 a National Health Insurance Act instituted free medical services for low-income families financed by compulsory contributions from employees and their employers, supplemented by Treasury grants. For most of the population, however, general medical and dental services had to be provided privately. Although medical specialists and hospitalization were available to a limited degree to low-income groups through philanthropic hospitals and clinics or medical schools, these too were available to the majority in adequate quantity and quality only if one had the money to pay for them.

[1]*National Health Service Act*, London: H.M. Stationery Office, 1946, sec. 1.
[2]The benefits rendered by the Service, however, are not confined to people insured under the National Insurance scheme.
[3]Quoted in Robert A. Brady, *Crisis in Britain*, Berkeley: University of California Press, 1950, p. 354.

In 1946 the Labour government changed this picture radically when its National Health Service offered on a virtually free basis whatever medical services or facilities the resident of Britain needed to maintain health and to cure or alleviate disease. In Parliament the bill creating the Service encountered only token opposition. The opposition accepted "the principle of a national, comprehensive, 100 percent health service."[4] However, opposition to the bill (and, after its passage, to the Minister of Health's execution of its provisions) came from the British Medical Association. Shortly before the Act was to become fully effective, the Association threatened to sabotage it by having its members refrain from participation in the Service. After certain assurances were given the Association by the Minister of Health, the medical profession cooperated in setting up the Service, and at present all but a very few members of the medical and dental professions are members of the Service.

ORGANIZATION AND OPERATION OF THE NATIONAL HEALTH SERVICE

The National Health Service is much too extensive and intricate to permit an adequate description of all its facets. Figure 1 presents an organizational sketch of the Service, omitting innumerable details. As in the case of the nationalized industries, a Minister of Social Services is responsible for the complete operations of the Service, and he, as a member of the cabinet, is responsible to Parliament. The Minister is assisted by an advisory Central Health Services Council, which consists of some 40 members appointed by the Minister and representing the medical and dental professions, hospital management, local government officials, nurses, midwives, and pharmacists. Its function is to advise the Minister on all phases of the Service and to publish reports from time to time on particular problems affecting its efficiency. Considered functionally, the National Health Service and its operations can best be described by treating each of its three parts separately. This description is in the present tense because, aside from changes in details, the Service remains the same in organization and operation as when it was established by the Labour government.

Hospitals and Specialists

Nearly all of the hospitals in Great Britain, some 3000, are owned by the government and managed by the Minister of Social Services. The nation is divided into 20 regions, in each of which is located one of the long-established medical schools that can act as a center of research and diffusion of knowledge of medical advance. In each region the hospitals are

---

[4]*Ibid.*, p. 369. See this source for a full account of the events leading up to this bill and the parliamentary debate on it.

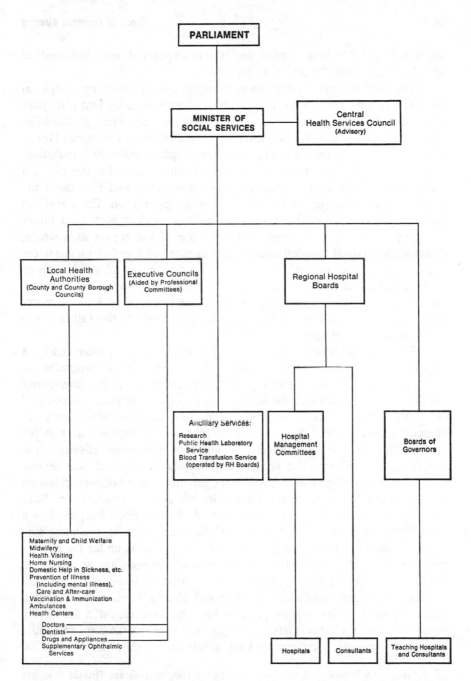

FIGURE 1. Organization of the National Health Service in Great Britain. (From *Britain—An Official Handbook*, London: H.M. Stationery Office, 1960, p. 140, as modified by subsequent changes.)

divided into two groups for management purposes: (1) those performing the usual services and not connected with medical schools ("nonteaching hospitals") and (2) those which are closely connected with the medical school of that region ("teaching hospitals").[5]

The nonteaching hospitals in each region are operated by a regional hospital board responsible to the Minister and appointed by him after consultation with all interested organizations in the region. Through the Minister, each regional hospital board receives an allotment of National Health Service funds to pay for the operation of the hospitals under its jurisdiction. It appoints the top *medical* staff of each hospital, cares for the physical maintenance of the hospital buildings and equipment, and lays down the practices to be followed by hospitals under its supervision. Each regional hospital board also provides certain centralized services such as a blood bank and special X-ray equipment for the use of the region as a whole. Under each regional hospital board are a number of hospital management committees, each responsible for the detailed day-to-day administration of one hospital or, in some cases, a group of hospitals. The membership of each such committee ranges from 15 to 20 and is supposed to be representative of the local community. This committee selects the full-time *administrative* staff that operates the hospital.

The teaching hospital (or hospitals) in each region is managed by a board of governors appointed by the Minister and directly responsible to him. Each board of governors includes representatives of the universities offering medical education, the teaching staffs of the medical schools, and the regional hospital board of that region. It is responsible not only for managing the one or more teaching hospitals in its region but also for coordinating such hospitals effectively with the universities offering medical education and with the nonteaching hospital services of that region.

An individual gets to a hospital for inpatient or outpatient diagnosis and treatment by being referred there by his general practitioner. Both inpatient and outpatient services are free of charge. Each hospital has a top medical director and a staff of specialists (consultants), including surgeons. Once under treatment in a hospital, the patient is under the care of one or more of these specialists. Specialists and surgeons are appointed to the hospital staffs on either a full-time or a part-time basis, the latter permitting private practice outside the National Health Service and including certain rights to bring private patients into the hospital on a fee-paying basis.[6] Hospital staff specialists and surgeons are remunerated on an annual basis, with salaries for top-ranking positions ranging from £3,200

---

[5]There are about 140 teaching hospitals throughout Great Britain that are equipped and staffed with an eye to their usefulness in medical education. The medical schools have remained under the same administrations they were under before 1946; each has its own governing body but receives grants from the government.

[6]These cases involve the use of the so-called amenity beds, of which each hospital has a few, reserved for patients who are being treated by their own physicians outside the National Health Service and who are therefore required to pay hospital fees.

($7,700) to £4,900 ($11,800) depending on length of experience; junior staff salaries are much lower, with house officers receiving as little as £1,300 ($3,100) annually.

Local Government

Under the National Health Service Act, each of the 146 county councils and county borough councils (the basic units of local government) is made a Local Health Authority with certain specific health functions vested in it. It is the responsibility of the local health authority to provide the following: prenatal and postnatal medical and dental care for mothers and for children under five years old by physicians employed by the authority; certified midwife and maternal nursing services (confinements in hospitals being reserved for women requiring special medical attention, having their first baby, or living where conditions are not suitable for home delivery); "health visitors" to advise on the care of children or ill persons in the home; nurses for attendance on people requiring nursing in their own homes; facilities for vaccination and immunization; ambulance service; pre- and posthospital assistance for the mentally ill; domestic help needed because of the presence of an ill person, a new or expectant mother, a mental defective, an aged person, or a child below compulsory school age. The local health authorities are authorized to arrange with charitable, religious, and philanthropic organizations for the performance of such services or to provide them directly. Although the local health authority is permitted to make minimal charges for domestic help it supplies, the other services are provided free of charge. The local health authorities meet about half the cost of these services through local taxation, and the Minister grants each authority an allotment of National Health Service funds to pay for the other half.

One function with which the local health authorities were charged has not been carried out. Under the Act, each authority was to provide, equip, and maintain "health centers" within its area where general practitioners, dentists, and oculists would maintain offices, pharmacies would be located, and the services of some specialists and the facilities for minor surgery would be available. In such centers, it was anticipated, medical practitioners and dentists could jointly use specialized equipment such as X-ray and laboratory apparatus. The centers were also expected to become the focal points of general health enlightenment. Actually, very few such centers have been established. At first their construction was hampered by shortages of materials and labor. More recently, there has been much doubt as to whether general medical practitioners or dentists, whose presence would be the heart of the health center, would be willing to remove their offices from locations that are usually near the homes of their patients. The health-center plan that has not come to fruition is represented in Figure 1 by a line stemming from Health Centers to Doctors, Dentists, Drugs and Appliances, and Supplementary Ophthalmic Services.

General-Practitioner Service

For the area covered by each local health authority, there is an executive council charged with making available general medical, dental, and optical services by physicians, dentists, and opticians who are members of and paid by the National Health Service. The Minister of Social Services appoints the chairman of the council and four members; other members are appointed by the local health authority and local medical, dental, optical, and pharmaceutical associations. Since the arrangements for dentists and opticians parallel those for medical doctors, the following description is in terms of physicians only. Each executive council publishes a list of physicians who have joined the National Health Service and provides facilities for each person to choose the practitioner who is to be his physician, subject to that physician's consent and to a prescribed limit on the number of patients on a physician's list. It assigns to a physician (presumably with his consent) people whose chosen physician has been unable or unwilling to accept them as patients. Each physician practicing at the time the Act became effective had the right to be included on the list of practitioners in the Service for the area in which he was practicing. Each physician subsequently applying for membership in the Service (now almost exclusively newly trained physicians) has his application passed upon by a national Medical Practices Committee. This agency, subject to the applicant's appeal to the Minister, can reject an applicant for a given area on the ground that it is already adequately supplied with physicians. Under this arrangement, a new entrant into the Service may be forced to take his second, third, or later choice of location before being admitted to the Service. Over the past decade this has resulted in decreasing substantially the patients per physician in the "underdoctored" areas and increasing the patients per physician in the "overdoctored" areas.

The objective, then, of each executive council is to see that each person who chooses to use the National Health Service will get onto the patient-list of a physician of his own choosing; that no physician will be forced to accept as a patient any person who, for reasonable cause, is unacceptable to him; and that each physician in the Service will have a list of patients not exceeding 3500. Apparently these objectives have been quite completely achieved. The average list is about 2500 patients per physician, and there are no indications that physicians are often forced to take unacceptable patients or that patients are often placed on the lists of physicians unacceptable to them. Once a person is on a physician's list, he looks to that physician for all his general-practitioner care, free of charge, and for reference to a specialist or a hospital if needed, also free of charge. A prescription issued by a physician is filled by a pharmacy, almost always a member of the Service, with any cost above a modest fixed charge paid by the Service. No individual, physician, or pharmacy is required to join the Service. As far as individuals are concerned, 97 percent of the population have joined, and all but about 600 of the 26,000 general practitioners in Great Britain have entered the Service. Although they are not compelled by the government to join, with almost everyone getting his medical services free through the National Health Service only a few physicians can afford to remain outside the Service. Those who do cater to high-income patients who prefer the luxury of a private physician to some of the inconveniences of diagnosis and treatment through the National Health Service. Although a physician who belongs to the Service is free to treat (for a private fee) patients not on his list, there is only a small amount of "private practice" of this sort because people are generally unwilling to pay for something they can get free.

The physician is paid an annual capitation fee for caring for his list of patients. This fee begins at one amount for each patient in the first 500 on the physician's list, rises substantially for each patient over 500 up to 1500, and drops back substantially for each patient over 1500. The purpose of this scale is to encourage the physician to accept the number of patients that will fully utilize his time, without putting too much pressure on him to extend it beyond the number he can comfortably handle. Since 1966 the basic capitation rate has been supplemented by increased allowances for such factors as seniority, service in unattractive areas, or treatment of elderly patients. The schedule of capitation fees currently in effect is estimated to yield general practitioners an annual average compensation of about £4000 ($9600), not including certain government contributions to physicians' retirement funds. In addition, the general practitioner receives from the Service an annual expense allowance based on its estimate of average expenses per physician. The scale of compensation in all phases of the National Health Service must be viewed against the background of a general level of incomes in Great Britain that is substantially lower than in the United States. British doctors do not fare significantly worse than British college professors, for instance, in salary comparisons with their respective counterparts in America.

At the time the National Health Service Act was passed, it was the custom in Great Britain for a retiring physician, or the estate of a deceased physician, to sell his practice to another physician, possibly one just entering practice, who would then make payments in installments running over some years. An established medical practice thus had come to have a capital value that the retiring physician or the widow of a deceased physician could count on as a source of support. The Act, of course, made it impossible for a physician entering the Service to sell his practice. To compensate physicians for their capital losses, the Act provided a fund from which each physician who suffered such a loss could be compensated. Once determined in amount, the individual physician's compensation is paid only upon his retirement or death, with interest added from the effective date of the Act.

PROBLEMS AND ACHIEVEMENTS

No significant body of opinion anywhere in Great Britain proposes the abolition of the National Health Service or any major modification of it. Although the British public recognizes the need for continual administrative improvement in the Service, it has no inclination to abandon the principles of the National Health Service as its means of searching for health and the alleviation of disease. The public is completely convinced that, whatever disadvantages may be inherent in the scheme, they are outweighed by the advantages of no longer forcing the burden of sickness and disease to be carried through either personal suffering without proper medical care or burdensome expense to obtain such care. This attitude is reflected in the following reply a foreigner is reported to have received when he asked a Briton whether he did not find some unpleasantness in the Health Service. He replied: "Yes, but not the unpleasantness of having to pay."

Although the British Medical Association was adamant in its initial opposition to the institution of the National Health Service, by the tenth anniversary of its founding its *Journal* published praise by the leaders of the profession. One referred to his opinion that "from the point of view of the 'consumer' it has been an enormous benefit and success" and that "the absence of any financial barrier between doctor and patient must make the doctor-patient relationship easier and more satisfactory." Another said, "I believe in the National Health Service with all my heart. Indeed I believe some sort of National Health Service, whatever it may be called, will come in every country in the world. Not necessarily our model; it might not survive export. . . . But other countries, including the United States, can and will benefit from our experiences, our successes and our mistakes."[7]

Popular acceptance or approval of the Service does not mean that it is free from problems. Complaints, questions, and suggestions for improvement constantly stream from the British public, newspapers, and political groups. Some of these run as follows: Why, in the light of its initial purposes, should there be any charge, no matter how nominal, for any service rendered under the National Health Service? Should some of the charges be higher or some new ones imposed in order to lighten the burden on the taxpayer? If a patient sees fit to pay for private service from a physician who is not in the Service or from a physician who is but takes him as a

[7]Quoted in *Harper's Magazine*, May 1959, pp. 32–33.

private patient in addition to those on his list, why should he not be able to have his prescription filled on the same basis as a patient under the National Health Service? Do private patients of hospital consultants, specialists, or surgeons get priority in the assignment of scarce hospital beds, and if they do, is this fair? Why should it not be made impossible for any physician to remain out of the Service, and especially, should not private patients be prohibited to physicians who are in the Service? If members of the Service also take private patients, do they not neglect the patients on their lists, since they are assured of payment for them? Do not physicians prescribe too expensive drugs—especially the new antibiotics—just because they are persuaded to by advertising by private pharmaceutical companies, when in many cases old, established, and cheaper drugs would be just as effective? If this happens, does it not mean that a large portion of the competitive sales promotion costs for new pharmaceuticals finally comes out of National Health Service funds?

These and many other questions pertain to the details of administration or policy issues that require continuing attention from the Minister of Social Services, his Central Council, and the House of Commons. However, they do not merit attention here. There are certain basic problems that the Service and the government must meet, however; these can be discussed briefly. One is the problem of overall costs. The National Health Service is only one of the major claimants on the government's budget and the taxpayer's pocketbook. The size of its valid claim must be judged in relation to the others. The consistent rise in the annual cost of the Service during its early years concerned the Conservative government in 1955. The Minister of Health appointed a high-caliber independent group, known as the Guillebaud Committee, to study the current and prospective cost of the Service and to determine whether modifications in organization or otherwise were needed to control costs and ensure the efficient use of public funds entrusted to it. After an intensive study of many phases of the Service, the Committee submitted its report in 1956.[8] It found that the cost of the Service, in terms of its proportionate use of the nation's resources, had not increased but that there were some vital needs in the Service—for instance, renovation and construction of hospital buildings—that should be met by increased government appropriations. The Committee found that in 1949–1950 the Service had cost 3.75 percent of the nation's gross national product and that this had fallen to 3.24 percent in 1953–1954. This may not be an accurate measure of trend, since during the Service's early days it was filling, completely free of charge, an accumulated need for dentures, eyeglasses, surgery, and so on. However, the Committee's findings disposed of the fear that costs, as of that time, were getting out of hand.

[8]Report of the Committee of Enquiry into the Cost of the National Health Service, London: H.M. Stationery Office, 1956.

Currently the annual cost of the National Health Service is about 4 percent of the country's national income compared with about 4.5 percent of the United States' national income going into medical care, 4.1 percent in Belgium, 4.4 percent in France, 3.8 percent in the Netherlands, and 4.6 percent in New Zealand. Since the National Health Service has some clear and basic unfilled needs, the question is being raised as to whether at least some slight increase in the percentage is not warranted in Great Britain. For instance, the average 2500-patient list of the general practitioner is too long and results in hasty or cursory attention to some patients who possibly should have more thorough contact with their physician. For the maximum list of 3500 patients, there is still less assurance that a professionally satisfactory relation between physician and patient can be maintained. Although in the late 1950s the government made funds available for expansion of the program of hospital construction and renovation, the pace of that program should be stepped up in order to get rid of the many submarginal hospital buildings now in use, particularly some used for mentally ill patients. The need for hospital construction is acute. When industries such as coal and transport were nationalized, large capital-investment programs were initiated to mechanize and modernize production facilities. No capital-investment program of anything like equivalent intensity has ever been undertaken by the National Health Service. The question of what is the right portion of the nation's gross national product to go into the National Health Service apparently needs some rethinking by the government in office.

An obviously basic question is what has happened under the National Health Service to the *quality* of medical service. Quantitatively, in the comprehensive meaning, medical services available to the masses of the population have expanded greatly. Has this been at the expense of quality? The question involves such subtleties pertaining to the patient-physician relationship, the quality of the applicant for medical training, and the ability and incentive on the part of the practicing physician to keep abreast of advances in medical knowledge and equipment that it is understandable that so little really serious work has been done in Great Britain to assess quality. The Guillebaud Committee referred to earlier reported that it found no lowering of standards of physicians' services to patients after 1948. However, it did recommend that the Service direct its attention to the serious problem of coordinating its three functional parts—the hospitals with their specialist staffs, the local health authorities, and the general-practitioner service—and this recommendation at least suggests a failure to realize certain quality potentials. The three divisions of the Service have been inclined to follow their separate paths rather than diligently seeking coordinated methods of improving the nation's health. One illustration of this may be permitted here: Prior to the establishment of the Service, the general practitioner maintained fairly close connections with a hospital by having patients there under his care. In this way he kept contact with specialists and research—especially if his was a "teaching" hospital—and gained fresh knowledge of advances in medical science. Now that the general practitioner is one branch of the Service and the hospitals with their staffs of specialists another, the tendency is for the specialists to take over a patient going into a hospital and for the general practitioner to lose contact with this source of information on new equipment, drugs, and techniques.

The Guillebaud Committee was not established primarily for investigating the quality of medical services and may not have delved deeply enough into criteria or facts pertaining to quality to warrant a final conclusion on this matter. As indicated previously, little objective attention has been directed to the question of quality in its comprehensive form. In the mid-1950s a committee was appointed by the British Medical Association to determine the effect of the National Health Service on the quality of the general practitioner's services. The committee, having had the assistance of research by a foundation, reported its findings as follows: About one-quarter of all general practice is of high quality; about half is sound and reliable; one-quarter "shows substantial room for improvement;" and, within this one-quarter, one-twentieth is so poor "it is hard to find excuses" for it. This one-twentieth comprises the work of some 1000 physicians with some two million patients.[9]

A later evaluating committee, set up by nine major British medical organizations and representing all branches of British medicine, reported in late 1962. The president of the Royal College of Physicians, as chairman, referred to the study as the "sharpest study medicine has made of itself in twenty years." The committee concluded that the basic concept of the National Health Service was sound and rejected one suggestion that had been considered for changing its basic nature. The committee reported that the physician had retained his professional freedom, that the arrangements for individuals to choose their physicians had not violated the principle of freedom of choice, and that there was little substance to the common allegation that the status of general practitioners had seriously deteriorated under the Service. It did suggest some administrative reforms that would shift certain responsibilities for policy making from civil servants to physicians, and it recommended drastic cuts in the maximum sizes of general practitioners' patient lists to 2500 in urban and 2000 in rural areas. Under the auspices of the committee, a "Gallup poll" of the British public was taken on the quality and quantity of their medical care. This showed that 90 percent of those polled were satisfied.

Several issues must be confronted by the National Health Service in years to come. A Ministry "green paper" released in 1968 pointed out the need for administrative reform to reduce the number of local health boards and to achieve better coordination between hospitals, general-practitioner

[9]As reported in the *London Economist*, March 27, 1954, p. 941.

services, and local health authorities. This tripartite division, established at the beginning of the National Health Service, has resulted in the relative isolation of family doctors from the more modern facilities and techniques available in hospitals. This is part of a larger concern for the general status of doctors in British society. A strike of doctors over wage levels was narrowly averted in 1965, but the issue will undoubtedly continue to arise periodically. The number of doctors emigrating is estimated to offset one-fourth of the annual total of new medical graduates. This can be viewed as part of the larger "brain drain" of highly skilled engineers, teachers, and scientists leaving the United Kingdom, but the absence of opportunities for promotion among qualified medical specialists in hospitals provides extra impetus to leave.

The election of a Conservative government in 1970 demonstrates how far removed from political shifts the National Health Service has become. Although the Tories are generally somewhat less committed to free health care on an ideological basis, they nevertheless increased expenditures on the Service and maintained the momentum of new-hospital construction.[10] They are attempting to keep costs in line by creating specialized administrative positions in health-care management. The problem of salaries and working conditions for doctors, especially those in hospitals, remains acute because of the absence of promotion opportunities for junior doctors. The Conservatives restored a pay increase that the Labour government had ruled out as part of its incomes policy, but the issue of pay levels will return regularly in the future and will no doubt someday result in strikes or slowdowns by medical personnel.

One of the authors spent a year in England and observed the operation of the National Health Service from the viewpoint of the patient. In his opinion the accessibility and quality of general-practitioner care he received was superior to that available to him in the United States. There is something appealingly democratic about waiting one's turn in a doctor's surgery with a cross section of British citizens. Once inside the office, the attention was somewhat brief but seemingly competent. On two occasions when specialist services were required, treatment was prompt and courteous. One hospital procedure (by American practices), childbirth, was carried out by competent nurse-midwives in a successful home delivery. All told, the author and his family received free medical services during the year that would have cost approximately $1000 in the United States.

The general practitioner shared office facilities and night duty with three other doctors. Because of the wide geographical area they covered, they had only about 8000 patients on their combined lists. The doctor claimed that he was satisfied with his economic situation and expressed distaste for "political" colleagues who agitated for higher salaries. He described his role as one of "looking at fifteen cases of bellyache a day and

[10]*The Economist*, February 12, 1972.

deciding which two are appendicitis" and seemed happy with the division of labor between himself and hospital specialists. No general conclusions can be drawn from a statistical sample of one, but direct observation justifies the conclusion that in this case, at least, a British doctor was favorably disposed toward the institutional structure of his profession.

However future problems of the National Health Service may be resolved by Parliament, the evidence warrants crediting the Service with some very solid improvements in the delivery of medical care to British citizens. Among those achievements are the following: General practitioners are better distributed relative to population density; specialists are now available in every part of the country; small-group practice allows doctors access to equipment and technical services they could not afford singly; refresher courses are attended by increasing numbers; antiquated hospital facilities are gradually being replaced with modern buildings. There is no pressure by any significant political or other group to remove the National Health Service from the aegis of government.

QUESTIONS FOR CLASS DISCUSSION

1. In what sense may the British National Health Service be regarded as a nationalization project? as a "communization" project?

2. Specifically how extensive are the health facilities supplied to the individual by the British National Health Service? To what extent are these provided completely free of charge to the beneficiary?

3. What was the initial attitude of the British Medical Association toward proposals for a National Health Service? How has this changed?

4. What are the main portions of the administrative apparatus through which the National Health Service operates?

5. How is the National Health Service related to British medical schools and teaching hospitals?

6. What is the role of hospitals in the National Health Service? How may this role have adversely affected the general practitioner?

7. How are general practitioners, consultants, and surgeons compensated for their work in the National Health Service? Are the levels of their respective compensations excessively low?

8. What parts do local health authorities play in the National Health Service? How are they related to health centers?

9. Does a general practitioner in the National Health Service have free choice as to where he will practice?

10. How extensively does the population of Great Britain rely on the National Health Service for its diagnostic and treatment needs, as compared with the citizen's freedom to be a private patient of a physician if he so desires?

11. What portion of British physicians are members of the National Health Service, and why do some not become members? May a member also have private patients who pay him directly for his services?

12. Why would anyone not elect to become a National Health Service patient of a physician in the Service? Does the fact that some choose to do so raise a question about the quality of the Service?

13. Some problems of the National Health Service are major and some are minor. Give examples of each kind.

14. Summarize the evidence available as to whether or not the quality of service under the National Health Service is such as to be severely criticized.

15. Does the fact that there is an annual net outflow of physicians from Great Britain indicate that the National Health Service is a failure?

SUGGESTED STUDENT REPORTS FOR PART V

1. The role of economic ideas in the history of the British Labour Party.

2. Evaluate the recommendation that all nationalized industries be grouped under a single ministry.

3. Differences in public policy toward nationalized industries under Labour and Conservative governments.

4. The sources of recent operating deficits in the public sector.

5. A comparison of the manager's position in a publicly owned industry with that of his counterpart in the private sector.

6. The extent to which nationalization can be blamed for Britain's postwar economic performance.

7. The experience of the United States with the investment tax credit as a device for economic stabilization.

8. The current status of economic planning in the Netherlands.

9. The attitudes of labor unions toward indicative economic planning in France.

10. A comparison of the French Sixth Plan with the targets and mechanisms of earlier plans.

11. A comparison of guidepost policies under Presidents Kennedy and Nixon.

12. A study of the effects of inflation on various occupational groups and income levels in the United States.

13. A history of the American Social Security program.

14. A study of the economic and ethical aspects of a guaranteed annual income.

15. How the British people feel about the organization and performance of the National Health Service.

16. How the British medical profession feels about the organization and performance of the National Health Service.

17. A comparison of the operation of British hospitals with that of large public hospitals in American cities.

SUGGESTED FURTHER READING FOR PART V

Bauchet, P., *Economic Planning: The French Experience*, London: Heinemann, 1964.

Beckerman, Wilfred, ed., *The Labour Government's Economic Record, 1964–70*, London: Duckworth, 1972.

Beveridge, W. H., *Full Employment in a Free Society*, New York: Norton, 1945.

Caves, R. E., and Associates, *Britain's Economic Prospects*, Washington, D.C.: Brookings, 1968.

Denton, Geoffrey, Murray Forsyth, and Malcolm MacLennan, *Economic Planning and Policy in Britain, France, and Germany*, London: Allen and Unwin, 1968.

Dobb, M. H., *Papers on Capitalism, Development, and Planning*, New York: International Publishers, 1967.

Edelman, M., and R. W. Flemming, *The Politics of Wage-Price Decisions: A Four-Country Analysis*, Urbana: University of Illinois Press, 1965.

Fleisher, F., *The New Sweden: The Challenge of a Disciplined Democracy*, New York: McKay, 1967.

Gemmill, P. F., *Britain's Search for Health*, Philadelphia: University of Pennsylvania Press, 1961.

Heller, Walter W., *New Dimensions of Political Economy*, Cambridge, Mass.: Harvard University Press, 1967.

International Labor Office, *Prices, Wages, and Income Policies*, Geneva: ILO, 1966.

Joint Economic Committee, *The Wage-Price Issue: The Need for Guideposts*, Washington, D.C.: Government Printing Office, 1967.

Lutz, V., *French Planning*, Washington, D.C.: American Enterprise Institute, 1965.

Myrdal, G., *Beyond the Welfare State*, New York: Twentieth Century, 1968.

Oulès, Firmin, *Economic Planning and Democracy*, London: Penguin, 1966.

Reid, Graham L. and Kevin Allen, *Nationalized Industries*, Baltimore: Penguin, 1970.

Robinson, E. A. G., *Economic Planning in the United Kingdom*, London: Cambridge University Press, 1967.

Robson, W. A., *Nationalized Industry and Public Ownership*, London: Allen and Unwin, 1960.

Sheahan, J., *The Wage-Price Guideposts*, Washington, D.C.: Brookings, 1967.

Shepherd, W. G., *Economic Performance Under Public Ownership: British Fuel and Power*, New Haven, Conn.: Yale University Press, 1965.

Shonfield, A., *Modern Capitalism: The Changing Balance of Public and*

Private Power, London: Oxford University Press, 1965.

Skinner, B. F. *Beyond Freedom and Dignity*, New York: Bantam/Vintage, 1972.

Spiller, R. E., ed., *Social Controls in a Free Society*, Philadelphia, University of Pennsylvania Press, 1960.

Theil, H., "Some Developments of Economic Thought in the Netherlands," *American Economic Review*, Supplement, March 1964, pp. 34–55.

Theobald, Robert, *Free Men and Free Markets*, Garden City, N.Y.: Doubleday, 1963.

Titmus, R. M., *Essays on the Welfare State*, London: Allen and Unwin, 1958.

Willmott, Phyllis, *Consumers' Guide to the British Social Services*, London: Penguin, 1967.

Wooton, B., *Freedom under Planning*, Chapel Hill: University of North Carolina Press, 1945.

PART VI: SOVIET ECONOMIC PLANNING

19. Historical and institutional background of the Soviet economic system

The Union of Soviet Socialist Republics has now existed for more than 50 years—a relatively long time for political and economic experiments that arise in revolutionary circumstances. The fact that Soviet Russia and Japan are the two nations to establish modern industrial economies outside the established framework of Western cultural values and economic institutions commands our attention. The additional fact that the Russians have performed this feat while proclaiming their loyalty to the views of Karl Marx creates an opportunity to study the link between ideology and the development of institutions based on that ideology. This chapter will establish the historical and institutional background for our subsequent study of how the Soviet economic system operates today.

RUSSIAN ECONOMIC HISTORY

The Economy of Czarist Russia

Russia's economy was, and to a considerable extent still is, agriculturally oriented. We begin our historical survey with a significant change in an agrarian institution—the emancipation of the peasant serfs in 1861. Serfdom was established in the seventeenth century. As a *quid pro quo* in return for obligations of service to the Czar, the landlord class claimed services from their peasant cultivators that amounted to virtual slavery. Even after formal noble obligations to the Czar ended in 1762, landlord-peasant relations were not significantly altered until the Emancipation Edict.

The details of land transfer at the time of emancipation were to have profound effects on the subsequent development of the Russian economy up to and long after the Revolution of 1917.

> The emancipation involved, first of all, a determination of the land area to be given over by the landowner to the peasants for permanent use. There is no question that over wide parts of the country (and particularly in the black-earth belt) the peasants received a good deal less land than had been customarily assigned to them before the reform. Second, there was the question of the magnitude of the quitrents (*obrok*) to be paid by the peasants as compensation for land allotments. . . .
> It might be argued that the two features of the Russian reform just mentioned should have provided a favorable climate for subsequent industrialization; the inadequacy of the peasants' landholdings in conjuncton with the considerable financial obligations imposed upon their households could have been expected to favor a flight from the countryside and thus to provide a large reservoir of labor supply to the nascent industry. Such might have been the consequences indeed, if the reform and the later legislative measures had not erected considerable barriers to land flight by strengthening the *obshehina*, the village commune, wherever it existed.[1]

The labor-supply bottleneck was not significantly dealt with until the Slotypin reforms of 1906–1911, which ultimately abolished redemption payments for land and allowed peasants freedom of movement. Russia meanwhile chose an alternative path to modernization—technological borrowing from abroad—a strategy the Soviet government has also relied on in critical periods of economic change. During the 1890s a program of railroad building, foreign borrowing (particularly from France), and tariff protection for heavy industry produced a spurt of industrialization that re-

[1]Alexander Gerschenkron, *Economic Backwardness in Historical Perspective*, Cambridge, Mass.: Harvard University Press, 1962, pp. 119–120. See also his essay, "Russia: Agrarian Policies and Industrialization, 1861–1914," in Alexander Gerschenkron, *Continuity in History and Other Essays*, Cambridge, Mass.: Harvard University Press, 1968.

sulted in an impressive doubling of the industrial sector in that decade. Industrial growth continued on a less steady and rapid basis up to the outbreak of World War I. The cumulative product of these developments was an economy that was considerably more sophisticated than many less developed countries today.[2] Despite the destruction and disorganization brought about by the war effort in Russia, the Soviet regime inherited a dual economy consisting of a huge agricultural sector combined with a much smaller, but more modern, industrial sector.

Economic Experiments of the First Postrevolutionary Decade

The end of the Czarist regime came amid food riots, troop mutinies, and peasant land seizures. The provisional government that assumed authority in 1917 was overwhelmed by the continuing deterioration of the economy, and the Bolsheviks, led by Lenin, in turn seized political control. A government espousing the principles of Marx was for the first time in a position of actual authority!

Marx had consistently belittled "utopian" socialists who drew up detailed blueprints for operating a socialist society. At any rate, his theory predicted that capitalism would be overthrown first by the proletariat of a modern industrial nation, not a relatively backward peasant agrarian economy like Russia.[3] It was the task of Lenin and his followers to develop a strategy for imposing the "dictatorship of the proletariat" on a country whose own proletariat was in the initial stages of formation and in which economic and administrative collapse and civil war demanded immediate remedies.

The combination of ideological principles and practical necessities produced the period of War Communism between 1918 and 1921 in the Soviet Union.

> During this period the Soviet Government succeeded in gaining control of the 'commanding heights' of the national economy. Large-scale industries, transport, banks, foreign trade, the main branches of the distributive system, municipal services, and even large private houses were taken over by Central Government institutions or by their local branches or local Soviets.[4]

This series of nationalizations made a virtue of the necessity of centralizing administration of industry in the absence of previous owners and managers. Industrial output and productivity continued to fall, however, until 1921;

[2]O. Hoeffding, "Soviet State Planning and Forced Industrialization as a Model for Asia," reprinted in Malcolm E. Falkus, ed., *Readings in the History of Economic Growth*, London: Oxford University Press, 1968, pp. 245–258.

[3]W. W. Rostow once entitled an essay on this subject, "Marx was a City Boy."

[4]Alexander Baykov, *The Development of the Soviet Economic System*, London: Cambridge University Press, 1950, p. 47.

the situation was even worse in agriculture, where, having given former estates to peasants, the government found that it had no means of securing food to feed the cities. Peasant cultivators responded to government edits requisitioning supplies or imposing socialism on the agricultural sector by cutting back acreage sown and slaughtering livestock. "As long as the city had nothing to offer him in return for his labor (the peasant) kept producing a bare minimum to stay alive and cared little about the fate of the city-dweller or the triumph of world revolution."[5]

It became distressingly evident that the government had neither the authority nor the ability to operate the economic institutions it had seized under War Communism and that a retreat to less extreme measures was in order. Under these conditions the New Economic Policy (NEP) era came into being with slogans like "Learn to trade."

The retreat was signaled by placing grain taxes at less than confiscatory levels and by leasing back smaller industrial establishments to private entrepreneurs while retaining the "commanding heights" of large-scale industry, banking, and foreign trade. Famine and shortages of fuel and raw materials plagued the early years of the NEP experiment, but 1923 brought a new problem—the "scissors crisis" in agriculture:

> From a situation in which the terms of trade between village and town were too favourable to the former—though under conditions of famine the peasants were unable to take much advantage of this—the changed circumstances led to an opposite distortion: a rapid move in relative prices in a direction unfavourable to the village, so unfavourable indeed as to discourage agricultural marketings and to constitute a menace, since the precarious political stability of the regime depended on peasant acquiescence, or at least a decision on their part *not* to rebel.[6]

The NEP system was a mixed economy with considerable private activity in both agriculture and industry. Central planning was confined mainly to strategic heavy industries; consumer-goods firms in the nationalized sector were grouped into trusts that planned their own output with little central interference.

Even as the New Economic Policy was stabilizing the economy and facilitating the return of production to something resembling pre-1914 levels, a debate was building over the future direction economic activity should take. The debate centered on the twin problems of agricultural procurement and speeding up industrialization; it was conducted in an atmosphere of political intrigue following the illness and eventual death of Lenin in 1924. Economists of many ideological persuasions contributed to the arguments, and it was their fate to rise or fall with the fortunes of

[5]Anatole G. Mazour, *Soviet Economic Development: Operation Outstrip, 1921–1965*, Princeton, N. J.: Van Nostrand Reinhold, 1967, p. 20.
[6]Alec Nove, *An Economic History of the U.S.S.R.*, London: Penguin, 1969, p. 93.

political factions that espoused corresponding economic programs. The gradualists argued that practical necessity required the encouragement of better-off peasants as a source of foodstuffs and industrial raw materials; therefore, they argued, the pace of industrialization must be balanced by the limits to growth in the private agricultural sector. They believed that attempts to squeeze the richer peasants (*kulaks*) would be disastrous economically and politically because of the danger of open revolt in the countryside, where Party control was weak or nonexistent.

The opposing faction was dismayed by the entrepreneurial vigor of "Nepmen" traders and *kulaks* who responded to opportunities for personal enrichment created by the New Economic Policy. They favored an immediate program of rapid industrialization as necessary for military and economic survival, and argued that peasant agriculture was the only possible source of resources to achieve this goal. Stalin began as a member of the gradualist camp, but as we will see, he was soon to rule over a drastically more rapid and confiscatory program than those envisioned by the original opposition to the gradualist position.[7]

From 1926 on, the private trading sector of the economy was progressively reduced through such devices as higher transport charges for private goods and discriminatory taxes. Central planning grew apace with the decline of private trading. A 1927 decree called for the creation of a comprehensive economic plan, a move made necessary by the rapid increase in heavy investment. This move, in turn, necessitated reinstatement of compulsory farm deliveries to the central government. "It (arbitrary confiscation) upset once and for all the delicate psychological balance upon which the relations between party and peasants rested, and it was also the first time that a major policy departure was undertaken by Stalin personally, without even the pretence of a central committee or politbureau decision."[8] These two developments—the beginnings of comprehensive planning and coercion of the peasantry—mark the beginning of a new era of Soviet economic planning in the late 1920s.

Collectivization and Five-Year Plans

The years between 1929 and 1934 are perhaps the most dramatic in the varied historical pattern of the Soviet economy. Confronted with the reluctance of independent peasants to supply grain at terms advantageous to the central government, Stalin daringly ignored Lenin's admonition to retain the loyalty of peasant cultivators by plunging headlong into reorganizing all agriculture into state-operated farms or into producers' collectives. The more prosperous peasants, or kulaks, were singled out as traitors, and

---

[7]The positions and personalities involved are detailed in Alexander Erlich, *The Soviet Industrialization Debate, 1924–1928*, Cambridge, Mass.: Harvard University Press, 1960.

[8]Nove, p. 153.

some five million were deported or killed for resisting. The brutality of collectivizing agriculture so abruptly remains a blot on the Soviet economic record that no series of subsequent achievements can completely erase.

The machinery created for the forceable collection of grain in 1928 was expanded. Farmers facing collectivization destroyed their crops and killed livestock rather than hand them over to authorities. The goal of rapidly absorbing all private lands was pushed, even though more gradual methods that left peasants some possessions might have worked better. Officials feared being labeled "deviationists" if they appeared unzealous in their work.

> Local officials announced: "He who does not join a kolkhoz (collective farm) is an enemy of Soviet power." They had "either to achieve 100 per cent in two days or hand in your party card." The assault was launched, regardless of lack of preparation, regardless of local conditions, of opinion, of everything except the great campaign. There was, one can see, some logic against going slow, peasants who knew what was coming would react by cutting down production, perhaps destroying their tools and livestock. Better get it over with, and before the spring sowing.[9]

The agricultural sector became demoralized and disorganized. The crop year was disrupted, and considerable output was lost through late planting or lack of harvesting manpower and tools. State procurement levels, if obeyed, left peasants and their livestock little to eat. Directions on how to organize collective units were lacking, and there was no clear-cut incentive system to encourage individual effort within the collective.

The Party exerted control over collective farms through Machine Tractor Stations (MTS), which centralized ownership of agricultural equipment. The urban officials sent out to administer them added little to the sum total of available technical expertise, but they were the eyes and ears of the Party in the countryside. Each MTS serviced between 60 and 300 collective farms, receiving grain in payment for their services.

Meanwhile, a less harrowing but not insignificant narrative of high-pressure development with attendant sacrifices in human terms was unfolding in the industrial sector. The targets of the first five-year plan period were revised upward to extremely unrealistic levels, resulting in bottlenecks and delivery failures.

> It was then that the government, by stages, imposed upon the economy its own priorities, by ever-tightening control over resource allocation, physical output, credit. The "Stalin" model was created in the process of trying to do the impossible, and therefore by facing every day the necessity of assuring supplies to the key projects or "shock-constructions," at the expense of others regarded as of lesser importance.[10]

[9]*Ibid.*, p. 165.
[10]*Ibid.*, p. 189.

The first plan called for a massive program of industrial investment. Modern chemical, metallurgical, and electrical complexes were developed from scratch. Machinery production made especially impressive gains in the years between 1927 and 1932. Many foreign technicians, some attracted by belief in the Soviet experiment and more by employment opportunities not available in the West during the Great Depression, came to Russia to build and operate the new facilities. As in the 1890s and the 1960s and 1970s, the effort to catch up rapidly was supplemented by technological borrowing from more advanced nations. In many ways this is a reasonable way to deal partially with a general lack of incentive for technological innovation at the enterprise level under the Soviet system.

The establishment of the central planning mechanism and the collectivization of agriculture produced, by the mid-1930s, a set of economic institutions fundamentally similar to those prevailing in the Soviet Union today. The political upheavals of the Stalinist purges of the late 1930s, the physical destruction of World War II, and above all, the increase in scale and complexity brought about by 40 years of rapid and relatively stable growth have occurred within the basic framework whose creation we have been describing. Until very recent times, the high rates of investment that propelled the modernization process have been achieved by holding back on the increase in real purchasing power for consumers. If there is a lesson for currently less developed nations in the Russian experience, it is perhaps to realize the magnitude of sacrifices to be imposed on the total population in order to sponsor massive investment programs when foreign capital is lacking. It is a lesson those nations will probably not relish learning.

We will have more to say about the long-term rate of economic growth in the Soviet Union in a later chapter. Our attention now turns to a description of the economic institutions on which the present system of economic planning is based.

SOVIET ECONOMIC INSTITUTIONS

In our discussion of a capitalist economic system, we first considered the existing economic institutions and then studied how the economy actually operates within that institutional framework. The primary characteristics of a command economy like the Soviet model have been outlined by Professor Montias:

1. Political authorities have the power to make ultimate decisions affecting the allocation of resources;
2. Basic allocation decisions are either taken directly by central organs or coordinated centrally;
3. Decisions regarding the future are enshrined in national economic plans;
4. The plans are broken down into concrete tasks "addressed" to specific organizations;

5. The plan and the operational decisions taken during the year to execute its provisions determine how the key resources of the economy will be rationed out;
6. The socialized enterprise (nationalized firm or producers' co-operative) represents the basic economic unit of the system;
7. Prices of both producer and consumer goods are either fixed by administrative organs or approved and controlled by such organs on the basis of enterprises' cost estimates.[11]

We will therefore discuss the institutions in the Soviet Union that provide political direction, plan the economy and keep track of financial accounts, and receive orders from central authorities concerning the production and distribution of goods and services.

The Communist Party

In the Soviet Union the Communist Party is the only political party; there is no other to represent any opposing point of view. Prerevolutionary parties disappeared, the Communist Party now alleges, not because they were violently stifled but because their policies were not attuned to the workings of historical forces as outlined by Marx. The rationale of the one-party system is "that after the expropriation of large-scale private ownership of the means of production society gradually moves toward homogeneity . . . as time goes on the social-political unit of the new society becomes stronger and stronger. . . . In those conditions there is no social basis for the political parties having different ideological and political platforms. The trend toward a one-party system can therefore be regarded as quite natural in a socialist society."[12]

The organizational structure of the party is based on the principle that for every geographic or functional government there should be a corresponding body of the party. Thus for the shop or department within an industrial enterprise, for the enterprise as a whole, for the collective farm, for the store, and so on, there are thousands of party units called cells. Some half-million of these cells are the base on which the entire party structure rests. Each cell is governed locally by a committee. The committee secretary is the individual who, through a hierarchy of area, district, and republic party organizations, draws instructions and authority ultimately from the secretariat of the Central Committee of the Communist Party. The party hierarchy thus parallels the economic planning bureaucracy and provides a dual system of reporting and control on the success of economic performance at the enterprise level, even though fewer than 5 percent of Soviet citizens are actually Party members.

---

[11]John Michael Montias, "Central Planning in Soviet-Type Economies: An Introduction to Basic Problems," in Montias et al., *The Soviet Economy in Theory and Practice*, Columbia, Mo.: University of Missouri Press, 1964, pp. 1–3.

[12]*Soviet Union Today*, New York: American Russian Institute, 1966, p. 6.

Planning Institutions

Virtually all the different general organs constituting the diverse governments are in some degree concerned with resource use, but from this standpoint the most important by far are bodies wielding executive power: in the all-union government, the Council of Ministers: at the republic level, the body with the same name: and at the local level, the executive committee. Headed by a chairman, the all-union council has a diverse membership, including chiefly persons occupying senior posts in subordinate organizations.[13]

The central planning agency, *Gosplan*, has responsibility for preparing economic plans to be approved by the Council of Ministers. Under it a vast planning machinery spreads out, characterized by vertical interconnections between its several layers, horizontal linkages, and regional connections with bodies that plan land use, city development, and so on.

The actual responsibility for plan implementation lies mainly with industrial ministries. Except during the experimental attempt to organize on the basis of geographic units between 1957 and 1965, product lines such as coal, iron and steel, or textiles have served as the basis for ministerial boundaries. The minister and his senior deputies and department heads form the collegium of the ministry; they function mainly as administrators and technicians rather than as politicians. Since ministry departments (*glavki*) usually administer a group of enterprises, an individual plant manager deals with only a small sector of the ministry bureaucracy.

Financial Institutions

It is possible for the Soviet economy to give priority to *physical* potentialities of production and to adapt financial arrangements to physical goals because of the nature of bookkeeping procedures in the Russian socialized economy. All accounts for the individual enterprises, industries, stores, farms, and so on, are ultimately merged into one gigantic set of accounts. This merging thwarts purely financial limitations on production and means that every functional part is coordinated with the planned goals of the economy as a whole.

In the Soviet system government finances, economic planning, and industrial production are intimately connected. The Ministry of Finance is the government agency responsible for most budgeting activity. A large share of investment projects are financed by grants from the government budget issued through investment banks.

The State Bank of the USSR plays an important part in auditing and controlling transactions between enterprises. It provides working capital to firms, settles contractual obligations with bookkeeping transactions, reg-

[13]Abram Bergson, *The Economics of Soviet Planning*, New Haven, Conn.: Yale University Press, 1964, p. 27.

ulates the money supply, and serves as banker to the government. Since enterprises and agencies are required to keep all liquid funds in the Bank as deposits, payment cannot be made in any other way; thus, the Bank becomes a key observation point in keeping track of specific financial obligations placed on any enterprise by the economic plan.

Of less importance are the savings banks that hold small deposits of individual savers. As income levels increase and there are more consumer durable goods to save up for, it is likely that the level of private savings will increase.

Productive Units

The enterprise is the unit for administering property owned by the state. Its director and other officials are civil servants. Profits are transferred to the state or deficits are made up by central-government grants. Output, of course, is dictated by the plan targets handed down by higher authorities.

State farms follow this general form, but collective farms are organized as producers' cooperatives, whose members share the surplus left over after expenses (including taxes) have been met. Often, as we shall see, the revenues have been outweighed by expenses at various stages of the effort to industrialize, leaving little incentive for farms to contribute toward the work of the collective as distinct from their own private plots.

Marketing Institutions

A system of state-owned retail stores accounts for most retail trade in the Soviet Union, with consumer cooperatives and collective farm markets also in the picture. State stores obtain their merchandise through contractual relations with producing enterprises or wholesale organizations. Prices are set by the central authority.[14]

One of the few remaining expressions of freedom of enterprise in the Soviet Union is the market where goods produced on collective farms and private plots are bought and sold. Prices are uncontrolled, and much of the fresh produce in Russia is obtained through this source. Limitations on freedom of enterprise are one reason why maintenance and repair services are generally poor. Some of this deficiency is the result of a lag in repair facilities behind the rapid introduction of new consumer durables. Americans who remember the early days of television will understand this phenomenon; life would be made considerably easier for the average Russian if a way were found to service the goods that are becoming widely distributed to private citizens.

This cursory survey of historical and institutional perspectives puts

[14]Marshall I. Goldman, *Soviet Marketing: Distribution in a Controlled Economy*, New York: Free Press, 1963, p. 84.

us in a position to see how the process of economic planning operates in the Soviet Union and how the individual industrial and agricultural enterprises respond to planning directives.

QUESTIONS FOR CLASS DISCUSSION

1. Why did the emancipation of the serfs in 1861 produce lasting consequences for the development of the Russian economy?

2. Discuss the advisability of importing modern technology in an effort to industrialize rapidly. What problems were created by technological borrowing at key stages of Russian industrialization?

3. What immediate problems did the Bolsheviks have to deal with after they came to power? How did War Communism combine their ideological beliefs with the practical necessities of that era?

4. Was a program of rapid or moderate industrialization better indicated for Russia in the 1920s? Speculate about what would have happened to the Russian economy if the NEP period had been continued indefinitely.

5. What was the "scissors crisis" in Soviet agriculture? Did collectivization resolve it?

6. In what ways were comprehensive economic planning and collectivization of agriculture interrelated? Large-scale investment and collectivization? Political stability and collectivization?

7. Compare the role of central planning during the New Economic Policy with that of the First Five-Year Plan.

8. What are the distinguishing characteristics of a Soviet type of command economy? Which of those characteristics excludes the American, British, and French economic systems from this category?

9. In what ways does the organization of the Communist Party in Russia supplement the economic planning apparatus?

10. How do financial institutions assist in the economic planning process in Russia?

20. The Russian planning system

Historical experience has largely answered the question of whether a centrally planned economic system *can* work. In 50 years the Soviet Union has climbed from a relatively backward, largely agrarian economy to a position among the industrial giants of the modern world economy. The relevant questions thus become, How was this growth record achieved and how much credit can be attributed to the institutions and processes for economic planning that the Soviets have evolved? This chapter looks at the planning process through the eyes of the central planner; the next two chapters investigate the effect of planning on the operation of individual industrial and agricultural units of production. Although the details of the planning process and the names of relevant agencies have varied somewhat over time, the following account catches the essential stages of plan construction.

"In its most general sense, economic planning is the working out of a description of a desired state of the economy at some future date, and the use of active instrumentalities to bring about this state of the economy."[1] The creation of an economic plan involves a choice of comprehensive goals and the allocation of tasks among the various economic units. These functions are performed by substituting central direction for the relatively free movement of prices that prevails in market-oriented economic systems. The plan document includes production targets, capital-investment schedules, domestic and foreign trade planning, and programs for social and cultural advancement.

The Soviets have chosen to use strict economic planning in its centralized form for both ideological and practical reasons. Marxist-Leninists (as Soviet ideologues refer to themselves) hold that the marketplace is a chaotic instrument for allocating resources because it reflects the financial power of the bidders instead of the needs of the state. Competition, they say, is wasteful and has no worthwhile role to play in the building of socialism.

Centralized planning, on the other hand, affords the Communist Party direct influence over the direction of the national economy. The command economy system has proved effective in achieving the structural transformation away from agriculture and toward industry, and the planned emphasis on investment at the expense of the consumer. Whether it has done this as efficiently as possible, in the sense of achieving maximum output with available resources in any given period and maximum growth over time, will be debated in later chapters. No one can dispute, however, that central planning has exerted a tremendous influence on the course of economic events in the Soviet Union.

STEPS IN THE PLANNING PROCESS

The Soviets prepare a number of social-economic plans varying in duration and comprehensiveness. The long- and intermediate-term plans are not binding but serve as a guide in the preparation of short-term plans. We will be concerned here with the annual economic plan, which is operational because it is concrete and legally binding on economic units. The planners seek to determine the composition of physical output, the rates of growth in productive capacity, and the improvement, if any, in the standard of living.

---

[1]Herbert S. Levine, "Growth and Planning in the Soviet Union," in Montias et al., *The Soviet Economy in Theory and Practice*, Columbia, Mo.: University of Missouri Press, 1964, p. 68.

Planning Targets and Instruments

Several instruments are at the disposal of central planners to assist in achieving these goals: the setting of output norms, the design of material incentives for managers and workers, the construction of prices, investment and financial plans, and the program of taxation.

Each enterprise receives a target for its annual output in physical terms of quantity and assortment that it is expected to fulfill. Recent reforms have also introduced a planned rate of profitability that the manager must keep in mind when appraising his costs of production. The profitability measure attempts to overcome deficiencies of physical-output targets in securing the results the central planners intend as contrasted with what managers see as the easiest way to meet output success indicators.

The Soviet system employs a set of material and nonmaterial incentives to induce labor and managers to act in accordance with the plan. In fact, much of the history of the Soviet economic system can be explained with reference to adjustments and transformations in the incentive system.

At this time, labor is not allocated by command in the Soviet Union —workers are largely free to choose their occupation and place of employment. In the past, labor passes were utilized to cut down on job turnover, and of course the forced labor camps of the Stalinist era represented a form of command control over a segment of the labor force. Wage differentials are designed to reward skill, education, and putting up with dangerous or unpleasant work conditions in occupations like mining. Piecework rates, bonuses, and payments in kind reflect extra effort on the part of workers. A chance for a better apartment in company-controlled housing provides considerable incentive, given the scarcity and overcrowding of residential facilities.

Managerial incentives center around bonuses, which make up a considerable portion of their total earnings if they fulfill plan targets. We will discuss the managerial reward system in greater detail in the next chapter —it plays a key role in the operation of the industrial sector. Benefits in the form of better housing, access to a company car, and perhaps a vacation cottage away from the city add considerably to the standard of living enjoyed by top management personnel.[2]

Prices, with the exception of some free-market trading by collective farmers and by artisans, are set by the state. Necessities, on the whole, are low priced; in fact, many such goods are in short supply at prevailing prices, as testified by the long queues in many shops and markets. Luxuries are usually priced far beyond the reach of the average consumer, although consumer durable goods such as television sets and washing machines have become more accessible in recent years. Private ownership of automobiles

[2]David Granick, *The Red Executive: A Study of the Organization Man in Russian Industry*, Garden City, N.Y.: Doubleday, 1960.

on any significant scale is still far in the future. Price setters must be careful not to destroy material incentives by not providing goods on which to spend extra income. Prices in the industrial sector do not serve the same rationing function as consumer prices; they serve largely as an accounting measure to set contract terms between firms and to trace financial flows through the state banking system.

Investment plans provide the firm with funds made available to expand capacity and improve techniques of production. Capital charges have been introduced in recent years to limit managers' requests to those investment projects which will prove profitable for the enterprise. (Considerable ingenuity was required to reconcile these charges to the Marxist belief that interest payments were a tool for capitalist exploitation that would disappear under socialism; Marx neglected the rationing function of interest rates.) Some internal funds may remain in the control of the enterprise for investment purposes, but the amount is limited by the fixed-price contracts procuring inputs and selling outputs under which the enterprise operates.

Purchasing power in the Soviet Union has consistently exceeded the supply of consumer goods, especially once the shoddy quality of many goods is taken into account. This purchasing power must be reduced to avoid the unpleasant effects of black markets and reduced incentive for productive effort. The turnover tax is aimed at this problem. By imposing differential tax rates on consumer goods at the wholesale level, the market price of commodities can be adjusted to curb excess buying power and steer purchasers toward relatively abundant items. Now that the Russian consumer has acquired the basic necessities of life, it becomes more necessary to permit a discernible rise in real living standards by increasing both the quantity and the quality of those goods which consumers really want to buy.

Construction of the Annual Plan

Central planners must have a statistical base from which to construct the annual plan. Data must be accumulated early in the year before the one being planned. This enormous task is undertaken by the Central Statistical Administration and involves literally millions of people. The planners must extract from this preliminary information an indication of areas in which production targets for the year are not being fulfilled.

These statistics are also the basis of production norms for the plan year. A *production norm* is the number of units of an input required to produce one unit of output; it thus becomes the fundamental source of estimates on requirements of raw materials and intermediate goods to achieve output goals. Working with fixed production norms requires strong assumptions about the nature of technology; economists disagree on whether the production process can be adequately described over short periods by fixed coefficients or norms. If input requirements are set too liberally, waste and excessive inventory costs result; if they are too taut, it is technologically impossible to achieve output targets with available resources. Since the selection of a set of norms is really a selection of a specific technology, it is not surprising that alternative methods have had to be used to induce Russian factory managers to experiment with new techniques of production. The Soviets are aware of the disincentive effect of production norms on innovation, and this has figured in their discussion of planning reform.

Political Ratification of Plan Goals

Political leaders, once they possess some knowledge of where the economy will be at the beginning of the plan year, can set forth their preferences on the directions the economy should take during the plan year. It is they who ultimately decide the overall growth rate and appropriate output mix to be attained. Their preferences take concrete form when directives are presented to the State Planning Committee, or *Gosplan*. The individual ministries then receive from *Gosplan* several hundred "control figures" for the planned output of major industrial products and the maximum amount of key inputs that ministries can expect to receive.

It must be emphasized that at this point the plan is in very crude form. It could not yet serve as a guide for every single enterprise or farm. These control figures embody the essential priority decisions for the economy as determined by the Council of Ministers and other political bodies. Before the priority decisions can be translated into specific planning directives, the control figures must be disaggregated into a workable plan of action for individual economic units.

Translating the Plan into Enterprise Norms

At this stage of plan construction, the industrial ministries subdivide the task of disaggregating control figures according to type of product. They inform subministries, organized along product and geographic lines, of the output that will be expected of them; these units, in turn, allocate production norms to the enterprises they oversee. Approximately 1500 different products are planned in this way. Once the firm knows its output target, it can apply production coefficients to request needed materials in order to produce that level of output.

We encounter here the first of a series of conflicts of interest between central planner and enterprise manager. It will be to the manager's benefit to underestimate his productive capability and to overestimate his input requirements. A manager who successfully conceals "reserves of productivity" can easily overfulfill the lower target set for his factory; if he hoards raw materials, he can survive future shortages or even (illegally) barter scarce commodities with other enterprises. From past experience the manager knows that the plan will be "taut," that is, that it will err on the optimistic side and demand his full effort. The manager can assume, moreover, that the planners are aware of his tendency to understate capacity and will routinely adjust output and input coefficients to recapture maximal output. This is a dangerous and potentially wasteful game to play, as shown by the concern expressed in official Soviet publications and in periodic legal trials of offending plant managers selected to serve as examples.[3]

The raw-material estimates of the enterprises make their way back to *Gosplan*. At each point in the hierarchy, the administrator will attempt to minimize the burden of requirements on himself or herself and to maximize the burden shifted to others. A great deal of negotiation takes place throughout this process and, although not officially sanctioned, becomes part of the adjustment process involved in balancing the plan. At one stage of Soviet development, a specialized group of "expediters" arose in Moscow who engaged in activities that a Washington lobbyist dealing with administrative bureaucracy would instantly recognize. These sorts of activities become very important to the success of a manager and are brought on by the prevailing tautness of the plan. The prudent manager, in fact, may be well advised to break, or severely bend, several laws and regulations in order to "lead a quiet life" free from prying investigators sent out by supervisory agencies.[4]

Balancing the Plan

Gosplan must now check that the figures for input requirements are not larger than the projected output of those commodities; otherwise bottlenecks and shortages will result. The *method of material balances* sums all the requirements for a product and compares the quantity with that available from all sources, including current production, imports, and inventory depletion. Uses of a product include inputs to domestic enterprises, final consumption, exports, inventory buildup, and an emergency reserve. Often it is found that requirements initially exceed planned availability, and adjustments must be made if the plan is to be rendered internally consistent.

One procedure for rectifying this situation is on the "uses" side. High-priority enterprises (military, heavy industry) still receive their full allocation, but distribution to low-priority areas is cut back. Reducing the flow of goods to final consumers has the least repercussions on related production; thus, consumers often bear the brunt of the materials-balancing operation.

---

[3]Professor Holland Hunter has developed the concept of "optimal tautness" to mediate between the polar evils of waste and inflexibility when norms are set too low or too high.

[4]This phrase often cropped up in interviews with former factory managers who were refugees or defectors from the Soviet Union after 1945. See Joseph S. Berliner, "The Informal Organization of the Soviet Union," *Quarterly Journal of Economics*, August 1952, pp. 342–365.

On the sources side of the account, imports of the goods in short supply may be increased. Recent grain purchases from Western countries in years of poor Russian harvests are an example of this remedy. Imports must ultimately be paid for with exports, of course, and this measure involves economic or political consequences. The planners may adjust to shortages by changing input norms for enterprises in order to force them to economize on raw-materials use. If there is slack in the plan due to underreporting, this is a healthy move; if the plan is already taut, evasive tactics that give the false appearance of plan fulfillment will necessarily be resorted to.

Approving the Plan

Gosplan submits a balanced version of the annual plan to the Council of Ministers. This is not a rubber-stamp gesture; approval is not automatic. The individual ministers have a large personal stake in the accomplishment of the goals set forth in the plan. They too try to get output targets reduced and input allocations increased. A number of changes are often made at this late stage, since ministers possess considerable political power. When a compromise is reached, the plan is finally approved as law.

The plan is not operational, however, until the enterprises receive "funds" to purchase required inputs. This term does not mean money or credit; it is a corruption of the Russian word for requisition permits that allow contractual agreements between suppliers and purchasers to be drawn up. Firms are then prepared to carry out the dictates of the annual plan, which affects every economic unit in the Soviet Union with the exception of a few consumer industries that must be responsive to rapidly changing needs and therefore operate with a shorter planning horizon.

We have followed the planning cycle from the initial phase of data collection to the moment when the final plan is implemented. Soviet planning machinery has grown considerably more complex and more sophisticated since the early plans of the 1930s, which were often forced to make ad hoc adjustments in coefficients or in priorities in the middle of the plan period. "After 1953, when the new leaders of the USSR pledged themselves to a gradual but steady rise in the population's living standards, consumer goods industries could no longer be used so conveniently as a buffer to break the impact of planning mistakes on the priority sectors of the economy."[5] Even as the ability to plan was improving, the task of planning was becoming increasingly difficult as industrial production experienced an explosion in the range and degree of fabrication involved. An army of planners was occupied in a losing battle to keep track of physical details of interindustry transactions; the development of computers and the reemer-

---

[5]John Michael Montias, "Central Planning in Soviet-Type Economies: An Introduction to Basic Problems," in Montias et al, p. 7.

gence of economic theories for decentralized decision making in the Soviet Union during the 1960s were no coincidence. A brief discussion of these trends is in order, because they point out possible future directions around which economic planning institutions may evolve.

IMPROVING THE PLANNING PROCESS

Computerization

The machinery and bureaucracy of plan construction in the Soviet Union are voracious users of manpower and time. If modern data processes were applied to the handling of economic statistics, resources could be freed for more constructive activities. Computerization of data collection has not proved an easy task, however, because of the lag in the Soviet computer industry.

> [The head of the computer branch of the Soviet Academy of Sciences] has estimated that more than 4,000 medium-to large-sized computers would be required [for a statistical network]. There probably are not more than 3,000 digital computers now [1966] installed in the U.S.S.R., of which very few are so deployed that they would belong to this system. This contrasts with the 28,000 general-purpose computers that had been installed in the United States by the end of 1965.[6]

The Russians are still far from closing this gap, as shown by recent interest in obtaining computers from the West. Even if computer hardware is imported, there will be a continuing shortage of technical workers with adequate training. In addition, certain institutional barriers discourage the creation of a unified system of accounting to replace the multitude of systems currently employed by various enterprises, industries, and ministries.

The task of computerization is enormous, but it will necessarily have to proceed at an accelerated pace if the economic planning system is to avoid being buried in its own paper work.

> Obtaining the annual-plan norms for the Ural Machine Building Factory required compilation of documents 17,000 pages long . . . . Soviet government agencies collect mountains of information. They then process the information so poorly and store it so inconveniently that only a fraction of it is ever used. The most famous description of the problem is the oft-quoted statement (outside Russia and within) of the prominent mathematician-cyberneticist, V. M. Glushkov, to the effect that, if nothing is done to modernize the planning system, by 1980 planning will occupy the entire adult population of the Soviet Union.[7]

[6]Joint Economic Committee, Congress of the United States, *New Directions in the Soviet Economy*, Washington, D.C.: Government Printing Office, 1966, p. 331.
[7]Herbert S. Levine, "Economics," in George Fisher, ed., *Science and Ideology in Soviet Society*, New York: Atherton, 1967.

Application of Mathematical Economics

Another suggestion for modernization of the Soviet planning process has come from the new mathematical approach to economics championed by the late V. S. Nemchinov. These suggestions had to be advanced most cautiously to avoid charges of anti-Marxist heresy. Fortunately Marx was very vague about exactly how the economy of a socialist state should be managed. Lenin severely underestimated the skills required for economic planning. Nemchinov tried to avoid any "bourgeois" stigma attached to the use of mathematics by documenting seemingly sympathetic statements of orthodox Marxists and by charging Western mathematical economists with perverting and misusing valuable tools of economic analysis.[8]

One tool advanced by this school is claimed as a Russian invention. Input-output analysis was developed by Professor Wassily Leontief of Harvard, who left Russia in the 1920s. Input-output analysis makes assumptions about the economy similar to those underlying the construction of production norms. The application of modern computing techniques makes input-output analysis a flexible and expandable alternative to the method of material balances for achieving internal consistency within a plan. Modern computers make it possible to construct several variants of the plan in order to compare the investment and consumer-welfare results of each, thus giving political leaders a range of choice among economic outcomes.

The success of input-output analysis depends critically on the accuracy and reliability of the data on which the model is based. Many observers believe that extensive reliance on the results of input-output analysis in the Soviet Union cannot occur until the quality of Soviet economic data improves.

In 1939 a Russian mathematician, Kantorovich, developed a technique for calculating the movement of goods over an existing transportation network at minimum cost. It became the basis for the development of what is called linear programming in the West. The importance of this technique for solving the economic problems confronting economies like that of the Soviets was not recognized in Russia until recent years. Linear programming has been used in the West to select the best technology and to evaluate the efficiency of industrial production. It can also reflect a rational valuation of commodities by means of shadow prices, which show the quantities of scarce resources devoted to their production. This would permit the Soviets to choose techniques of production that maximize production in terms of objectively determined criteria without resorting to capitalist-tainted profit-maximizing techniques. The use of linear programming is spreading throughout Soviet industry now that its usefulness is finally being recognized.

Mathematical economics has gained tremendously in prestige in re-

[8]See V. S. Nemchinov, *The Use of Mathematics in Economics*, Cambridge, Mass.: MIT Press, 1964.

cent years. When it is combined with computerization, there is increased probability that the ponderous apparatus of Soviet planning can be reformed. Mathematical techniques are well suited for incorporating consumer desires into planning considerations, thus creating a mechanism in which genuine consumer sovereignty could exist outside a market economy if the political leaders ever gave top priority to increased living standards and freedom of consumer choice. These advances, along with some decentralization of decision making in recent years, have caused some Western observers to attribute capitalist tendencies to Soviet planners. It is more likely, however, that these developments will be used to preserve the socialist character and command structure of Russian economic institutions. The viability of the Soviet experiment with central planning has been strengthened by the ability to overcome ideological barriers to the consideration of new ideas and new methods of facilitating economic decision making. The sum total of these intellectual currents is the revitalization of Russian economics for the first time since the 1920s.[9]

QUESTIONS FOR CLASS DISCUSSION

1. How does economic planning differ from economic forecasting? from the day-to-day operations of an enterprise?

2. Can capitalist firms engage in economic planning? Can they avoid engaging in economic planning?

3. Discuss the points at which the preferences of political leaders and the recommendations of economic planners intersect during the process of plan construction in Russia.

4. Why do errors or deficiencies in statistical reporting endanger the Soviet planning process?

5. Discuss the importance of production norms in Soviet planning. What is meant by a "taut" plan?

6. Why is the method of materials balancing employed during the final stages of plan construction?

7. Discuss possible methods for persuading managers to state their productive capacity and input requirements more honestly.

8. Discuss the role of the turnover tax in Soviet planning.

9. How are control figures translated into enterprise production targets?

10. Discuss what computers can do and what they cannot do to solve the problems confronting Soviet planners.

11. How can input-output analysis and linear programming solve the types of problems that exist in economic planning?

12. Why does the Soviet consumer stand to benefit from adoption of mathematical planning techniques?

---

[9]W. W. Leontief, "The Decline and Rise of Soviet Economic Science," *Foreign Affairs*, January 1960, pp. 261–272.

21. Russian industrial planning

Soviet industry is organized vertically into a number of ministries, each concerned with a specific set of related industrial enterprises; they include the Ministry of Machine Building and Metal Working, the Ministry of Petroleum Refining, the Ministry of Ferrous Metallurgy, and so forth. For some industries the ministry is at the all-Union level; that is, there is one ministry for the entire Soviet Union. For others, the enterprises are part of the ministry of the republic in which they are located. Each ministry is represented by a member of the Council of Ministers of the USSR or the republic with which it is concerned. The number and responsibilities of the ministries have been subject to frequent change.

The ministries are further subdivided into main administrations, which supervise enterprises grouped by product type and geographic considerations. The managers of enterprises are responsible directly to their ministries, and ministers are responsible to the political leadership for the performance of their enterprises.

The bureaucratic apparatus of the Soviet industrial sector resembles the hierarchy of one of the West's giant corporations. Like a capitalist corporation, moreover, the Soviets do not expect the bureaucracy to supply each individual in the system with all the instructions and supervision necessary to carry on all the various facets of production. The system therefore employs material incentives to make the goals of the individual coincident with those of the leaders. As we will see, the design of these material incentives is vital to the smooth operation of the system and must be carefully constructed to avoid undesirable responses.

OPERATION OF THE INDUSTRIAL ENTERPRISE

Motivating Management

The manager of a successful Soviet industrial enterprise is a remarkable person and is well rewarded for his efforts. Because of the nature of Soviet planning—tight plans and optimistic targets—a manager's job is complicated. He must be certain that the enterprise will have the inputs it requires to meet its targets. He may get a call from his ministry (the telephone is a crucial instrument in Soviet industrial administration) informing him that his targets have been increased but that no extra inputs will be forthcoming. He may be informed that a shipment of parts the enterprise has just received does not fit his machinery. If he refuses to accept the parts, however, he may never get replacements. He could organize a workshop to adapt the parts for his use, but there are no workers to be spared from the assembly line.

What does he do? He uses his connections and ingenuity. He phones his (unofficial) representative at the ministry in Moscow, calls the secretary of the local cell of the Communist Party, or sends his expediter to make a deal for more inputs, new parts, or the use of a workshop. As reformers realize, he may also adjust the assortment or quality of his output in order to fulfill the targets with less strain on his limited resources. If the quality of output suffers, this is the price paid for taut planning and for material incentives that are not adequate to ensure that quality standards can be met along with output targets.

What does the manager receive for his resourcefulness? The rewards are both monetary and nonmonetary. The nonmonetary awards include social status, consumer amenities—a chauffeur-driven car, a nice apartment—and the possibility of further advancement. The monetary reward is very significant; the manager's bonus may be as much as 50 percent of his base salary.

When the manager decides to put one order into production ahead of another, or to substitute one material for another, it is not his salary he is thinking about. It is usually the size of the month's bonus that will depend on the decision taken. It is in this sense that the bonus is the principal incentive in the operational decisions of the Soviet enterprise.[1]

The bonus, therefore, must cause the manager to make decisions consistent with the preferences of the political leaders if central economic planning is to be successful. Under the system instituted by Kosygin in 1965, managers' bonuses depend on the rate of profitability of the enterprise. The rate of profitability will rise if the output is increased or costs are reduced, given the amount of fixed capital owned by the enterprise. These two responses are desirable in the eyes of the political leaders. The rate of profitability was proposed by Yevsey Liberman as an answer to abuses arising from use of physical output targets as the base for bonuses. It was adopted by the political leaders in 1965. Output targets are still constructed and are still binding, but there is also a planned rate of profitability that gains the manager a larger bonus if he exceeds it.

The Soviet industrial manager is usually an engineer by education. Soviet business education is usually limited to learning to use standardized forms. If the manager is a good engineer, he can increase his output or reduce his costs and thus increase his bonus. As we have discussed, he must also know how to circumvent bureaucracy! It is in this capacity that adverse responses to material incentives appear.

Motivating the Worker

The wages of the Soviet worker depend on his productivity. Time-work rates, comparable to straight hourly rates in American industry, are related to the demands of the job in terms of skill and effort. Time rates are used only when quantity or quality of output is difficult to assess by standards of performance, and no more than one-quarter of the production workers in industrial plants are paid simple time rates. The majority of workers receive wages based on some piece rate or bonus scale. Piece rates and bonuses may reflect individual, workshop, and enterprise achievement. A fund is set aside from the profits of the enterprise to be used for bonuses. These rewards are calculated, as are the managers', on the bases of planned norms and thus serve as an incentive to overfulfill those targets.

Workers also receive nonmonetary rewards. The enterprise budget includes a fund for social and cultural projects for workers. Soviet enterprises often make housing available to their workers. They may even have resort facilities where industrial workers can spend their annual two-

---

[1]Joint Economic Committee, *Comparisons of the United States and Soviet Economies*, Washington, D.C.: Government Printing Office, 1959, p. 1.

week paid vacation. A productive year may bring the workers a new lunch-room or expanded recreational facilities. Specific awards are often made for outstanding individual achievement; these are both material and hon-orary, such as the Order of the Red Banner of Labor.

Trade unions in the Soviet Union do not act as collective bargaining agents for labor. They serve more as fraternal benevolent associations and also help management obtain the degree of labor performance necessary to enable the enterprise to fulfill its plan. They are expected to ensure that the Uniform Labor Code is enforced. Material reward for the Soviet worker is a direct result of his own effort and that of his fellow workers; his in-structions from the political hierarchy are clear-cut in a way those for managers are not.

Managerial Success Indicators as Operational Communications

It is a fairly simple matter to provide instructions for a factory producing a single homogeneous product and using a single inflexible production pro-cess. Most modern factories, however, are capable of producing a broad range of commodities displaying subtle variations in performance charac-teristics, style, size, and durability. Central planners would have to spend an inordinate amount of time and effort to supervise the infinite detail of completely specified production orders. They naturally resort to "success indicators" that incorporate some, but not all, of the dimensions of product variations; managers facing the task of conforming to these success indica-tors just as naturally seek the easiest way to measure up by slighting aspects, such as quality or variety of assortment, that have not been spelled out in detail by the central authorities.[2]

Managerial incentives have changed in form because of the previous failure to provide adequate communication of the intentions of political leaders to managers of enterprises. The aspect under most severe attack is that of rewards for fulfilling output targets in physical units that adversely affect the quality, assortment, and innovativeness of Soviet industrial pro-duction.

It is very difficult to find a physical unit of output that will suffice to include all of the desired qualities of that output. Consider the case of chandeliers, once mentioned in an official Soviet speech as an offending industry. The original physical production description chosen was weight. The Soviets could soon boast the heaviest chandeliers in the world, but the real output target was not satisfactorily fulfilled. An alternate choice might be a measurement of the amount of light produced, or candle power,

2The importance of success indicators for Russian planning has been docu-mented in Alec Nove, *The Soviet Economy: An Introduction* (rev. ed.), New York: Praeger, 1965, pp. 161–178.

since this is the purpose of chandeliers. It is doubtful that every room could use chandeliers with as much candle power as might be produced.

> A factory manufacturing parts for tractors, for example, was rewarded for over-fulfilling its output plan by 60 per cent. This feat was achieved by lowering the quality and reducing the useful life of the parts produced to 40-50 per cent of what it had been. Not only are incentives for quality improvement lacking. The planned goals often set up actually penalise it. When the personnel of the Moscow ZIL plant managed to reduce the weight of the automobiles they produce by 100 kilograms, they received a commendation but suffered a reduction in earnings: the factory's output goals are set in tons.[3]

Nicolas Spulber cites two examples of the distortions in communication caused by physical targets in two other industries:

> An official textbook indicates that in 1954 the ministry of the coal industry delivered coal with an ash content exceeding by 2 per cent the standard set in 1940. Owing to this, coal consumers received 6 million tons of waste rock, the transportation of which required no fewer than 6,000 railroad trains. Nikita Khrushchev threw some additional light on these questions by citing the example of a machine tool plant in Saratov: "Why should that plant cease to produce obsolete machine tools," remarked the Soviet Premier ironically, "when this would alter the output plan, . . . and when workers have already been paid several thousands of rubles in bonuses, including 21,000 rubles to the plant director for over-fulfilling the production plan?" (*Pravda*, July 2, 1959)[4]

Most Western authorities on the Soviet planning system have their own collection of anecdotes about success indicators that fail to achieve their original goals: Unusable bricks are delivered because the norm does not penalize breakage during dumping; trucking enterprises chalk up ton-miles by needlessly shuttling goods from terminal to terminal; a shoe factory produces only small sizes in order to save on leather and avoid the bother of adjusting machinery for larger sizes; unwanted ladies' dresses pile up in warehouses because there is no incentive to pay attention to the style preferences of potential consumers. Efforts to set output targets in terms of "roubles worth" meet with a different set of obstacles: Price credits are often out of line with resources absorbed, resulting in easy-to-produce but unwanted assortments of output; unnecessarily expensive raw materials are used to boost the value of each unit produced; spare parts are usually undervalued and hence underproduced.

---

[3]Leon Smolinsky "Soviet Industry: A Fascinating Mixture of Modern Sophistication and Primitive Backwardness," in Harry G. Shaffer, ed., *The Soviet Economy: A collection of Western and Soviet Views* (2nd ed.), New York: Appleton, 1969, p. 180.

[4]Nicolas Spulber, *The Soviet Economy: Structure, Principles, Problems*, New York: Norton, 1962, p. 59.

Through all of the efforts to adjust the incentive system there is the inexorable tendency for quality to decline and. for little attention to be devoted to consumer preferences in style, color, and size.

These difficulties with the design of material incentives have been discussed extensively in the Soviet official press. As the obvious sources of gains in economic productivity were exhausted in the industrialization of the Soviet Union, the emphasis on efficiency grew. Such abuses as we have mentioned could no longer be tolerated. The incentives discouraging innovation were particularly abhorrent to the political leaders. The Soviet Union could not expect to remain in the forefront of industrial nations if its managers had to play it safe and stick to current methods of production rather than experimenting with new techniques. The plight of the consumer could not be alleviated if concern with the fulfillment of physical output targets must supersede concern for meeting the needs of the consumer. The need for reform was evident. The action for reform began in 1957 with Nikita Khrushchev's reorganization of industry and took a new form with the 1965 reforms of Alexei Kosygin. These reforms did not change the command nature of the Soviet economy. They were an attempt to decentralize some of the decision making in industry. They tried to improve the means by which the communication of the political leaders' instructions might take place.

ECONOMIC REFORM IN INDUSTRY

The 1957 Regionalization of Administration

Under Stalin the industrial ministries had become very powerful. In an effort to control receipt of inputs, the ministries often set up facilities within their own bounds to produce as many of the inputs required as possible. A ministry would transport materials from its own factory in Vladivostok in the east to a factory near Moscow, rather than purchasing them from a Muscovite factory of another ministry, to ensure quality and delivery times. These activities were called empire-building and were greatly disparaged in official circles. There was much discussion of the inefficiency of decisions made by ministries in Moscow for enterprises spread throughout a land of many contrasting economic environments.

In 1957, to combat this centralization of decision making, Nikita Khrushchev reorganized the industry of the Soviet Union on a regional basis. Administration of enterprises was transferred to some 100 newly created Regional Economic Councils (*Sovnarkhoz*), each responsible for *all* industry in one of the Economic Administrative Areas into which the nation was divided. The regional councils were responsible to the Council of Ministers in the republic in which they were located. This regional organization is similar to that of the Communist Party, and it was hoped that the Party would influence industrial efficiency.

The councils were expected to remedy the abuses of the empire-building ministries as well as to make better use of local resources and ensure the reliability of input supply. This was not the case. The regional economic councils set about empire building of their own. They desired their regions to be self-sufficient and ignored potential advantages of trade across regional boundaries. The councils had to regulate all types of industry for which they lacked the technical knowledge of ministry officials. They could take advantage of local resources but in the process lost the advantages of specialization. It became increasingly obvious that the 1957 reform had not dealt with the fundamental problem—communication of economic instructions.

The 1957 reform attracted considerable attention in the West when it was first announced. In retrospect it appears to have been based more on expediency than on any fundamental ideological commitment. Organizational changes are often designed to produce one-time increases in productivity simply by shaking things up and exposing areas of inefficiency. In addition, it is possible that the 1957 action was aimed partly at demoting ministry bureaucrats in Moscow who represented a potential source of political opposition. Reforms may involve not only new policies but also new people to carry them out.

Reforms of Managerial Incentives

The question of more basic reforms appeared in a 1962 *Pravda* article by Professor Yevsey Liberman of Kharkov. The resulting scheme, termed *Libermanism* by some in the West, centered on new criteria of managerial performance and greater freedom of decision making at the enterprise level.

> How is it possible to entrust the enterprises with the drafting of plans
> if all their calculations are, as a rule, far lower than their true potentials?
> It can be done if the enterprises have the greatest possible moral
> and material interest in making full use of reserves not only in plan
> fulfillment but also in the very compilation of plans. To this end, planning
> norms of profitability must be worked out for each branch of industry
> and must be firmly established for an extended period.[5]

The profitability criteria provided dual motivations to cut costs and to be frugal in asking for investment funds, since profits were to be calculated as a percentage of total capital. A progressive bonus rate structure was to encourage each firm to set its own production goals close to full-capacity levels because overfulfillment bonus rates were lower. Finally, an extended plan period was to be instituted to encourage innovation, since

[5]Yevsey G. Liberman, "The Plan, Profit, and Bonuses," in Shaffer, ed., *The Soviet Economy: A Collection of Western and Soviet Views*, p. 474.

more productive firms would not face immediate upward revisions in their output targets.

The wastefulness of existing investment-allocation procedures became most obvious in the electric power industry, where huge investments of resources were tied up in giant hydroelectric sites without adequate consideration of the ultimate savings from alternative generating sources. The search was on for a system of capital rationing taking into account the durability of investment projects.

All this discussion took on concrete form with the establishment of Khrushchev's successors. The new order was set forth in a report by Alexei Kosygin to the Central Committee of the Party in September 1965. Measures were proposed as follows:

> A system of measures to expand the economic independence of enterprises and raising their role as the main economic unit; To strengthen and develop self-accountancy, to increase economic stimulation of production with the help of such means as price, profit, bonus credit;
> Resolutely intensify the incentives for workers and employees in improving the general results of the work of the enterprise;
> To improve the management of industry, to set up agencies built on the branch of industry pattern, i.e., industrial ministries vested with all rights and fully responsible for the development of these branches.[6]

What were the 1965 reforms designed to accomplish? In addition to signaling the end of the 1957 attempt at regional administration, there were significant changes at the enterprise level. The addition of profitability criteria as a significant element in managerial bonuses coincided with an overall reduction in the number of restrictions on managerial discretion. For instance, for the first time the manager was free to choose between various categories of labor if he could reduce costs in doing so. Innovation was encouraged because the new incentives would guarantee bonuses for the entire planning period for any innovations that were profitable to the enterprise.

The 1965 reforms have not proved to be as sweeping as most Western observers at first thought. They are more accurately regarded as a change in the incentive system for managers rather than a fundamental move toward a profit-directed economic system. Centrally provided output plans still exist; managers now have more freedom in the way they meet the new criteria of cost and quality. There is some measure of decentralization in budgeting and technical planning at the enterprise level. Capital charges discourage hoarding of capital and facilitate the calculation of profitability.

The effect of the reforms has been blunted to some extent by the lukewarm reception, bordering on sabotage, accorded them by ministry planners or Party officials who found their functions superseded by new

[6]*Soviet News Bulletin*, Special Issue, September 29, 1965.

regulations. Reports appeared that bureaucrats sometimes refused to pay bonuses on the new basis or were slow in releasing discretionary funds that were supposed to be controlled by individual enterprises. Although the initial reform has been extended to almost all industrial enterprises, there appears little possibility of the next stage of decentralization—some control over pricing, allocation of raw materials by supply and demand instead of through the plan, and freedom to fix wages and dispose of profits. Liberman himself appears to have backed away from heavy reliance on profit criteria in his later writings.[7] The dialectical process whereby change combines features of the old and the new is again demonstrated in these efforts to change the institutions of Soviet economic planning.

Reforms for the Consumer

Another concern of reformers is the response of industry to the needs of the consumer. Under the conditions of excess demand that formerly existed in the USSR, industry expected that whatever it produced for the consumer sector would be purchased. With the increase in output of consumer goods initiated by the post-Stalin leaders, it became clear that such an assumption was unwarranted; some undesirable goods were left on the shelves. The preferences of consumers could not be communicated by the output plans of political leaders alone. Reform in this area was first explored through experiments in the feasibility of producing what consumers wanted.

In July 1964 two textile factories engaged in manufacturing men's suits, the Bolshevichka and Mayak enterprises, were released from their output plans and instructed instead to produce to fill the orders of their retail customers. To meet output targets, such enterprises might formerly have concentrated on manufacturing styles and sizes requiring the least manpower or material, whichever was in short supply. Now their retailers could expect shipments that customers would be eager to buy. These experiments met with great success, and the system was soon applied to similar enterprises. The Soviets have even become interested in Western marketing techniques, conducting surveys and interviewing consumers about their reactions to experimental models in retail stores. This too represents a great change from the thinking of the Stalin era, which served the Soviet Union well in an earlier period but eventually threatened to slow its economic progress.

It is evident that increased emphasis is being placed on consumer needs. The ninth five-year plan, covering the years 1971–1975, is the first to project a higher growth rate for light industry than for heavy industry.[8] Long queues, limited selection, and poor quality are still part of the consumer's lot, however, and it does not appear that any major breakthrough

[7] *The Economist*, February 13, 1971.
[8] *The Economist*, February 20, 1971.

will occur until the forces of supply and demand come to play a much larger role in determining what gets produced.

The reforms we have discussed were motivated by a need for increased economic efficiency once the easily attacked reserves of productivity no longer existed. They were not "creeping capitalism." A great need for reform was and is obvious also in the agricultural sector, the great weak spot in the Soviet economy. We now turn our attention to Soviet agricultural production.

QUESTIONS FOR CLASS DISCUSSION

1. Discuss the motivation effects of the bonus system of managerial compensation in the Soviet Union.

2. What is meant by the term "success indicator"?

3. Discuss the limitations to more detailed specification of product characteristics by central planners. Can targets stated in "rouble values" avoid problems of noncompliance with planners' goals?

4. Why is technological innovation difficult to achieve within the Soviet incentive system?

5. In what situations could a geographic organization for industrial production be expected to be more advantageous than an industry structure?

6. Why do Western observers consistently overestimate the importance of newly promulgated economic reforms in Russia?

7. What are the primary facets of the Liberman proposals for economic reform?

8. How would consumers benefit from releasing consumer-goods factories from output targets in favor of direct contracting with sales outlets?

22. Russian agricultural planning

Agriculture is of key importance to the Soviet economy. It employs one-third of the labor force and provides essential raw materials for industries and food for the industrial work force. We have seen that agriculture was squeezed to provide resources for the industrialization drive of the 1930s; until about a decade ago, in fact, little was done to confront the related problems of low yields, low productivity, low incentives, and administrative inefficiency. Soviet leaders now recognize the need to modernize agriculture by increasing the level of farm investment and streamlining the incentive system for workers and managers. Despite this new emphasis, there have been recurrent harvest failures (in 1963, 1965, and 1972), making it necessary to import grain. Because of the importance of farming in the total

Russian economy, poor crop years have a large adverse impact on the over-all growth rate. We will attempt to identify sources of low productivity by examining the organization and planning of agricultural output, including the various attempts at agrarian reform during the past 15 years.

It should be kept in mind that the state of Soviet agriculture is an extremely important domestic political issue; in fact, improvements in the planning structure have sometimes failed because of political meddling. Khrushchev's failure to deal effectively with the agricultural crisis was an important factor in his premature retirement.

THE ORGANIZATION OF AGRICULTURE

Agricultural units in the Soviet Union are organized either as state farms (*soukhoz*) or collective farms (*kolkhoz*). State farms employ laborers at standard wages, just as an industrial enterprise might. Profits of the state farm accrue to the state budget. State-farm employees and managers, like factory workers, are paid on an incentive basis. including bonuses, social insurance, and other benefits.

A collective farm is a cooperative and owns its equipment and live-stock. The collective farm is nominally self-governing, and its profits are distributed among the members of the collective according to their con-tribution to production. In reality, the Communist Party cells are very active in influencing the management of the collective farms. Historically the lot of the state-farm worker has been somewhat better than that of the collective-farm worker because the state-farm worker is guaranteed an in-come, while the income of the collective farmers depends on the vagaries of the weather and the price policies of the government.

By 1966 there were over 12,000 state farms in the Soviet Union. They employed about eight million people and averaged about 18,000 sown acres per farm. The responsibilities of the manager of a state farm are much the same as that of a factory manager, and so are his rewards. An employee of a state farm has a private plot of about one-third of an acre on which he may build his own home and cultivate his own crops. State farms usually specialize in a few products and need not be as self-sufficient as collective farms since they have access to the state budget and pay regular wages. Having met with increasing recent success after long years of deficit operations, the state-farm system has absorbed a number of formerly collective enterprises.

The comparable figures for collective farms are 36,500 farms, em-ploying over 18 million workers on an average of about 7,000 sown acres. Thus the average size of Russian farms is very large by American stand-ards. Collective farms account for nearly 80 percent of the country's cotton output, half the total grain, and one-third of total livestock, milk, and eggs. The collective is much more self-sufficient than the state farm.

In spite of a "model charter," which ensures democratic self-government consisting of a farm chairman and a committee responsible to a meeting of the general membership, government and Party planning and influence dominate the collective farm. Collective farmers are also allocated private plots to cultivate for their own use. They are larger than in the previous case—½ to 2½ acres, depending on climate and fertility—and in the past have occupied a position of prime importance to the collective farm workers. The product of work on his private plot accrues entirely to the worker and can provide him with his necessities plus a cash crop that he may take to market. Collective-farm markets selling produce above government prices are prominent in Soviet cities. Private plots on collective farms, although only 3 percent of total cultivated land, were responsible for nearly ⅓ of gross farm output and ½ of livestock production in 1964.

Before 1966, collective-farm workers received no guaranteed wage for their labor on behalf of the cooperative. Each task was assigned a "workday" value. At the end of the year, when all expenses had been deducted from the collective's revenues, the workday unit was assigned a value and the remaining revenues distributed to members according to their accumulation of workdays. A particularly skilled or difficult job might be assigned a workday value of two, while a simple task would be evaluated at half a workday per day's labor. Owing to large compulsory deliveries to the government at low prices, the income received by the worker from the collective was very low. The incentive for the worker to devote his energy to collective pursuits was small, and he had to depend on his private plot. This problem was peculiar to collective farms before 1966; after 1966 tasks were assigned rouble values, and workers are now paid monthly wages from farm revenues. Profits are distributed at the end of the year in the form of bonuses on the basis of the year's wages for each worker. Current Soviet policy recommends that collective workers' incomes should be at least as high as those of state-farm workers. Private plots are recognized as essential to peasant morale and welfare, but each member must work at least a minimum number of days in his collective brigade.

AGRICULTURAL PROBLEMS

Low Productivity and Yield

Soviet agricultural productivity lags significantly behind the industrial sector and behind Western agriculture. At the fiftieth anniversary of the Revolution, the Russians could proudly boast of gains in industrial commodities, but agricultural output was only 1.8 times the 1914 production of butter. In the United States it requires six farmers to provide food for 100 people, while in the USSR 40 farmers are needed for the same task. We must recognize that the Soviet Union, while rich in natural resources, does not possess a great deal of arable land. Much of the land under cultivation receives too little moisture or experiences a very short growing season, while other areas are too marshy. The Soviet Union has a great diversity of climates and soils, but centralized agricultural policy has made this a more serious handicap than it need be. The wide swings of agricultural policy, which periodically has met with great temporary success, eventually caused progress to grind to a halt in the face of nature's adversity. Thus as in industry, a need for decentralized decision making became obvious.

Agricultural Incentives

Another problem in agriculture was the failure of incentives for collective farm workers. Farm chairmen had to be ruthless in exacting work on behalf of the collective from members whose only concrete hope for a livelihood centered around their private plots. The brighter and more industrious peasants made their way to the cities and the state farms, which further aggravated the manpower shortage due to the casualties of World War II. The compulsory deliveries to the state at very low prices kept the collectives short of funds to distribute and invest. The farm chairman could not calculate the costs and revenues of crops, and most of what was grown was determined by what had to be delivered. The chairman had to answer to the agricultural ministry, the local Communist Party secretary, the Machine Tractor Station (which controlled all the mechanized equipment for the neighboring collective farms), and the farm members. Investment in agriculture, mainly of tractors and some increased fertilizer production, was far from adequate, being neglected in favor of strategic production in heavy industry. When investments were finally made, they typically failed to consider local needs and advantages.

An Illustration from Russian Fiction

The student of economic systems can sometimes learn a great deal from works of fiction. One example is a short novel that appeared in 1963, during the post-Stalin thaw in literary expression. "The New Life" is the name of the collective farm on which the hero, Comrade Anany Yegorovich, is the manager.[1] He is sensible and conscientious in performing his duties, a task made infinitely more difficult by bureaucrats and Party officials who do not understand the realities of farming and by the collective farm members, who have a discouraging list of excuses and disabilities that prevent them from working efficiently.

The story is simple enough: The manager puts first priority on harvesting hay while the weather is dry; higher officials order him to switch to silage (green fodder) cutting in order to meet the district production quota on time, even though the silage could survive rainy weather and the

[1]Fyodor Abramov, *The New Life: A Day on a Collective Farm*, New York: Grove, 1963.

hay could not; the rains come, and in a desperate effort to save the crop Yegorovich attempts to organize a crash program of Sunday work among the collective farm members.

As he trudges from cottage to cottage in the kolkhoz village, many of the troubles that have haunted Russian agricultural planning are revealed in miniature. The chairman of the construction brigade is home drunk, and the cow barns may not get finished before winter; a group of old women are picking mushrooms for sale in the free market rather than working for the collective; workers in the timber industry who remained in the village after they quit the kolkhoz for better wages and working conditions are out of the chairman's control; a disgruntled peasant refuses, bemoaning the fact that the farm is too poor to allow each member to keep a cow. Even the milkmaids, the only young and enthusiastic workers present, are dreaming of marrying city officials and escaping the drudgery of farm life. The Party is no help; members on the collective are bureaucrats, teachers, or others out of contact with day-to-day farming decisions.

Discouraged, the chairman spends the evening at the village club; he drinks too much and awakes very late the next morning to find the whole village single-mindedly at work bringing in the hay. He is amazed to learn that the night before he promised a 30 percent bonus for all who would work on Sunday. The prospect of extra earnings is enough to lure malingerers away from their private plots, home improvements, and imaginary bad health.

The author's diagnosis of the situation is clear—too much bureaucratic meddling, too few incentives to keep younger workers from drifting off to better jobs, too few amenities for those who remain.

> The same old story. It was like a vicious circle! To make the daily labor norm attractive, people had to work. What other source of income was there for the kolkhoz? But to get people to work, you had to have an attractive daily norm. Where was the solution? In the district committee they had told him, "You're giving bad leadership. You've softpedaled agitational and educational work." But how were you going to bring agitational pressure on the kolkhoz worker of today? Without money, agitation didn't get you anywhere.[2]

Money, exemplified by the 30 percent bonus, got the hay crop harvested. In solving a short-term problem on "The New Life," it also pointed the way toward upgrading the quality of labor in the agricultural sector and making it attractive for young workers to stay. Finally, the novel indicates that there are reserves of motivation and productivity waiting to be tapped if central planners would alter the incentive system and provide funds for modernization. Recent reforms in Soviet agriculture indicate that some of these suggestions are beginning to be acted upon.

[2]*Ibid.*, pp. 72–73.

AGRICULTURAL REFORMS

Khrushchev and his successors recognized the problems of agriculture and set about coping with them. At first they dealt with them as they dealt with any economic bottleneck—by supplying more state directives. It soon became obvious that radically new approaches to farm problems were required. Some of Khrushchev's schemes were called harebrained, but they led to basic changes in the organization of the agricultural sector.

The Virgin-Lands Campaign

In the years immediately following Stalin's death, his successors realized the neglect into which Soviet agriculture had fallen and the abominable conditions that characterized peasant life. Farm prices were raised, and the disparity in price between compulsory deliveries and sales to the state was reduced and finally abolished by 1957. The output response was encouraging; from 1956 to 1958 gross agricultural output exceeded the 1950–1952 yield by 48.7 percent.[3] The new Soviet leaders, struggling to consolidate their positions, wanted quicker and even greater success in agriculture.

Khrushchev hit upon the idea of opening up new lands for crops. These lands had either too little moisture or too short a growing season to be profitably farmed. During the 1950s some 90 million acres of virgin land were brought under cultivation. Students from universities left their studies for a volunteer tour in the virgin lands; others were attracted by promises of better housing and living conditions. In the first years the program was an overwhelming success, and the lands yielded to their full capacity with very little investment. By the beginning of the next decade, however, dust-bowl conditions, similar to those prevailing in the American Southwest in the 1930s, caused many of the virgin-land experiments to be abandoned. Such conditions developed because the land was abused in a centralized campaign that was unresponsive to local conditions. In addition, the failure to deliver on promises of amenities in the newly settled areas discouraged migration and caused many of the pioneers to return to older farming regions.

Machine Tractor Station Reform

Before 1958, all heavy farm machinery was controlled by government-owned and operated Machine Tractor Stations (MTS). Collective farms paid for the services of the machinery with shares of its crops. The MTS served as a source of Party influence on collective farms and was an added limitation on the freedom of farm chairmen to decide what and how crops should be raised. It paid no capital charges and absorbed more investment

---

[3]See Jerzy F. Karcz, "Khrushchev's Agricultural Policies," in Morris Bornstein and Daniel Fusfeld, *The Soviet Economy: A Book of Readings* (3rd ed.), Homewood, Ill.: Irwin, 1970, pp. 226.

funds than was desirable. Farm chairmen complained bitterly of the inefficiency of the MTS and of the undue influence it exerted over their management. By 1958, however, because collective farms were being consolidated and financial reserves were being built, liquidation of the MTS became feasible. It also symbolized how far the Communist Party had come in pacifying and unifying the countryside since the bitter resistance of the original collectivization drives.

In March 1958 the decision was made to sell the equipment controlled by MTS to the collective farms and to transform the stations into repair centers. Credit arrangements were made, and by the middle of 1959 half a million tractors, several hundred thousand grain-harvesting combines, and other equipment totaling over 17 billion roubles ($4 billion) in value, were transferred to collective farms. The MTS became supply depots for new equipment as well as repair centers. The three million MTS employees displaced by the reform were attached to the collective farms they had formerly served. They were originally given special compensation because the income of collective farmers was low, but this was equalized by later guaranteed-wage reforms for members of collectives.

At this time the dual compulsory-delivery–state-purchase system was eliminated and replaced by a compulsory-purchase quota system that further limited the decision-making authority of farm chairmen. Collectives were no longer permitted to substitute types of crops in their deliveries. Thus the government gave with one hand and took with the other. On balance, prosperous collective farms were rewarded by the reforms, while poor farms suffered the increased burden of paying for the equipment. Much of the equipment was in deplorable condition and had to be retired in the next year or so.[4] Thereafter, government campaigns dealt with introducing new crops such as corn and winter wheat, which had been successful in other countries but were doomed to less than moderate success in the varied climates of the Soviet Union. Khrushchev's corn program (the result of his visit to an Iowa farm) was extensively ridiculed after his retirement.

Recent Reforms

The reforms made by Khrushchev's successors have centered on two main areas: increased monetary reward for the collective-farm workers and increased investment in the agricultural sector. In addition, some state farms have been put on a profit-bonus basis with fewer quotas; this is similar to the industrial system. These reforms have been successful in increasing output and reducing costs, and it is clear that the practice is being extended throughout the state-farm system. On collective farms, the guaranteed-wage system discussed previously has been instituted and the disparity between state- and collective-farm incomes thereby reduced. Farm prices have been raised, the incidence of taxes on poor farms decreased, and the price of

[4]*Ibid.*, p. 230.

some machinery and of electricity reduced. The emphasis on agricultural investment in recent plans is greatly increased, and drainage and irrigation programs are being pursued extensively. It seems that the importance of material incentives and of some degree of local autonomy have finally been recognized by the political leaders of the Soviet Union. It is interesting to note that charges of mismanagement in the agricultural sector seem to be the point of greatest vulnerability for political authorities.

> Secret dispatches from the U.S. embassy suggest the Communist Party leader Leonid Brezhnev, the top man in the Kremlin, has fought off a challenge to his leadership. He got into trouble over the same issues that led to the late Nikita Khrushchev's fall from power in 1964. Khrushchev was blamed for agriculture failures which forced him to exchange Soviet gold for Western grain. . . . Now another disastrous harvest has compelled Brezhnev to lay out gold for grain.
> The late-ripening harvest in the Asian territories had been promising. But cold rains flattened the fields, and mismanagement compounded the catastrophe. Farm machinery broke down and went unrepaired for lack of parts. Wet grain turned mouldy for lack of drying facilities. Grain shipments bogged down for lack of trucks.[5]

Soviet agriculture can thus be seen as still far from matching the achievements of the industrial sector. Farm output is still extremely vulnerable to climatic variability, a situation that could be partly alleviated by greater attention to irrigation, to application of fertilizer, and to development of faster-maturing varieties of feed grains. Output of farm machinery must be increased and its design made compatible with the skills of the people available to operate and repair such equipment.

Even assuming all of these items are given priority, however, the twin problems of effective central management and of an effective incentive system for the individual collective-farm member will remain. A recent account by American travelers documents these problems:

> Everywhere we have travelled in the Soviet farm areas we have seen administrative and organizational shortcomings, low operational efficiency, low productivity of labor and land, and backward conditions of village life. Collective farm fields have too many weeds, and collective and state farms produce crop yields that would be considered very poor in Czechoslovakia and Poland, in Western Europe and the United States. Indeed, Soviet average yields would spell bankruptcy for the individual farmer in Western Europe.
> During our journey in 1967 we saw sugar beets languishing where they should not have been planted and corn which (for the same reason) would never be over three feet tall. When we asked why these crops were sown, the answer was always "It's in the plan."[6]

[5]Jack Anderson in *The Philadelphia Bulletin*, October 9, 1972.
[6]Arthur E. Adams and Jan S. Adams, *Men Versus Systems: Agriculture in the USSR, Poland, and Czechoslovakia*, New York: Free Press, 1971, p. 89.

There is increasing emphasis on state farms and economic self-accounting (profit-bonus) management for state farms. Observing the success of large corporate farms in the United States, this may prove a profitable turn of events. Some of the new consolidated farms, however, are much larger than most American commercial and even corporate farms. The imbalance of Soviet economic growth that has led to the conditions just described figures heavily in the evaluation of Soviet economic performance that follows.

QUESTIONS FOR CLASS DISCUSSION

1. Compare the incentives for workers on Soviet state farms and for collective-farm members. How would you expect a guaranteed minimum annual income for collective-farm members to affect productivity?

2. What lessons can be learned from the novel *The New Life*?

3. Is it possible to decentralize decision making in Soviet agriculture and still ensure that enough food and industrial raw materials get produced?

4. Was the virgin-lands program doomed to failure?

5. How is Communist Party influence exerted in collective-farm operations?

6. It is sometimes claimed that economic planning, particularly in agriculture, faces the following dilemma: Enthusiasm for a new program can be generated only through a propaganda campaign that has the unfortunate consequence of causing overcompliance by officials who neglect everything else for the project of the moment. Discuss this assertion.

7. Discuss the advantages of disbanding the Machine Tractor Station system.

8. Why are Russian political leaders sensitive to criticisms of their agricultural policies?

23. An evaluation of the Soviet economic system

A half-century of historical experience has been accumulated on which to base an evaluation of the Soviet economic system. A provisional judgment involves measuring the increase in goods and services produced (and how much of that increase benefited individual citizens) and an inquiry into how nonmaterial dimensions such as creativity, diversity, and individual freedoms have fared under a regime of centralized economic planning. In making such a judgment, we will follow the example of Abram Bergson, the foremost American expert on the Soviet economy, in applying economists' criteria to an assessment of the Russian experience.[1] These criteria are

[1]Abram Bergson, *Planning and Productivity Under Soviet Socialism*, Pittsburgh: Carnegie-Mellon University, 1968.

growth, productivity, and efficiency in output; material living standards for consumers; and job satisfaction and advancement opportunities for workers. In addition, the latitude to express individual preferences will be considered in an attempt to appreciate the global changes in Russian life brought about by the political and economic revolution that occurred after 1917.

ECONOMIC GROWTH UNDER CENTRAL PLANNING

Many students believe that an economy's rate of growth is an unambiguous fact that is beyond dispute. They are surprised to learn that there is a considerable discrepancy between various measures of Soviet economic performance since 1917; they are even more surprised to learn that several "right" answers can be derived from similar data, depending on which basis for comparison is selected. If an economy produced only a single homogeneous commodity, a reasonable physical measure could be found to keep track of the tons, yards, or dozens turned out; with a variety of products, however, a monetary standard is needed—adding tons of coal and tons of diamonds certainly distorts the value of carbon products.

Relative prices vary over time; thus, the core of the "index-number problem" is the discrepancy between measured growth rates depending on the base-year prices selected as a standard. Early-year weights give high price weights to new products that are growing rapidly; late-year weights give low price weights to the same products. In the Soviet Union, during periods of extremely rapid growth, this gives rise to extreme variations; one reputable estimate shows only 4.8 percent average annual growth between 1928 and 1937, if 1937 prices are used as weights, but an 11.9 percent rate if 1928 prices are used instead.[2]

Whatever the exact measure, it is undeniable that a rapid increase in output (especially industrial output) occurred during the first two five-year plans. The growth rate fell, however, during the Stalinist purges of the late 1930s and fell still further before and during World War II. Cohn's figures show a 7.1 percent annual growth rate for 1950–1958 and a slower pace of 5.5 percent for 1958–1967. Estimates for later years are provisional, but there is evidence that the 6.7 percent planned rate of increase for the 1971–1975 period is probably on the optimistic side.

> To find rates of sustained growth in the capitalist world one must go back
> to historical instances such as the U.S. in the 1870s and 1880s,
> Australia in the 1860s and 1870s and Japan in the 1920s and 1930s.
> Even those growth rates are only on the order of 5 or 5.5 percent. Taking
> into account the fact that the U.S.S.R.'s growth was set back severely
> by World War II and that its average annual rate for the 38-year period

[2]Stanley N. Cohn, "The Soviet Economy: Performance and Growth," in Marshall I. Goldman, ed., *Comparative Economic Systems: A Reader*, New York: Random House, 1971, p. 342.

since 1928 nevertheless ranges between 5.4 and 6.7 percent, the Soviet accomplishment appears to be essentially unprecedented.[3]

How did this impressive accomplishment occur? To help answer that question, we can rely on a simple model disaggregating the sources of economic growth in the Soviet economy.

A Model for Analyzing Sources of Economic Growth

The following symbols measure output per capita (O/P) and show that it equals the participation rate (W/P) of workers in the total population multiplied by the overall sum of each sector's productivity times its share in the total work force. For simplicity we will divide the entire economy into three sectors—agriculture (A), industry (I), and services (S). The complete formula is:

$$\frac{O}{P} = \frac{W}{P} \left[\left(\frac{O_A}{W_A} \cdot \frac{W_A}{W} \right) + \left(\frac{O_I}{W_I} \cdot \frac{W_I}{W} \right) + \left(\frac{O_S}{W_S} \cdot \frac{W_S}{W} \right) \right]$$

There are three basic sources of increasing output in this simple algebraic model: (1) The participation rate (W/P) can increase so that a larger share of the population is in the economically active group; (2) productivity per worker can increase within one or more of the sectors; (3) the proportion of workers in a high-productivity sector can be increased by shifting workers out of a low-productivity sector, even if productivity per se within each sector remains unchanged. In fact, all three of these sources play an important role in the economic history of the Soviet Union. The participation rate jumped when the labor force grew three times as fast as population between 1928 and 1937, a result mainly of eliminating hidden underemployment in agriculture.[4] More recently, the increased utilization of women, who now constitute fully half of the Soviet work force (compared with one-fourth to one-third in the West), has allowed a continued upward climb in this source of increased output per head.

The most important source of increasing output per capita in the Soviet Union has been the radical shift of resources out of low-productivity agriculture during the process of industrialization. The proportion of agricultural employment has fallen from roughly 70 percent in 1928 to the present level of approximately 30 percent. This is still a very high proportion (the United States was in a similar position on the eve of World War I); nevertheless, the structural transformation from agriculture to an industrial base has been a major factor in explaining the changes of the past 40 years.

[3]Raymond P. Powell, "Economic Growth in the U.S.S.R.," *Scientific American,* December 1968, p. 21.
[4]Cohn, p. 344.

To some extent these two elements—participation rates and structural shifts between sectors—represent "one shot" sources of gains in output that cannot continue. There are demographic limits to how high participation rates can go and natural-resource endowments that dictate a continued role for agriculture. The future outlook, in fact, may reverse past gains from these sources. To the extent that the services sector grows more rapidly than the others, there will probably be a slight drag on overall growth.

Finally, there have been increases in sectoral labor productivity. Detailed evidence is sketchy on this point, but it appears that agricultural productivity increased very slowly between 1930 and 1950, and then approximately doubled between 1950 and 1965.[5] Since the agricultural labor force has remained constant since 1950, any increases in output are reflected in labor-productivity measures. Nonagricultural productivity likewise showed its major increase in the postwar period, partly as a result of technological borrowing from abroad.

Future Soviet economic growth must come from increasing productivity. This is the purpose behind accentuated attention to investment in agriculture during the past decade and, to some extent, the importation of entire factories from the West to update industries like automobile manufacture, chemicals, and petroleum refining. Increased productivity in the services sector may be considerably more difficult to attain; at the same time, pressure will grow for more housing services, repair facilities, and other symbols of a consumer-oriented economy.

Static Efficiency

Economic performance can be judged according to two kinds of efficiency: "static efficiency, or the degree to which a community is able to exploit material opportunities that are open to it within the limits of available technological knowledge, and dynamic efficiency, which relates to the community's capacity to add to its technological knowledge and to exploit such knowledge with increasing effect."[6] We will consider the criterion of static efficiency in this section and that of dynamic efficiency in the next one.

Efficiency is related to growth, but in some ways it represents a more realistic standard of Soviet economic performance by not assessing fault for factors beyond the control of central planners. Achieving static efficiency provides a larger surplus for investment in future productive capacity and thus facilitates rapid growth; achieving dynamic efficiency pushes the economy along the highest feasible growth path as limited by resource endowments, labor-force growth, and environmental conditions. Since these vary among nations, the growth rate produced under dynamic-efficiency conditions varies also.

[5]Powell, p. 20.
[6]Bergson, p. 52.

Referring back to our model, the question of the static efficiency of the Soviet economy at any moment becomes the following: Given the existing participation rates and the sectoral allocation of labor, did productivity in each sector achieve the maximum level made possible by existing technology? Previous chapters chronicled the sources of static inefficiency. They can be summarized under three categories—shortcomings of the incentive system, waste at the enterprise level, and obstacles instigated by central planning per se.

The morale problem on collective farms remains unsolved, as does the unwieldy size of farm units and the bureaucratic interference with managerial decision making. Although there is an increased commitment of investment funds to agriculture, fundamental administrative reforms of the organizational structure imposed in the 1930s have not occurred. Equally remote is a move toward reliance on the price mechanism as a basic motivating device for securing agricultural production. Thus the same forces that precluded static efficiency in agriculture up to now will continue to operate in the future.

Our chapter on industrial planning listed similar difficulties in the industrial and services sectors, with the significant difference that industry was not systematically and deliberately starved of capital the way agriculture was. Reforms in the incentive and administrative systems have been attempted in industry, but it is questionable whether they have done much more than keep up with the demands imposed by the increased scope and complexity of centrally planning a mature industrial economy.

It is doubtful, moreover, that the Soviets fully realize the task that confronts them in creating a services sector commensurate with the standard of living they envision for the near future. The quality of consumer-durable goods is notoriously low; there are periodic publicity campaigns in which immediate breakdowns of long-awaited television sets or refrigerators are documented, together with the virtual absence of any means of getting them repaired. The recent decision to embark upon the mass production of automobiles will eventually involve millions of people in related service activities. One does not have to envision a full range of shopping centers and drive-in movies to predict that the automobile will revolutionize Russian living patterns and mobility, and will absorb resources in ways similar to the American experience.

We conclude, therefore, that static inefficiency has been and will continue to be a fact of Russian economic life. Precise measurement of the extent of wasted resources from this source is extremely tenuous, but one bold attempt estimated that if the bundle of resources available in the Soviet Union in 1960 had been utilized with American techniques and organizational skills, a 5 to 20 percent greater output would have resulted.[7]

[7]Joseph S. Berliner, "The Static Efficiency of the Soviet Economy," *American Economic Review*, May 1964, pp. 480–489.

Dynamic Efficiency

Dynamic efficiency, it will be remembered, refers to an economy's ability to add to its stock of usable technological knowledge. Achieving dynamic efficiency is a two-phase process in a modern economic system: First, a high rate of saving out of current output must take place in order that capital formation can occur; second, a scientific and administrative structure must be created that encourages new technological discoveries to be incorporated into additions to the capital stock.

The ability to achieve high rates of investment has been one of the greatest areas of success for the Soviet economy. Except during World War II, the capital stock has been growing at an average rate of 8 to 9 percent annually since 1928.[8] This rate implies a doubling of the capital stock every eight years. This is about twice the rate achieved by the United States during our period of most rapid economic growth, at the end of the nineteenth century. On top of this rapid accumulation, the Russians have been able to direct investment toward areas of the economy where the output payoff has been immediate and substantial. Activities with high capital/output ratios, of which housing is the most blatant example, have been systematically starved to prevent them from absorbing scarce resources while generating relatively little additional output. If this situation is ever reversed, the implications for future economic growth in Russia are profound.

Dynamic inefficiency thus arises predominantly from how capital is used once it has been allocated to sectoral distinctions. Considerable waste has occurred as a result of the ideological proscription on capital charges as a rationing device for allocating capital. Individual enterprises, moreover, have been understandably reluctant to incorporate new technology into additions to productive capacity.

> In the Soviet industrial context, any increases in the degree of dependence of an enterprise on outside organizations increases the risk of plan underfulfillment. The traditional efforts at enterprise "autarky" reflect the aversion to such dependence. The enterprise undertaking an innovation, particularly if it is of large scale and if it is the first instance of its introduction in the USSR, becomes heavily dependent on outside R and D [Research and Development] organizations for the supply of vital services.[9]

Despite these drawbacks, the Soviet record of productivity growth in the postwar period is roughly comparable to that of the United States. The difference between the growth rate of total output and that for combined inputs is a composite of organizational improvements, economies of scale, improvements in the quality of labor and capital inputs, and the increasing

[8]Abram Bergson, "Future Growth Strategy for the Soviet Economy," *The ACES Bulletin.* Association for Comparative Economic Studies, Spring 1972, p. 3.
[9]Berliner, "Innovation and Economic Structure in Soviet Industry," *The ACES Bulletin,* 1970, p. 3.

proficiency resulting from accumulated experience in advance production techniques. One estimate places the annual advance in this measure of "total factor productivity" at 3.9 percent for 1950–1958 and 2.3 percent for 1958–1964.[10] Initial figures for the subsequent period point to the possibility of a dramatic slowing of the recent rate of technical advance in the Soviet Union.[11]

> The Soviet record of economic growth has been impressive and in terms of the objectives of Soviet political leaders, which have not rated human welfare very highly, it has been quite successful. Further, we have tried to show that the main impact of Soviet centralized planning on Soviet economic growth has been felt in the ability of the central planners to force structural change in outputs and inputs on the economy. This has been reflected in the more rapid growth of industry and construction relative to total national product and within industry by the relatively more rapid growth of producers' goods in comparison with consumers' goods. And it has been reflected in the rapid increase in the quantity and quality of capital and labor. Finally, we have argued that Soviet central planners were not so effective in fostering growth in the realm of micro resource allocation, that is, they were not too successful in getting the economy in a given year with its given resources to produce an output close to its potential maximum. However, we have also argued that they have been relatively successful in achieving dynamic efficiency. The growth of outputs per unit of aggregate inputs in the Soviet economy has generally been equal to that of the leading capitalist economies.[12]

The continued accuracy of this summary evaluation hinges on the two sources of dynamic efficiency. As the rate of capital formation reaches the limits to which it can be pushed, given present needs on the consumer front, there must be a corresponding increase in both the supply of technical innovations within the Soviet Union or borrowed from abroad and the receptivity of establishments to adopt such innovations because adequate incentives exist for doing so. It is clear that neither can Soviet central planning achieve this necessary transformation nor does sufficient flexibility exist for institutional adaptation to the ending of growth primarily through structural shifts and a high rate of capital formation. No one can predict the final outcome of the forces that have been set in inexorable motion.

ECONOMIC WELFARE UNDER CENTRAL PLANNING

Two facts documented in the previous section are the rapid growth in total and per-capita output in the Soviet Union since the era of five-year plans

[10]Cohn, p. 348.

[11]Bergson, "Future Growth Strategy for the Soviet Economy," p. 3.

[12]Herbert S. Levine, "Growth and Planning in the Soviet Union," in Montias et al., *The Soviet Economy in Theory and Practice*, Columbia, Mo.: University of Missouri Press, 1964, p. 87.

was launched in 1928 and the high portion of output devoted to capital formation during this period. These two magnitudes determine a third, namely what was left over for private consumpton and how per-capita consumption varied over time. Economic growth can thus be seen as partly a question of the division of the bounty of economic activity between the present generation of consumers and a receding horizon of future generations; the "sacrifices" made now to allow a high rate of capital formation expand potential output in the future. In a market economy the choice between present and future consumption results indirectly from the voluntary savings generated by individuals anticipating the future needs of themselves and their heirs. Centrally planned economic systems make the same choice directly and arbitrarily when the planned rate of capital formation is specified.

Living Standards

When attention is focused on Russian consumption since 1928, the abruptness and totality of the Soviet industrialization effort becomes evident. Recognizing all of the measurement difficulties that were discussed in relation to the growth of output, the evidence leads one to the initial conclusion that the real per-capita consumption of the typical Russian citizen did not increase significantly during the quarter-century preceding Stalin's death in 1953.[13] In other words, Russian workers were enlisted in a massive, frantic rush to industrialize, which more than doubled per-capita output without any of the benefits showing up in per-capita *consumption*. It can be argued that every historical example of successful industrialization probably involved some temporary lag of consumption standards behind the rate of output growth, but it is doubtful whether any other country can match the duration and severity of restricted consumption that occurred in the Soviet Union.

It is idle to speculate about how much longer these conditions could have continued unaltered beyond 1953. The succession of political leaders were all committed to some degree of emphasis on increasing the standard of living. The broadest generalizations that can safely be made about recent living standards in the Soviet Union are the following: (1) They rose substantially from 1950 to the early 1960s. (2) The impact of the adverse trend in the rate of economic growth in the early 1960s was permitted to fall principally on consumer-goods rather than producer-goods industries, causing a pause in the rate of increase. (3) The level of welfare of the Soviet population has improved conspicuously in recent years. (4) Overall average living standards are at about one-quarter to one-third of the prevailing average in the United States. (5) Standards vary in degree from housing, where their average is far below one-quarter of ours, to food and clothing,

[13]Cohn, pp. 350–351.

where it may be nearly half of ours, to medical services, education, and certain public services, such as urban transportation, where it may approximately equal ours. (6) The Soviet standard of living encompasses extreme degrees of inequality, extending from the most comfortable or even luxurious living standard of the popular writer, artist, musician, actor, outstanding professor, scientist, engineer, or Party leader to the dire poverty of many members of poor collective farms. (7) Soviet average living standards, barring severe recession in the United States or a major reversal of the Soviet priority on planned allocation of productive resources, will lag far behind ours for the foreseeable future.

Any attempt to generalize about comparative living standards between the Soviet Union and the United States is made at considerable peril. It is extremely easy to draw generalizations from too restricted or irrelevant sets of facts. Several illustrations of this will suffice. The paucity of privately owned automobiles, by American standards, might well be taken to reflect poor national living standards. The fact is that Party policy makers and planners, at least until recently, have held that urban populations will be better served by channeling resources into the improvement of bus and subway urban transportation. They point with derision to what they regard as a misdirection of productive resources resulting in a scourge of traffic jams and accidents in urban communities in the United States and Western Europe.

Similarly, the logic of another frequently cited criterion of living standards could be challenged. It is sometimes noted that, comparing average workers in Moscow and New York City, the former works 4 times as long as the latter to be able to buy a pound of beef, 1½ times as long for a loaf of bread, 11 times as long for a man's wool suit, 4 times as long for a quart of milk or a package of cigarettes, and so on.[14] Such references disregard established basic differences in patterns of consumer desires in the two countries. Also, many comparisons of living standards make the false assumption that the Soviet citizen looks to public agencies for the same portion and the same elements of his living standards as does the citizen of the United States. The fact is that the Soviet citizen acquires a larger portion of his total consumption from public sources, thereby supplementing his expenditure of personal income.

Though this cannot be quantified accurately, it is illustrated by certain facts. Whereas the American industrial worker spends about 25 percent of his income for living quarters, the Soviet worker spends 4 or 5 percent for this purpose because worker housing is very heavily subsidized from public funds in the Soviet Union. The Soviet citizen faces no bills for medical services—even for hospitalization and surgery, of a quality near the American level—because these costs are met entirely from government funds. The same is true for education at all levels. In the Soviet Union, fares on

14United States Bureau of Labor Statistics. See *Business Week*, July 16, 1960.

public transportation far from cover the costs of rendering this service, and the citizen contributes nothing to the cost of his old-age pension and sickness and disability insurance. Nursery services for children of working parents are made available at a nominal charge. This larger area of communal consumption by the Soviet citizen is a factor that should not be neglected when living standards are judged on the basis of private consumption expenditures.

The position of consumers in the Soviet Union has improved considerably in the past few years, owing largely to normal wage raises for improved skills, higher labor productivity, and greater welfare payments such as pensions, educational stipends, and so on.

> More important, however, were wage and welfare reforms begun by Khrushchev in 1964 and continued and embellished by the Brezhnev-Kosygin regime. Welfare measures implemented in 1965 brought 25 to 30 million collective farmers and their families under a state social insurance program, raised by 20 percent the average wage of 18 million workers in the service sector, and increased the minimum monthly wage by more than one third. Further increases in 1967 added approximately 15 percent a month to the incomes of 4.5 million workers in lumbering, consumer goods industries, and certain occupations on state farms.[15]

This upward spiral of incomes may well continue as a result of new welfare measures currently being implemented.

In order that such a sizable increase in the rouble incomes of so large a portion of the population may represent a rise in the recipient's real living standard, it obviously is necessary that the supplies of consumer goods be considerably expanded. The Soviet economy has made significant progress in this direction, including some liberalization in the importation of consumer goods. There is clear evidence that the Soviet retail buyer is now measurably better able to be selective in his shopping for consumer-durable goods and to avoid the poorer qualities and styles he does not like.[16]

Health, Education, and Scientific Progress

Health, education, and scientific progress are especially crucial indicators of future expansion in the Soviet economy. There are said to be over 12 percent more physicians in the Soviet Union per 100,000 people than there are in the United States. About 70 percent of them are women. Each has completed a six-year medical education in one of the country's 80 medical schools. All medical, dental, surgical, diagnostic, hospital, and related services are free of charge to any Soviet citizen, the patient paying only for

---

[15]Joint Economic Committee, *Soviet Economic Performance*, Washington, D.C.: Government Printing Office, 1968, p. 91.
[16]*The Economist*, May 29, 1971.

medicines he uses at home. In addition to physicians, there are trained physicians' assistants, midwives, pharmacists, and nurses. The medical training program in the Soviet Union is the largest in the world. Medical students pay no tuition, and 85 percent of them receive stipends to meet living costs. Apparently the quality of medical services is high, although the quality of medical training probably is not quite comparable to that available in the United States. Although there are occasional complaints about the limited time a physician has for a patient, the need for more equipment in the polyclinics where out-patient services are rendered, and unsatisfactory services in agricultural or outlying industrial regions, these are relatively minor compared to the impressive achievements in expanding the quantity and quality of medical services under Soviet rule.

In 1959 the basic elementary-school period was made eight years, with courses in fundamentals of science, Russian, mathematics, history, physics, foreign language, and geography. Thereafter all students are expected to engage in some kind of regular productive work, with opportunities afforded to continue their studies in three-year evening secondary schools; those who do well have their regular working hours reduced. Here courses of study include general educational and technical subjects, with the greatest number of hours being allocated to mathematics and physics. While a small number of especially able students continue directly from the eight-year school into full-time high-school academic courses and then into the universities, the main paths to be followed above the eight-year school are (1) to a work-study high school and thence to either a job or a university (for those who meet the high entrance requirements) or (2) to a technical training school and thence to a job.

Qualified Americans who have studied the Soviet educational system firsthand are impressed with the way they educate and train for the specific manpower and professional needs of their system, whereas in the United States we emphasize much more general aspects of education while giving students leeway to choose majors and courses to fit their individual interests. The zeal of the Soviet population for education and the rapid increase in educational opportunities are highly commended. Also noted are the high quality of equipment, the favorable teacher-student ratio, the emphasis on productive work, the work of the Pioneers (a school-age Communist organization) in keeping discipline and supervising extracurricular activities, and the emphasis on physical education and health. Some of the questions or criticisms pertain to the lack of emphasis on the humanities and the absence of instruction in economic systems and societies other than their own.

So much has been published in popular sources about the Soviet Union's progress in the physical sciences that little need be said here. Their scientific advance comes from precisely the same sources ours must come from—generous allocations of resources to higher education and scientific research and devoted work by students, teachers, and researchers. Scientific research, like everything else, is highly organized in the Soviet Union.

The top scientific organizations are the USSR Academy of Sciences, responsible to and reporting annually to the Council of Ministers, and 15 other Academies of Sciences, each responsible to the Council of Ministers of its republic. The USSR Academy of Sciences consists of many institutes for the respective scientific fields; an example is the Institute of Economics. The actual research activity occurs in an array of research institutions. The Academy, which is financed wholly from the government budget, constructs both annual and longer-term research plans. To be elected an Academy member is the highest professional honor for a scientist, and all of the leading scientists are among its 500 members.

The Individual and the State

When one examines the Soviet system from the viewpoint of the traditional values of the Western world, considerable doubts about its ultimate merit arise. Western traditions hold the individual to be the end toward which political and economic activity is directed. The individual's freedom and ability to develop personal potentialities to the full is the final criterion by which our institutions, processes, and historical trends are judged. Although activities are limited by law, these limitations are grounded on the necessity to restrict one individual's actions in order to assure others their inherent rights. We have a concept of the common good—the necessity for group or communal action in certain limited spheres—in order that individuals, as such, may enjoy full lives. The great force protecting the individual is pluralism: in a multiparty political system; in relatively free economic enterprise and competition; in independent newspapers, books, and magazines; in religious freedom and tolerance; in varied state and private educational systems and institutions; and in unrestrained activities in the sciences and the arts.

The absence of pluralism in the Soviet system opposes it to Western philosophies and ideals. As noted in our brief study of political institutions, sovereignty in the Soviet Union resides in the Communist Party—the single legal party—and not in the government with its ostensibly popularly elected assemblies (soviets). Within the Party, sovereignty centers in a small circle of Party officials, which, while the personages change, remains a self-selected, self-perpetuating, all-dominating power bloc. This is not to say that this self-selected power elite does or can do whatever it personally may prefer; there is an outside limit in the tolerance of the masses. In the Soviet Union this outside limit is kept inactive by the ubiquity of government as an agent of the Party. The government owns and operates practically all industrial enterprises and a constantly enlarging portion of agricultural units; government or Party appointees edit and government presses publish all newspapers and journals, and government presses publish all books; religion in any traditional sense is experiencing a planned withering away; and education is exclusively a function of government. Only in the arts and sciences does pluralism have some reality, and in the arts this is well confined by Party influence.

The persistence of restrictions on the free flow of artistic and intellectual ideas long after they represent any immediate threat to political stability may indicate an ingrained bureaucratic distrust of creative expression in nonpluralistic societies. Although the methods of repressing dissent have become more subtle, the possibility of loss of privileges, bans on publication, or even involuntary incarceration in "mental" hospitals exerts a chilling effect on intellectual activity. Life for most Russian citizens goes on in a bland, routine way; any society imposes sanctions on rebellious or deviant behavior, but in Russia the detection mechanism is omnipresent and the price of misbehaving greater than in the West.

Our interest centers in the economic aspects of this monolithic society. Its detailed organizational and operational phases have been discussed. It remains for us to take a sweeping look at their implications from the viewpoint of our own Western scale of values. First, the individual consumer has little, if any, of the sovereignty that exists in very substantial measure in Western nations. Decisions involving the division of productive resources between building capital facilities and producing goods for consumption are made by top-level Party bodies. The subdivision of resource use within these broad categories is made by a centralized economic-planning hierarchy reaching into every crevice of the economy. Admittedly, many detailed plan goals are related to the quantities of goods the populace buys in retail stores. However, the prices at which consumers make their choices are aggregates of many and important arbitrary cost elements, the turnover tax being a visible example (many are invisible to the public eye). Even if one accepts as accurate the most severe estimates of the power in the United States of misleading advertising and sales promotions, the inability of the consumer to judge quality, durability, and usability of consumer goods, and the consumer's failure to initiate counterforces to these, consumer sovereignty remains a vital pluralistic aspect of our economy.

In the Soviet Union all industrial employees work for the government, either directly in state-owned and operated enterprises or in closely controlled producers' cooperatives. The peasant farmer either works directly for the government on a state farm or, aside from time spent on his private plot, in collective-farm activities. The skill or type of ability the industrial worker achieves and the attainments of the professional worker are related directly to the amount and type of education or training the government makes available. In addition, an enormous number of people are employed by the hierarchy of governmental administrative, planning, and management agencies, and by the Communist Party apparatus.

Finally, our evaluation of the Soviet system must not be concluded without noting the reply of Soviet Marxism to these questions. The contemporary domination of government and Party, they declare, is simply a way station along the path to full communism; it is only in this latter stage of human living that complete consumer sovereignty can prevail. Only then will a person be really free, the hard and disagreeable work having been taken over by machinery and some measure of socially useful effort having become an inherent ingredient of individual happiness; only then will class divisions and distinctions have disappeared, and no symbols of class remain; and only then will true pluralism in its full meaning prevail, with its benefits freely available to all. This surely has the ring of the highest idealism. The present Soviet Communist Party leaders admit that entry into such a stage of human society first requires proliferation of society's economic productive power—now sought through powerful government and Party use of planned scientific development and industrial automation. The leaders also contend that the beginnings of ultimate full communism and the attendant absence of restrictive government are now visible in the Soviet Union.

This, of course, raises the question of the goals and motivations of present and future political leaders in the Soviet Union. Is affluence a goal in itself, or is it also a means of increasing the freedom and dignity of the individual? Will the levers of economic and social control be relinquished now that the initial rationale for them—rapid modernization of the economy—has largely been achieved? Will a pent-up mass demand for greater civil liberties emerge the way the demand for consumer-durable goods has recently required the attention of economic planners? Indications are that a further loosening of individual choice will occur, but like all processes of social change it will occur unevenly and with unforeseen side effects and political ramifications.

PAST ACCOMPLISHMENTS AND FUTURE PROSPECTS

In November 1967, *Monthly Review*, the leading journal of socialist economics in the United States, devoted an entire issue to commemorating 50 years of Soviet power. It included essays by many of the best-known Western proponents of socialism. To a surprising extent the overall appraisal of the current Soviet economy was that in the process of acquiring material comforts it had somehow lost its "soul." The following quotation exemplifies this consensus view.

> The Revolution brought industrialization, urbanization, a rise in living standards, and the achievement of universal literacy along with other basic elements of human culture. Formerly, these advances were achieved under capitalist auspices, but for well-known reasons this is no longer possible in backward countries today. No less significant is the fact that while the capitalist nations required two and three centuries for their accomplishment, the Russian Revolution, using a socialist framework, required only 30 years. (In this connection, we must not forget that it took a decade to recover from the First World War and the civil war, and that a second decade was consumed by the Second World War and its aftermath.)

Thus in the performance of "capitalist" tasks, the Russian Revolution has achieved great successes. But, compared to the aims and aspirations of the inspirers of the Revolution, the story is different. The Russian Revolution, like the French, was a climactic event for a world-wide body of idealists. They aspired to a true communal life, genuine equality, the abolition of classes, rank, and distinction, the emancipation of women and sexual freedom, the liberation of the arts, the birth of a cooperative commonwealth in which men would at last find harmony among themselves and with their environment. . . .

But the direction of Soviet society today is such that there seems to be little will to move toward socialism, now that it is at last becoming possible. In the years of the hard ascent, the Revolution seems to have lost its way. Everything was sacrificed so that the Revolution might survive and industrialize; and now the very instruments created for survival, the modes of rule, the habits of thought, the institutions, the ideological crudities seem to form a solid barrier across the road to socialism. . . .

This is why the Soviet experiment has, with remarkable suddenness, lost the center of the international stage.[17]

Has the idealized "new socialist man" become simply another wage worker responding to material inducements in a "bourgeois" environment? Are Russian political leaders just another group of bureaucrats, technocrats, and manipulators of public opinion? Has the Russian economic system grown fat and complacent now that the tremendous challenges of achieving political stability and economic modernization in a hostile world have been largely accomplished? It becomes obvious that even the most fervid admirers of past Soviet economic accomplishments are not content to let the growth rate stand as the sole criterion for evaluating the costs and benefits of the experiment that has been going on in Russia for the past 50 years. Economics is ill-suited for judging monumental accomplishments brought about through monumental sacrifices in human lives and efforts and under the most adverse of conditions. Rapidly raising the Soviet economic system to a position among the industrial leaders of the world is a tremendous success story judged by narrow economic criteria alone. How these factors compare to those desired by sympathetic critics—"more equality and fewer privileges to the bureaucracy, more confidence and trust in the masses, greater inner party democracy"[18]—must be left to the value judgments of the individual evaluator. We might add, however, that a utopia without laughter and flowers doesn't seem to us to be much of a utopia.

If the Soviet experiment has indeed lost the center of the international stage, as the passage just cited indicates, it is because experiments aimed at creating a socialist economy while using alternate incentive systems have

---

[17]Harry Braverman, "The Successes, the Failures, and the Prospects," in *50 Years of Soviet Power, Monthly Review*, November 1967, pp. 23–24.
[18]*Ibid.*, p. 5.

appeared to break down the image of socialism as a monolithic entity slavishly imitating the Russian pattern. The next chapter treats the incentive systems of Yugoslavia, China, and Cuba—the three most widely discussed variations of the Soviet prototype.

QUESTIONS FOR CLASS DISCUSSION

1. Why does the index-number problem occur? How does it affect discussions of Soviet economic performance?

2. Distinguish between static and dynamic efficiency. How does each affect the rate of growth of an economy?

3. How did the Russian economy achieve such high rates of growth during the past 45 years? How does the simple model presented in this chapter help identify sources of growth?

4. Discuss the impact of the high participation rate of women in the Russian labor force on the economy and society.

5. How does a market economy shift resources from one sector to another? How did the Soviets achieve similar sectoral shifts?

6. Why is labor productivity so low in Soviet industry and agriculture compared with productivity levels in other developed nations?

7. Discuss the past and present condition of the consumer in the Soviet economy. What problems arise in comparing living standards in different countries?

8. Why are Soviet enterprises reluctant to adopt technological innovations? With all the obstacles to dynamic efficiency, why have the Russians done relatively well in this respect? What is the future outlook for achieving dynamic efficiency?

9. Place yourself in the position of a typical Russian citizen. From this viewpoint, state the good and bad things you perceive in your day-to-day living conditions.

10. Why have political authorities been so loath to allow greater freedom of artistic and intellectual expression in the Soviet Union?

11. Is pluralism compatible with a Soviet type of economic system?

12. Do you agree with the conclusion that the Soviet Union has opted for material comforts for individuals instead of advancing toward "real" socialism?

13. How does the incentive system of the Soviet Union affect the general "tone" of economic life?

24. Variations on the Soviet model—incentive systems in Yugoslavia, China, and Cuba

Not too many years ago, American high-school students, were asked examination questions like the following: "Name three reasons why socialism is bound to fail." Among the "correct" answers was that socialism offered no incentives whatsoever for human endeavor. It is doubly ironic to note that many recent reforms in centrally planned economic systems turn out to be largely efforts to adjust incentive mechanisms—if no incentives exist, why pay so much attention to them?

The sources of human motivation are complex in any economic system, but to say that no incentives exist is simply untrue. The industrial growth of the Soviet Union followed a zig-zag course of methods to bring forth productive effort; contrary to the impression held by many Americans, economic motivation was not a result of unmitigated police-state tactics.

To illustrate the variety of incentive systems that can prevail within the command type of economic systems, we will survey three nations that have deviated from the Soviet model: Yugoslavia, the People's Republic of China, and Cuba. In stressing only the aspect of incentive systems, we go to the heart of the problem of harnessing economic institutions to the task of achieving rapid economic development. This seems the quickest way to understand innovations that have aroused considerable interest among outside observers.

Incentives may exist in material or nonmaterial form. Higher wages and salaries, access to housing or other scarce goods and services, and free vacations at company resorts are examples of increased material living standards. Honorary titles, an audience with a top political leader, and more decision-making responsibility on the job are nonmaterial incentives, as are the internal sanctions that seek the favorable regard of one's relatives and fellow workers. Nor should we underestimate the negative incentives involved in the prospect of incurring the displeasure of one's immediate boss or higher authorities; leading a "quiet life" free from investigative scrutiny was seen to be one of the major factors in the mind of the Soviet plant manager.

It is appropriate to speak of an incentive system because the tangible and psychological motivating elements together form a pattern of stimuli that produce the overall effect. The incentive system changes when new elements are added (profitability as a bonus criterion in the Soviet Union, for example) or when the relative emphasis on existing factors shifts (the periodic waxing and waning of tolerance for private agricultural plots on the part of Russian economic planners). Once the incentive system is conceptualized, consideration can be given to how the individual goes about achieving his "quota" of effort. A cynical view might hold that people are inherently lazy and therefore try to meet personal goals while minimizing inputs into the life of the community, but a reading of history and of our own personalities reveals periods when people get "carried away" into "unselfish" actions by the force of events or by inspiring leadership. Whether such unselfishness works for extended periods is an interesting question for study and debate.

Goals must be set, performance evaluated, and rewards dispensed at all levels of a planned economy. Planning bureaucrats, managers of farms and factories, and individual workers all respond to their own pattern of incentives. The possibility that one group, in meeting its goals, may sabotage the efforts of another group is always present. Adjusting success indicators so that the spirit as well as the formal provisions of rules are met is a problem every central planner, like every parent, experiences. Considerable ingenuity is demonstrated in the ability to subvert the intent of new regulations designed to patch up weaknesses in old ones.

The development of the incentive systems of Yugoslavia, China, and Cuba is closely connected with political developments in each nation. War or revolution played a leading role in the establishment of their present political structures. In each case there remained an external political threat that served to rally the population and, incidentally, to provide a rationale for the austere living conditions that are a concomitant feature of efforts to achieve a high rate of investment. It is probably not coincidental that charismatic leadership existed in the critical period of innovation in the persons of Marshal Tito in Yugoslavia, Chairman Mao Tse-tung in China, and Premier Fidel Castro in Cuba. Radical changes in incentive systems are undoubtedly made more easily if a forceful appeal for support is made by a generally respected and trusted political leader.

In each of these nations significant experimentation with incentive systems occurred and is still going on. This presents no small problem of justification, since each phase must be made consistent with the prevailing political and economic ideology. Each policy shift also dislocates administrators who have a vested interest in the implementation of the old policy. Finally, there is likely to be an unsettled interval calling for interpretation of pronouncements when incentive systems are changed. The overstatement needed to publicize desired changes in direction seems to lead to "overcompliance" in some situations where the new policy is inappropriate. The agricultural sector seems especially vulnerable to this dilemma.

We will use a unique feature of each nation as the focus for discussion of their incentive systems. In Yugoslavia that feature is an institution—the Workers' Councils, which attempt to give some degree of control over economic decision making at the corporate level to the employees who actually work there. In China it is an event—the Cultural Revolution of the late 1960s, which among other things seems to have been aimed at eliminating the elitist authority and prestige usually associated with responsible positions in an economic hierarchy. In Cuba our interest will center on a product—sugar—and how the existence of a sugar monoculture prior to Castro's revolution imposes significant constraints on attempts to modify economic incentives.

ECONOMIC INCENTIVES IN YUGOSLAVIA

Yugoslavia is a nation of 20 million people inhabiting an area about the size of Wyoming. It is a federation of republics, consisting of Slovenia and Croatia in the north and Bosnia-Herzegovina, Serbia, Montenegro, and Macedonia in the south. These diverse areas were bound together as part of the political realignments following World War I. Regional animosities have continued in recent years and now represent a threat to continued economic and political progress. Yugoslavia is a poor country whose population is predominantly agricultural. There exist, nevertheless, wide discrepancies in living standards and industrial development between the relatively prosperous republics of Croatia and Slovenia and the rest of the nation.

Yugoslavia is an interesting case study. First, it has the only communist political system in Europe that is and has been completely independent of the Soviet Union; the satellite nations have been subservient to Moscow. Since 1950 Yugoslavia has deliberately departed from the political and economic institutions of the Soviet model. A kind of democratic and decentralized communist system has developed, in which workers formally share in the management of the socialized industry and peasants own and till their own land with the assistance of agricultural cooperatives.

The present government grew out of internal guerrilla resistance to the German invasion in 1941. With the end of the war, political unification and economic recovery became major goals.

> In a country as diverse as Yugoslavia, "building of socialism" must have posed difficult problems and choices. There was a problem of priority: Which parts of the country should be developed first? Slovenia and Croatia, because of existing infrastructure and manufacturing tradition, offered a less expensive road to progress. But one of the main goals of the other republics was to catch up with Slovenia and Croatia, and it would have been politically inopportune to frustrate their desires. Then there was the problem of financing: Which of the social strata were to bear the costs of development? Taking into consideration that the great majority of the population and a sizable portion of the partisan army were peasants, the decision was not an easy one to make.[1]

Yugoslavia first embarked on a development scheme closely paralleling the Russian example, complete with a Five Year Plan and an attempt to collectivize the agricultural sector. A combination of unrealistic planning, the withdrawal of Soviet aid and export markets, and harvest failures in agriculture due to droughts and disruption produced an economic crisis in the early 1950s. This situation resulted in the creation of the present Yugoslav incentive system, called "Our Own Road to Socialism."

Economic Planning in Yugloslavia

With Yugoslavia's severance of political ties with fellow communist countries, the second period of the First Plan (1953–1956) was marked by a reconsideration of the plan model. More emphasis was put on agriculture and light industry instead of on heavy industry. The introduction of workers' self-management and the decentralization of governmental and economic functions provided powerful incentives for economic revival. Emphasis was shifted from comprehensive planning to regionally and functionally decentralized plans. The general *federal* plan was confined to the basic proportions for economic development. The five basic proportions set up were:

[1]Joseph T. Bombelles, *Economic Development of Communist Yugoslavia,* Palo Alto, Calif.: The Hoover Institution, 1968, p. 11.

1. Proportions between different sectors of the economy—industry, agriculture, and services.

2. Proportion between saving and consumption, ensuring an accelerated rate of capital accumulation.

3. Proportions of basic wages among sectors.

4. Proportions of contributions to the Social Fund from individual taxation, profits of productive enterprises, and so on.

5. Proportion of administrative expenditures for such traditional items as defense, law and order, and so on.

The year 1953 also brought a change in the system of financing capital-investment projects. Previously these had been supported almost entirely by outright grants from the national government's budget; now investment comes from repayable loans from the Federal Bank or the reinvestment by enterprises of their own earnings. For a time in the mid-1950s, loans were granted through a system of competitive auctions—an institutional form that caught the attention of Western observers because of its ability, in theory at least, to achieve efficiency in allocating scarce capital within a socialist economy. The investment auction was replaced by administrative rationing of loans for centrally favored projects (those promoting tourism or regional balance, for instance). The rapid turnover among plant managers encouraged bidding to finance short-term, high-risk projects under the investment-auction system.

Also in 1953, the agricultural collectivization program was abandoned. Collectivization failed because of the slow rate of mechanization, the lack of agricultural technicians, and the weak incentives on the part of collective-farm members. Many collectives were dissolved by majority vote of their members, and the land reverted to private operation by independent peasant households. The government's primary agricultural institution, the General Cooperative, provides access to cheaper fertilizer and agricultural equipment, and to government credit and extension services. Through voluntary membership in cooperatives, the government hopes to achieve some of the advantages of large-scale collective farming within a system of small, private landholdings.

The problem of agriculture remains essentially unsolved. The story of the collapse of the collective-farm movement merits scrutiny. Although the Soviet collective-farm pattern of organization was followed superficially, there were no attempts to mechanize farms rapidly as in Russia, no counterparts of the Soviet Machine Tractor Stations, and no large-scale governmental investment in agriculture. The result was failure to raise agricultural productivity. Of course Yugoslavia is handicapped in these matters by the fact that two-thirds of its terrain is too mountainous to be suitable for large-scale farming. Moreover, the hold of private, small-scale farming on the ideology of the peasant has been firm, and his at least tacit support is needed by the Communist League in a country where the agricultural peasantry embraces about half the population. To make the peasant production minded beyond the limits of supplying food for his own family and feed for his livestock, and to introduce mechanized production methods are the big problems. The small size of the private holding is an enormous handicap to mechanization. However, a start is being made through cooperatives supplying their machinery to prepare soil, sow it with high-yielding varieties of seed, and harvest the crop on land belonging to peasant families under contractual arrangements providing for the division of products between the cooperative and the private peasant.

Workers' Councils

Karl Marx had a vision of a better life for the proletariat after the predicted overthrow of capitalism occurred. The vision did not extend, however, to a situation in which the workers themselves would make the actual management decisions. Yet that is the legal status of the Workers' Councils— employees participate in deciding on the use of an enterprise's resources, on how much of its earnings to invest and how much to use in raising wages, and on which managers should be hired to implement these decisions. Western observers have differing opinions about the extent to which the central-planning apparatus erodes the de facto powers of workers' councils, but all agree that worker participation is a novel means of promoting effort in a market-oriented economy.

The workers' council is the supreme body of management in an enterprise. At its meetings it decides basic policy matters for the enterprise. The members of the council are elected to one-year terms by the workers in the particular enterprise. Candidates for membership are nominated by the local trade union or by any group of workers comprising at least one-tenth of the total number of employees. The usual workers' council consists of between 15 and 20 members, depending on the size and organization of the enterprise. The members are elected by secret ballot. The council works as a body and adopts all of its decisions at its meetings, which are held at least once every six weeks. Decisions are made by majority vote of the members present. Meetings are attended by the director of the enterprise and by the members of the managing board, the executive committee of a workers' council.

The managing board directly manages the enterprise in accordance with the policy decisions and directives of the workers' council and in keeping with laws and rules enacted by the national government. The board consists of between three and eleven members, including, ex officio, the director of the enterprise. The board is elected by secret ballot at the first meeting of the workers' council for a one-year term. In order to secure proper composition of the board and prevent bureaucratic tendencies therein, at least three-quarters of its members must be workers engaged directly in the process of production. The members of the workers' council and the managing board receive no remuneration for membership in these bodies aside from their regular wages, which are paid while they perform the duties entailed by their office. During their terms they continue to work at their regular jobs in the enterprise.

The director, responsible for the day-to-day operating management of a given enterprise, is chosen from openly competing candidates drawn from outside the enterprise, the final choice being made by a joint commission composed of representatives of the workers' council and representatives of pertinent professional associations nominated by the commune (local government) of the area where the enterprise is located. The director organizes the process of production in the enterprise and directs operations in accordance with the policies and decisions of the workers' council and the managing board. He represents the enterprise in negotiations and contractual relationships with other enterprises. Ordinarily the council and the director stay out of each other's domain, although there are close advisory and consultative relations between them. If an irreconcilable dispute were to arise, causing the council to wish to get a new director, the matter would be finally resolved by the local commune or, in the case of a very large enterprise, by a higher governmental body.

With regard to purchasing raw materials and equipment, enterprises are free to enter into contracts with each other. The markets for most finished commodities have been free and open, and each enterprise decides what quantity of a particular commodity to produce and what price to charge for it according to supply and demand conditions. Central planning of output and price occurs for public services such as transportation, communication, and other utilities, and for new enterprises in certain basic industries. Overall targets for the various industries are usually set in general planning. But these are strictly advisory, designed primarily to give the individual enterprise an idea of what may occur in the economy as a whole during the year, just as a firm in an American industry may look to the President's Economic Report for some guidance in policy making. The general economic plan does not determine the obligations of the enterprises by administrative fiat. They carry on their business according to their economic interests, while general economic regulations (on credit, on the distribution of an enterprise's net earnings, and so on) are designed to induce the enterprise to conduct business according to the course set and the provisions of the general economic plan.

In general, it can be said that centralized planning of the economy as a whole has been curtailed since 1953. Most raw-material prices, formerly controlled by the state, have been decontrolled. Capital accumulation has also been freed from central control to a certain extent. After an enterprise has met its costs for materials, wages and managerial salaries, taxes and depreciation, and other costs, the workers' council decides how to dispose of the surplus, if any. Under outside limits imposed by government regulations, they decide what portion of the net earnings of the enterprise will be distributed in bonuses to workers and how much will be used for capital expansion. The established enterprises get perhaps as much as half of their new capital needs by reinvesting their own earnings.

In the matter of wage setting, the workers' council again plays an important role. Preliminary scales of wages for particular jobs are drawn up by the management board of the enterprise. If the workers' council, the pertinent commune officials, and the local trade union all agree to these proposed scales, they are put into effect. If agreement among these bodies is not reached, however, the whole case is referred to an arbitration commission and thus leaves the domain of the workers' council. The arbitration commission includes representatives of the commune and the trade union. A representative of the government of the republic acts as chairman of the commission and has the deciding vote if the other two groups do not agree. In practice, however, the proposals of the management board are usually agreed to by all concerned.

It is evident that the Yugoslav regime has tried to organize industrial production in such a way as to induce the worker to perform efficiently and contribute his creative energies to his job rather than sabotaging his enterprise through absenteeism and unconcern. It seems to be in his own best interest that his enterprise should sharpen its efficiency in order that it may realize as large a net earning as possible, for only in this way can his own wage and his bonus from net earnings be maximized. However, the degree to which so-called economic democracy has been attained is very difficult to assess. The triple controls—(1) the party—the Communist League members in key positions; (2) the state, with its powers to make and revise laws pertaining to the economy; (3) the general plan—the overall blueprint with clear indications of targets and indirect regulatory provisions (as on credit)—are real and doubtless quite effective. Any sort of democratic planning faces the query as to how *decentralization* and *planning* can effectively go hand in hand. If it is planning, it involves some degree of regimentation and centralization of power. The Yugoslavs face the hard task of demonstrating that "economic democracy" can ensure planned development where means of production, at least in the industrial sector, are completely nationalized.

Notwithstanding the rapid progress of workers' self-management, it has some well-publicized deficiencies. The level of efficiency at which its organizational parts function leaves much to be desired. There are considerable differences in degree of success in various sectors of the economy; for example, the construction industry has been a conspicuous laggard in this respect. In recent years the government has complained of a tendency of workers' councils to participate in monopolistic price setting in some products. Since the individual enterprise sets its own prices, an enterprise finding itself without competition in supplying a particular market area may be able to charge a higher price than it could if there were a modicum of competition. Enterprises have been known to join in group price-stabilizing arrangements or understandings. At one time punishment was actually meted out to several enterprises believed to have been guilty of such offenses. Yugoslavia thus became the first communist country to take anti-trust action.

A Workers' Council Meeting

To give the student an opportunity to gain something of the flavor of an actual workers' council meeting, the following is an account of a regular meeting of the workers' council of an enterprise in Belgrade with some 700 employees that manufactures tar paper, insulation materials, and cork products.[2]

> All nineteen members of the Workers' Council, which included two women, attended the meeting. The six members of the Managing Board were present, as well as the Director of the enterprise and the Chief Engineer, who took active part in the dicussions but not in the actual decision-making. The session was well conducted, the soft-spoken President using a minimum of parliamentary procedure to keep the meeting in order and focused on the agenda. About one-half of the members participated frequently in the dicussion of the various items of business, while most of the others spoke only occasionally. The Secretary took minutes of all that was said and decided. Although each of the members appeared to be most articulate on matters relevant to the department from which he had been elected, it was quite clear that many of them were acutely aware that the interrelationship of departments was vitally connected with the success of the whole enterprise, and discussed detailed matters against such a background. The President gave no indication of trying to force his views on the group, although he let them be known. No formal vote was taken on any issue. When those wishing to discuss a matter had finished, the President would state what appeared to him to be the consensus and ask whether there was any disagreement with his conclusion. In no case was any expressed and in this way each issue was resolved, although some matters were held over for further study or consultation with plant workers involved, according to the procedure outlined by the President in his summation of the issue. The Director of the enterprise spoke, sometimes at length, on each matter on the agenda. He seemed to be an able, forceful man with qualities of leadership. The positions he took on the several issues, and the recommendations he made, were not quietly accepted by the members. Numerous questions were raised about statements he made, and he was pressed for more details in defense of his positions. It appeared that the members respected the Director but had no compunction about differing with him. The Chief Engineer spoke at length on the engineering aspects of several matters discussed. The members seemed to have less confidence in him than in the Director and, in at least one instance, the consensus of the meeting ran counter to his position. On this, after the discussion, the Director

[2]It was the privilege of one of the authors to attend this meeting. See W. N. Loucks, "Workers' Self-government in Yugoslav Industry," *World Politics*, October 1958. This journal has kindly granted permission to reprint a portion of this article.

sided with the Council members and appeared quite critical of the Engineer's failure to perform satisfactorily certain functions relative to the revision of piecework production norms.

If the full notes of the business of the meeting were reproduced here, they would indicate that the Workers' Council was performing those functions described earlier. . . . A brief summary of the items discussed and decided upon will show that the Council was dealing with fundamental management problems. The same had been true of the previous meeting, judging by the minutes which were read.

The first item taken up was the report of the Director on the fulfillment of the [enterprise's] plan for the first nine months of 1957. Each member had before him a typed copy of this report. The Director discussed individual items at length and answered numerous questions. The Director's report was broken down by departments, and through the members' questions and comments it became clear that the prevailing sentiment was that one of the departments was not operating efficiently. The Director went on the defensive, speaking at length about unavoidable handicaps under which that department had worked. One was a cutthroat competitive situation in which each of the three competitors selling the commodity produced by this department had had its price forced below cost. The Director reported that this situation finally had been stabilized by a price agreement among the three enterprises, an act which a government official later told the writer was absolutely illegal. The Director also pointed out that the distribution of certain plant overhead among the several departments was a quite arbitrary procedure and that, if some other equally logical method of distribution had been used, the financial results in the department under discussion would have been quite different. The Chief Engineer entered the discussion, also in defense of the department under attack, although he was forced to concede that the incentive-rate production norms in this department were obsolete and that this affected performance. He was asked pointed questions as to why the situation on norms had not been rectified. It was entirely apparent that the members generally were not satisfied with the Director's or the Chief Engineer's explanations and, as one member put it, were convinced that "the work in this department is not properly organized." The discussion ended with the Director issuing orders to the Chief Engineer to gather the needed data personally and revise the norms. The matter was placed on the agenda of the next meeting and the members agreed to make individual investigations of conditions in the department.

The Chief Engineer submitted detailed recommendations for the reconstruction and rehabilitation of numerous pieces of plant equipment. The members asked many questions about his proposals, one inquiring whether the proposals were merely the Chief Engineer's ideas or were officially being placed before the Workers' Council by the Managing Board and the Director. The Chief Engineer answered that the proposals were merely offered for discussion and that they were not in final form for official submission to the Council. The proposals were approved "in principle" and the Council asked for more specific data on the self-disposal funds available for capital improvement, and for more time to consider some of the numerous alternative suggestions made by members in the course of the discussion. It was the President's suggestion that each member prepare himself to decide upon "the whole plan of reconstruction" at the next meeting.

After brief discussion it was decided to supply certain workers with special work clothes at the enterprise's expense. The Council discussed the proper wage rates for two new employees who had been added to the staff of the employees' kitchen. This discussion ended with the Council, upon the fervent plea of one of the women members, setting the wage rates in question at a higher level than that recommended by the Director. The Council received a written complaint from a worker to the effect that, after he returned from an absence due to an industrial injury, he had been downgraded to a common laborer. There was active discussion of this case, the consensus being that the complainant, a relatively new employee, was not industrious, had come to this plant with the injury he alleged was responsible for his absence, and had been absent frequently without notice and without adequate subsequent explanation. There was considerable sentiment for discharging him, but it was noted that this would be illegal since a sick leave was involved. Finally, the matter was disposed of by a decision that the complainant could retain the job to which he was objecting but had no legitimate claim to his former job.

All of the matters discussed at this meeting were such as would be decided unilaterally by representatives of private owners in a capitalist economy, or would be bargained out with representatives of a union. In the Soviet economy they would have been decided by the plant manager or a superior agency of control.

An Evaluation of the Yugoslav Incentive System

To understand workers' self-management in industry, one must understand how the financial affairs of an industrial enterprise are managed. From the total receipts derived from the sale of its product, the current costs of operations must come first: outlays for materials, power, and so on; depreciation charges on physical equipment and plant buildings; an interest charge paid to the national government as the legal owner of the production facilities used by the enterprise; and the regular wages and salaries to the director and his staff. What is left after these deductions is then distributed as follows: The federal government levies a substantial profits tax on net earnings, and the commune where the enterprise is located has a legal claim to a portion. What remains is at the disposal of the workers' council, which, within certain legal restrictions, divides it among the following uses: reinvestment in the physical facilities of the enterprise to supplement grants or loans it may get from the government; expenditure on a variety of projects to benefit employees, such as construction of housing facilities; and bonuses to production workers, supervisors, and the director and his staff. Although manufacturing enterprises feature piece-rate and incentive-wage schemes, this last portion of distributed earnings is expected to stimulate the workers of an enterprise not only to perform their own jobs efficiently but, especially, to take avid interest in increasing efficiency everywhere in the enterprise.

It is extremely difficult to keep track of changes in discretionary control over funds at the enterprise level. Yet the portion left available to the firm and the freedom to allocate these funds between reinvestment and immediate wage supplements and fringe benefits is the key to evaluating the degree of autonomy vested in the institution of workers' councils. Within the limitations on available data, it is possible to distinguish three distinct periods.

During the first period, extending from the creation of workers' councils until 1961, the federal government's goals of achieving a high level of investment, of reallocating funds toward the poorer republics, and of allowing local governments the resources to start new enterprises meant that already-established firms faced a heavy burden—up to 80 percent of gross profits—in various forms of taxes and levies. Furthermore, the latitude granted to use the remaining share for bonuses was subject to government regulation. All in all, it seems that cooperative self-management was never granted the full measure of flexibility and autonomy that a reading of the 1950 *Law on the Management of Economic Organizations by Working Collectives* would indicate.

Beginning in 1961 it became evident that the Yugoslav economy was entering a period of extremely serious strain; the rapid industrialization of the 1950s gave way to what the British call "stag-flation"—a combination of stagnation in real output combined with inflation in money wages and product prices. The government responded with an attempt to stimulate enterprises by reducing the heavy taxes previously owed to local commune governments.

It appears that this change more than doubled the percentage of enterprises' net earnings at the discretion of workers' councils—some estimates are that it rose from 20 percent to as much as 55 percent. Promptly, workers' councils materially expanded their appropriations. Although increased appropriations to new equipment and renovation of old were of course directed to "investment purposes," they increased the pressure exerted by industrial expansion on the nation's productive resources. It is also reported that in allocating these newly acquired free funds workers' councils tended particularly to expand allocations for consumer goods such as sports stadiums and other recreational facilities, for enterprise-owned workers' housing, and for increased bonuses—the last, of course, going almost entirely to expand consumer demand. No explanation has been offered for proceeding so drastically to enlarge the funds at the disposal of workers' councils. The result, which should have been foreseen but apparently was not, was a rapid increase in aggregate monetary demand, with consequent further pressure on productive resources, serious imbalance in the rise of imports over exports, and jeopardy to the very bases of the Yugoslav economic experiment in self-government of industry.

The seriousness of this situation was quickly sensed by party and government leaders. Two sets of centralized compulsory controls were instituted. One was a decreed rollback of prices and wages (including bonuses) and an immediate increase in consumption taxation to take the momentum out of the inflationary forces at play. Private-profit endeavors, which stood to gain immeasurably from inflation, were prohibited by government decree. The other set of controls concerned matters of a still more basic nature. The workers' councils were placed under very strict centralized regulations governing the allocations of the net earnings of each enterprise: requiring increases in appropriations to amortization, working capital, and reserves; restricting increases in bonuses to cases of higher labor productivity, plant by plant; restricting government investment loans to enterprises; and channeling into the national government's possession earnings available for reinvestment in the enterprise accumulating them (such funds to be allocated back to an enterprise only if its investment plans for use of those funds corresponded with the national plan). Some important prices that had previously been left to the play of market forces were fixed by central authority. Both the immediate and the more basic controls imposed for those purposes in 1962 tended to be much more centralized in their administration than earlier doctrine or practice in Yugoslavia had provided for.

In 1965 Yugoslavia introduced a third basic set of economic reforms designed to stabilize its overextended inflationary condition. The dominant themes of the reforms were an emphasis on decentralization of economic controls from the federal government to the republics and increased exposure of industrial enterprises to competitive market forces to increase efficiency and thereby drastically cut production costs. Although Yugoslav employees would theoretically benefit most if their firms maximized returns per worker, it appears that many enterprises had been harboring excess workers under the previously existing incentive system.[3]

Under the 1965 reform, investment criteria were shifted from a political emphasis toward much greater reliance on economic indicators of potential worthiness. Individual firms thus had to be more responsible for ensuring that capital would be available for their own investment needs, either from retained earnings or from bank loans, which could be secured only if the firm were operating efficiently enough to repay the loan. The immediate effect seems to have been an effort to reduce payrolls significantly.[4]

The Yugoslav experiment in worker self-management can succeed only if a very delicate balance is maintained between the workers' council and hired managers within the firm. Evidence points to moderate success on this front: Managers have not dominated enterprises by retaining vital information or by browbeating members, as had been feared. Managers must use tact and persuasion; the frequency with which they are fired testifies to the existence of real power in workers' councils. At the same time, there appears to be little enthusiasm generated among workers for direct involvement in the planning process at the firm level. "Several recent opinion polls have pointed to a mood of bitter and resentful apprehension

[3]See Benjamin N. Ward, *The Socialist Economy: A Study of Organizational Alternatives*, New York: Random House, 1967, for a theoretical discussion of behavior under decentralized socialism.

[4]*New York Times*, October 20, 1965.

among the workers."[5] The low level of productivity in Yugoslav industry is indirect evidence that morale and incentive problems still exist 20 years after the initial formation of workers' councils.

The delicate balance extends to relations between the individual firm and the central economic planning bureaucracy. Economic decision making has been alternately centralized and decentralized, tightened and relaxed, adjusted and readjusted since 1953. Whatever the policy at any given moment, the problems of low productivity, periods of slow growth, rapid inflation, and balance-of-payments deficits appear to become ever more severe. The correspondence between this list of difficulties and those facing England (or, for that matter, the United States) is striking. So is the list of attempted solutions—devaluation of the dinar, credit controls, measures to curb consumption. "There are growing doubts whether the whole idea of a 'self-managing' economy, with firms controlled by workers, can really work after all, without Latin American style inflation."[6] Unless some means is found of prodding workers' councils to make fundamental adjustments in output and productivity instead of responding with price and wage increases based on monopoly influence, it seems likely that another swing toward centralized planning is in store for Yugoslavia. Even though workers' councils will probably be retained as the institutional basis for the organization of industrial enterprises, further controls to discourage wage-price inflation seem necessary.

> The question that no Yugoslav expert can answer with complete certainty is: how much of the undoubted and spectacular improvement in Yugoslavia's economic performance in the late 1950s and throughout the 1960s was the direct result of workers' enthusiasm and co-operation within the self-management system and how much was due to other factors, especially huge western aid, the removal of the worst managers and the lessening of direct bureaucratic interference? Whatever the conclusion, and the Yugoslavs admit that a complete proof one way or the other is impossible, one thing is clear: workers' self-management cannot be pronounced an economic failure, as its many critics in communist countries shrilly insist. The best that can be said is that it has quite a few uses, from the workers' and managers' point of view, and that certainly from the workers' angle it is preferable to a centralized system of state management. But the workers are certainly in no mood to see all-powerful state bureaucrats replaced by all-powerful manager-technocrats.[7]

ECONOMIC INCENTIVES IN CHINA

It is difficult to believe that an economic system serving more than 800 million human beings could disappear from observation for a decade, but

---

[5]*The Economist*, August 21, 1971, p. xxii.
[6]*The Economist*, January 8, 1972, p. 62.
[7]*The Economist*, August 21, 1971, p. xxv. This issue contains a comprehensive review of the state of the Yugoslav economic system as of that date.

that is largely what happened to the People's Republic of China during the 1960s. In part the lack of information resulted from continued U.S. recognition of the Nationalist government in exile on Formosa. More important were the cataclysmic political and economic events of the Great Leap Forward (1958–1960) and the Great Proletarian Cultural Revolution (1966–1969), which obscured internal developments in Mainland China. In recent years economic data and eyewitness accounts allow an appraisal of the remarkable incentive system the Chinese have created.

> They're not trying merely to revolutionize people and establish a sense of social conscience; they're trying to change the character of these people. The place is one vast school of moral philosophy. I think that's the main thing; whether they make it or not, it's a heroic attempt. I don't think anything in the Soviet revolution or even in our own compares in magnitude with trying to change a quarter of the human race.[8]

A bit of history is necessary to understand how the current situation arose. The Manchus, the last of the succession of dynasties that had ruled China since ancient times, fell in 1912. Sun Yat-sen and his fellow revolutionaries became the government of China. The Constitution of 1924 made the Kuomintang the only legal party, but an internal split within the Nationalist Kuomintang between Chiang Kai-shek and the Communists in 1927 began a long civil conflict for control of the country. There was an uneasy alliance during World War II against the invading Japanese. After the close of the war, however, Communist forces controlled more and more of the country until at last Chiang Kai-shek resigned as premier and eventually removed his remaining troops to Formosa. Soon afterwards the communist People's Republic of China, led by ·Chairman Mao Tse-tung and Premier Chou En-lai, declared itself to be the only legal Chinese government. The United States did not initiate direct diplomatic relations with that government until 1971.

Economic Planning in China

Great damage had been suffered by the Chinese economy during almost a half-century of political turmoil before 1949. Communication was disrupted, industry at a standstill, and the agricultural sector constrained by traditional land ownership and techniques of production. The tremendous natural-resource base and manpower supply could alleviate this dire situation, but only if they could be effectively mobilized. As in Yugoslavia, a beginning was made on the classic pattern pioneered in the Soviet Union— government ownership of major facilities, a Five-Year Plan, and movement

---

[8]New York Times, *Report from Red China*, New York: Avon, 1972, p. 339. From a transcript of a television interview with James and Sally Reston. This collection of dispatches by *Times* reporters is a convenient source of information on life in China.

toward collectivized farming. Agriculture occupied four out of every five workers in 1950 and directly accounted for about half of total output; much of the industrial sector, moreover, was dependent on agricultural raw materials.

> The Communist Party of China adopted the solution of collectivization as a means of increasing the size of the operating unit because it was, and still is, ideologically opposed to the emergence of a "rich peasant" economy. However, for political reasons it went about collectivization in a roundabout manner, first advocating and then carrying out a land-redistribution program. The advocacy of land reform earned the Communists the reputation of being agrarian reformers, which was exceedingly helpful in foreign as well as domestic propaganda. The implementation of the land-reform program, carried out in most parts of the country during 1950–52, was instrumental in redistributing wealth as well as political and economic power in rural areas. The process of collectivization or formation of cooperatives, carried out largely in 1954–56, was spearheaded by the formation of "mutual aid" teams. In 1958, the cooperatives were further merged into communes, although the operating unit was the "production brigade," which corresponded to the cooperative farm in size.[9]

At the same time, a concerted effort was made to build up heavy industry. With the help of Russian equipment and technical assistance, new plants were constructed incorporating modern technology. Impediments to increased efficiency and productivity were progressively removed.

> The First Five-Year Plan (1953–1957) was a solid success. The small industrial base inherited by the new government and located mainly in Manchuria and a few major port cities was rapidly expanded, and a beginning was made on the development of major industrial centers in the interior. Overall industrial production doubled, led by advances in key industrial materials—coal, steel, cement, and crude oil.[10]

The Second Five-Year Plan, which was to cover the years 1958 to 1962, never materialized. Instead, the government under Mao embarked upon an ill-fated Great Leap Forward, attempting to speed up the already-impressive rate of industrialization achieved during the previous period. There was a realistic basis for expecting gains from the newly constructed plants coming into production and from extensive irrigation and land-reclamation projects in agriculture, but these factors were completely over-

[9]Yuan-Li Wu, *The Economy of Communist China*, New York: Praeger, 1965, p. 135.

[10]Arthur G. Ashbrook, Jr., "China: Economic Policy and Economic Results, 1949–1971," in Joint Economic Committee, Congress of the United States, *People's Republic of China: An Economic Assessment*, Washington, D.C.: Government Printing Office, 1971. This document presents a thorough evaluation by government intelligence agencies of the impact of the Cultural Revolution on China's economy. It is the source of much of the factual information presented on the following pages.

whelmed by a frenzy to achieve, or at least announce, ever-larger production norms inspired by the example and teachings of Mao Tse-tung. In the process, statistical reporting became so exaggerated that the economic bureaucracy was unable to plan realistically or to coordinate supplies with output requirements. Decentralized planning meant lack of coordination between local units. On top of all this, an ideological dispute between China and Russia resulted in the 1960 withdrawal of Soviet technicians and discontinuation of Soviet-backed aid projects.

The situation was equally bleak in agriculture. The abundant harvest of 1958 was followed by three extremely bad years, necessitating massive grain imports that were both an embarrassment to Chinese leaders and a drain on precious foreign-exchange reserves. The giant communes formed in 1958 were designed to equalize rural consumption (at a modest level) and to assume planning responsibilities as part of a move toward economic decentralization. They proved to be administratively unwieldy and an inadequate source of motivation for the peasant working in production teams. Some labor-intensive efforts at building irrigation systems and other agricultural capital were carried out by communes, but the policy known as "walking on two legs," which aimed to build up small-scale industry, largely failed owing to lack of technical know-how and inability to meet quality standards. The "backyard furnace" movement to produce iron and steel has come to symbolize the excesses of the Great Leap period.

> Between September 1958 and February 1959, we experimented producing iron by our local method. We have, of course, both coal and iron-ore up in the hills. We built a blast furnace and I was responsible for organizing the work. There were seventy of us working on this. We were given work points for all other work. But this was a non-recurrent phenomenon. I can't remember the exact figures now, but as far I can remember, it didn't pay.[11]

The strengthening of the Communist Party at the local level, which had been counted upon to provide coordination, proved inadequate to the task. Beginning in 1961, the central communist leadership drastically redirected industrial and agricultural policy. Communes lost their nonagricultural functions to the central bureaucracy, and the operational responsibility for agricultural production was located below the commune level. Private plots were returned to peasants, and compensation was brought more into line with the amount of work performed. Agriculture was granted priority for investment funds, reversing the industrial emphasis prevailing previously. Industrial production was geared to chemical fertilizers and agricultural machinery.

---

[11]Jan Myrdal, *Report from a Chinese Village*, New York: Vintage, 1972, pp. 165–166. This sensitive series of interviews in the village of Liu Ling, together with the sequel *China: The Revolution Continued*, New York: Pantheon, 1970, is an excellent source of information on the changes communism has made in rural China.

Thus the situation of the economy at the beginning of China's Cultural Revolution had more than made up the ground lost during the Great Leap Forward; it appeared that rapid growth could once again proceed on a more realistic basis in the agriculture and raw-material sectors. The extreme attempts to create small-scale heavy industry had ended, and Japan and Western Europe began to supply some of the modern industrial facilities that had been curtailed by the Russian pullout.

"In 1964 it was announced that the Third Five-Year Plan was being prepared and would start in 1966. But by 1964 the Maoist pendulum had begun to swing back to the Great Leap Forward strategy."[12] The events of the Cultural Revolution that followed represent a mixture of ideological dispute, political factionalism, and economic development strategy that is almost impossible to disentangle. While postponing a discussion of the impact on economic incentives, we can briefly state the rationale and immediate economic effects of the events of 1966–1969.

> According to the Chinese view, Russian experience shows that a capitalist-type superstructure can grow up on a socialist base. When there are no capitalists to run industry and direct investment, the State develops organs to take over these functions, and the individuals put into control of them may suffer deformations of character sometimes even more unpleasant, from the point of view of socialist ideals, than those of the old bourgeoisie.
>
> In China the Party persons in authority taking the capitalist road, whom we may call Rightists for short, were accused of imitating the Soviet model. They were accused of carrying out their work in an authoritarian manner, developing a superior attitude toward the workers, forming gangs to protect each other, and taking advantage of their position to gain privilege and amenities for themselves. They were taking the capitalist road in the sense that they obstructed socialism in the superstructure.[13]

From the initial skirmish between students and the head of Peking University in June 1966 until the new stage of consolidation was instituted in 1968, the vortex of the Cultural Revolution was the Red Guards, 15 to 20 million students organized on the basis of their educational institutions. Intellectuals, Party officials, and former members of the landlord class were subjected to harassment, occasional violence, and public humiliation. Often they were demoted or sent to rural areas for ideological reindoctrination. History has few, if any, examples of a political leader encouraging rebellion against his own regime, but that, in effect, was what Chairman Mao did during this period. His Sixteen Points, adopted August 16, 1966, provided

[12]E. L. Wheelwright and Bruce McFarlane, *The Chinese Road to Socialism: Economics of the Cultural Revolution*, New York: Monthly Review Press, 1970, p. 203.

[13]Joan Robinson, *The Cultural Revolution in China*, Baltimore: Penguin, 1969, pp. 12–14.

guidelines for the Great Proletarian Cultural Revolution supporting primacy for workers and peasants over bureaucrats and for the countryside over cities. In all this, Mao Tse-tung's thought was to serve as a source of inspiration and guidance.

This political turmoil and challenge to authority unavoidably led to economic losses. The leaders of economic-planning agencies, factories, and local government units were all targets of the Red Guards. Many factories were shut down by strikes and shortages of power and raw materials. Industrial output fell by some 15 to 20 percent during 1967 and 1968[14] but unlike the situation during the Great Leap period, agricultural output and industrial construction were only slightly affected. Industry rebounded quickly once order was restored (in mid-1968, when the Army was called out in a nonviolent show of force and many of the Red Guards were dispatched to work in remote rural areas).

"Three-in-one" revolutionary committees were established at all levels of planning. Revolutionary Party cadres, army representatives, and the workers themselves were joined in the actual management of farms and factories to prevent the reappearance of "capitalist road" behavior among higher officials.

> The struggle-criticism-transformation in a factory, on the whole, goes through the following stages: establishing a revolutionary committee based on the "three-in-one" combination, mass criticism and repudiation, purifying the class ranks, rectifying the Party organization, simplifying organizational structure, changing irrational rules and regulations and sending people who work in offices to grassroots levels.[15]

Little is known about the economic-planning apparatus currently operating in China. It would seem that the new emphasis on self-reliance at the enterprise level should reduce the bureaucratic input to more of a coordinating role. In 1970 references to the Third Five-Year Plan (1966–1970) reappeared, and an unpublished Fourth Plan exists for 1971–1975. Whatever its targets, an excellent start has been made in the years following the transformation of the Cultural Revolution into a more constructive phase. Barring disastrous harvests, it appears that a basis for sustained economic growth has been established.

The Chinese Incentive System

The Maoist incentive system, which is now becoming institutionalized in China, is subject to varying interpretations depending on the view taken of the optimal form of economic planning. If one happens to exalt orderliness above zeal, for instance,

---

[14]Joint Economic Committee, *People's Republic of China*, p. 27.
[15]Quotation from Chairman Mao Tse-tung in Yao Wen-yuan, *The Working Class Must Exercise Leadership in Everything*, Peking: Foreign Languages Press, p. 16.

Mao appears to have been the despair of economic planners. He seems to have been bored by the economic affairs, and by his own testimony did not involve himself deeply in economic work for 13 of the 16 years of PRC existence up to 1966. Yet in this period he has brought to a halt two soundly functioning economic programs and strategies. His calculus differs from the planners'. He is not concerned with the return on invested resources, but rather with how many people were affected and how it did alter their thinking. His predilection for political campaign disrupts orderly development.[16]

The basic contrast between Mao's views and a system stressing material incentives can begin by exploring the emphasis on the latter during the 1953–1957 First Plan. In industry increased labor productivity was to be achieved by creation of piece rates that directly related reward to performance. Egalitarian features in the wage system were regarded as barriers to increased production. "Some of the wage increases given in June, 1956, were aimed at widening skill differentials and making readjustments for groups whose activities were important to society."[17] The organization of agricultural collectives during this period was also based on the socialist principle of reward according to labor. The initial dividend for labor and equipment pooled into the collective was to be gradually reduced so that income would eventually be based on labor input alone.[18]

It is interesting to compare the forms of nonmaterial incentives that appeared during the Great Leap Forward with those of the Cultural Revolution. During the Great Leap period of 1958–1960, the emphasis was on decentralization and the formation of giant agricultural communes.

The Water Conservation Campaign was built on moral rather than material incentives; the idea of sharing things in common, irrespective of the individual's contribution, made progress in the communes. The August, 1958, Resolution spoke of the need to promote "the social consciousness and morality of the whole people to a higher degree," to institute universal education, and "to break down the differences between workers and peasants"; and later in 1958, shipbuilding workers in Shanghai abolished the systems of bonuses and piecework. All of these became central motifs again during the Cultural Revolution.[19]

Piece-rate wages largely disappeared from the industrial sector during the Great Leap period. In their place emphasis was shifted to group performance as the basis for bonus incentives, if bonuses were given at all.

[16]Edwin F. Jones, "Cultural Revolution: In Search of a Maoist Model," in Joint Economic Committee, *People's Republic of China*, p. 54. Jones' grudging recognition of high growth rates currently being achieved with Maoist incentives makes interesting reading.

[17]Charles Hoffman, "Work Incentive Policy in Communist China," in Choh-Ming Li, ed., *Industrial Development in Communist China*, New York: Praeger, 1964, p. 95.

[18]*Ibid.*, p. 98.

[19]Wheelwright and McFarlane, p. 145.

Competition between production teams, between factories, or between regions was established, with banners and titles serving as the prizes in most cases, instead of material incentives. Outstanding efforts received widespread publicity and resulted in challenges from other production units. This frenzy of enthusiasm could not be maintained permanently, especially in the face of food shortages resulting from harvest failures, and piece-rate wage systems reappeared after 1960. Just as an adequate industrial raw-material supply system did not exist to sustain the Great Leap ideology, a basis for sustaining incentives beyond the first burst of enthusiasm was not established either.

The failures of the Great Leap mentality were most apparent in agriculture. Although the precise division of blame between disastrous harvests in three consecutive years (1959–1961) and shortcomings in the incentives provided by the newly formed communes is a moot point, it appears obvious that nonmaterial incentive schemes were not readily applicable to peasant agriculture. As in Russia, the abolition of small private plots had serious demoralizing effects. The "free supply" system of providing meals and other consumption goods on an egalitarian basis removed the link between work and living standard for the commune, and the decision to use the commune as the accounting unit to judge productive effort instead of smaller work teams diffused responsibility for failure. The inability of nonmaterial incentives to persuade agricultural workers is shown in this statement by the leader of the Liu Ling village production brigade:

> We had heard about that business of free food. But we didn't think it would be suitable here with us. We simply did not believe in it. We were afraid that it would undermine our members' trust in the principle of the day's work as the unit. It would make consumption independent of the work contributed, and we did not think that would work well. . . . If any such discussion was to start [among the members], we could check it. But no one took the idea up.[20]

It became increasingly evident that neither productive capacity nor ideological purity existed to make moral incentives a sufficient basis for diverting investment funds from agriculture to heavy industry. With the shift in emphasis toward the rural sector came a new incentive policy. "In the communes the policy had two main patterns: a sharpening of the effect of money payments for collective work and a return to individual initiative in side-line activities including use of small private plots again. The aims were to boost production and deliveries to the State and to raise peasant income and enthusiasm."[21] Thus for both industry and agriculture the years after 1961 until the Cultural Revolution represented a de facto return to material incentives in spite of the veneer of rhetoric that continued to

[20]Myrdal, p. 163.
[21]Li, p. 108.

appear in pronouncements concerning economic development policy. "With this came the reemergence of intellectuals, technocrats, and managers—all with close connections with regional Party authorities. 'Expertness,' rather than 'redness,' was what counted in making economic decisions."[22]

It is no coincidence that Mao Tse-tung was gradually being reduced to an honorific role during this period. Although he continued to make statements criticizing the policy of reactivating material incentives, it was not until the Cultural Revolution that Mao's return to supreme political authority made slogans like "Learn from Tachai" the watchword for the new incentive policy.

> Tachai Brigade in North Shansi operated in the worst possible condi-
> tions—stony hills and eroded gullies. The brigade painfully and success-
> fully terraced the hillsides and filled them with desperately scarce
> soil. In 1963 a deluge destroyed the terraces. However, the brigade
> refused state aid (to which it was entitled) and rebuilt its cultivation plots,
> achieving very high yields. In 1965, opponents of Mao challenged
> the figures of crop yields put out by Tachai, but after an expert team
> was sent in by Chou En-lai to measure every plot and count every grain,
> the brigade was vindicated.[23]

The Cultural Revolution

The Great Proletarian Cultural Revolution (to use its full official title) re-asserted the role of people's thoughts and motivations in achieving economic goals. Instead of giving mere lip service to the unity of interests between the ruling elite and the masses, the Cultural Revolution appeared as a genuine attempt to erase both the overt and the unconscious symbols of rank and privilege from Chinese society. As Westerners, we are skeptical of such drastic changes in what we regard as basic human nature. "But the opportunity to hear the words in person, even on a carefully controlled tour of the country does make a difference. One discovers that real people not only mouth the stock phrases and depict the stock situations described by official releases for the outside world, but actually live them from day to day and, moreover, can be pressed for details and amplifications," concluded one of the reporters from the *New York Times* group that visited China.[24] Where else would it happen that "the new Ambassador to Canada and his

[22]Wheelwright and McFarlane, p. 69.

[23]*Ibid.*, p. 92. An American college student who lived and worked at Tachai for a month with one of the first groups admitted to China as official visitors reports that it has become something of a mecca for Chinese and foreign travellers. Lynnette Wright, "The Chinese People Discuss their Economic Development," unpublished independent study paper completed for Bill Whitney, May 1972.

[24]New York Times, *Report from Red China*, p. 172. Selected headlines reveal a generally favorable impression of economic conditions in 1971: "Welfare plan assures minimum living standard; stores give customers a better deal; factory foreman and family live well; mass efforts achieve great feats; for most of the peasants things are better."

wife have just returned from protracted work-study in Hunan, where they spent much of their time laboring in the rice fields."?[25]

Eyewitness accounts of Western visitors allow a far better basis for judging the continuing impact of the Cultural Revolution than would be possible if China's virtual blackout on economic information had not been lifted. We will consider briefly how the incentive system is currently affected by wage policy, internal management practices, and efforts to eliminate what one group aptly termed "the manipulative character of expertise."[26]

> "We are still in the stage of struggle-criticism-transformation on this matter [of wages]," Liu Wentao, the 44-year-old deputy chairman of the factory's Revolutionary Committee, said. Struggle-criticism-transformation is the phrase used to describe the discussions under leadership guidance that go on in the process of working out agreements with a group.
> The wage question came up when Mr. Liu and others in the factory management were asked what had been done about the system of bonus incentives that prevailed for workers before the Cultural Revolution. . . .
> More pay for extra output and overtime work appears to have been eliminated everywhere and it has been a fairly general policy to increase base pay to some extent to make up for the disappearance of incentive pay.
> The machine plant management declined to say specifically what the problem was in the wage debate, but the wage level after elimination of incentive pay seemed to be the issue.[27]

In both industry and agriculture, wage differentials based on skill levels have been reduced but not eliminated. How this system works in agriculture is demonstrated by Hongqiao, a prosperous vegetable-growing commune near Shanghai visited by American scholars.

> Hongqiao also follows Tachai's system for determining wages. Under the "Tachai system" peasants work together on tasks determined by team leaders. Meetings are held at regular intervals in which peasants evaluate their own work and suggest a work-point rating for themselves. Then other peasants discuss the ratings and adjust them if necessary. The factors considered in determining work points for each person are first that person's attitude toward work and then his or her level of skill and degree of strength. . . .
> The value of the work point is figured on the annual income of the production brigade (at Tachai) or team (at Hongqiao or Huadong). The total number of work points is divided into the income left after all other expenses are met. In Hongqiao, for example, 60 percent of the total

---

[25]*Ibid.*, p. 178.
[26]Committee of Concerned Asian Scholars, *China! Inside the People's Republic*, New York: Bantam, 1972, p. 73. This book reports the observations of the first group of American scholars to visit China after the 1971 thaw in Sino-American relations.
[27]New York Times, *Report from Red China*, p. 184.

income is distributed to the workers; 5 percent goes to the state for tax; 7 percent for capital improvements to the commune; 3 percent to a fund for public benefit (medical services, social welfare for the aged and disabled, nurseries, and schools); and the remaining 25 percent meets the costs of production. . . .

Peasants also maintain small private plots to grow vegetables for their own consumption. Government policy has never been to completely work for the collective. In Huadong each family head is allowed ⅛ mu [i.e., ⅟₄₈ acre]. In addition some raise their own hogs, ducks, and abolish these small bits of land which the peasants till in addition to their chickens. Twenty-five percent of the families' income was said to come in this way.[28]

The Cultural Revolution has produced a significant increase in worker participation in economic affairs. Workers are included prominently on the revolutionary committees that form the basic administrative unit for each farm and factory; party committees coexist with revolutionary committees at each level but are only minimally involved in day-to-day operations. The campaign slogan of "self-reliance" has produced many innovations by workers; a cotton-textile mill in Shanghai, for instance, invented a knot-tying machine that doubled productivity.[29] In addition, schools have been established in factories to produce technicians from the ranks of experienced workers. All of these measures are aimed at breaking down distinctions between professional managers or engineers and ordinary workers. Although it appears that the role of workers in managerial decision making is limited in many instances, the Chinese system, by all reports, has given workers a feeling of direct involvement in the production process without reliance on individualistic enrichment as in the Yugoslav experiment with worker self-management. Just how important worker participation is to be in China will become clearer as the three-in-one principle of organization becomes more firmly rooted.

Equally important for China's future is the effort to abolish traditional distinctions between city dwellers and the rural population. Millions of young Chinese have gone to "reform themselves through labor" on communes. Some will be chosen for further education partially on the basis of their work performance, but for most it represents a permanent move away from overcrowded cities. In addition, schools training new party leaders are now located in the countryside and are essentially farms with cadre students providing the needed labor. "Why should bureaucrats plant corn? The idea is that they learn to respect and understand the vast majority of Chinese people who do manual labor, break down their own attitudes of white-collar superiority, and become more physically fit through labor."[30]

[28]Committee of Concerned Asian Scholars, *China! Inside the People's Republic*, pp. 168–170.
    [29]Wright, p. 12.
    [30]Committee of Concerned Asian Scholars, *China! Inside the People's Republic*, pp. 100–101.

Imagine a similar program for civil servants, professors, doctors, and other professionals in the United States!

One of the most interesting manifestations of this movement arises from Chairman Mao's slogan, "In medical and health work, put the stress on rural areas." Not only do doctors routinely spend part or all of their careers in rural areas, but they are also training "barefoot doctors"—commune members selected for training as the first level of the medical system.

> Miss Chang has had a year of medical schooling over a period of three years and says she knows how to diagnose and treat most common illnesses and even how to set simple fractures and to stitch up cuts. If she thinks the illness is one she cannot deal with, she sends the patient to the commune hospital where university trained doctors are on duty.
>
> When Miss Chang is not administering to the sick, she works in the fields like other members of the collective. She is credited with work points—the index of how much she will get of the collective's earnings at the end of the year—equivalent to the number given to a full-time field worker. This comes to about $15 a month.[31]

It is now time to attempt an impossible task—a summing up of the Chinese experience. Monumental changes have occurred in China in recent years. It appears that a vast majority of the Chinese people, especially the young, really believe and practice the precepts of the Cultural Revolution. Maoist thought will undoubtedly survive Mao, regardless of the struggles over succession that may follow his death. "The People's Republic of China has become an economically strong, unified nation. Its capability simultaneously to meet requirements of feeding its population, modernizing its military forces, and expanding its civilian economic base must now be assumed from its record to date."[32]

Can China sustain its economic performance while continuing to rely heavily on moral or nonmaterial incentives? We all recognize the value of enthusiasm and high morale in a family, classroom, or athletic team; why not for an economic system as well? Economists have begun to realize that motivation factors may play a larger role in economic development than marginal shifts in resources.[33] The Chinese appear to be attempting to institutionalize a system of moral incentives on an economy-wide basis in the most populous nation in the world.

Is the Chinese road to socialism a "reasonable" economic system, given conditions and attitudes prevailing there? Perhaps Western standards of reasonableness are not easily applied to China. One sympathetic Amer-

---

[31]New York Times, *Report from Red China*, pp. 206–207.

[32]Joint Economic Committee, *People's Republic of China: An Economic Assessment*, p. xiv.

[33]Harvey Leibenstein, "Allocative Efficiency vs. X-Efficiency," *American Economic Review*, June 1966. Reprinted in Marshall I. Goldman, ed., *Comparative Economic Systems: A Reader*, New York: Random House, 1971.

ican scholar points out that much of what is happening in China does not show up in conventional measures of economic performance. "Maoists believe that rapid economic development is not likely to occur *unless* everyone rises together."[34] Efficiency is thus sacrificed by building on weakness rather than strength and by forgoing the benefits of extreme division of labor. In addition, many of the gains of insuring against famine, taking preventive public-health measures, and spreading educational opportunities are not measurable in terms of the human satisfaction provided. "Most surprising perhaps, was the contrast between physical China, which to an American is still a very poor and struggling country, and the people of China. For the overwhelming impression of China is vitality—the enthusiasm, the humor, and the tremendous commitment of her people to this new China."[35]

ECONOMIC INCENTIVES IN CUBA

Although there is only one Cuban citizen for each 100 Chinese—8 million to 800 million—there are several similarities in their efforts to generate economic systems suited to their particular circumstances. "Outstanding characteristics of this line are a highly centralized economy and planning system; a trend toward nationalization of all means of production; nonmaterial or 'moral' incentives (such as revolutionary enthusiasm, socialist emulation, granting of medals, banners, pennants, and diplomas); political education to eliminate selfish inclinations, and develop 'a new man'; and financing of enterprises through a state budget (that is, most enterprise profits are taxed away by the state, which follows its own criteria for investment, disregarding profitability.)"[36] We will focus on how these features affect the incentive system that has evolved since Castro came to power in 1959.

The ideological basis of the Cuban brand of socialism is not the thought of Mao Tse-tung; rather, it seems traceable to Che Guevara, Castro's fellow revolutionary and Minister of Industry, who was later to die in the jungles of Bolivia. He advocated that "Cuba always stresses the ideological aspect, the education of the minds of the people, and the call to duty. . . . Then comes the necessary material stimulation to mobilize the people."[37] As in China, the relative predominance accorded nonmaterial

[34]John G. Gurley, "Capitalist and Maoist Economic Development," *Monthly Review*, February 1971, p. 17.

[35]Committee of Concerned Asian Scholars, *China! Inside the People's Republic*, p. 2.

[36]Carmelo Mesa-Lugo, "The Revolutionary Offensive," in Irving Louis Horowitz, ed., *Cuban Communism*, Chicago: Aldine, 1970, p. 79. Some of the information contained in this section is based on a speech by Mesa-Lago at the University of Pennsylvania in April 1971.

[37]Quoted in Robert M. Bernardo, *The Theory of Moral Incentives in Cuba*, University, Ala.: University of Alabama Press, 1971, p. 8.

incentives has fluctuated from time to time in Cuba, but the ideal form of economic motivation continues to be one that strives to deemphasize individual enrichment in favor of collective goals.

Discussion of Cuban socialism cannot proceed without some historical perspective on the economic and political situation prior to the Revolution. The economic history of Cuba is dominated by a single product: sugar. As early as 1883 the national hero Jose Marti warned that "A people that puts its trust in a single product in order to subsist is committing suicide."[38] Yet Cuba was and still is the most fertile sugar-growing region in the world, and the opportunity cost of diversification away from sugar monoculture became apparent in the abortive attempts to shift resources away from that product. Actually, sugar production is a two-stage process; freshly cut cane must be taken immediately to sugar mills, or *centrals*, to be crushed and refined in a technologically sophisticated process. "It is not like cutting bananas off a tree," was one Cuban's derisive reply to an uninformed professor who lumped sugar with other products of tropical agriculture.

With reliance on sugar came reliance on Uncle Sam as customer, supplier, and investor. American investors owned many of the giant sugar plantations before 1929. Specialization was so great that Cuba imported not only manufactured products but foodstuffs and raw materials as well. The Great Depression of the 1930s was thus transmitted from the U.S. to Cuba with increased virulence; half the Cuban working population was unemployed when foreign income fell and American policy favored domestic sugar growers over Cubans.

Sugar monoculture also had profound implications for the Cuban labor force. Agricultural workers were primarily a landless proletariat employed on the plantations; others owned only enough land to eke out a bare living. Sugar production is concentrated during the first half of the year, so many workers were effectively unemployed from July to December. In addition, wages were sufficiently low for sugar workers to limit their effective demand and thus discourage the potential market for consumer goods.

The tourist industry, based on sunshine and gambling, grew in importance after World War II. Over one-third of the labor force was employed in the service sector in the 1950s, although they were concentrated in the casinos, nightclubs, and brothels of Havana. Tourism, too, was extremely sensitive to fluctuations in the American economy.

Thus beneath the surface prosperity and cultural sophistication of prerevolutionary Cuba there were severely unbalanced conditions: a per-

[38]Quoted in Rene Dumont, *Cuba: Socialism and Development*, New York: Grove, 1970, p. 6. Dumont served as an agricultural expert in Cuba between 1960 and 1963. His obvious expertise and sympathy, combined with his candid criticisms of many policy decisions made by Castro and Guevara, make this one of the most useful reports on the Cuban economy.

capita income level of $400 divided disproportionately between the masses of rural underemployed or underpaid and those made rich by sugar and tourism, a foreign-trade sector completely reliant on American economic conditions, and a growing contrast between the glitter of Havana and the abject poverty of the countryside.

The Cuban political system was similarly subservient to the United States. The Platt Amendment, in force until 1933 as part of the settlement following the Spanish-American War, allowed the United States to intervene militarily when "in their judgment, lives, property, or individual freedoms were endangered."[39] A succession of political leaders, operating with American support, made Cuba a country of increasing corruption. This trend culminated in the 1952 military coup of F. Batista, who adopted repressive measures against political opponents.

Fidel Castro appeared on the scene in opposition to the Batista regime. Imprisoned in 1953 for leading an extremely unsuccessful attack on an army garrison, he regrouped his guerrilla forces in Mexico after he was freed in 1955. From there he and 80 supporters launched another ill-fated invasion attempt. The 12 survivors escaped to the mountains of Oriente Province in eastern Cuba, where they mounted guerrilla attacks with increasing public support. As Castro's volunteer army grew amid the repressive atmosphere of the government in power, Batista was forced to flee, and after a brief interim Castro became prime minister.

The political relations between Cuba, the United States, and the Soviet Union were tangled in the years immediately following the 1959 Revolution, so a brief attempt at straightening them out is required before proceeding to the economic problems confronting the new regime. The United States protested the execution of Batista supporters and the expropriation of large estates; Castro visited the United States in April 1959, but the U.S. government refused to seek better relations; early in 1960 a Soviet-Cuban trade agreement was signed; Castro seized American-owned oil refineries that refused to handle Russian crude oil in the summer of 1960; the United States then canceled Cuban sugar imports; Castro retaliated by expropriating most of the remaining U.S. property in Cuba; the United States, in turn, declared an economic boycott on all trade with Cuba.

The belligerence of the Eisenhower Administration in 1960 may be partially explained by the training of a Cuban exile army to recapture the island. After Castro openly affiliated with Cuban communists in the fall of 1960, the preparations for the Bay of Pigs invasion speeded up. The mistaken assessment of Castro's popularity that the CIA provided newly inaugurated President Kennedy resulted in a profound blunder in American foreign policy and a source of increased Cuban support for Castro's anti-American stance. The end of the Cuban Missile Crisis of October 1962 finally brought about a somewhat calmer political situation.

[39] *Ibid.*, p. 8.

Economic Planning in Cuba

Carmelo Mesa-Lugo identifies four distinct phases of Cuban economic policy before 1970: the liquidation of the prerevolutionary economy, 1959–1961; the introduction of socialist institutions, 1961–1963; experimentation with alternative models, 1963–1966; and the radicalization of the economy during the next four years.[40] As might be expected, political and economic circumstances played a role in bringing about the transition from one phase to another; ideological considerations, however, must also be credited with the tendency toward greater emphasis on moral incentives. "The guiding principles of economic policy in the first years of the Revolution were agricultural diversification, industrialization, and the cultivation of new trading partners."[41] The Cuban leaders actually welcomed the break in economic relations with the United States; they had deceived themselves with rhetoric claiming that previous trade had been to the sole advantage of the United States.

The principle economic acts of the first two years of the new regime were agrarian reform; nationalization of banks, public utilities, and American-owned firms; and the construction of housing and social-overhead capital in rural areas. The Agrarian Reform Law of 1959 expropriated large estates and all rented lands. The large farms were reorganized as cooperatives under the National Institute of Agrarian Reform (INRA), which was also in charge of building roads and public buildings.

Nationalization of firms was largely in reaction to worsening international relations with the United States. The technicians and managers of these firms overwhelmingly fled Cuba as part of the exodus of 500,000 (one-eighth of the population) who opposed Castro. The 1960 trade agreement with the Soviet Union was designed to provide technical advice for both new industry and existing enterprises.

In contrast to the initial Russian and Chinese phases of socialism, which squeezed resources out of agriculture to finance industrialization, the Cuban Revolution is unique in the attention devoted to the social condition of the agricultural peasantry, whose living conditions were extremely primitive.[42] Most construction activity was directed toward rural areas, where housing was built for agricultural workers. In addition, salaries of farm workers were increased, and goods were distributed through state-supported stores. One of the most successful programs was the effort of volunteer teachers to teach reading and writing to illiterate adults. "On December 22, 1961, the alphabetization program was officially ended—and illiteracy had plummeted from 23.6 percent when it had opened to only 3.9

---

[40]Carmelo Mesa-Lugo, speech at the University of Pennsylvania, April 1971.
[41]Leo Huberman and Paul M. Sweezy, *Socialism in Cuba*, New York: Monthly Review Press, 1969, p. 66.
[42]RIUS, *Cuba for Beginners*, New York: Pathfinder Press, 1970, p. 77. An anti-American cartoon book in praise of Cuba.

percent when it closed."[43] It is not surpising that poor peasants were among the most fervent supporters of the Revolution.

The Cuban economy made rapid progress in the years after 1959 through a combination of the good fortune of near-record sugar harvests, the enthusiasm generated by opposition to the Bay of Pigs invasion, and the reserves of manpower and industrial capacity that existed under the old system. By 1962, however, it became apparent that these achievements had not been based on a viable set of economic policies, and the facade of economic success showed flaws in several places simultaneously. "The former guerrilla fighters were thinking in social terms, wanting to give everyone wealth and work, without having the economic bases that would have opened up better paths for reaching this goal."[44]

Some factors made eventual difficulties inevitable: the departure of most of the island's managers, doctors, technicians, and white-collar workers; the embargo on spare parts for American-made machines and vehicles; inflationary pressures generated by increasing salaries more rapidly than commodities became available. More important, however, were the bad planning and distortions of the incentive system that prevailed in both agriculture and industry. The ideological insistence on extreme centralization of authority in Havana and elimination of profitability criteria meant that individual farms and factories were not accountable for their own economic performance.

Castro regarded collective farms as an inferior form of socialism; in 1961 he therefore created giant *granjas del pueblo* (people's farms) on which all work was to be done for wages and all profits (an optimistic fantasy) were to go to the state. "These shortcomings of the *granjas* were easy to predict because of their scanty knowledge, their lack of autonomy, and the fact they had to turn all their receipts over to the Treasury. *No one had any direct material interest in whether they were profitable; as a matter of fact, none of them has been*."[45] Agricultural wages were guaranteed at a level that made loafing and absenteeism the norm.

The situation was equally bleak in the industrial sector, where some 50 "consolidated enterprises" were created in the Ministry of Industry under Che Guevara. Again, accountability was not imposed on the separate enterprises; Guevara believed that the compactness and good communications network of Cuba made central management feasible without the "capitalistic taint" of profit criteria. Factories were often idle for lack of raw materials or spare parts. In the haste to diversify the economy, little thought was given to problems of organizing industrial production. Not surprisingly, the Soviet Union began to have second thoughts about how their aid was being used and pressed for more attention to costs and productivity.

[43]Huberman and Sweezy, p. 27.
[44]Dumont, p. 40.
[45]*Ibid.*, p. 67. Italics in original.

Economic chaos soon created a balance-of-payments crisis. Sugar production fell from 6.9 million metric tons in 1961 to 4.8 million in 1962 and 3.8 million the following year. While exports were falling, the need for imported raw materials and manufactured products was rising. "By this time (1962) it was already clear that import substitution through industrialization, from which so much had initially been expected, would provide no solution to the balance-of-payments problem and in fact might even contribute to making it worse for a long time to come."[46]

In spite of the poor record of agricultural cooperatives and people's farms, Castro decided in 1963 to nationalize medium-sized farms—that is, those between 5 and 30 *caballerias* (165 and 1000 acres) in area. This decision was in keeping with his ideological opposition to private enterprise; it might also have helped cut down on the black market in farm produce that had grown up since rationing was imposed. Dumont, the agricultural expert Castro had invited, strongly protested this move because of the lack of civil servants to run the farms and because of the disincentive effects on owners of smaller farms, who feared further nationalization. He accused Cuban leaders of "a certain *lack of humility in the face of the facts, in the name of very questionable interpretations of a doctrine that was never intended to be rigid.*"[47] Except for some retail trade (which was expropriated in 1968) and the remaining small private farms, virtually the entire economy was nationalized before 1964. The extent and pace of public control of the economy thus exceeded that of Russia or China.

In 1963 Guevara admitted "two fundamental errors" in economic planning—the war against sugar cane and the desire for factories without adequate provision for raw materials.[48] Soon after a new strategy for development was adopted, one that emphasized sugar and beef as agricultural products and geared industry toward meeting the demand for agricultural inputs (like fertilizer) and domestic consumer goods. This implies an interesting international division of labor among the socialist nations of the world; the 1964 Cuban-Russian trade agreement makes Cuba permanently dependent on Russian oil and machinery, and allows Russia to expand its sugar consumption with low-cost imported sugar.

At about the same time, a debate occurred concerning the twin questions of the financial autonomy of individual enterprises and the relative importance of material versus moral incentives.[49] Che Guevara's position emphasized budgetary control of enterprises by central authority and reliance on moral incentives; it eventually prevailed and became official policy. In seeking to solve its economic problems, Cuba therefore opted for an approach that is much closer to Maoist China's than the market orientation

---

[46]Huberman and Sweezy, p. 73.

[47]Dumont, p. 102. Italics in original.

[48]Theodore Draper, *Castroism: Theory and Practice*, New York: Praeger, 1965, p. 153.

[49]Huberman and Sweezy, p. 163.

of the Liberman reforms in the Soviet Union. The Central Planning Commission (JUCEPLAN) appears to negotiate directly with each enterprise concerning receipts and disbursements anticipated to occur in the next planning period. Although Professor Leontief found awareness of input-output methods during his visit to Cuba in 1969, there is little evidence of effective coordination between sectors by means of a central plan. The present weak state of administrative sophistication, the lack of economic data, and Castro's penchant for ad hoc projects make true central planning unlikely in the present Cuban political context.

To dramatize the new trends in the economy, Premier Castro announced a target for the 1970 sugar harvest, or *zafra*, of 10 million tons—a record that had not been approached either before or since 1959. He made this goal a symbol of the success of the Revolution and pledged that extraordinary efforts would be made by everybody to achieve it. The only comparison an American can attempt is with President Kennedy's promise to land a man on the moon in the 1960s; the same fervor, neglect of cost considerations, and sense of national prestige was present in Cuba, with far greater force. Since this goal was to be achieved through reliance on nonmaterial incentives, it is worthwhile to keep the reader in suspense concerning the outcome of the 10 million ton harvest while we discuss the evolution of the Cuban incentive system.

The Cuban Incentive System

On July 26, 1968, Castro gave his blueprint for the future. Material incentives will be phased out and replaced by moral ones; the connection between work for and wages from an enterprise will be broken, and citizens will develop a relationship between their effort on behalf of the society and the free goods and services directly granted by the state. (The government already supplies free education, medical care, social security, burials, telephone calls, nurseries—and, for some, recreation and housing.) In the future, all housing, meals, clothing, transportation, communication, public utilities, and entertainment will be free. Income differences will be gradually abolished and distribution made according to needs. Hence, there will be no social classes. In the future Cuban society, an engineer will earn as much as a cane cutter.[50]

How did this extreme reliance on nonmaterial incentives come about? In one sense the economy has always operated on a form of moral incentive —the popular support of Fidel Castro (among those who stayed in Cuba) and the opposition to American military and economic threats to Cuba. The primary source of motivation in the years after 1959, however, was material rewards. In agriculture, renters of small plots received de facto

[50]Mesa-Lugo, "The Revolutionary Offensive," in Horowitz, p. 82. See Martin Kenner and James Petras, eds., *Fidel Castro Speaks*, New York: Grove, 1969 for a transcript of this and other Castro speeches.

ownership in the initial Agrarian Reform, and workers on sugar-cane co-operatives and people's farms received guaranteed wages. As peasant incomes rose, the incentive for greater productive effort declined. "All his traditional, one might almost say inborn, reasons for working hard disappeared. Unless new reasons could be substituted, the most natural and human thing in the world was for him to stop working any harder than required to enjoy his new and much higher standard of life."[51] The 1970 harvest campaign thus became an attempt to supply a new set of reasons for working hard.

"Apart from land, the most commanding rewards for farmers in all of Latin America are schools, hospitals, roads, teachers, doctors, and transport."[52] After 1962 more and more emphasis was placed on these collective material incentives. Doctors and teachers were strongly encouraged to serve periodically in rural areas; thousands of rural children were sent to boarding schools, where they received a combination of political indoctrination and basic education. One is impressed, in recent accounts of everyday life, by the pride that ordinary Cubans take in the educational achievements of their children under the present system.[53]

Wage policy outside the agricultural sector went through several stages:

> We saw that wages inherited from the capitalist period were frozen. Then in 1962–63 the new system of "wage scales and work norms" was painstakingly adopted from Soviet manuals and soon implemented, as it was in China. In fact, there was confusion in the implementation of the new wage policy, although Cuban officials claim actual completion of the process of introducing the new wage policy by late 1964 or early 1965. In late 1966 and early 1967, there was a gradual reversal of policy in favor of straight time payments and a severe narrowing of the moderately wide salary differentials of the new wage scales.[54]

Workers have generally renounced any remaining vestiges of overtime wages (which have become something of a symbol of an unpatriotic attitude). Managers are paid on the scale of civil servants and often receive no more than veteran workers. Except for a few scarce technical skills, wage differentials are not widely used today as a labor-allocating device.

The shortage of consumer goods and the rationing of meat, rice, coffee, and many other items meant that there was little to buy when material incentives were increased in the mid-1960s. Rationing quotas became

[51]Huberman and Sweezy, pp. 144–145.
[52]Adolfo Gilly, "Inside the Cuban Revolution," *Monthly Review*, October 1964, p. 24.
[53]Jose Yglesias, *In the Fist of the Revolution: Life in a Cuban Country Town*, New York: Vintage, 1969; and Barry Reckord, *Does Fidel Eat More than Your Father?* New York: New American Library, 1972.
[54]Bernardo, p. 69.

the effective determinant of real income. All available evidence points to even greater equalization of wages in the future. As the system of free supply gains further headway, it is possible that moral incentives will almost completely replace wages as a stimulus to labor.

The core of the system of moral incentives, however, is the system of voluntary labor, which sends thousands of students and office workers to work in the cane fields every year. No one has ever claimed that cutting sugar cane under the tropical sun is much fun for a bureaucrat or an intellectual; the cane is sharp, flies abound, and backs and arms soon give out. By rational measures the cost of transporting and feeding volunteer workers largely outweighs the work they produce. Cuban leaders place such a high premium on the moral value of volunteer labor that they disregard such considerations.

How many "volunteer," and for what reasons? "The following facts were widely publicized in 1968 and were typical: 240,000 renounced payment for overtime work; 25,350 men turned their jobs over to women in order to join agricultural brigades; 3448 switched from city to country for two years and thousands upon thousands aspired for Heroes of Moncada Banners, and so on. '[55] Also important in this respect is the increasing use of elite army units or semimilitary youth groups as agricultural task forces. The contrasts in attitudes of volunteers are shown in the following reports:

> I asked a friend of mine whether he cut cane. He said shortly, "Enough."
> Why does he go? Because there is moral pressure on him to go. But
> it is *moral* pressure. If he has no *morality* he needn't go. He can stay in
> the office and still draw his salary. There is a legal necessity to go
> to the fields only one day a week. . . . The militant twenty per cent set
> the work pace in Cuba and most of the country follows. . . . The
> hostile twenty per cent neither attend meetings nor do the extra work.
> They get cold-shouldered, called *gusano* [worm], a lift attendant
> might force them to walk up the stairs. Food gets roughly shovelled on
> to their plate in the cafeteria.[56]

> One daughter bubbled in, the mechancial engineer. She was muddy. She
> chatted, waiting to get into a shower which they shared with about
> twelve neighbors. She'd been doing voluntary work in the fields. "How
> many hours?" "Oh, a few." "Don't you watch the clock?" She laughed.
> All the people she'd been responsible for had turned out, she said.
> The work wasn't all that efficient, the daughter said, but at least it
> wouldn't have to be done all over again.[57]

Che Guevara believed that moral incentives would eventually prevail if only a few enthusiastic workers in each group would serve as examples for others. There are strong incentives for at least "going through the mo-

[55]*Ibid.*, pp. 77–78.
[56]Reckord, p. 24.
[57]*Ibid.*, p. 50.

tions" of participating in voluntary work projects—the local Committee for the Defense of the Revolution is on the alert for slackers. It seems that more government officials and other administrators in Cuba, as compared to China, do so with a sense of reluctance and duty, in the spirit of an American boss putting in an appearance at the annual company picnic. "The second stage [of volunteer labor], now under way, is to deepen people's understanding of shared labor as the key to a classless, educated society and to raise individual productivity, express revolutionary idealism in work, break economic bottlenecks that choke men with hunger and frustrate their ideals everywhere."[58] Much depends on the generation of post-revolutionary young people now entering the labor force.

The 1970 Harvest and Its Aftermath

Many observers, both inside and outside Cuba, were doubtful about the feasibility of achieving a 10 million ton harvest in 1970. To push production beyond the natural "capacity" level of about 8.5 million tons, they claimed, would pull resources and administrative talent out of vital uses and create a subsequent letdown in economic activity. They were largely correct. But moral crusades do not spring from rational calculation. In 1968, facing a harvest of only half the 1970 goal, Castro reaffirmed that "we understand how the 10-million-ton goal has become a yardstick by which to judge the Revolution; and, if a yardstick is put up to the Revolution, there is no doubt about the Revolution's meeting the mark."[59]

The Revolution in fact fell about 1.5 million tons short of the mark. Although the harvest was a record and entailed monumental efforts (such as postponing Christmas until after the can was cut), it nevertheless represented a failure of the claim that anything was possible if only an all-out effort were made. On July 26, 1970 Castro made an extraordinary speech, taking personal responsibility for errors of economic policy and revealing the damage to the economy that had occurred. Summarizing a Castro speech is like trying to summarize a Beethoven symphony; it is hoped that these excerpts capture the essence of his recent views on economic matters:

> I repeat that we were incapable of waging what we called the simultaneous battle. And actually, the heroic effort to increase production, to raise our purchasing power, resulted in imbalances in the economy, in diminished production in other sectors, and in short, in an increase in our difficulties. . . .
>
> Difficulties have been encountered in highways as well as railroad transportation. These difficulties have been determined partly by the priorities given to the transportation of sugar cane and by-products, and by a lack of spare parts. The result has been a decrease in the number

58*Ibid.*, p. 105.
59Kenner and Petras, pp. 248–249.

of available vehicles, which has led to operational problems and seriously interfered with economic activities during that period. . . .

I believe that we, the leaders of this Revolution, have cost the people too much in our process of learning. . . .

Why should a manager have to be absolutely in charge? Why shouldn't we begin to introduce representatives of the factory's workers into its management? Why not have confidence? Why not put our trust in the tremendous proletarian spirit of men who, at times in torn shoes and clothes, nevertheless keep up production? . . .

We must also add that nobody here is going to solve a problem if he doesn't obtain the cooperation of others. Seeing only one's own section is inadmissible and absurd! More than a crime it is a stupidity! In a society where the means of production are collective, lack of coordination is stupid. Thus the need for coordinating different sectors and linking them to a coordinating team at the highest level. . . .

We must use our heads to solve problems. If the ten-million-ton sugar harvest was a problem of brawn, what we now have before us is a problem of brains. . . .[60]

The attention to administrative skills, coordination between sectors, and economizing behavior marks a departure from the view that revolutionary spirit could make up for deficiencies in these facets of economic planning. New, also, is the possibility of giving workers a significant voice in management at the corporate level. The basic features of the Cuban economic system remain virtually unchanged, however. Moral incentives and volunteer labor will continue, the free-supply system will equalize living standards further, and the budgetary system that centralizes planning will rule out reliance on market incentives or profitability criteria as success indicators. There seems to be no obvious way in which rational calculations can be carried out unless firms are held more strictly accountable for their own efficiency.

Thus the Cuban economy faces serious problems in the years ahead. The risks of sugar monoculture have not been eradicated under the Castro regime. Soviet loans are coming due, and an increasing share of sugar revenues will be earmarked for debt repayment. The Cuban national character seems much less suited for wholehearted adherence to moral incentives at this time than appears to be the case in China. There is some question as to whether Castro's charismatic leadership can weather a continued series of economic disasters.

Nevertheless, the very survival of the Cuban economic system in the face of lost American markets and continued U.S. political harassment (which seems increasingly outmoded in the light of present world conditions) constitutes some measure of success for the Revolution. The material conditions of many people have been improved. More important, their

[60]Fidel Castro, "This Shame Will Be Welcome. . . .," *New York Review of Books*, September 24, 1970, pp. 20–33.

spirits and expectations have been raised. "Castro's (and Cuba's) predicament is that his own style—one can even say his life style—is at odds with the only hope for Cuban socialism, the growth of effective popular institutions for decision making and administration. . . . Since the Revolution without Fidel is unthinkable if not impossible, there seems nothing left for him to do but to adapt himself to the realities he revealed to the public on July 26 [1970]. It will be interesting to see what he does."[61]

QUESTIONS FOR CLASS DISCUSSION

1. What is an incentive system? How does it change?
2. Why is the regional allocation of resources such an important issue in Yugoslavia?
3. How much decision-making power do workers' councils possess?
4. What conflicts of interest exist between workers and managers in Yugoslavia? Between firms and central planning agencies?
5. Why is efficiency so low in Yugoslav industry?
6. Why did information about China become scarce in the 1960s?
7. Compare the incentive systems of the Great Leap Forward period with that of the Cultural Revolution.
8. What is the difference between an agricultural cooperative and a commune in China? between a cooperative and a people's farm in Cuba?
9. What were the essential features of the Cultural Revolution? What was the "capitalist road" mentality? the three-in-one principle of economic organization? struggle-criticism-transformation?
10. What is the difference in motivating effects between piecework and daily or hourly wage rates?
11. What is the significance of the Tachai Brigade? the self-reliance campaign? the barefoot doctors?
12. How did sugar monoculture affect the Cuban economy before the Revolution? Which of these conditions still remain?
13. Evaluate the argument of Che Guevara that a single centrally controlled budget could cover several firms because of the good communications network in Cuba.
14. Was the shift back to reliance on sugar after 1963 a "good" choice? Was the Second Agrarian Reform?
15. Discuss the relation between moral incentives and volunteer labor in Cuba.
16. Compare the balance of gains and losses of Cuban peasants from the Revolution. Compare for factory workers. Compare for white-collar workers.
17. In the present political context, should the United States resume diplomatic and economic relations with Cuba?

[61]Lee Lockwood, "Introduction [to Castro's July 26 speech]," *New York Review of Books,* September 24, 1970, p. 18.

18. Discuss the economic significance of the 1970 10-million ton sugar-harvest target.

SUGGESTED STUDENT REPORTS FOR PART VI

1. A study of Russian economic development before 1917.
2. A reenactment of the Great Industrialization Debate of the 1920s in Russia.
3. Causes and results of the NEP era in Soviet Russia.
4. A study of achievements under the various five-year plans, including the movement of living standards.
5. The effects of World War II on the Russian economy.
6. The extent of *Gosplan's* role in Soviet economic planning.
7. Reasons for continued problems in the agricultural sector.
8. Current Western views on the success of the Liberman reforms.
9. A discussion of the pros and cons of the decision to produce automobiles.
10. The living standard of middle-income Russians as compared with middle-income Americans.
11. The role of economists in the Soviet Union.
12. The reliability of Soviet economic data.
13. The international trade position of the Soviet Union.
14. The quality of Soviet goods and the availability of spare parts and repair facilities.
15. Examples of the failure of economic indicators to achieve the goals planners had in mind.
16. The economic effects of nationalistic movements in Yugoslavia.
17. Cyclic changes in Yugoslav growth rates.
18. Worker attitudes toward workers' councils.
19. Reasons for the migration of Yugoslav workers to temporary jobs in West Germany.
20. The role of the Yugoslav banking sector.
21. A study of the economic writings of Mao Tse-tung.
22. A survey of the accounts of recent visitors to China.
23. A comparison of urban and rural living conditions in China today.
24. A report on what has become of the Red Guards in the aftermath of the Cultural Revolution.
25. The availability of consumer goods in China.
26. A comparison of the economic views of Fidel Castro and Che Guevara.
27. An economic analysis of Castro's recent speeches.
28. A survey of accounts of recent visitors to Cuba.
29. Technological and economic aspects of sugar production.
30. Possible types of moral incentives that might be tried in the American economic system.

SUGGESTED FURTHER READING FOR PART VI
Russia
Adams, Arthur E., and Jan S. Adams, *Men Versus Systems: Agriculture in the U.S.S.R., Poland, and Czechoslovakia*, New York: Free Press, 1971.
Bergson, Abram, *The Economics of Soviet Planning*, New Haven, Conn.: Yale University Press, 1964.
Bornstein, Morris, and Daniel Fusfeld, eds., *The Soviet Economy: A Book of Readings* (3rd ed.), Homewood, Ill. Irwin, 1970.
Dobb, M., *Soviet Economic Development since 1917* (3rd ed.), London: Routledge & Kegan Paul, 1966.
Erlich, A., *The Soviet Industrialization Debate 1924–1928*, Cambridge, Mass.: Harvard University Press, 1960.
Gerschenkron, Alexander, *Continuity in History and Other Essays*, Cambridge, Mass.: Harvard University Press, 1968.
Goldman, Marshall I., ed., *The Soviet Economy: Myth and Reality*, Englewood Cliffs, N.J.: Prentice-Hall, 1968.
Joint Economic Committee, Congress of the United States, *New Directions in the Soviet Economy*, Washington, D.C.: Government Printing Office, 1966.
Maynard, Sir John, *The Russian Peasant and Other Studies*, New York: Collier, 1962.
Montias, John Michael, et al., *The Soviet Economy in Theory and Practice*, Columbia, Mo.: University of Missouri, 1964.
Nove, Alec, *An Economic History of the U.S.S.R.*, London: Penguin, 1969.
Shaffer, Harry G., ed., *The Soviet Economy: A Collection of Western and Soviet Views* (2nd ed.), New York: Appleton, 1969.
Talbott, Strobe, trans. and ed., *Khrushchev Remembers*, Boston: Little, Brown, 1970.

Yugoslavia
Bombelles, Joseph T., *Economic Development of Communist Yugoslavia*, Palo Alto, Calif.: The Hoover Institution, 1968.
Horvat, Branko, "Yugoslav Economic Policy in the Post-War Period: Problems, Ideas, Institutional Developments," *American Economic Review*, Supplement, June 1971, pp. 71–169.
Sturmthal, Adolf, *Workers Council*, Cambridge, Mass.: Harvard University Press, 1964.
Vanek, Jaroslav, "Economic Planning in Yugoslavia," in Max F. Millikan, ed., *National Economic Planning*, New York: Columbia University Press, 1967.
Ward, Benjamin N., *The Socialist Economy: A Study of Organizational Alternatives*, New York: Random House, 1967.

Waterston, Albert, *Planning in Yugoslavia*, Baltimore: Johns Hopkins University Press, 1962.

People's Republic of China

Committee of Concerned Asian Scholars, *China! Inside the People's Republic*, New York: Bantam, 1972.

Joint Economic Committee, Congress of the United States, *People's Republic of China: An Economic Assessment*, Washington, D.C.: Government Printing Office, 1971.

Li, Choh-Ming, ed., *Industrial Development in Communist China*, New York: Praeger, 1964.

Myrdal, Jan, *Report from a Chinese Village*, New York: Vintage, 1972.

New York Times, *Report from Red China*, New York: Avon, 1972.

Wheelwright, E. L., and Bruce McFarlane, *The Chinese Road to Socialism: Economic of the Cultural Revolution*, New York: Monthly Review Press, 1970.

Cuba

Bernardo, Robert M., *The Theory of Moral Incentives in Cuba*, University, Ala.: University of Alabama Press, 1971.

Draper, Theodore, *Castroism: Theory and Practice*, New York: Praeger, 1965.

Dumont, Rene, *Cuba: Socialism and Development*, New York: Grove, 1970.

Huberman, Leo, and Paul M. Sweezy, *Socialism in Cuba*, New York: Monthly Review Press, 1969.

Reckord, Barry, *Does Fidel Eat More than Your Father?* New York: New American Library, 1972.

Yglesias, Jose, *In the Fist of the Revolution: Life in a Cuban Country Town*, New York: Vintage, 1969.

PART VII: CONCLUSIONS

25. The convergence hypothesis

In recent years the most lively topic of discussion among economists interested in the kinds of questions covered in this book has been the Convergence Hypothesis—the supposition that the diverse economic systems of the world are moving toward the adoption of similar institutional structures to cope with similar economic problems. An extraordinary development, if true!

EVIDENCE PRO

Several events during the early 1960s contributed to making belief in the Convergence Hypothesis plausible. The global spread of modern methods of communication and transportation gave rise to the expectation that other innovations would be universally adopted. Jacques Ellul, a noted French philosopher, speaks of "technique" (by which he means not only machines but also the scientific basis of applied technology and the social organization of which the economic structure is a part) in these terms:

> Technique has been extended geographically so that is covers the whole earth. It is evolving with a rapidity disconcerting not only to the man in the street but to the technician himself. It poses problems which recur endlessly and ever more acutely in human social groups. Moreover, technique has become objective and is transmitted like a physical thing; it leads thereby to a certain unity of civilization, regardless of the environment or the country in which it operates.[1]

Belief in these phenomena and in the rationality of scientific technicians, whatever their idcological background, were palpable in a plan for *rapprochement* between East and West proposed by the Russian physicist Sakharov to eliminate such dangers as thermonuclear war, poverty, dictatorship, and threats to intellectual freedom. The basis for collaboration, in his view, is economic in nature.

> The continuing economic progress being achieved under capitalism should be a fact of great theoretical significance for any dogmatic Marxist. It is precisely this fact that lies at the basis of peaceful coexistence and it suggests, in principle, that if capitalism ever runs into an economic blind alley it will not necessarily have to leap into a desperate military adventure. Both capitalism and socialism are capable of long-term development, borrowing positive elements from each other and actually coming closer to each other in a number of essential aspects.[2]

Conditions on both sides of the Iron Curtain during the early 1960s tended to support the Convergence Hypothesis. The evidence that the countries of Western Europe exceeded their long-term growth rates during the first two postwar decades was seen by many as verification that a new era for economic planning had arrived.

> There is every reason to believe that the successful experience of Europe in managing demand represents a permanent sophistication in the technique of managing a capitalist economy with fairly general policy instruments. Further refinements would help, but the basic equipment of fiscal and monetary policy has been rather fully used in Europe. Unfortunately this is not true of the United States. . . . The United States has thus a good deal to learn from Europe in the art of economic management. It particularly needs to develop an active fiscal policy.[3]

---

[1]Jacques Ellul, *The Technological Society*, paperback edition, New York: Vintage, 1967, p. 78.

[2]From a translation appearing in *New York Times*, July 22, 1968, p. 1.

[3]Angus Maddison, *Economic Growth in the West*, New York: Twentieth Century, 1964, pp. 18–19.

If a failure of policy was seen as the root cause of the performance of the laggards—the United States, the United Kingdom, and Canada— then correct policy could confidently be expected to rectify the situation; the U.S. tax cut of 1964 and the formation of the National Economic Development Council in Great Britain would represent steps in that direction. Eventually, if this line of argument proved correct, every nation could reach and maintain a permanent position of rapid economic growth.

A new era of planning implies further experimentation with new institutional arrangements. The most successful features from each nation could perhaps be adapted to other situations. Thus the fostering of cooperation between industries and government that was thought to exist in the German industrial organizations or under French indicative planning might be tried elsewhere, or the construction and use of econometric models along Dutch lines might be tried. This was the time when all nations suddenly became interested in incomes policies and searched for effective means of holding wages within productivity guidelines. A convergence of growth rates in the Western nations was thought to portend a similar tendency among patterns of economic organization.

If the nations on both sides of the North Atlantic gave evidence of similar economic tendencies, it was also apparent by 1965 that economic reforms in the Eastern European nations of the Soviet Bloc and in the Soviet Union itself were under way. Although Yugoslavia had pursued its own road to socialism for 15 years, relying heavily on market forces to allocate resources and on decentralized decision making by workers' councils at the corporate level, it was the Russian reform movement that prompted headline writers to surmise, "Soviet is Leaning to Profit System . . . Party Reorganization May Bring Western-style Economy to Russia."[4] The Soviet Union, after 30 years of single-minded adherence to five-year plans aimed at developing heavy industry for military purposes, found that goal largely achieved and faced the question of future economic targets. At about the same time, it became apparent that the system of highly centralized decision making did not always achieve the results envisioned by the planners; the opportunities for violating the spirit of planning directives at the corporate level, while formally complying, were too numerous.

A plenary session of the Central Committee in September, 1965, approved guidelines for dissolving the ramshackle structure of planning and administrative agencies which Khrushchev had set up and restoring the ministerial principle of organization, reforming the system of prices according to new principles, and altering the system of planning and controlling enterprise behavior. The general goal of these reforms might be summarized briefly as an attempt to give enterprise decision-makers more freedom to make decisions about resource use and to give

[4]*New York Times,* November 22, 1964.

them a reformed set of incentives and signals that would encourage
them to use this new freedom in ways consistent with the general welfare.[5]

These reforms constitute a major departure from the old system, but
they are only a small part of the innovative thought concerning economic
planning going on in the Soviet Union. The ultimate effect of many of these
proposals is to establish a system of rational prices to achieve an efficient
allocation of economic resources along the lines of Lange market socialism.

A possible transitional step toward that end can perhaps be seen in
the planning system adopted in Czechoslovakia late in 1964 and put into
full operation at the beginning of 1967. Czechoslovakia is the most industrialized of the Communist nations of Eastern Europe, but its economy,
which had developed rapidly during the 1950s, came to a virtual standstill
between 1961 and 1965. "Even though Czechoslovakia's economic problems are manifold, the economists are convinced that one single systematic
defect—*detailed economic planning from the center*—is at the root of the
trouble, and that only the elimination of the existing planning structure
will provide the fundamental cure."[6]

The reforms were aimed at rectifying not only the lagging growth rate
but also the shoddy quality of many consumer goods, the low productivity
of labor, and the burgeoning of an entrenched planning bureaucracy. The
view was stated that economic centralism might be appropriate for a backward economy or one requiring forced capital accumulation or large structural shifts in the relative importance of industrial sectors, but it could
actually prove counterproductive for the Czech attempt to consolidate and
perpetuate a complex economic system. The New Economic Model provided for a larger degree of autonomy for individual economic enterprises
to produce and sell products, and to secure raw materials and labor services as they chose. Firms were responsible for their own investment from
profits or borrowed funds, subject only to the broad outlines of national
investment policy. A three-price system was to prevail, with price controls
on basic commodities, flexibility within limits for most industrial products,
and freely fluctuating prices for the remainder. "The state intends to
achieve its economic goals; first, by retaining a few features of the command economy; second, by controlling wage rates and prices; third, by
taxation, subsidies, and special levies; and fourth, by regulation of credit
availability exercised through the State Bank."[7]

The preceding statement makes it clear that the Czech reform, even
if fully implemented, would still have made it unlikely for that nation's eco-

[5]Robert Campbell, "Economic Reform in the U.S.S.R.," *American Economic Review*, May 1968, p. 547.

[6]Harry G. Shaffer, "Czechoslovakia's New Economic Model," *Problems of Communism*, September–October 1965, p. 35.

[7]George J. Staller, "Czechoslovakia: The New Model of Planning and Manage-ment," *American Economic Review*, May 1968, p. 560.

nomic system to be mistakenly viewed as identical to the mixed economies of France or Sweden. The point is, however, that the reform movements in Eastern Europe marked a significant departure from rigid central planning in the direction of democratic socialism. It is this fact that adds credence to the Convergence Hypothesis.

EVIDENCE CON

The vision that national economic systems will become essentially similar at some time in the future is one of those long-range predictions that, like the Marxist prophecy of the downfall of capitalism, is impossible to refute unequivocally because the proponent can always argue that "the time is not yet ripe." A meaningful discussion of the Convergence Hypothesis must therefore focus on trends in the institutional evolution of economic systems. The main evidence cited in favor of the proposition is the rapid growth and policy-making innovations of the nations of Western Europe in the postwar period and the economic reforms of the Soviet Bloc nations over the past decade. As often occurs when long-term generalizations are constructed from short-term observations, subsequent events have weakened the pro-convergence position.

These trends might be symbolized by the tarnishing of the West German "Wirtschaftswunder" or "economic miracle" with the recession of 1965. The formation of the European Common Market had increased the economic ties between the nations of Western Europe, spreading the effects of a slowdown or currency crisis in one to its trading partners. The precarious international economic position of the British economy, despite the drastic remedies of a wage freeze and currency devaluation, and the U.S. exposure to inflationary pressures and balance-of-payments deficits are examples of the weaknesses that appeared after 1965. No country can view its economic performance during this period with unalloyed enthusiasm.

The postwar growth spurt that was thought to be a permanent shift upward in long-run trends turned out, on close investigation, to contain several one-time contributing factors. A careful quantitative study of European nations concluded that the shift of resources away from low-productivity sectors, primarily agriculture, into the modern industrial sector was the single most important source of accelerated economic growth.[8] Other nonrecurring elements were U.S. Marshall Plan aid, borrowing from the backlog of advanced American technology, and the initial expansion of consumer-durable goods.[9]

The end of the economic boom cast doubt on the institutions devised to avoid the very problems that were so much in evidence. Wage-price

[8]Edward F. Denison, *Why Growth Rates Differ*, Washington, D.C.: Brookings, 1967.

[9]Richard B. DuBoff, "Western Europe's Postwar Boom: The End of an Era," *Monthly Review*, February 1968, pp. 34–41.

guideposts became largely exercises in futility in countries where enforcement was a politically sensitive issue; indicative planning in France faltered before the growing independence of businessmen and the vague discontent of workers, who supposedly were becoming more affluent as the economy developed. Welfare programs, in many cases, had to be sacrificed when the growth rate ceased its upward climb. When the components originally cited as evidence of the unification of the economic systems are diminished in importance, so of course is the plausibility of the Convergence Hypothesis proper.

The economic reforms of the Soviet Bloc also lost momentum when exposed to the harsh realities of underlying conditions in those countries. In the first place, the reforms themselves turned out to be less sweeping than they had originally been considered. The emphasis on profits in Russia, for example, was much more a change in the incentives to which enterprise managers respond than a transformation of the fundamental precepts of the Soviet system. Moreover, most Western observers underestimated the resistance of old officials to new administrative proposals.

> Today discussion of Eastern Europe centers around the stalling of the reforms, the strong tendencies everywhere to postpone decisions on reorganization, or to eliminate the more radical proposals. The vision of developing market socialist economies throughout this area, including the Soviet Union, seems to be fading, and the reasons are everywhere the same: not so much fears that the reforms won't work or the inability of reformers to agree on a program, but rather fears that the political consequences of reforming may be unacceptable to the present leadership, that in some fundamental way markets and Communist parties don't mix.[10]

The complex interaction between economic reform and political stability in economies of the Soviet type is nowhere more evident than in the case of Czechoslovakia. The inability and unwillingness of the party bureaucracy to make the reforms instituted in 1967 work effectively fostered the downfall of the old political leaders as 1968 began. Ferment in the press, in the arts, and in the political arena indicated that a major social upheaval was under way. Several citizens were quoted to the effect that once economic reforms began it became inevitable that the tight reins on personal action in other areas could not long be maintained. The statements issued by the new leaders made it clear that interference by party officials in all kinds of economic activity would be halted.[11]

Political turmoil led to the invasion of Czechoslovakia by the Soviet Union and her allies in the summer of 1968. The spectacle of the abrogation of a reform movement by armed force within the Soviet Bloc empha-

[10]Benjamin Ward, "Political Power and Economic Change in Yugoslavia," *American Economic Review*, May 1968, p. 568.
[11]*The Economist*, July 15, 1972.

sizes the crucial role of political factors. This is not to say that change cannot occur or is not occurring within the planning apparatus of the nations of Eastern Europe. The pressure of economic circumstances requires a corresponding adjustment of institutions for securing the goals of the economy; the essential point is that these solutions will be sought within the limits of change imposed by those groups holding ultimate political power rather than in the direction indicated by any criteria of economic efficiency.

CONCLUSIONS

The Economist sums up the economic outlook for the predictable future in the following headline: "The world's economic prospect is for good growth, bad inflation, and silly decisions at international conferences which fortunately will not really matter."[12] What does this relative uniformity in economic performance portend for the Convergence Hypothesis as applied to the economic systems of the West? There is little evidence for institutional restructuring on purely philosophical or ideological grounds; the exigencies of political or economic events are a more likely source of pragmatic actions.

Foremost among these pressures is inflation, which affects every industrialized nation. If no nation has found a definitive cure for inflation, it follows that no nation provides a model for other nations to converge upon. Just as every capitalist nation has adopted broadly similar monetary and fiscal policy tools, they will also probably be forced to institute some form of wage and price controls in an effort to mitigate the domestic and international trade consequences of a chronically rising price level. This will represent a significant convergence of institutional forms, in our opinion, only when some variant of the guideline medicine is found that cures the inflationary disease. The increasing militancy of public-sector employees means, as the United Kingdom can testify, that the problem is not likely to be more manageable where industries have been nationalized.

Neither do the following two examples for possible emulation appear to be copyable. The European Common Market, even with British participation, appears more like a federation to realize economies of scale arising from unified markets and tariff protection than a move toward corresponding economic institutions. The participating nations have largely resisted proposals that might be interpreted as creating a single economic system in the European Economic Community. The Japanese success story likewise seems exportable only to a limited degree. The close cooperation of the government and industrial combines in promoting exports, for example, is receiving close attention in the United States and other countries; the paternalistic relationship between employer and employee that is a major source of productive effort and receptivity to technological innovation,

---

[12]*The Economist*, July 15, 1972.

however, is so alien to Western cultural patterns that it is difficult to imagine the Japanese incentive system in operation anywhere else.

The nations of the Communist world show equally wide disparities among economic systems and equally little observable tendency toward convergence. The reliance on nonmaterial incentives adopted by the Peoples Republic of China and, to a lesser extent, by Cuba is light-years removed from the considerable material incentives provided by the private cars, vacation cottages, and foreign holidays of consumer-oriented Yugoslavia. The countries located between these extremes—Russia, Poland, Hungary, the German Democratic Republic, etc.—may continue to experiment with various planning reforms and adjustments in incentive systems, but it is likely that ideological considerations and internal political realities will rule out significant emulation of either the Chinese or the Yugoslav prototype.

The first cracks in the Convergence Hypothesis appeared when the "miraculous" examples of West Germany and France proved susceptible to common economic ills. Its shaky foundations were demonstrated by worldwide unrest among the young and by the failure to confront the crucial issues of income distribution and inflation head on. The hypothesis collapsed, perhaps permanently, when Russian tanks put down the liberalization of the Czech society that followed genuine economic reforms in the direction of convergence.

There is no magic formula for achieving orderly change in the economic institutions of either capitalist or socialist economic systems. The choice among economic systems is unavoidably a political question, with no guarantee that economic and political stability can be attained simultaneously. This means, above all, that political leaders will continue to limit the range of feasible economic reforms if the price in ideological terms is judged too high. The implications of these observations for the economic system of the United States is the topic of the final chapter.

QUESTIONS FOR CLASS DISCUSSION

1. What is the essence of the Convergence Hypothesis? How could it be conclusively proved or disproved?

2. What specific conditions in various countries appeared to support the Convergence Hypothesis? Why, in particular, did the Liberman proposals in the Soviet Union give a fillip to the pro-convergence position?

3. Is there a central theme running through recent economic reforms in Eastern Europe? Is a highly centralized planning structure appropriate to the current conditions prevailing in countries like Poland, East Germany, and Hungary?

4. To what extent was the post-World War II growth record of Western Europe the result of "one shot" favorable circumstances?

5. Does the convergence of economic systems necessarily imply the convergence of incentive systems? Why or why not? If you believe in an

eventual convergence of incentive systems, where on the material-nonmaterial spectrum will it end up?

6. Try to imagine life in the American economic system if the Chinese incentive system were somehow imposed by government fiat. Could the Chinese approach fit any more readily into the current Russian economic system?

7. Why is inflation so persistent and ubiquitous in the West?

8. In what economic systems is a more equal distribution of income a primary goal at the present time?

9. To what extent, in your opinion, can economic necessity overcome political opposition to alteration of economic systems? Does your answer differ for democracies and for dictatorships?

10. Name and defend three generalizations about economic systems that you would make on the basis of what you have learned from a course in comparative economic systems.

26. The future of American capitalism

The first edition of this book, published 30 years ago, noted that "education . . . is to face the future where the problems to be solved lie, and to avoid facing the past." In this concluding chapter of the ninth edition, we face the future of the American economic and political system. The economic indicators of all phases of our domestic economic operations have been climbing steadily. Gross national product, national income, aggregate personal incomes, new capital investment, percentage of employables employed, wage rates, and corporate net profits have soared to new heights. The outward evidences of economic prosperity are unsurpassed in their glow of economic well-being.

Concurrently, however, dissatisfaction, strife, antagonisms, racial and class cleavages, employer-union disagreements, and indeed doubt and fear for the future basic well-being of American society as a whole, appear to be at a peak unmatched in recent decades. Just as the physician first carefully determines *what* disease is present before he seeks to cure it, so must we first seek the the root causes of the economic illness that now afflicts us, despite the appearance of health.

INFLATION AND CAPITALISM'S FUTURE

Appearances of well-being are easily taken as evidence of real basic social well-being when they are not. For instance, a rise in the national income must be corrected for rises in the prices of the goods it embraces before it can have great significance. Adjustments of this sort cause some economic indicators to experience major reversals during periods of sustained general price increases.

An illustration of practical significance is found in the field of labor relations. Unions and companies are currently bargaining for new agreements with average hourly increases in wage rates of nearly 6 percent per year. This to the rank-and-file wage earner may seem like real prosperity. However, if 4 percent of this is taken away by regular increases in living costs, labor is left with a 2 percent *real* gain rather than the apparent 6 percent. Eventually, of course, this hard fact is sensed, dissatisfaction results, and labor leaders respond with demands for still-greater increases. When these exceed increases in man-hour labor productivity, the result is higher prices, increases in living costs, and still-higher wage demands, backed by the power of unionization and passed along through rises in administered prices.

This confusion of appearance with reality has assumed another form, which is of major significance. In a general and somewhat haphazard way, monetary and fiscal policies in the United States during the past several decades have followed Keynesian lines. They may have assisted in achieving a high level of employment at most times and may have caused real living standards to rise somewhat among all but the most seriously disadvantaged of our population. However, the degree of success of such policies must be tempered by the acknowledgment that over this entire period a decline in the general purchasing power of the dollar has been occurring. The success of the economics and practice of Keynesian monetary and fiscal policies must be held seriously in question when betterment of real per-capita national income is accompanied by substantial inflationary trends.

There is little doubt that under capitalism real per-capita national income can be held on an upward trend *if inflation is a part of the context within which the capitalist system functions.* The crucial question is whether a capitalist system whose operation is bolstered by the stimulant of inflation can build soundly for its own future. History does not reveal much affirmative experience. Automatically, a little inflation continually enhances the potency of the profit motive—a key incentive factor in a capitalist economy—by lowering the cost of borrowing. No one has invented the means whereby a politically democratic society can prevent continuous inflation (even "a little," at the beginning) from feeding on itself and finally creating major problems for the capitalist economy it was supposed to be sustaining.

What happens then is a question worth pondering. Perhaps powerful unions and oligopolistic industries will see the wisdom of mutual self-restraint to abort the spiral of wage-price inflation. Perhaps those consigned to relatively fixed incomes—pensioners, welfare recipients, employees of nonprofit institutions, unskilled workers, other categories of the poor—will form a coalition to make politicians, fearing retribution at the polls, as wary of inflation as they are of depression. Joseph Schumpeter envisioned a different scenario—one that makes interesting reading in the era following Republican President Nixon's New Economic Policy, imposed in 1971.

> Perennial inflationary pressure can play an important part in the eventual conquest of the private enterprise economy by the bureaucracy—the resultant frictions and deadlocks being attributed to the private enterprise and used as arguments for further restrictions and regulations. I do not say any group follows this line with conscious purpose, but purposes are never wholly conscious. A situation may well emerge in which most people will consider planning as the smallest of possible evils. They will certainly not call it Socialism or Communism, and presumedly they will make exceptions for the farmer, the retailer, and the small producer; under these circumstances, capitalism (the free-enterprise system) as a scheme of values, a way of life, and a civilization may not be worth bothering about.[1]

GOVERNMENT AND CAPITALISM'S FUTURE

In seeking to cure the economic ills besetting our economy, our economic and political systems must be regarded as so basically interrelated that reform will have to come simultaneously and harmoniously to both. The experiences of the past five to ten years of two great democracies, Great Britain and the United States, afford proof beyond doubt of this fact. Both have been faced with serious basic problems of inflation and resultant distortions in their international balance of payments, which both attempted to meet by first seeking voluntary restraint on private action by business, labor, and citizens at large. They failed in these efforts, and both eventually conceded the failure and shifted to governmentally imposed legal restraints on the actions of individuals and powerfully organized economic interest groups.

It would now appear incontrovertible that we in the United States

[1]Joseph A. Schumpeter, "The March into Socialism," reprinted in his *Socialism, Capitalism, and Democracy* (3rd ed.), New York: Harper & Row, 1960, p. 424.

must reorient ourselves with respect to the basic propriety of the use of governmental agencies to make our capitalist system function as it should to serve human needs. It is oversimplified, but true, that the tremendous emphasis capitalism places on individual freedom of action—when that freedom is extended to huge private business corporations, unions, and a plethora of effective organized economic interest groups—simply overwhelms competitive forces, which theoretically mold all efforts for private gain into a massive drive to serve the common good. Government is the only institution capable of coping with the multiplicity of strengths attained by powerful, organized, and astute economic interests.

The present ability of our federal government to assume and successfully play such a role in the near future is woefully weak. Congressional and presidential reform is essential for the performance of functional tasks such as are suggested here. An antiquated committee system grinding out national legislation under leadership selected by seniority in the House and Senate does not conform with the role here envisioned for our federal government. The speed with which proposed federal legislation is either defeated or enacted must be stepped up immeasurably, but without sacrificing careful assessment of its wisdom by the membership of Congress. It is wholly unacceptable that a congressional bill levying a surtax on personal and corporate incomes, designed to curb inflation, should not be finally acted upon by Congress until approximately two years after it was first introduced. It is a sage epitome that "we are changing the world faster than we can change our institutions."[2] Unless political scientists develop sound and practical ways of reducing the lag so far as economic problems are concerned, the future of our system of capitalism is in jeopardy.

Retaining in mind that we must develop the ability to separate the *reality* from the *appearance* as far as the operations of our capitalist economy are concerned and that the speed with which sound governmental (especially federal) control and guidance of economic operations are put into effect must be increased, some delineation of broad areas of *proper* control and guidance is in order. Here again one must be fully cognizant of the minimum and maximum limits of the program of governmental control and guidance of economic action here posed by Schumpeter's well-meaning but lethal bureaucrats.

It would be meaningless to leave the student at this juncture without more specific suggestions as to possible control and guidance measures that, with due foresight, appear to be practicable components of such a program. These, offered with the greatest humility, are suggestions for immediate action, for possible delayed action, and finally, for some long-run goals consistent with the indefinite continuation of a capitalist type of economic system in the United States.

---

[2]James Reston, *Indianapolis News*, May 16, 1968.

MEASURES OF CONTROL AND
GUIDANCE FOR AMERICAN CAPITALISM

Immediate Needs

It is imperative that we find measures to strengthen our established, but mild and wavering, commitment to the effective use of monetary and fiscal measures to stabilize economic activity. If, as we believe is a fact, the American public is firmly convinced that their future well-being rests upon the continuance of a capitalist type of economic organization, the first requisite is this proposal. *Coordinated duality* of monetary and fiscal policies is crucial. With the Keynesian revolution in economic theory, the nature of this duality was described, and means to its realization for the control and guidance of the economy were noted in their crude form. This theory has been worked over and over by academic theoreticians and practitioners in private business and government service. A new area of economic research and teaching has developed under the titles of mathematical economics and econometrics. Refined to great sharpness, these tools and methods of economic analysis supply reliable means of determining how much of a stimulus our capitalist economy needs from time to time, and when it is approaching "overheating" and needs deflationary influences injected into it.

Just as medical science does not await the final possible iota of knowledge on a newly discovered potential cure of a disease before beginning to use it, so we cannot afford to await the development of the final niceties of technique in econometrics and mathematical economics before we begin to apply them to manipulations of monetary and fiscal policies. We are now sufficiently knowledgeable in these areas to proceed with implementation in the practical affairs of day-to-day economic operations, although constant refinement and correction must occur in monetary and fiscal tools of control. If some errors are made, the chances are overwhelmingly greater that their adverse effects on the capitalist economy, and the people of our nation, will be less serious than not applying these devices now to the best of our abilities.

Indeed, with respect to monetary policies, the facilities for theoretical analysis and policy making are in good working order. However, there is need to reconsider some phases of operative monetary policy. The Federal Reserve Board has the authority to effect basic policies of this type. It is independent of political control so far as its policy decisions are concerned, but of necessity its cooperation with the Treasury Department is close. Through its authority over and relationships with the operations of our Federal Reserve central banking system, the volume of monetary funds available for use in our economy and the cost of borrowing funds are very firmly influenced by deliberate policy decisions, which the Board makes and implements.

We need to enlarge greatly our ability and willingness to utilize fiscal means of stabilizing noninflationary, solid economic growth. Fiscal policies and actions have to do with federal, state, and local governments spending, taxing, borrowing funds, and repaying them. The 50 state governments, along with their county, township, and municipal subdivisions, have independent fiscal authority derived from their basic sovereignty. Because of the great number of sovereign units of government, it is unrealistic to believe that they, as independent governmental units, will seriously undertake to gear their fiscal policies to national needs to stimulate or retard overall economic activity. As far as fiscal policies for economic stability and growth are concerned, it is fortunate that our federal government has, both directly and through subsidization of states and their subdivisions, become the giant spender, taxer, borrower, and repayer in our nation.

The potential of revenue-sharing proposals lies both in their stabilizing and their redistributive aspects. The types of taxes that have become the domain of state and local governments—property taxes, sales taxes, and users' fees—are regressive and vary relatively little over the business cycle. Federal corporate and personal income taxes can be redistributed to even out the inequalities that exist between taxing powers of poor communities as well as the heavier burden of providing municipal services that they bear. Revenue sharing would also increase the effectiveness of fiscal policies.

The built-in reluctance of Congress to increase taxes and its built-in temptation to initiate new spending programs creates an inflationary bias in fiscal policy. Some discretionary Presidential power in adjusting tax rates is one possible remedy, but one that Congress is reluctant to grant. The timing of large public-works projects and the rate at which construction is carried out could be deliberately varied. Considering the deteriorated condition of American cities and the high rate of unemployment among teenagers and unskilled workers, federal programs to clean up cities during periods of economic slack appear to be an effective type of fiscal policy.

We must face the question of whether it is a sign of health or sickness in our capitalist system that some Americans, as private businessmen, made huge profits out of producing war materiel, while other Americans on the front lines of conflict were forced to risk and lose their lives in putting such materiel to its final use. Whatever the practices on procurement, whatever the precise private profits made on war contracts, there can be no doubt that many large corporations have found very lucrative profits in the manufacture of war supplies. While presumably an economic system per se is amoral, and although incentives for military-preparedness equipment produced during times of peace can justifiably yield a reasonable profit to the private producer, it is morally shocking to ponder the coexistence of *higher than normal profits* made on the United States' Vietnam War effort while young American citizens were drafted to use that equipment and paid only nominal *wages* for bearing the risk of death. The moral stigma of excessive private business profit made from a war in which the lives of fellow citizens are blighted or ended should be expunged from our capitalist system immediately. If a draft of manpower for the military forces is morally justifiable, it is grossly immoral not to draft the financial returns to privately owned productive resources supplying the materiel with which the manpower fights. It is strange and astounding how strong commitment to the capitalistic profit motive can blind a nation to a moral issue like this.

Delayed Reforms

The immediate reforms of the capitalist system that we have discussed should be instituted expeditiously. Achieving this—which is fully possible if the nation has a compelling desire to do so—would quickly enhance the soundness, health, and durability of capitalism in the United States. There is a second layer of reforms that should be planned now for somewhat later realization. They generally would tend to correct inequities existing among individuals or groups of individuals making up our population and therefore involve value judgments on appropriate priorities among many possibilities. Here it will be possible to elaborate only one of these, but it is by common consensus a fundamental issue.

Any modern capitalist system, predominately *private* in initiative and yielding *private* profit, must allow for a public sector producing a sizable group of commodities and services that individuals cannot provide for themselves. A major question is, Insofar as these are provided by our federal government, how should they be paid for? In our capitalist society the basic principle is not debated: (1) Individuals should pay taxes levied on the basis of ability to pay—that is, at progressive rates, under which the higher the net income of the individual the greater the percentage thereof paid in taxes. (2) Business corporations should pay a flat percentage of their net profits. Although there are unending debates over the proper degree of progression in the federal personal-income tax and the proper level for the flat-rate corporate-income tax, in our judgment such debate involves details that are not pertinent to the basic questions of how a capitalistic system like ours can be better prepared to meet the needs of the future.

A problem supremely important to the future of our capitalist system is this: Are the federal personal-income tax and the corporate income tax, as these actually operate, in conformity with basic principles of equity and justice? A proper coordination of the basic features of the federal income tax, acting in this role, is absolutely essential to the continued existence of a capitalist type of economy. The words *just, fair*, and *equitable* defy absolute definition—they carry heavy overtones of ethical considerations. However, it is our view that using any defensible concept of these words there are such obvious injustices, unfairnesses, and inequities in the federal income tax, as now defined in statutes and administered by the Internal Revenue Service, that this tax must be subjected to major reform. The change cannot be made immediately within some reasonable period of time; however, tax reform is absolutely essential to capitalism's future health and longevity in the United States.

To explore this area thoroughly would require several volumes; therefore, only the illustrative essence of selected problems can be mentioned. As a practical matter, any reform must avoid serious impairment of the capitalistic principle that individuals and corporations retain vital incentives to engage in productive activities for private or personal gain. As several prospective reforms are proposed, it will be evident that they would generally strengthen rather than weaken these incentives.

Serious real inequity among personal-income taxpayers also arises from the capital-gains portion of the personal-income tax. Under this statute, a taxpayer who sells personally owned property, which he has held for a certain minimum length of time, at a higher price than he paid for it pays on that gain a maximum tax of 25 percent, regardless of how high his *total income* is. The inequities and injustice of this arrangement are rife. An illustration reveals the elemental inequity. A certain physician adds to the services he has been rendering by lengthening his office hours and extending his list of patients, thereby materially increasing his personal income in a given year. On this *increment* in his income, he might well pay a tax of 50 percent. In contrast, another physician, with the same income as the first, buys a vacant piece of urban land that he believes will increase in value. In a year he sells it for apartment-house construction at a price exceeding the price he paid for it by the same amount as that by which the first physician increased his income in the same year by caring for more patients. The recipient of the increment in land value would pay a tax of 25 percent on that *increment* in his income. Thus one person, who has increased his income by performing more productive services than he previously did, is taxed 50 percent of that increment; the other, who has increased his income by the same increment but has performed no productive services (he has merely been lucky, or perspicacious, in foreseeing a purely speculative increase in the value of something he did not make or physically preserve) is taxed only half as much as the first person.

This illustration reflects only one small aspect of the adverse effects of inequities and injustices flowing from the capital-gains portion of the personal-income tax. It is estimated that this loophole results in the government's collecting some $7.5 billion less than it would if net capital gains from the ownership of property were taxed like other personal income.

Actually this aspect of the income tax creates more than a mere inequity or injustice as between persons or between types of income of equal expendable benefit to recipients. One of the foundations of capitalism is that each individual should be rewarded commensurately with the value of the productive services he makes available to society. In our example of the two physicians, the first was *penalized* because his increment in income was derived from *rendering a productive service*, and the second was *re-*

warded because his was not. Thus the federal capital-gains income tax works relatively to discourage truly productive activities as a source of income and encourage purely speculative activities that do not result in new or more products. This is precisely the reverse of the theory that under capitalism the basic incentive to productive economic activity is the personal-income reward received.

Perhaps one more illustration may be permitted. An oil-producing company, under present tax statutes, is privileged to deduct over one-fifth of its taxable net income before declaring the income on which its corporate-income tax is paid. This is euphemistically called an "oil depletion" allowance, on the theory that as the petroleum pool under a given well is pumped out the reserve therein is gradually exhausted. It is also justified as a supposed stimulator of more active search for new reserves of petroleum in the United States. In fact, neither of these explanations is a bona fide justification for special tax treatment of this industry. Both are based on the assumption that there is an impending shortage of known underground reserves of crude petroleum. This assumption is not true for the United States or for the world as a whole, particularly when one includes oil-shale reserves. The continuation of the allowance in corporate income-tax laws is apparently due simply to the strategic position of the oil industry in national politics. Many giant oil companies pay only token amounts of corporate-income tax.

These and other federal income-tax loopholes are estimated to reduce the proceeds from that tax, personal and corporate, by approximately $20 billion per year. Assuming the total federal budget is at its proper level, these $20 billion must be made up by taxpayers who have no loopholes available, or possibly by those who have moral scruples against seeking out and utilizing loopholes. When an income taxpayer supporting a family on, say, as little as $5000 per year must pay *some* income tax, can there be any question that such tax windfalls as we have discussed incite justified indignation at the inequity and injustices of our federal income-tax system? When one realizes that the ordinary taxpayer regards the federal income tax as part of the system, and when it is in fact an integral part of the *current* capitalist system, it is difficult to argue seriously that this portion of our system is not in dire need of modification. The examples cited do not exhaust the needs for reform, for instance, in the tax advantages of stock options or other deferred compensation for corporate executives. Reform should not be hasty, but it should be undertaken if we are seriously interested in preserving capitalism in the United States.

Indeed, the need has not gone unrecognized. There is talk of a possible "taxpayers' revolt" among middle-income groups whose income arises from wages and salaries and who bear a disproportionate share of the tax bite. One of the authors recently amused himself while working on his income tax by calculating that over a five-year span in which his gross income increased approximately 20 percent his take-home pay rose only 5 percent, primarily because of increased withholding of various taxes. When the effects of inflation were computed in, the result was a net *decrease* in real purchasing power of some 12 percent—one dollar out of every eight—during a relatively brief period. At that time, also, newspapers reported the instance of an owner of a professional football team, whose income was $1.5 million in the previous year but who paid no income tax whatsoever because of the "depletion allowance" on the players whose contracts he acquired. The Tax Reform Act of 1969 left several spacious tax shelters of this kind untouched.

Alleviations of confrontations between white and black, employer and employee, ruler and ruled would surely flow from effective pursuit of reforms in our political-economic system. They would tend to counteract the strong strains of cynicism and despair that clearly are developing in the political and economic dimensions of our national life.

Long-Run Change

Finally to be considered is the matter of what long-run reforms or changes in capitalism as we know it today in the United States are essential to prolong the usefulness of that system indefinitely. The phrase "long run" is not entirely appropriate. As used here, it carries no inference that initiation of such reform must await implementation of any of the changes already proposed. The gradual installation of such change characterized as "long term" could well *start* immediately. However, we refer to quite fundamental change in certain aspects of what has traditionally been regarded as capitalism—changes whose repercussions will require further adaptive changes. Topics discussed earlier in this chapter could be treated in quite specific terms; those referred to here cannot be specified except in their broadest and most basic features, because details must evolve step by step as interrelated parts of the whole.

It would appear that for the next decade or two the most basic problem of capitalism in the United States will be that of what can be done within its framework of private enterprise and the profit motive to elevate the economic and social status of racially separated or economically disadvantaged groups in our population. These are largely concentrated in large metropolitan centers and are most closely related to the industrial sector of our economy. Scattered disadvantaged groups in the agricultural sector are not to be neglected, but the trend of population movement of low-income groups continues to be toward the cities; hence, our attention will focus upon them. It may very well be that the final test of whether capitalism in the United States will survive indefinitely in recognizable form rests in the question of what it can do to improve the lot of extremely disadvantaged urban masses—to lift the levels of their economic and social life, their education, their skills, their hopes, and their ultimate achievements. Before the emergence of the poverty problem and the racial riots of the 1960s, these disadvantaged masses were the forgotten segment of our population. They can no longer remain forgotten.

The magnitude of the problem as here envisaged is reflected in the estimate that some 30 million people would have to be touched by such a reform. In about two-thirds of poor families, the family head is effectively removed from the labor force by age, child-care responsibilities, or disability; in the remaining number of poor families the wage earner (or earners) falls in such a low wage category that this group would have to be included in any scheme of assistance.

When one takes a hard and long look at this problem, in its probable context in the next decade and in the light of all of its ramifications, there appears to be only one satisfactory approach—a guaranteed annual income or "negative income tax." The former proposal involves: (1) setting a minimum decent family living standard, adjusted to family size and with some built-in incentive to induce employables in the family to earn more than the minimum, but (2) guaranteeing that if they do not, the government will make up whatever dollars are lacking to attain the minimum. The negative income tax would tie the plan to the federal income tax in that if the family income were above the minimum standard, it would automatically be subject to *payment* of that tax, but if it fell below that minimum it would *receive* "negative taxes" through the income-tax system. The principle underlying both schemes is the same: supplemental income from public funds to enable every family to live at least at the minimum family-living-standard level. This would be paid whether or not the head of the family, or the most likely breadwinner, did or did not work.

The major merits of this proposal as an adjunct to a capitalist economy are evident: (1) It would absorb into itself a maze of social-welfare agencies administering a wide range of public-benefit and relief plans for the poor, the sick, the physically handicapped, the unemployable, and so on, with their currently inconsistent scales of benefits and conflicting jurisdictions. (2) It would set a minimum *money* income qualification for benefits and thereby avoid difficult problems of qualifying for present assistance programs. (3) It would not interfere with or replace various publicly supported programs of training for industrial jobs. (4) By being national in scope, it would eliminate confusing problems of eligibility attached to change of residence.

The difficulties of instituting such a program are also clear. Some "chiselers" would undoubtedly find ways of qualifying for benefits who were not entitled to them. It might cause some people who were formerly employed to remain idle and live on the minimum; but these would necessarily be from the lowest-paid and least economically productive segment of employed labor. It looks like a free handout by government, and to some extent it would be. However, the minimum, at least at the beginning, would be quite low and not above conservatively estimated minimum family needs.

Possibly the most acute question in the minds of Americans would be the cost of such a scheme. Estimates are that the total annual cost would be somewhere between $11 billion and $26 billion a year. Of this, about $3 billion would be saved by replacement of existing public-assistance schemes. If defense expenditures could be reduced by some $20 billion, the project appears manageable if the citizenry of the nation chose to make this switch in allocation of public funds. In a May 1968 public statement, such a plan was approved by 1000 economists from 125 colleges and universities in the United States who presumably were motivated in part by a benefit-cost evaluation. Earlier, a New York State committee of 12 business and financial leaders appointed by the governor recommended adoption of a negative-income-tax plan. There is no doubt that a solid foundation of intelligent public support for the project now exists.

The most difficult question to answer is whether or not the implementation of a guaranteed income or a negative-income-tax plan would, over time, have a debilitating effect on the American industrial labor force so far as its willingness to work for compensation is concerned. If this proved to be the fact, it obviously would not assist in the preservation of American capitalism. Any answer anyone gives to this question must be purely speculative. No one can judge in advance what the balance would turn out to be between the two possible psychological impacts on industrial labor: one in the direction of reduced incentive to hold a steady job because income would not cease if one's work ceased; the other in the direction of less concern about the insecurities of illness, accident, unemployment, or other misfortune, and hence a more responsive attitude toward finding job satisfaction in a society providing blanket security up to some minimum. Hence, the real question to be pondered is whether, balancing the speculative pros and cons, the *chance of success* is worth the *chance of failure*. We believe that it is, for we see no other effective attack on the problem of the vast unmet basic human needs of the disadvantaged fifth or sixth of our population living in the midst of apparent general affluence in the nation as a whole.

Finally, we must search for some resolution of the long-run problem of an American capitalism that has developed enormously powerful centers or focal points of economic interest: large corporations, powerful and astute trade associations, labor unions, professional associations, agricultural organizations, and so on, each bent primarily if not exclusively on serving its own relatively narrow economic interests—that is, "narrow" when compared with the overall national interest. Conflict among power centers creates centripetal influences within a capitalist economy, whereas a single overall national economic objective requires centrifugal influences. Joining of special interests for the attainment of a common group goal is not wrong in any ethical sense, nor is it necessarily contrary to the healthy functioning of a capitalist economy—provided that no single organized economic-interest power center serves itself by infringing upon the valid interests or well-being of any other economic interest group or upon the common national interest.

In a capitalist system characterized by freedom to organize common economic interests into a power center, there is no automatic governor that restrains each economic power center from such infringements. The net result, hence, is distorted in the direction of the *most* powerful organized economic group or groups. Power then becomes an end in itself, to be attained and used for self-aggrandizement by the most powerful group or groups, and the capitalist system could thereby be brought to the verge of a kind of neo-Marxian intergroup power struggle—an intolerable and doomed form of capitalism, if it should be termed "capitalism" at all.

Although the future policies of the United States in the areas referred to here are still indeterminate, there is really only one basic policy that can be followed without jeopardizing the future existence of our capitalistic system, and that is one of self-imposed restraint in the struggle among economic-interest power centers. This means, in plain language, a willingness of large corporations, unions, trade associations, and all other powerful organized economic interest groups to exercise self restraint where it is clear that pressing a given interest further will significantly damage the well-being of the economy as a whole.

The challenge of this situation cannot be evaded by asking, with feigned sincerity, how a power center is to know that it is entering the danger zone of infringement upon the national interest. There is only one source of information for external guidance on this question—the economic agencies of the federal government and the President of the United States as their spokesman. These are not infallible sources of guidance on the timing, nature, and degree of self-restraint needed, but with the President's Council of Economic Advisors, a quite highly professionalized agency, making the judgments, there is no better existing source of guidance. The problem is not that reasonably reliable guidance is unavailable. It is rather that no organized center of economic power is willing to forgo the potential spoils of exercising unrestrained power for the sake of protecting a national interest in stable economic operations generating reasonably rapid rates of economic growth without inflation. The President and his Council of Economic Advisors have repeatedly directed specific requests or demands to organized economic interest groups to exercise voluntary restraint in a matter affecting the public interest. With only an occasional insignificant exception, every such request has been rejected with either silent or defiantly stated noncompliance.

Evidence is beginning to accumulate that receptivity to basic changes is increasing in a broad cross section of the American population. The relative ease with which President Nixon's 90-day freeze on wages, prices, and rents, and the subsequent Phase II and Phase III programs became part of the institutional framework, is one indication. A survey of over 400 of America's most powerful leaders is another:

> The survey showed that a majority of those in every category of leadership favored some kind of Government action to help the poor, deficit spending in times of recession, anti-inflationary wage and price controls and Federal creation of jobs for the unemployed. "Keynesian economics and the welfare state in some form are now orthodoxy among American leaders," the survey director said. But leaders in all fields reject such socialistic concepts as a top limit on incomes and the nationalization of large corporations. Even among labor leaders, only one in six gives so much as qualified approval to socializing industrial giants.[3]

Ironically, the deteriorating American position in international competition may cause business leaders to seek a larger governmental role in economic affairs in order to avoid being priced out of foreign markets. Elements in what former Treasury Secretary John Connally called a "transformation" of business-labor-government relationships might include:

> Turning antitrust policy inside out so that in many cases the government would encourage mergers instead of discourage them. More long-range government planning for the economy. Much more federal assistance to key industries—along with much more influence over them. Diverting many young people away from the universities and into vocational training. Convincing—or compelling—unions to abandon lengthy strikes.[4]

The other side of our vision of the governmental role—*reducing* government involvement in areas of the economy that survive only through subsidies and lobbying activities—is equally needed. Unhealthy alliances exist between government agencies and their most frequent clients in such activities as agriculture, defense industries, highway users, and environmental control. Influence peddling to procure contracts, favorable administrative decisions, and exemptions from taxes is a way of life in Washington. Those lacking real power—most notably the consumers—foot the bill, but the avarice that grants economic favors for political considerations may ultimately bleed the capitalist system dry.

This is an intolerable situation for American capitalism. There is no magic formula whereby anyone can generate self-restraint or long-range vision in himself or in anyone else—including the inner circle of any economic-interest power center. Either it is self-generated in order to assist in the preservation of American capitalism, or it is not. If it is not, anyone is free to predict whether that system will merely become shackled by debilitating rigid governmental control or will gravitate toward some essentially noncapitalist institutional form of organization. In either case, the American

[3]*New York Times,* August 8, 1972, p. 9.
[4]*Wall Street Journal,* April 24, 1972, p. 1.

capitalist system we have known, which has served us well in many ways for a long time, will have disappeared, and the United States will have entered a different era of its economic history—for good or for ill.

QUESTIONS FOR CLASS DISCUSSION

1. Name several ways indicators of economic activity may be seriously misleading. What factors should be considered in a proposed measure of net national economic welfare that would incorporate both the "bads" and the "goods" of economic activity?

2. How would you propose to eliminate inflation if you were President of the United States?

3. Why is there a need to reorient our ideas on the relationship between government and private business in the United States?

4. What issues arise from the effort to coordinate monetary and fiscal policies? What is the role of the Federal Reserve System? Of Congress? of the President?

5. What basic questions arise from reliance on the profit motive during wartime? How would you resolve them?

6. "Loopholes" are what the other guy benefits from; my tax breaks are well-merited relief from the intolerable burden of arbitrary and confiscatory tax gouging. Discuss.

7. Would a program of fundamental tax reform in the United States sharpen or dull the incentive to work?

8. Would a guaranteed annual income such as the negative-income-tax proposal sharpen or dull the incentive to work? In periods of high unemployment, why motivate people to search for jobs that may not exist?

9. What conclusions do you draw from the survey results indicating that a sampling of America's most powerful leaders indicates considerable tolerance for federal intervention in the economy?

10. Isn't there an inconsistency in our suggestion that the government is the only institution that can point out what forms of self-restraint are needed in the private sector?

SUGGESTED STUDENT REPORTS FOR PART VII

1. A study of the compatibility between advanced technology and economic systems.

2. A survey of recent international economic conferences.

3. Reasons for Japanese economic success in the postwar period.

4. A comparison of rates of inflation in the leading industrial nations and their efforts at inflation control.

5. Long-run philosophical implications of the Convergence Hypothesis.

6. The possible effects of tax avoidance and tax evasion on the general ethical attitudes of American citizens.

7. The role of economic lobby groups in financing political parties.

8. A historical analysis of the expansion of the government's economic role in times of war and depression.

9. An evaluation of the effect of inflation on the distribution of real income in the United States during the 1960s.

10. A report on the purpose and accomplishments of the Joint Economic Committee of the U.S. Congress.

11. The balance between self-restraint and government regulation during Phase II of President Nixon's program of economic controls. A similar analysis of Phase III.

SUGGESTED FURTHER READING FOR PART VII

Bazelton, D. T., *The Paper Economy*, New York: Random House, 1963.

Berle, A. A., *Power Without Property*, New York: Harcourt Brace Jovanovich, 1959.

Bowen, Howard R., *Social Responsibilities of the Businessman,* New York: Harper & Row, 1953.

The Brookings Institution, *Agenda for the Nation*, Washington, D.C.: Brookings, 1968.

Ellul, Jacques, *The Technological Society*, New York: Vintage, 1967.

Heilbroner, R. L., *The Limits of American Capitalism*, New York: Harper & Row, 1966.

Kolko, Gabriel, *Wealth and Power in America: An Analysis of Social Class and Income Distribution*, New York: Praeger, 1962.

Lundberg, F., *The Rich and the Super-Rich*, New York: Lyle Stuart, 1968.

Miller, A. S., *The Supreme Court and American Capitalism*, New York: Free Press, 1968.

Nossiter, B. N., *The Myth Makers: An Essay on Power and Wealth*, Boston: Houghton Mifflin, 1964.

Rothschild, K. W., ed., *Power in Economics: Selected Readings*, Baltimore: Penguin, 1971.

Shonfeld, A., *Modern Capitalism: The Changing Balance of Public and Private Power*, London: Oxford University Press, 1965.

Weisskopf, Walter A., *Alienation and Economics*, New York: E. P. Dutton, 1971.

Index